Design and the Economics of Building

D1199588

Also available from E & FN Spon

A Concise Introduction to Engineering Economics
P. Cassimatis

Construction Tendering and Estimating
J.I.W. Bentley

Property Valuation: The Five Methods
D. Scarrett

Construction Contracts: Law and Management
J. Murdoch and W. Hughes

Arbitration Practice in Construction Contracts
D.A. Stephenson

Architectural Management
M.P. Nicholson

Building Economics: Theory and Practice
R.T. Ruegg and H.E. Marshall

Building Regulations Explained 1992 Revision
J. Stephenson

A Concise Introduction to Engineering Economics
P. Cassimatis

Construction Conflict Management and Resolution
P. Fenn and R. Gameson

Effective Speaking: Communicating in Speech
C.C.R. Turk

Effective Writing
Improving scientific, technical and business communication
C.C.R. Turk

Good Style
Writing for science and technology
J. Kirkman

Economics: A Foundation Course for the Built Environment
J.E. Manser

The Idea of Building
Thought and action in the design and procurement of buildings
S. Groák

Collaborative Practice in the Built Environment
T. Collier

For more information about these and other titles, contact The Promotion Department, E & FN Spon, 2–6 Boundary Row, London SE1 8HN, Telephone 0171 865 0066.

Design and the Economics of Building

Ralph Morton
Formerly Director
School of the Built Environment
Liverpool John Moores University, UK

and

David Jaggar
Director of Research and Development
School of the Built Environment
Liverpool John Moores University, UK

E & FN SPON
An Imprint of Chapman & Hall

London · Glasgow · Weinheim · New York · Tokyo · Melbourne

Published by
E & FN Spon, an imprint of Chapman & Hall, 2–6 Boundary Row,
London SE1 8HN, UK

Chapman & Hall, 2–6 Boundary Row, London SE1 8HN, UK

Blackie Academic & Professional, Wester Cleddens Road, Bishopbriggs, Glasgow
G64 2NZ, UK

Chapman & Hall GmbH, Pappelallee 3, 69469 Weinheim, Germany

Chapman & Hall USA, 115 Fifth Avenue, New York, NY 10003, USA

Chapman & Hall Japan, ITP-Japan, Kyowa Building, 3F, 2-2-1 Hirakawacho, Chiyoda-ku,
Tokyo 102, Japan

Chapman & Hall Australia, 102 Dodds Street, South Melbourne,
Victoria 3205, Australia

Chapman & Hall India, R. Seshadri, 32 Second Main Road, CIT East, Madras 600 035,
India

First edition 1995

© 1995 Ralph Morton and David Jaggar

Typeset in 11/13pt Bembo by Gray Publishing, Tunbridge Wells, Kent

Printed in England by Clays Ltd, St Ives plc

ISBN   0 419 19200 X

Apart from any fair dealing for the purposes of research or private study, or criticism or
review, as permitted under the UK Copyright Designs and Patents Act, 1988, this
publication may not be reproduced, stored, or transmitted, in any form or by any means,
without the prior permission in writing of the publishers, or in the case of reprographic
reproduction only in accordance with the terms of the licences issued by the Copyright
Licensing Agency in the UK, or in accordance with the terms of licences issued by the
appropriate Reproduction Rights Organization outside the UK. Enquiries concerning
reproduction outside the terms stated here should be sent to the publishers at the London
address printed on this page.

   The publisher makes no representation, express or implied, with regard to the accuracy of
the information contained in the book and cannot accept any legal responsibility or liability
for any errors or omissions that may be made.

A catalogue record for this book is available from the British Library

Library of Congress Catalog Card Number: 95–069071

♾ Printed on permanent acid-free text paper, manufactured in accordance with
ANSI/NISO Z 39.48-1992 and ANSI/NISO Z 39.48-1984 (Permanence of Paper).

Contents

Part II: The economic context: materials, labour and physical capital

Part III: Economic aspects of design decisions

Part IV: Relating design choices to building and its management

Foreword

It would be difficult to imagine better timing for the publication of this comprehensive, sound and important book. This is for three very different reasons.

The first is that this is the first full scale review of building economics to be published since Sir Michael Latham proposed in 1994 his extensive reforms for improving the performance of the British construction industry. Latham's vision of an industry which spent less of its resources on confrontation and demarcation disputes and more on meeting the needs of clients, users and society is a compelling one. This book has the breadth and width to explain why things are the way they are in the construction industry as well as what will be involved in reconciling within a coherent economic framework so many diverse contradictory and often conflicting interests. This book is exactly what is needed to help forward the re-construction of the construction industry.

The second reason is that this book about building economics puts architectural design right into the centre of building economics as the key issue in determining whether buildings are worth constructing or not. The authors make use of some of the excellent examples of fine buildings by contemporary British architects who have obviously worked hard to make sure that the highest standards of design are properly aligned with the procurement and construction process to meet emerging client needs. We are lucky to have the high quality of architects we enjoy today in the UK and it is timely to see their wide range of value adding skills explained coolly, clearly and exactly within the same coherent economic framework. Good, well directed design multiplies the value of every penny invested in it.

The third reason for congratulating the authors on their timeliness is that they have chosen exactly the right moment to present the whole range of techniques which building economics currently has to offer from comparative building morphology to analysis of procurement methods to costs in use. Building economics has now come of age. What the authors' synoptic view does – exactly like the exhilarating experience of reaching the crest of a range of hills – is to reveal an entrancing new perspective which I believe will be nothing less than the development of building economics in relation to emerging client needs.

It is no longer enough to consider the costs and value of construction independent of the way clients look at buildings. Ultimately clients are interested not just in the productivity of the building process but in occupancy costs in relation to their own economic objectives. Clients are now becoming interested in a new and most important concept: measuring the productivity of building use through time.

Building economics has developed enormously since pioneering work of Peter Stone, Duccio Turin and Bernard Williams in the sixties and early seventies. The reward of all this good work is the prospect opened up by this book of systematically relating the all too often introverted world of design and construction to the values of the real world and to what clients really want.

Francis Duffy
President of the RIBA
23 April 1995

Acknowledgements

This book would not and could not have been written without the help, advice and information given so willingly by very many people – colleagues with specialist knowledge, architects in practice, managers and foremen in construction firms, trade union representatives, members of research organizations and many others. We cannot name them all but would like to express our real appreciation and thanks; we have depended heavily on their guidance and hope that it has been properly interpreted. The inaccuracies and errors that will inevitably remain in an attempt to describe such a complex and volatile industry as construction are entirely our responsibility.

The diagrams were drawn by our colleague Paul Hodgkinson and we would like to thank him not only for his skilful interpretation of our requests and suggestions but for his remarkable patience in accommodating our frequent changes of mind.

Copyright permissions

The authors and publishers would like to thank the following for kind permission to use the materials described.

The Architects' Journal for Figure 6.5, Table 8.1, Figures 9.5, 9.6, 9.8, 9.10, 9.13, 9.14, 10.4, 11.1.

Building for Figures 4.2, 4.5, 5.6, 5.8, 7.7, 7.8, 7.9, Tables 7.1 and 7.2.

RIBA Publications for Figures 2.3 and 2.4 from the *Handbook of Architectural Practice and Management*.

Brian Lawson for Figure 2.1, Factors to be considered in designing a window, from *How Designers Think* (2nd edn, 1990), Butterworth.

The Building Cost Information Service of the Royal Institution of Chartered Surveyors for information used in Figure 3.1, Indices of building cost and tender prices; Figure 3.3, Tables 3.1, 3.2, 3.3 and Figure 9.16.

Magnet Ltd. of Royal Ings Avenue, Keighly, Yorkshire, for Figure 4.1, a promotional advertisement of a trading division of Magnet Ltd. for the UK exhibition Interbuild 1993, held at the National Exhibition Centre, Birmingham.

The Construction Industry Training Board for Figures 5.5, 5.7 and 5.9.

The National Joint Council for the Building Industry for Figure 5.3 and quotations from the Working Rule Agreement, 1994 edition.

HMSO for Figure 8.8, extract for PSA Cost in use tables; for Figure 9.7 and Table 9.1 from P.F. Bottle and L.J. Piper (1970) *Deep or Shallow Buildings?*, the Laboratories Investigation Unit, Paper no. 2.

Dr. Frank Duffy for Figure 9.15 from Duffy, F., Cave, C. and Worthington, R. (eds) (1976) *Planning Office Space*.

Austin Smith Lord, Architects for Figure 9.17 the plan of the Adam Robarts Learning Resource Centre, Liverpool John Moores University.

Carl Thompson for Figure 9.18 and the photograph of the Cricket pavilion in Birkenhead Park.

Cambridge University Press for Table 10.1, from Marian Bowley (1966) *The British Building Industry*.

Sutherland Associates for information used in Figure 11.2, Comparative Costs of Fuels, from Sutherlands Comparative Domestic Heating Tables.

The National Building Specification for Figures 13.2–13.7.

The Royal Institution of Chartered Surveyors which owns the copyright for Table 14.1, Trends in methods of procurement.

Blackwell Science Ltd. for Figure 14.1 from Hugh Clamp (1993) *The Shorter Forms of Building Contract*.

Routledge; for Figure 15.1 from C. Guy, *The Retail Development Process*.

The National Federation of Housing Associations for Figures 16.3 from the Private Finance Loans Monitoring Bulletins Nos. 3 and 4.

Linda Clarke for permission to quote from her paper, 'Value output time relationships in the British Construction Industry', given at the Bartlett International Summer School in 1988.

CIRIA for permission to use the list of buildability criteria from S. Adams (1993) *Practical Buildability*.

The Institute of Advanced Architectural Education for permission to quote from Research Paper 19, *Design Decision Making in Architectural Practice*, by Margaret Mackinder and Heather Marvin.

Penguin Books Ltd for permission to quote from p. 55 of *Building Materials* by Kenneth Hudson.

Stephen Gill for the quotation in Chapter 6 from *Imprint*.

Nicholas Kane kindly provided the photograph of the Learning Resource Centre at the Liverpool John Moores University, and John Ellis the picture of Gaudi's Casa Mila in Barcelona. All other photographs were taken by the authors.

Every effort has been made to trace all copyright holders but if any have been inadvertently overlooked, the publishers will be pleased to make the necessary arrangements at the first opportunity.

The Building Project Information Committee for Figures 13.2, 13.3 and 13.4.

The CIB for the SfB basic cost tables in Appendix 2.

About the authors

Ralph Morton MA (Oxon) Ph.D. was until his retirement Director of the School of the Built Environment at Liverpool John Moores University; during the previous twenty years he lectured on social and economic aspects of architecture both in the School of Architecture and other University departments. He has written and researched on housing and on architectural education, was a member of the CNAA Architecture Board and author of a report to the RIBA on economics teaching in Schools of Architecture across the world.

David Jaggar M.Phil. FRICS, MACostE is Professor of Construction Economics in the School of the Built Environment at Liverpool John Moores University. He has many years of experience in industry and higher education as practitioner and consultant, teacher and researcher in the field of construction economics. He has published widely and given conference papers in many parts of the world; his consultancy has included work for the World Bank, North West Water and the Royal Institute of Chartered Surveyors. He is joint co-ordinator of CIB W 92 Procurement Systems, which is concerned with international building procurement issues.

Introduction

A central argument of the book is that there is no necessary conflict between good design and good economics; that in fact as Sir Norman Foster has said, 'good design **is** good economics'.

However, there is, in practice, frequent and bitter conflict between those whose major concern is design and those whose major concern is obtaining buildings as cheaply as possible; and it certainly is the case that there are cost limits below which good building is hardly feasible. The reasons for conflict and failure are partly to do with misunderstanding between clients, builders and architects on what good building is, but there are also genuine difficulties, exacerbated by the industry's methods of working, in translating design concepts into actual buildings which can be built within some realistic cost limits.

Certainly, the relationship between design and the economics of building is well appreciated by working architects, who have learned through hard experience that the making of beautiful and effective buildings cannot be detached entirely from the mundane business of money and profit; yet there seems to be plenty of evidence that there are aspects of that relationship which are not well understood. Quantity surveyors and building managers are constantly concerned with the cost of buildings and have to estimate and try to control them as a fundamental part of their work; but they are rarely concerned with the design process itself, at least in its early stages, and again there is much evidence that their understanding of the nature and possibilities of design can be limited.

Despite recent pressures for change, it is still true that generally students in architecture, surveying and construction are trained in isolation; that they develop very quickly a set of ideas about the rôle of their own and the other professions which can soon harden into prejudice. Architectural education places very little emphasis on the economic aspects of building (Morton, 1991), while the education of surveyors and construction managers touches only superficially, if at all, on the process of design as architects understand it.

There is little easily available written material which can help students and inexperienced practitioners comprehend how deeply and inevitably the design and the cost of buildings are interrelated and thus to avoid some of the misunderstanding and conflict that seem endemic in the industry. The aim of this book is to develop and extend this understanding; it is not a 'how to do it' book attempting to teach cost estimation, cost control or valuation (a purpose for which many excellent texts are available). It does however attempt to explain some basic principles, describe current practice and explore interrelationships in ways which the authors believe can help to clarify how design decisions affect the total economics of building and how economic realities affect design.

There is – and some may find this surprising – hardly any 'economic theory'. This is quite deliberate and there are a number of reasons for it. First, there are already many texts at different levels introducing students to the application of elementary economic theory to construction; secondly in the author's experience, students frequently remain unconvinced about the subject's relevance at the elementary levels; and thirdly we have some sympathy with the view, expressed recently and strongly by Paul Ormerod (Ormerod, 1994), that marginal economics is not the most appropriate mode of analysis for many aspects of economic behaviour; if there is one industry which does not fit easily into the textbook model, it is construction (see also Rutter, 1993).

This does not mean that one can do without some of the central concepts of economics; concepts such as technological advance, economies of scale, competition, cost and price are of course essential but they can be understood sufficiently well without any need to trot through the conventional analyses. If this is, however, felt to be essential then we would suggest using this text along with others.

The central focus of this book is the link between design and cost. Inevitably all design decisions have cost implications; the shape of a proposed building, the materials from which it is to be made and the method by which it is to be built will ultimately determine its cost – and its expected cost may determine whether it will be built at all. Furthermore, when it is completed and in use, whether it be a house, an office block or a factory, its design will have important, perhaps predominating, effects on the costs incurred in using it, as well as the effectiveness with which it can fufil the purpose of its users.

The architect is not solely responsible, of course, for either the costs of producing the building or for the costs of using it. Much depends on the efficiency and quality of the building process, which is largely the responsibility of the builder. Market conditions in the construction industry, themselves reflecting the wider national and international economic situation, will help to determine not only what buildings are likely to be wanted but at what costs such buildings can be produced and how they can be financed. And there are other important factors, and people, involved in the whole complex process by which a building grows from a set of drawings – or an idea – into a realized and used object in space. Even the initial design itself may be very much influenced by the client, by the engineers, by quantity surveyors and other professionals working in, or with, the design team; the financial institutions may have an important influence; planners and other local authority officials will have powers of control which affect costs and may restrict alternatives.

Nevertheless, the designer of a building bears a very large part of the responsibility for the building's cost and for many aspects of the economy of its construction. For example, the efficiency with which the builder can operate may be partly determined by the way the design facilitates or impedes the optimum use of men and machines; the availability of finance may itself be influenced by the perceived quality of the building; the price of land may be affected by the amount of usable space which is going to be provided on it; and the efficiency with which the building can ultimately be used will depend very largely on how successfully the design allows the needs of the users to be met.

Synopsis and reader's guide

The book is designed to be worked through in the conventional way, as a reasonably comprehensive text; but for a really serious study of any of the topics, it is important for the reader to follow up the references at the end of the chapters which have been selected carefully for their current relevance, availability and quality. All the topics covered here cannot be dealt with in great detail in one book, and are brought together to demonstrate their importance and their interrelationship. Each chapter is accompanied by exercises and questions for discussion; to get the best out of the book it is essential to work through these either independently or in groups.

The text is divided into five parts. Part I introduces, in three chapters, some basic issues. Chapter 1 deals with the many interconnections between the design, the costs and the overall economics of building. Chapter 2 examines the respective roles of the main professions responsible for design and the control of costs, and discusses the changing relationship between those professions. Chapter 3 takes a preliminary look at the nature and structure of building costs.

Part II is concerned with the economic context of building, the historical and economic forces which affect the three basic resources, materials, labour and physical capital. This section is included in the belief that, although it is certainly possible for people working in one part of the industry to do their job by treating the other parts as a sort of 'black box' and be concerned only with the output, some understanding of why things are as they are might help them to do the job better. For example, the volatility of materials prices seems to take architects, surveyors and builders by surprise; the present is often extrapolated unjustifiably into the future (e.g. by submitting and accepting tenders at unrealistic prices). Some understanding of why materials output and prices behave as they do, which is the subject of Chapter 4, will, we believe be of value. Chapter 5 considers the issues of construction labour – and particularly the problems stemming from its fragmentation – and Chapter 6 looks briefly at the impact of technology. The section concludes with a short chapter on the structure of the building production industry. It is short partly because the topic is dealt with at length in many current texts (e.g. Ball, 1988, Harvey and Ashworth, 1993); however it is felt necessary at this point both to bring some ideas in the earlier chapter together and to provide a basis for further exploration of particular aspects in later chapters.

Part III examines the economic aspects of particular design decisions. Chapter 8 describes the criteria on which choices can, are and should be made, including the need to take account of costs incurred over the lifetime of buildings by building owners and users; it concludes with some examples and case studies of specific decisions on elements of the building which generally represent a relatively small part of total costs. There follow three chapters on the major strategic decisions which the design team has to take: determination of the fundamental shape and plan of the building (Chapter 9), the choice of structural system and envelope (Chapter 10) and environmental control systems (Chapter 11).

Part IV relates these design choices to the process of building and its management, demonstrating that costs cannot be properly understood without considering the specific activities and methods of building and the various managerial and contractual arrangements under which the process is arranged and managed. Chapter 12 describes programming and control of building activity, stressing the need for mutual understanding between designers, builders and quantity surveyors if costly delays and mistakes are to be avoided. In Chapter 13, methods of cost prediction and control are examined, with some suggestions as to ways forward. Part IV ends with a synoptic view of the impact on costs of the various procurement systems.

Part V is about cost limits and values. Up to this point the book has concentrated on the way costs are generated – through factors affecting the costs of resources, through design decisions and through the building process. But for the vast majority of buildings, we have to understand not only how costs are determined but how they have to be manipulated and controlled within some overall limit. That limit will sometimes be determined by available finance, sometimes by cost norms imposed by client bodies (such as public authorities) and usually in the private sector by commercial values established through market forces. Two examples are explored – the establishment of commercial values in the property market (Chapter 15) and the cost limits operating in the 'social housing' sector (Chapter 16).

A final chapter poses some questions on wider issues, on the whole concept of 'value' in the context of buildings, asking how we might relate their historical, social, aesthetic and environmental importance to the market-driven priorities which, inevitably perhaps, dominate the industry today.

Basic issues in the design and economics of building

1 The economic significance of building design

1.1 Too many horror stories?

In July 1994 a parliamentary select committee demanded an inquiry into the building of the new British Library – not for the first time. The Public Accounts Committee and the National Audit Office had already chronicled, in the words of one newspaper, 'a saga of incompetence and mismanagement'. Headlines such as THE LIBRARY FIASCO *(Independent on Sunday)* seem to have prefaced every article on the building's progress. Predicted in 1978 to cost around £164 million and be finished by the late 1980s, it was still unfinished in 1994 and the budget, now reckoned at £450 million was expected to be considerably exceeded.

The British Library is however only one of the latest in a long history of construction projects, often for public-sector clients, which have overrun their budgets and taken years longer to build than intended.

Some buildings seem to have established themselves in a sort of rogue's gallery of classic failures or even disasters. The building of the Sydney Opera House in Australia is frequently quoted as an example of how virtually everything can go wrong: misunderstanding and misinterpretation of the brief; technical failures in the design; breakdown of relationships between architect, engineer, contractor and client; and a final cost 35 times the original budget. We will refer several times during the book to the case of the Sydney Opera House and will return in the last chapter to question the whole notion of the building as any sort of 'failure'; but that things went badly wrong during its construction there can be no doubt.

Sometimes whole programmes of building have been dismissed as 'disasters': the high-rise housing of the 1950s and 1960s in the UK for example. Again, it is undeniable that fundamental mistakes were made; but exactly what sort of failures they were is less certain – failures of housing policy, of design, construction, of planning. And, encouraged now by critics in high places, it is not uncommon to hear the whole of something called 'modern architecture' roundly condemned as if modern architecture represented some easily defined and homogeneous way of designing and building.

But the bad news drives out the good; and the many examples of buildings which are successful in almost every way do not often make the headline news, though many are discussed, illustrated and praised in the professional journals. Sometimes the successes may seem modest in architectural terms but are important for the building's occupiers. For example in the late 1980s and early 1990s, very many housing association schemes have won design awards and energy-saving awards, have been built within quite stringent cost limits and, on the evidence of tenant surveys, provided very high levels of satisfaction; it is difficult to see what more one could ask. They were mostly designed by local architectural practices and even if there were many problems and plenty of not so successful schemes, the overall result is something the architectural profession should be proud of. And there have been many other modest buildings – some reported in the journals, some not – for clubs, schools, doctors, vets, health authorities, local authorities, commercial firms, and private individuals which have delighted their clients and met their budgets.

There are too the high-profile successes (though there is always a danger of being premature – a building's real success cannot be judged until it has been in use for many years). The story of the new Glyndebourne designed by Michael Hopkins is very different from that of Sydney Opera House; Norman Foster's library for Cranfield College has a very different history from that of the National Library. In both cases, the projects are considerably less ambitious, but they are major schemes none the less.

At Glyndebourne the £33 million budget fixed in 1991 was kept to throughout and the building completed in the 16 month 2 week time-scale predicted. It has been widely praised by both architectural and music critics as a major achievement both aesthetically and technically. (For good accounts of its construction see *New Builders,* 20 May 1994, *Building*, 10 December 1993, *Architects Journal*, 10 October 1994).

Norman Foster's library at Cranfield was described by one critic as 'delicate and transparent, a glorious antidote to the surrounding brick bunkers ... a seminal work of architecture' (Spring, 1994). The budget was fixed absolutely at £7.5 million and the completion date at 30 August 1992. Despite many problems, including a rise in VAT, both targets were met.

Stansted airport's terminal building (again Foster Associates were lead designers, page 28) has received some high praise indeed, such as this from Martin Pawley:

> *A claimed 20% cheaper than Gatwick's terminal, itself cheaper than Heathrow's Terminal Four, Stansted is a triumph of engineering, aesthetics and function unconfused by irrelevant styling or forced architectural jokes ... the roof is as perfect a roofing machine as a racing yacht is a perfect sailing machine: shorn of auxiliary functions it achieves a quality of light and space as awe inspiring as the great Gothic naves of 800 years ago* (Pawley, 1991).

From these examples and dozens more that could be quoted, it is clear that, despite the notorious cases, many buildings do give value for money even in terms of current commercial criteria. Yet more general questions are constantly raised, as we shall see in the next chapter, about the overall level of costs in building; it is frequently argued that the whole process of building construction is too inefficient and hence too expensive.

1.2 Value for money

The fact is, of course, that buildings are inevitably expensive objects; they are expensive to construct, expensive to own and often expensive to use. For individuals, the cost of housing represents usually a large part of their total budget, perhaps the largest single item of expenditure, and for owner-occupiers, their house will usually be the most expensive single item they will ever buy. This is true too of many businesses which own rather than rent their premises: office and factories may be their biggest capital outlay. For many commercial organizations, the costs of using buildings represent a substantial part of their total costs; not only as rent where buildings are owned outright, but in maintenance, cleaning, local taxes and insurance.

People who are committing large amounts of capital to investment in buildings expect value for money. But what is value for money? How are we supposed to know what buildings ought to cost? Is the British Library actually worth £450 million and if so why is there so much fuss; if not, what is it – or rather what will it ultimately be – worth?

These are difficult questions – and this is a particularly difficult case – but nevertheless in order to have any idea of whether a building is too expensive or not, we have to have some idea of its value.

But the word is used in very different senses even in the narrow context of building. There is a relatively straightforward meaning to 'value' in a commercial or market sense (discussed in detail in Chapter 15); figures can be and are attached to the values of buildings such as offices, shops and factories. Such values will vary with economic conditions and there may be disagreement on those values even among those expert in determining them. But at a particular time for a particular building a supposed commercial value will be an extremely important figure for the building team; for it may represent the upper limits of cost to which they have to work.

Public clients may perceive and calculate value in a different way or they may use the same techniques as in the private sector. But their perception of what a building is worth will be expected to set a limit on the costs that may be incurred and the quality of building expected; when things do go wrong, architects, builders or both will become targets for fierce criticism, or even legal action.

But there are wider questions of value. A building which is seen by passers-by, neighbours or visitors as, for example, excessively ugly and perhaps oppressive may be what the client wanted; it may have been cheap and it may allow activities within to proceed efficiently. But there are questions to be asked about the negative values that it holds for the local community and whether in some way that should be accounted for. Is that also the responsibility of architect or builder? And how can we account for the value of the building that brings positive delight to its neighbourhood and possibly to a much wider community? This is a question we will take up again right at the end of the book. Before that, however, the more measurable and conventional aspects of costs and value will have been discussed in more detail.

Social values such as these may imply higher expenditures; architects may argue with some justification that quality of building cannot be achieved by skimping on the costs and that one has to judge value in terms of the ultimate benefit to society of good architecture.

Yet buildings cannot be conceived solely as beautiful (or otherwise) objects in space. They are part of any country's fundamental economic resources; without buildings modern economies cannot work; even housing is part of that basic economic as well as social framework. There are therefore perfectly general economic reasons why all buildings should achieve value for money. New building represents only a very small proportion of the total building stock (perhaps no more than 1% is added each year in the UK though the figure is probably much higher in rapidly developing countries), but it is an important element of total capital expenditure. Figure 1.1 shows the distribution of capital spending in Britain in 1992 and we can see that investment in new building was approximately two-thirds of all government and over a half of all private-sector capital spending. In other words the construction industry is responsible for the major part of the country's investment.

Figure 1.2 shows how spending was distributed between the different categories of client and the approximate distribution of spending on

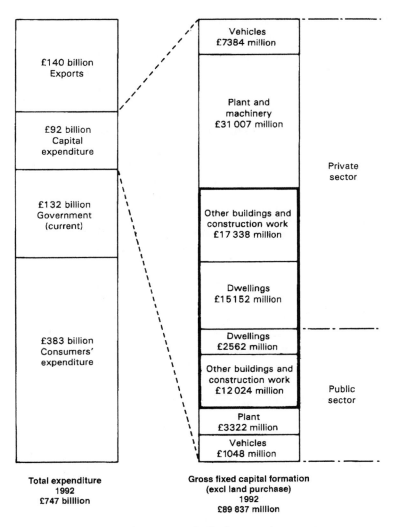

Figure 1.1   Construction expenditure makes up over half of national investment.
Source: UK National Accounts, 1993, Tables 1.2 and 13.1.

different types of building and infrastructure in 1982 and 1992. Although the economic significance of building for each type of client varies, there are few sectors of society which are not at some time directly concerned with and affected by construction activity.

This imposes therefore an obligation on the industry not only to produce good buildings within a specific client's budget, but to ensure long-term value for users and, given the dominance of buildings in our everyday environment, a considerable economic responsibility also to society as a whole.

Those responsible for managing and controlling that construction process from design through to the final building need therefore to understand how value for money can be achieved – how design decisions and construction process may produce or fail to produce buildings which meet the requirements of users effectively and efficiently.

1.3 Why buildings cost what they do

What is clear from the examples quoted above is that success is possible but failure common; what may also be true is that neither success nor failure is easily predictable. And the fundamental question explored in this book is: **how can designers, surveyors, builders and clients themselves seek to ensure the efficient and effective use of resources in the production and use of buildings?**

To answer that question we need, however, some answers to other underlying questions such as: what are the determinants and components of cost? Why do buildings cost what they do? What contribution do those involved with procuring, designing and producing buildings make, separately and collectively to the determination of those costs? How are effectiveness and value for money to be defined and achieved? Do architectural and economic values necessarily conflict?

In one sense the answers to some of these questions are very simple: a building's cost, that is the total resource it is going to require, depends on:

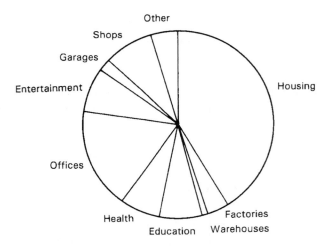

Figure 1.2   Distribution of spending on buildings, 1992.
Source: Construction Statistics.

- its size, shape and constructional system;
- the amount and type of materials used (the building's specification) and how much they cost;
- the costs of human resources involved in design and construction;
- the cost of plant, machinery and tools;
- the efficiency and integration of the design, procurement and construction;
- the effectiveness of the design in allowing efficient, low-cost use of the building when completed.

Each of these raises complex issues which are explored in the following chapters. But they can nearly all be seen immediately to involve design. The size and shape of the building – its overall design – determine the quantity of material, labour and plant required; although it will not determine their individual costs. Although different procurement methods (defined and discussed in Chapter 13) may result in different costs, the design function and its effectiveness remain crucial.

The long-term efficiency of a building – whether, that is, it continues to be value for money to its owners and occupants – will to some degree depend on the way it is used and the quality of maintenance but it is the initial design and the quality of construction which determines whether such long-term efficiency is in fact achievable.

So, to summarize the argument of this brief chapter, the economic importance of buildings to individuals, to companies, to communities and to society as a whole lays a heavy responsibility on the producers of building to achieve value for money. It is the building's design that establishes the parameters; it is the design which determines whether value can be achieved at acceptable costs; the construction process can only achieve value to the degree the design allows. But that construction may not fulfil the possibilities unless it is well managed and unless costs are controlled. There are many examples of failure and many examples of success; the differences lie not only in the nature of the design but in the relationship between the design, construction management and the control of costs. The way in which the functions of design, construction and cost control are related is examined in the next chapter.

2 Value for money – whose responsibility?

2.1 Introduction

When things do go wrong in construction – and they often do – there seems to be a fairly strong tendency to assume, on the part of most people involved, that it is someone else's fault. 'The Buck Stops Nowhere' was a *Daily Telegraph* headline on the British Library project; the article quoted a representative of the management contractors: 'the reasons for delay are many and varied – we do not consider ourselves responsible'. In 1991 an Audit Office report on the same project blamed some delay on late drawings from the architects; the architects blamed the treasury for 'stop–go funding'; the client said 'we are not happy with the way the project is being run – but we are not responsible for it'; the architect said he 'didn't know it was going to become such a scandal'. Only Sir Richard Luce, former Arts Minister, would say, 'if there were mistakes in my time, the man responsible must be me'!

But the habit of blaming everybody else extends to the supposed general inefficiencies of the industry. A report commissioned by the British Airports Authority in 1993 claimed to show that American building costs were 33% lower than those in Britain; the main reason for the difference was claimed to be inadequacies in the design technique in the UK, not any greater efficiency of the production process in the USA. The detailed arguments were translated into headlines, in the technical press, proclaiming 'architects to blame' for high British building costs. When architects were invited by *Building* magazine to comment, they argued that the report did not compare like with like, that it ignored differences in quality, ignored life-cycle costs, and, most importantly, ignored the fact that it was the client who had insisted on a higher level of specification in the UK building used in comparison (*Building*, 30 Apr. 1993; 14 May 1993).

This was only one example of the arguments which rumble incessantly through pages of the building press, occasionally breaking out into major storms. Only months before that report was published, the President of the RIBA was reported to be 'livid' at charges made by contractors' organizations that architects were primarily responsible for disputes costing the industry about £250m a year in legal fees alone, about 6% of its total turnover.

These rather ill-tempered disputes between the representatives of the design and construction professions arise from some real and deep-seated problems which will concern us throughout this book: the problem of identifying who is actually responsible for costs of a building, the problem of actually knowing what those costs are or are likely to be and the problem of understanding how they are incurred.

The completion of a building project from its inception to its handover is a complex operation involving a whole range of skills in design, management and technology; and it is not surprising that achieving the most successful solution in terms of value for money is therefore fraught with problems of communication and co-ordination.

These difficulties are exacerbated by the fact that building projects, unlike most other manufacturing enterprises, tend to be unique; each building produces new problems needing new solutions; there is a new 'learning curve' to be climbed each time. Further, the building industry, unlike many others, has evolved a compartmentalized structure where the design and construction processes have traditionally been seen as separate activities carried out by different people sequentially.

All these difficulties affect quality and cost but they may be made even more damaging by conflict, as separate interest groups struggle to preserve their own roles and delimit or extend their responsibilities. Roles have, over centuries, been constantly redefined and the present rate of change makes it more difficult than ever to identify them clearly. Yet it is easy to exaggerate the changes; for the two basic functions in the production of buildings remain: they are design and construction; both can be done well or badly and both will affect the ultimate cost of a building. Historically the two fundamental functions have been fulfilled by two distinct groups of people – the architects (though in fact architects are responsible for the design of a minority of buildings) and the builders. At different periods the roles have overlapped, have separated and, particularly in the last two centuries, been mediated and supported by other groups of people, the structural and other engineers, the quantity surveyors in the UK and now project managers (who may in fact be from a contracting, surveying, engineering or other background); and as contracts become increasingly complex and disputes almost standard, lawyers have become more and more significant participants.

It has often been argued in recent years that architects have been losing much of their traditional functions; until recently they have been seen as 'leaders of the building team', not only designers, but supervisors and project managers; but now it is said, for example, that 'the growth of specialist project managers' has led to 'disquiet among architects who see their traditional role as head of the team being snatched from their noses' and even 'the architect's traditional role as leading specifier is being challenged' (*Building*, 1992a, 1993d).

The RIBA's own *Strategic Study of the Profession* published in 1992 recognized that 'architects can no longer claim, as a matter of right, the leadership of the building team'. It was a role they should not relinquish but if they were to retain and expand it, they would need to regain a thorough understanding of building economics and management (RIBA, 1992). In early 1994 a complete television programme was devoted to the increasingly limited role of architects and what was called the consequential 'architectural Armageddon'; a pessimistic view of architecture which was widely disputed.

Surveyors, on the other hand, have pushed forward their claim to play a more significant part, not only in the management and control of projects, but also in design, with building surveyors claiming an independent design function, particularly in rehabilitation and refurbishment schemes.

Contractors too, particularly the larger ones, no longer see themselves as simply taking instructions – from architect, engineer or surveyor – but as active controllers of the whole process of producing a building through design, specification, finance and physical production. Furthermore, the detailed design of technical elements of a building has increasingly become the responsibility of specialist subcontractors, often engineers.

How responsibilities are in fact distributed on a particular project depends partly on the method of procurement used; the responsibilities of an architect, for example, under a 'design build' contract may be very different than his or her responsibilities in the traditional system using a contract such as JCT80. It is still true, however, that the two fundamental functions are the design of a building and its construction; it is those two activities and the effective relationship between them which determines whether a building can be efficiently built, can in fact achieve value for money. And to ensure that cost limits are not exceeded, careful cost prediction and control (the role in Britain of the quantity surveyor) are essential.

The purpose of this chapter is not to enter the discussion about the extent of each profession's role — important though that is; the aim is merely to describe the core of those functions themselves — design, cost control, production, showing how each affects overall building costs. And as it is important, given the potential for conflict, that people working in the industry should understand the roles of others as well as their own, we try to describe these functions in a way which not only highlights their cost implications but might help to dispel some common misunderstandings.

2.2 The design function and cost

2.2.1 The nature of design

One of the most damaging misunderstandings, common even among people in the industry, is about design. In particular there is a widely held view, outside architecture itself, that design is solely concerned with appearance, that the aesthetics of form or even worse, of façade, are the architect's chief concern. These aspects of design are of course extremely important: we recognize and remember a building of Palladio, Wren, Corbusier, Frank Lloyd Wright by their external forms and the quality of their internal spaces. But as every architectural student soon discovers, not only is the creation of form itself difficult, but design is far more than that.

Architects, in fact, have to be concerned with every aspect of a building's function, structure and appearance. To take one objective as an example, the effective planning of internal spaces. Designers need to assess the probable movements between parts of a building: which rooms need to be near which others? which further away? There are a virtually infinite number of ways of arranging and designing spaces for specific functions even in a relatively simple building so the planning problem itself can quickly become complex. But, in making decisions about internal spaces, the architect will also be concerned with the quality of the internal environment, the effective use of daylight and artificial light, thermal comfort, efficient ventilation, the need to minimize energy use, problems of sound transmission where some activities will be quiet and some noisy. All these aspects require thought about the building's orientation in its external environment, the size, shape, position and design of windows, building envelope and internal partitions. The designer will need to assess the most appropriate materials in terms of performance, look, and feel, for every part of the building. The list of issues to be considered can become very long indeed and they all have to be related to each other. Even the design of a window raises all sorts of issues which need resolution in relationship to many other aspects of the design. Figure 2.1 sets out some of

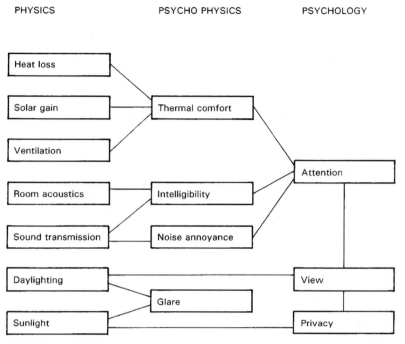

PHYSICS   PSYCHO PHYSICS   PSYCHOLOGY

Figure 2.1   Factors to be considered in designing a window (note this excludes problems of construction, cost, availability of materials etc.).
Source: Lawson (1980).

the issues – but even that only addresses part of the problem – there are issues of cost, long- and short-term, material availability, buildability etc.

The overall objective of building design has still not been better expressed than by Sir Henry Wooton's much-quoted eighteenth-century translation of Vitruvius's phrase as 'Firmnesse, Commoditie, Delight' or to put it in the more prosaic and banal language of today, a building has to be structurally sound, it has to suit the needs of users in every sense and it has to be enjoyable for its occupiers and those who pass by or through. Figure 2.2 reflects how a large modern practice specified the characteristics of a successful building, without suggesting that simply by following the guidelines, a 'good' building would result (Draper, 1984). To get it all right, to design a building which not only fulfils its function, but gives pleasure and satisfaction and to achieve all this within a tight budget is no easy task. It requires a great deal of knowledge, judgement and experience.

So how is it done? What is the activity of designing that the architect undertakes? What **is** design as the architect perceives it? What relationship does that activity have to the economics of building?

Some fundamental requirements of good design

Function:	concept clearly related to function relationship of spaces, internal and external, satisfies the functional requirements circulation of people and things efficient space provision adequate for each function growth and change allowed for internal environment comfortable, thermally, aurally, visually
Form	relationship to site and surroundings carefully considered imaginative and relevant expression of function and its location structure, services, spaces well integrated creates positive psychological response
Economy	planning economical yet able to meet functional requirements choices of materials and components maximise value for money in the short and the long term future operation and maintenance considered relationship of design to construction programme carefully considered

Figure 2.2   Some fundamental requirements of effective design.
Source: Draper (1984).

There is a vast literature, spanning centuries, on the objectives and practice of architectural design and it is not possible here even to sketch an outline of that long debate. Design 'methods' have often been articulated and described – sometimes as an attempt to describe what architects do, sometimes to prescribe what they should be doing, often attempting to rationalize an activity which does not yield easily to simply analysis. As Brian Lawson has argued, the study of the design process remains a methodological minefield:

> *We can theorize about the design process, we can watch designers at work, we can ask them to describe what they do and we can conduct experiments on them . . . but unfortunately all these strategies are inadequate. The early work of the design methodology movement, which tended to rely on theorizing, was most notable for its lack of realism. Quite simply, practising architects did not recognize what they did from the descriptions of these theorizers* (Lawson, 1993).

We will not attempt to enter this minefield. All this section attempts is to use some evidence available on the actual current practice of architecture to show the ways in which the decisions that designers make affect the ultimate economics of the building; and to stress that if a design is to be realized as a building, economics has to be considered right from the early stage – even before the physical design process has begun.

The designer is fundamentally responsible for determining the general level of a building's cost. If, as is usually the case, a client has a budget limit, it is the basic design which determines whether the building can in fact be built to that limit. Many things may and probably will intervene to make that original design more (or occasionally less) difficult to achieve within the costs originally envisaged. The budget may have to be exceeded or the design altered and that may or may not be the fault of the architect; it is equally likely to be the result of unforeseen contractual and building problems. The fact remains that it is the design which sets the level of costs which can be achieved; a point which cannot be too strongly emphasized.

The RIBA plan of work (Figure 2.3) sets out in a schematic way the functions the architect needs to fulfil at each stage of the building and design programme; cost considerations are shown to be relevant at each stage, as the second diagram, from the BCIS, based on the RIBA scheme, makes clear (Figure 2.4).

Of course design is not as straightforward as the RIBA programme seems to imply. Nevertheless, as investigations such as that carried out for the Institute of Advanced Architectural Studies at York have shown, the actual process of design **is** mainly one of sequential decisions but one which incorporates many 'feedback loops'; decisions at a late stage might require rethinking of decisions taken earlier. Figure 2.5 shows one possible representation of this process. For example, when problems of the detailed relationship of one room to another are examined it might be that the solution requires a rethinking of earlier decisions on the actual shape of part of the building. Often architects will be thinking of minor details right from the beginning; and in fact most would claim to be thinking of all aspects of the building simultaneously though concentrating on one particular aspect at a particular time.

Inevitably therefore design incorporates much reconsideration, re-testing and recycling of ideas; it requires the capacity to imagine and evaluate many possibilities at once. But for the purposes of simple exposition here we will treat it as essentially sequential, taking place roughly in the order suggested by the RIBA plan of work. Our main concern is to show how decisions at each stage have cost implications and that those implications must be understood and tested by the designer; they cannot simply be left to the quantity surveyor to evaluate at a later stage. What those implications are is the subject of later chapters.

2.2.2 The brief

'Design' may well begin even before a full brief is established — as soon as the client (that is the person or institution for which the building is to be built) has decided he or she wants a building of a particular sort in a particular place (though the identification of the site might also be a part of the design process in some instances). For there are implications for cost

RIBA
Outline plan of work   Reproduced by permission of the RIBA

Stage	Purpose of work and decisions to be reached	Tasks to be done	People directly involved	Usual Terminology
A. Inception	To prepare general outline of requirements and plan future action.	Set up client organisation for briefing. Consider requirements, appoint architect.	All client interests, architect.	Briefing
B. Feasibility	To provide the client with an appraisal and recommendation in order that he may determine the form in which the project is to proceed, ensuring that it is feasible, functionally, technically and financially.	Carry out studies of user requirements, site conditions, planning, design, and cost, etc., as necessary to reach decisions.	Clients' representatives, architects, engineers, and QS according to nature of project.	
C. Outline Proposals	To determine general approach to layout, design and construction in order to obtain authoritative approval of the client on the outline proposals and accompanying report.	Develop the brief further. Carry out studies on user requirements, technical problems, planning, design and costs, as necessary to reach decisions.	All client interests, architects, engineers, QS and specialists as required.	Sketch Plans
D. Scheme Design	To complete the brief and decide on particular proposals including planning arrangement, appearance, constructional method, outline specification and cost, and to obtain all approvals.	Final development of the brief, full design of the project by architect, preliminary design by engineers, preparation of cost plan and full explanatory report. Submission of proposals for all approvals.	All client interests, architects, engineers, QS and specialists and all statutory and other approving authorities.	
Brief should not be modified after this point.				
E. Detail Design	To obtain final decision on every matter related to design, specification, construction and cost.	Full design of every part and component of the building by collaboration of all concerned. Complete cost checking of designs.	Architects, QS, engineers and specialists, contractor (if appointed).	Working Drawings
Any further change in location, size, shape, or cost after this time will result in abortive work.				
F. Production Information	To prepare production information and make final detailed decisions to carry out work.	Preparation of final production information, i.e. drawings, schedules and specifications.	Architect, engineers and specialists, contractor (if appointed).	Working Drawings
G. Bill of Quantities	To prepare and complete all information and arrangements for obtaining tender.	Preparation of Bills of Quantities and tender documents.	Architects, QS, contractor (if appointed).	
H. Tender Action	Action as recommended in NJCC *Code of Procedure for Single Stage Selective Tendering 1977.*	Action as recommended in NJCC *Code of Procedure for Single Stage Selective Tendering 1977.*	Architects, QS, engineers, contractor, client.	
J. Project Planning	To enable the contractor to programme the work in accordance with contract conditions; brief site inspectorate; and make arrangements to commence work on site.	Action in accordance with *The Management of Building Contracts* and Diagram 9.	Contractor, sub-contractors.	Site Operations
K. Operations on Site	To follow plans through to practical completion of the building.	Action in accordance with *The Management of building Contracts* and Diagram 10.	Architects, engineers, contractors, sub-contractors, QS, client.	
L. Completion	To hand over the building to the client for occupation, remedy any defects, settle the final account, and complete all work in accordance with the contract.	Action in accordance with *The Management of Building Contracts* and Diagram 11.	Architects, engineers, contractor, QS, client.	
M. Feed-back	To analyse the management, construction and performance of the project.	Analysis of job records. Inspection of completed building. Studies of building in use.	Architect, engineers, QS, contractor, client.	

Figure 2.3   RIBA outline plan of work. Reproduced by permission of the RIBA.

and viability even at the early stage of defining the brief and the sooner the designer is involved, the less likely are costly misunderstandings or failures to match building to client's need likely to occur. A client, particularly one with no experience of building as is frequently the case, may have no real

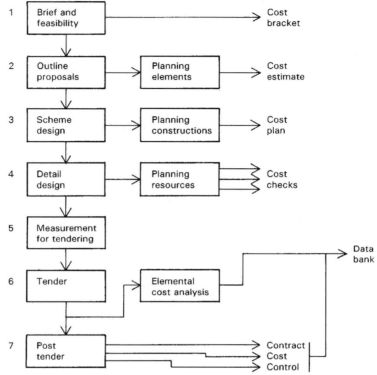

Figure 2.4   RIBA plan of work – cost stages.

idea of how much it will cost to meet his or her requirements and may, in discussion with the architect, have to adjust his or her brief to make it feasible within the proposed budget. Often the architect will be able to suggest ways of meeting – or even redefining – the client's needs, for example by suggesting a more effective use of space than the client originally had in mind. As Richard MacCormac, former RIBA president, wrote in his introduction to the Art of the Process exhibition in 1993, 'successful design transcends expectation'.

At this first stage, as the brief is considered and developed, some idea of cost has to be established quickly (we examine some simple ways in which this can be done in Chapter 3). There may already be a budget limit but if not the client will need to know what order of cost is likely to be involved, the 'cost bracket' in Figure 2.4. Feasibility involves financial as well as functional and technical requirements.

Although there is bound to be much rethinking in the early stages, it is critically important to get as much as possible settled as soon as possible for it becomes increasingly expensive and unrealistic to make changes as design

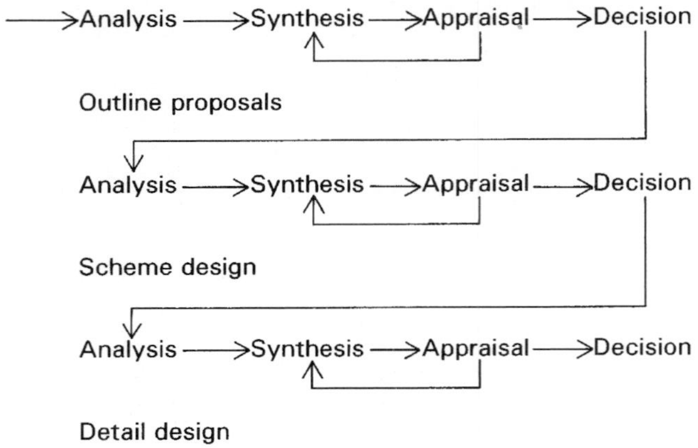

Analysis ⟶ Synthesis ⟶ Appraisal ⟶ Decision

Outline proposals

Analysis ⟶ Synthesis ⟶ Appraisal ⟶ Decision

Scheme design

Analysis ⟶ Synthesis ⟶ Appraisal ⟶ Decision

Detail design

Figure 2.5   The feedback loops in design.

and building proceeds. A late realization by the client that a building is not going to meet requirements fully can be the result of the client's own failure to specify them correctly in the first place. But it is the architect's role to tease out those requirements fully in terms of a building to identify what they are and how they can best be met.

2.2.3 The site

The study of the site (part of the feasibility stage in Figure 2.4) may itself indicate difficulties which will need resolving but may prove expensive. Ground conditions need of course to be properly appraised as mistakes or oversights can prove extremely expensive; but there is a problem here which recurs throughout the whole building process: the problem of balancing one risk against another. Full site investigations are themselves expensive and their cost has to be balanced against the risk of overlooking some serious problems (see Figure 2.6 – an extract from an architect's letter to the client).

The general character of the site and its immediate surroundings – adjacent buildings or landscapes – may be a predominant consideration in deciding the basic form and material of the proposed building; architects and clients may wish the building to merge in with and match the surroundings or stand out from them; or even, when the surroundings are particularly unpleasant, may wish a building to defy its context as does Ralph Erskine's extraordinary London Ark (Spring, 1994).

Another important aspect of the site is of course its accessibility for construction plant: roads may have to be closed and it may be very difficult

.".....based upon our experience of the adjacent site
any number of boreholes would have missed the well,
although would have indicated the sand and peat layers.
The cost of providing boreholes suficient to cover the site
would prove prohibitive and more expensive than the
remedial works necessary to counter the difficulty......"

Extract from architect's letter to client, 1985

Figure 2.6   Site problems identified – but late (extract from an architect's letter to a client).

to bring in tall cranes or other heavy equipment. The problems can usually
be overcome – but it may be expensive to do so and the understanding of
the possible difficulties is an essential element of the designer's initial
thinking. This again raises an important general issue: designers have to
think right from the start about the **process** of building; some contractors
argue that failure of designers to do this is one of the most important causes
of site problems and unnecessary additional cost.

2.2.4 The concept

As the brief is developed and the site is more fully understood a general
concept of the proposed building will emerge and the number of
possibilities on a specific site to meet a specific brief may be virtually
unlimited. It is this fact, the fact that when a designer is faced with a blank
sheet almost anything is possible, that makes design both exciting and
difficult. In reality the possibilities will be limited not only by the architect's
imagination and experience, but by planning requirements and budget
limitations; yet these factors can never fully predetermine a design.

The initial concept may be generated in many different ways. It may start
from a detailed analysis of the building's internal functions and elements
(the rooms or spaces required and their relationship) or it may begin as an
overall concept of what it should look like, the sort of building it is going
to be – one that boldly stands out as a symbol of a company's prestige
perhaps or as a work of art in its own right; or one that self-effacingly
settles into its context.

It was said of the Sydney Opera House, when difficulties arose in fitting
all the required seats in the auditorium, that it was a building designed from
the outside in rather than the inside out. This was a rather exceptional case:
the competition had been won by Utzon on the basis of a very sketchy
submission in which the formal concept was everything. But it illustrates
one extreme – the outside-in approach and its dangers. Most architects
would argue that they work in both directions at once and the greater their
experience and imagination the more likely they are to be able to
conceptualize the building in this way.

However arrived at, the overall size and shape implied by the basic concept of the building and the relationship of its component parts predetermine whether it is likely to be expensive or relatively cheap; a complex form for example, is, other things being equal (and often they are not), likely to be relatively expensive both because it may use more material and because its complexity may make it more difficult to build, an issue discussed in detail in Chapter 9.

The importance of thinking of economic implications right at the conceptual stage was brought out by the study of professional practice referred to above carried out for the Institute of Advanced Architectural studies at York in the 1980s which found that for most of the buildings studied the initial concept was the one that, with modifications, was eventually realized. This happens partly because there is no time in the real world of building for architects to work through a large range of possibilities in great detail, partly because experienced designers will have in fact taken account of many aspects including potential cost. But if the early concept is developed rapidly without a thorough understanding of the levels of cost implied, one of two things will happen: the design will be in the end so modified in detail as perhaps to spoil the overall and original concept (by for example incorporating cheaper materials); or it will run over budget, with serious consequences for the client, the architect and everyone else involved.

2.2.5 Detailed design

At the level of detailed design every decision will present a complex trade-off between function, aesthetics and cost; the designer will not necessarily have time or resources to explore all the cost alternatives; that is largely the role of the quantity surveyor as cost adviser, to which we turn in the next section; but it is precisely because there is not the time to explore all possibilities as part of the design that it is important for architects themselves to understand the many ways in which design choices, which may be made primarily on functional and aesthetic criteria, affect the overall economics of the project.

As the design progresses, through stages D and E, of the RIBA plan of work more of the total costs become determined and to an extent the range of possible alternatives for remaining stages becomes limited. Again there is an important general point here which is in fact brought out in the RIBA diagram itself: late changes in design can be expensive; obviously the more fundamental the revisions are; the more they are likely to cost but even minor changes can prove surprisingly expensive once the contractor's programme is already determined and materials ordered.

All these elements will be examined as the book progresses; the intention here is to stress that the designer's every decision, right from the start, implies an economic as well as an aesthetic or functional choice. And although cost advisers may be on hand to work out the implications of those choices in detail, the designer's responsibility remains fundamental.

2.3 The engineer's design role

Architects are not however the only members of the team involved in design; again this has become an area of considerable controversy – the degree to which the architect should design the detail. To many architects in the past, the ideal was to design every part of a building, including all fittings and furniture, to create a coherent total work of architecture. Some are as well known for their successful interior design as for their buildings – Le Corbusier, Frank Lloyd Wright and Rennie Mackintosh are examples that spring immediately to mind. That this opportunity does appear to arise so often is a matter of great regret to many architects. But the reality is that many interior fittings are designed by manufacturers and that many specialists such as interior designers have encroached on the earlier role of architects.

There is probably less dispute about the design function of engineers, though it is important to understand that the engineer's concept of design is often different from that of the architect. Engineering design is concerned more often with designing elements to meet a predetermined performance specification (which does not of course preclude an aesthetic and creative contribution) and as buildings have become more technically sophisticated, much of the equipment as well as the structure has come to be designed by the specialist engineers.

There are essentially two groups of engineers involved in the design of most medium- and large-scale buildings. The first comprises those concerned with structural stability and these may include a whole array of specialists depending on the size, complexity and physical environment of a particular building: difficult ground conditions, danger of earthquakes, exposure to extreme weather all require the consideration of specialists. The cost of major structural components such as the frame can be over a fifth of total construction costs and their design will have significant implications for the duration and phasing of building construction. The engineers' contribution to the design efficiency of the building is therefore considerable.

There is plenty of evidence that while so much controversy surrounds the breakdown in relationships between different actors in the building process, the collaboration between architect and structural engineer can be one of the most fruitful and creative; indeed without it most of the best modern buildings could not have been built. In some major practices the functions of architect and engineer have effectively been fused – Ove Arup, Norman Foster, Renzo Piano and many others. The sort of creative relationship that develops even in relatively modest buildings is well illustrated in Nicholas Haneka's three roofs shown in an exhibition (the Art of the Structural Engineer), in commenting on which he said:

> They are all contemporary versions of traditional structural forms, modified by close collaboration with sensitive architects to satisfy their requirements and the structural constraints imposed by the site. In all three early synthesis of aesthetic concept and practical considerations resulted in a roof designed ideally for its purpose. The relationship between architect and engineer was crucial (*Architect's Journal*, 1993).

The second group of engineers is concerned with the provision and maintenance of appropriate environmental conditions within a building and suitable transportation systems for goods, people and information. Solutions will again depend on the complexity and prestige of the building and the external environment in which it is located. They may vary from the extremely simple (technically) such as conventional lighting and heating, through to 'intelligent' buildings capable of responding automatically to environmental changes and requirements. Again the engineers' contribution will have an important effect on overall building costs and their integration with the design team becomes more important as the complexity of buildings increases. Although often thought of still simply as one group, 'mechanical and electrical engineers', this group comprises a very wide range of specialists concerned with very many different systems (as can be seen from Figure 13.2, an extract from the recently published *Common Arrangements*).

2.4 Quantity surveyor as cost adviser

Predicting and managing costs for a large modern building is a task requiring some expertise in itself; and although in other countries the 'quantity surveyors' or their equivalents may not be recognized as a separate or necessary specialism, their development in Britain does mean that there is a group of people trained to undertake that increasingly difficult job.

Although the work of quantity surveyors has now extended beyond their original functions, they are still primarily engaged in establishing the probable cost of building to a given design. They may be working in private practice, large multidisciplinary offices or for contractors, but one of their prime functions will be working out the resources required to produce the building. They are familiar with and expert in using the information sources available on resource costs and have a knowledge of the building processes.

Quantity surveyors evolved as a specialism in Britain to facilitate the tendering procedure which evolved at the beginning of the nineteenth century. This involved a number of contractors being invited to tender for the construction of a building on the basis of a more or less complete design and specification. To enable the competing contractors to prepare their tenders on a comparable basis it was recognized that a detailed statement in the form of a 'bill of quantities' could be helpful. This presented in a convenient schedule a description of the work involved together with the quantities required to complete it (see Figure 2.7). The implications of this method of approach will be discussed later; it is sufficient to say here that the preparation of bills of quantities still remains an integral part of the quantity surveyor's role and their use a significant part of the tendering process. Today, of course, methods are very much more sophisticated than they were, using statistical and computer-aided techniques to produce bills quickly and accurately.

However the point to stress is that despite advances in sophistication the priced bills of quantities is still the primary source of cost and resource data and that it is from this information refined in various ways, that the quantity surveyor is able to give cost advice at various stages during the development of the design and during the construction process itself.

Referring again to Figure 2.3, the RIBA plan of work, the quantity surveyor should be involved from the very early stages; by providing the information and quickly assessing the costs of alternative proposals, he or she can allow a wider range of alternatives to be considered and help to prevent financially unrealistic proposals progressing too far without alteration.

Unfortunately, owing to the structure of the professions, and to normal human frailty, the partnership does not always work in that way, except in the multidisciplinary practices which are so organized to ensure that it does. Cost advice often becomes reactive rather than promoting new options so design is refined through the cost planning process without sufficient consideration being given to various alternatives. Thus cost advice may become the costing of a design rather than giving guidance which helps the architect to explore a range of design solutions which might keep the building's ultimate cost within the allowed budget.

This problem is now well recognized and the use of cost modelling techniques based on computer-aided systems is doing much to put in place a more dynamic and responsive system of design cost management. A fundamental problem, discussed in detail later, is the fact that, cost

Item	STRUCTURE F10 BRICK/BLOCK WALLING	Quantity	Unit	Rate	£	p
	Common brickwork					
	Walls:					
A	215 mm thick facework bagged joints one side	40	m²			
B	215 mm thick facework bagged joints both sides	23	m²			
C	102.5 mm thick facework struck joints one side	40	m²			
	Facing brickwork					
	Walls					
D	102.5 mm thick facework one side	443	m²			
	Closing cavities					
E	50 mm wide brickwork 102.5mm thick	20	m²			
	Blockwork					
	Walls		m²			
F	100 mm thick	248				
G	100 mm thick facework bagged joints one side	102	m²			
H	100 mm thick facework bagged joints both sides	6	m²			
J	200 mm thick	142	m²			
K	200 mm thick facework bagged joints one side	15	m²			
L	200 mm thick facework bagged joints both side	55	m²			
			To collection £			

Figure 2.7   Extract from a bill of quantities.

information is normally based on 'unit rates' which assume that costs bear a simple and direct relationship to units of finished work, such as the area of a wall; it is suggested in later chapters that as this does not accurately reflect the way costs are generated in the building process, the method is a considerable barrier to accurate prediction and control, though alternatives are not easy to put in place (Chapter 3 and Chapter 13 in particular examine these issues).

The single figure estimates which are usually presented to the client all through the design and construction period can be misleading. With an industry as uncertain as construction such predictions are bound to be hostages to fortune. The problem with the British Library may have been at least partly due to an absurdly low and fixed initial estimate. If an estimate is unrealistic, a project is always going to be running over budget and in constant crisis. Again recent developments in estimating techniques concerned with both cost and time have recognized these limitations and much attention is now being given to the problems of risk management, underpinned by computer-aided systems.

As the design develops, the basis of cost prediction changes. At outline stage, predictions of likely cost are based on comparisons with other similar buildings; their reliability will depend very much on the type of building concerned (see Chapter 3). But as the design evolves and more information becomes available, the system of cost prediction becomes based on the establishment and use of simple algebraic and causal relationships. For example once it is known how large the floor slab is going to be, the cost can be estimated by multiplying out of the current costs per square metre for that particular specification by the size of the slab required. The calculations may become much more complex but the basic principle remains the same.

Quantity surveyors play a role in the management of the cost of the building both during the design and construction process and the techniques they deploy are still largely based on information derived from bills of quantities. This can be an almost mechanical procedure, made even more automatic by the availability of computers. But if quantity surveyors are to be really effective in using their expertise they need to have an appreciation and understanding of the objectives and problems of both architects and contractors

2.5 The contractor

In terms of controlling costs and producing a building of quality within a specific budget, the contractors have in many ways the most difficult task. First they have the complex problem of deciding how best to carry out the process on site and identifying the resources required, when they are

The Passenger
Terminal at
Stansted Airport

required and how much they will cost. Secondly they have the even more difficult task of actually making it all happen. Obviously it is in their interest, indeed it might well be a question of the firm's survival, to ensure that the building is completed at or below the amount for which they have accepted the contract (leaving aside for now the complicated issues that may allow variations in that figure). But the obstacles in their way will be many and sometimes become insuperable. Even for efficient contractors there will be inevitable delays and even disasters brought on by difficulties with the site, late deliveries, unavailable or poor materials problems with subcontractors (who have their own problems) – and simply the apparently inevitable mistakes and miscalculations that may be made, by clients, architects, surveyors or the builders themselves.

As we saw at the beginning of the chapter, contractors frequently blame architects – for failing to design in ways that allow efficient construction, for making changes at late stages, for lack of clarity in drawings and specifications or unavailability of drawings at the required time. On the other hand, architects blame contractors for misinterpreting drawings, for failing to understand what is required, for deliberately ignoring the design specifications. At its best, however, the relationship, under whatever procurement method, can be and should be creative.

It has not been customary, for example in traditional tendering procedures, for contractors to be consulted on the buildability of design details at an early stage and there are a number of reasons for this. Obviously, under a system of competitive tender, the contractor will not be known at the early stage. The architect will in any case feel himself well qualified to comprehend the feasibility of his proposals and will tend to consult specialists only for new or particularly complex ideas. Whether this attitude is justified or not depends clearly on the real skills and experience of the designer; there is no shortage of horror stories from contractors but it is of course the bad examples which make news; the continuous flow of good, buildable design raises no comment. With procedures such as design and build and management contracting (all to be described later in the book), the relationship between designer and contractor may be much closer at the early stages of design development. But neither new procurement methods nor changing of contract conditions can alter the fundamental responsibilities of the contractor on the one hand to interpret the design correctly and the architect on the other hand to make the design information clear and the design itself buildable within the conditions, financial and physical, that the contractor has to work to.

The most successful contractors are those who can make best estimates of the resources needed and then make the best use of them; this will allow them, all other things being equal, to tender successfully for a project and, having secured it, actually produce the building at a level of real cost which allows them sufficient profit to stay in business.

However it is increasingly the case that the main contractor will organize most of the work through subcontractors – either selected by the contractor (sometimes after a further tendering procedure) or selected by the architect. The subcontractors themselves may be individual tradesmen on small projects or very large engineering companies on large specialized projects. This clearly adds to the complexity of cost control; for although each of the subcontracts may be at a fixed price which allows contractors to meet their overall budgets, things can and do go wrong; indeed the court cases reported in the technical building press are now often dominated by contractor/subcontractor disputes.

The contractor's problems are therefore in many ways very different from those of architect, engineer or surveyor. At the tendering stage contractors may use the same sources of cost information, or indeed employ a quantity surveyor, to make estimates of likely cost; or if experienced in a particular type of construction, they may be able to make a quick commercial judgement on what tender price is likely to be acceptable and within which they believe they can build. Once the contract is won, however, they are faced with a quite different set of challenges, which can only be met effectively by the careful analysis and planning of the actual resources required and then effective control of their use. That they are not always successful is of course one of the reasons both for the high failure rate of contracting firms and for the frequent cost overruns on particular projects.

2.6 Conclusion

We have attempted in this chapter to give a broad picture of the ways in which the work of designers, quantity surveyors and contractors jointly determines whether or not a building is constructed to give maximum value for money. Obviously, as the aim has been simply to **introduce** some important issues, much has been left unsaid and many topics will be developed in later chapters. The essential points to grasp at this stage are that design implies cost; the designer must therefore, with the help when necessary of cost advisers, accept a large degree of responsibility. But construction costs are incurred through the use of resources and it is the contractor who has to manage that use. For the whole business to work effectively, each group needs not merely to know what the others do but to understand how and why.

FOR FURTHER STUDY

1 Recommended reading

On the design process itself, Brian Lawson's *How Designers Think* is an excellent introduction for non-designers as well as having much of interest to designers themselves. It has a wide-ranging bibliography, though more recent references should be checked. Lawson's latest book *Design in Mind* (1994) is based on interviews with 11 well-known architects. Geoffrey

Broadbent has also written widely on design method and references are given in the bibliography (e.g. Broadbent, 1973, 1984).

Chapters 1, 2 and 8 of Alan Holgate's *The Art in Structural Design* are particularly relevant to this chapter; Chapter 2 is a case study of the Sydney Opera House but that story is dealt with more fully in *The Sydney Opera House Affair* by Michael Baume and in Chapter 6 of Peter Hall's *Great Planning Disasters.*

A fascinating insight into the different roles of the architectural profession throughout history is given in Kostoff's (1977) *The Architect – Chapters in the History of a Profession*. The classic history of the surveying professions is F.M.L. Thompson (1968) *Chartered Surveyors – The Growth of a Profession*.

Chapter 4 of Denis Harper's *Building, the Process and the Product*, published in a new edition in 1990, is an interesting discussion of the design–cost–buildability relationship.

2 Discussion question

(Ideally these should be discussed with groups including students from different construction disciplines.)

a The construction industry is often said to be 'adversarial': there seems to be frequent confrontation between people fulfilling different roles (including clients). Yet they should all be interested in the same objective: getting a good building on time and at a reasonable cost. Why does the problem exist and what realistic measures can be taken to alleviate it?

b Sir Norman Foster, one of Britain's most successful architects by any criterion, is reported to have said that his best buildings were the ones that were never built. How could this be? Is it a sad comment on architecture or a sad comment on clients?

c Specify as clearly as possible the ways in which the work of the architect, the quantity surveyor and the contractor affect the cost of a building. Is it true, as claimed in the chapter, that design is the fundamental determinant of cost?

d If quantity surveyors exist, why should architects need to know much about costs or the more general economics of building?

3 Project or essay

Using library references (e.g. indexes to *The Times*, the *Architects, Journal, Building* etc.) explore the history of the new British Library, the Channel Tunnel or a similar major project and try to identify what, if anything, went wrong, why, and who was to blame. Similarly trace the history of the new Glyndebourne Opera House, Stansted Terminal, the Nottingham Tax Office etc.; what went right – and why?

<table>
<tr><td>

3

</td><td>

The structure of building costs – a first approach

</td></tr>
</table>

3.1 Introduction

To people outside the industry and particularly to alarmed clients, the apparent unpredictability of building costs is a puzzle; the same problem doesn't seem to arise with most other purchases as a buyer knows the price beforehand. Before buying a car you know what the price is going to be (though there can be surprises); before the commissioning of a new building, the degree of uncertainty about the price can seem astonishing. It is not surprising that much effort has been put recently into the development of procurement systems which claim to guarantee quality and to meet cost and time budgets; these inevitably have great appeal to clients.

There appears to be plenty, even a surfeit, of information on the costs of buildings; the professional journals regularly produce costs analyses of recently completed buildings; there is a national database of building costs; there are a number of price books giving current levels of costs for materials, labour and building components in great detail and most of this information is now available in various computer formats accessible by modem and direct electronic links. And yet, in spite of all this easily available information, and a profession skilled in its analysis, there still seem to be serious problems in assessing, predicting and controlling the costs of buildings.

The reasons for these problems are complex; they include the specific circumstances and modes of operation of the construction industry, the volatility of construction markets and perhaps the fact that much published cost analysis hides more than it reveals; we seem to know more about costs than we actually do. These problems will be explored in the course of this book. This chapter has three main purposes: first to provide some working definitions, particularly of the fundamental phrase 'building cost'; secondly to develop familiarity with some published data, using that information to gain a general idea of cost levels and cost structures; thirdly it raises some fundamental questions about why buildings cost what they do, suggesting that we need to think in terms of real resources.

Having worked through this chapter and its accompanying exercises, readers should be able to find and use some basic cost information and be able to guess roughly how much buildings of a certain type are likely to have cost. They should also have an understanding of how those costs are incurred. Acquiring this basic 'feel' for the level and distribution of costs is an important first stage in developing an understanding of the more detailed analysis of the relation between design and cost which follows in later chapters.

3.2 Some definitions

First it is necessary to clarify what is meant by 'the costs of a building', to produce at least some first working definitions. In its everyday use, the meaning of 'cost' is of course perfectly straightforward; the cost of something is simply what we have to pay to obtain it. But you have only to glance at any economics textbooks to see that this simple view of cost has not satisfied economists. Many different types of cost are referred to: average, marginal, total, direct, indirect, capital, fixed, variable; and there are plenty more. Most elementary economics textbooks devote a considerable part of their early chapters to explaining the meaning of these terms and introducing the established body of cost theory; this may already be familiar to some readers.

For our immediate purpose we can ignore more of this conventional theory, though this might seem surprising, even shocking to those who have laboured through the economics literature. There are two reasons why we believe it is, nevertheless, reasonable. First the actual cost information which is published in relation to buildings is based on a very simple, common-sense approach. Costs are simply assumed to be the sums of money paid out by clients or purchasers and are assumed to be attributable to specific building elements and to a range of overheads or 'preliminaries'. Though it will be argued that this approach can be misleading (indeed it is misleading precisely because it ignores some aspects of cost theory), its widespread use in the industry makes it a reasonable starting point.

The second reason for ignoring textbook cost theory at this stage is that most of it is concerned with long production runs, with outputs of many similar objects or large quantities of similar material. With some very important exceptions, including housing, to which we will return, buildings of most types are unique objects and we cannot easily relate conventional elementary theory to their production. This does not mean that the traditional concepts are inapplicable to construction; the distinction between indirect and direct costs, for example, is fundamental to an understanding of the economics of the site production process; the concepts of opportunity cost and marginal cost are crucial to understanding many aspects of the industry as a whole. But for the moment the issues of concern in this chapter can be discussed adequately without delving into cost theory.

We still need at this stage however to be aware that there are many different possible meanings of such an apparently simple phrase as 'the costs of a building' and that it is important to be clear how in fact it is being used.

Consider, for example, Figure 3.1 which shows the course of two indices over the period 1984–94; they are the 'all–in tender price index' and the 'average building cost index', two of a number of such indices published by the Building Cost Information Service for the Department of the Environment. (If you are not familiar with the notion or the manipulation of indices see Appendix 1.)

Both of these represent the costs of building. The Tender Price series is an indicator of how much clients had to pay contractors to have their buildings constructed; it excludes external works and figures for contingencies. The Building cost index on the other hand measures (the official definition) 'changes in costs of labour, materials and plant, i.e. basic costs to the contractor' (BCIS, 1994). We can see how these two measures changed

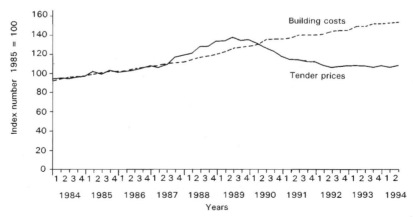

Figure 3.1   Indices of building costs and tender prices, 1984–94.
Source: BCIS.

at different rates and in different directions over the decade, a fact of considerable significance which we will need to investigate. But which one represents **the** cost of building? The answer is, of course, both; but each represents a different level of costs.

There are other levels to be considered, each of which can also be claimed to be a building cost. For example, the cost to a client of actually acquiring a building will include more than the tender price (even assuming that is what is eventually paid to the contractor), such as the cost of land and the fees paid to professional advisers including architects.

For many years it has also been recognized that any assessment of the true costs of a building must include costs incurred through its use over its whole life, usually referred to as 'life-cycle costs'. These will include the costs of maintenance, of heating and lighting and of security; they may also be taken to include the cost of property taxes. Figure 3.2 sets out these different levels of cost and their relationship in diagrammatic form. Finally, there will be the costs that a building may impose on people other than its owners and users: costs to society at large. Theoretically a building's total environmental impact could be assessed, including environmental damage implied by the use of some materials and excessive energy, against which could be set the social benefits derived from the building's existence. This is a complex and important area to which we return briefly in the final section of the book.

For our present purposes we concentrate on the first or initial costs, represented by the two primary levels discussed above – the tender price and the resource costs. In Chapter 13 we will examine again the validity of the cost definitions and analysis that are actually used in the industry. The following sections of this chapter, accepting the validity of the published figures, discusses the overall total cost of buildings, how and why they vary and suggests that there are different perspectives on ways of understanding what buildings cost and why they cost that much.

3.3 Size, type and cost

The two most obvious determinants of the overall cost of a building are its function and its size; indeed a very crude and simple way of estimating what a building is going to cost, often used by architects and surveyors as a first guess – and sometimes surprisingly accurate – is to take the proposed size of a building (in square metres of floor area) and multiply that by the average current costs per square metre for buildings of that type, in that region. (It is, incidentally, worth spending some time developing a sense of the actual sizes of buildings if you are not used to thinking of them in this way: what does a 20 000 sq. m. building look like? How big in square metres is a medium-sized house, small library, a large hotel?)

+ running costs,
(maintenance,
energy, cleaning etc.)

Procurement costs   = **Construction costs**
                                         +cost of land
                                         +consultants' fees
                                         +cost of finnance
                                         +any "excess" builder's profit*

Construction Costs   = costs of materials
                                         + costs of labour
                                         +costs of plant
                                         +costs of management
                                         +builder's finance
                                         +"normal " profit*

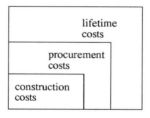

* Note on Builder's profit: The so-called "normal profit" the level
required to keep the builder in business is legitimately treated as part
of the costs of construction. Any profit above this, which may arise
because market conditions have allowed high tender prices, is part of
the total cost to the client. It may happen of course that the builder
makes a loss (because his tender price was too low for example), In this
case the client gains; he pays for the building less than it really
cost.
*

Figure 3.2   The hierarchy of cost levels.

Figures for average costs of particular building types are published and easily available in several sources. Table 3.1 shows some examples, taken from the Building Cost Information Service, for the last quarter of 1993 and it is important to devote some time to understanding both the usefulness and limitations of this sort of information. The figures are calculated from a survey of projects undertaken in the latest period and are based on priced bills of quantities at tender stage; they represent, therefore, insofar as they are accurate, the lowest of our cost levels as defined above.

The meanings of each column are fairly self explanatory but a few supplementary comments might be useful. The first column (building type) defines buildings by their major function; but of course there are other ways of categorizing, by size for example, or structure. The full tables produced by BCIS do categorize in several ways – steel-framed office blocks by type of construction and by number of storeys, for example. Obviously not every characteristic of a building can be identified in this way; some differences between buildings in a sample are bound to be obscured.

The second column gives the mean or arithmetic average in costs per square metre of all the buildings in the sample. The number in the sample is given in the final column and as can be seen this varies widely; it should be obvious that the usefulness of the average as representative of the costs of that building type is likely to be greater, the bigger the sample. In the extreme cases of Table 3.1 – the opera house and the teaching hospital – there was only one example of that type of project in the survey. So without knowing a great deal more about the particular cases, we have no way of knowing whether the cost quoted is likely to give any guidance at all to future projects. The sample size itself simply depends on how many buildings of that type were built and how many of those figures could be obtained by BCIS.

Columns 2 and 3 give the lowest and highest costs reported, showing the range from least to most expensive. It is quite obvious from the table that one problem in using these figures is the very wide range of costs for each building type. Although the mean cost per square metre for 'railway stations' for example, is given as £1080, at least one apparently cost only

Table 3.1   Average building costs per square metre for several building types. *Source:* BCIS.

Building type	Mean £/m^2	Lowest £/m^2	Highest £/m^2	sd £/m^2	Sample size No.
Opera house	1607				1
Railway stations	1080	257	2003	385	17
Law courts	731	346	1100	171	33
Banks	728	273	1518	219	40
Teaching hospitals	631				1
Offices (generally)	588	112	1434	215	588
Health centres	480	232	1005	123	275
Shops (generally)	349	131	872	162	68
Housing (mixed)	342	85	740	85	266
Houses (single)	524	174	2046	303	60
Warehouses	85	85	770	116	197
Car parks (multi-storey)	152	91	229	44	20

£257 while another, at the other extreme, cost £2003. Similar ranges are evident for most other building types quoted. And although the full BCIS tables give greater detail on the distribution of costs across the sample, and other statistical measures such as the standard deviation in column 4, these only marginally improve the quality of the information.

A clearer sense of the spread of costs for a given building type can be gained from the histograms also published by BCIS, some examples of which are given in Figure 3.3. Many distributions have a long 'tail' of high-

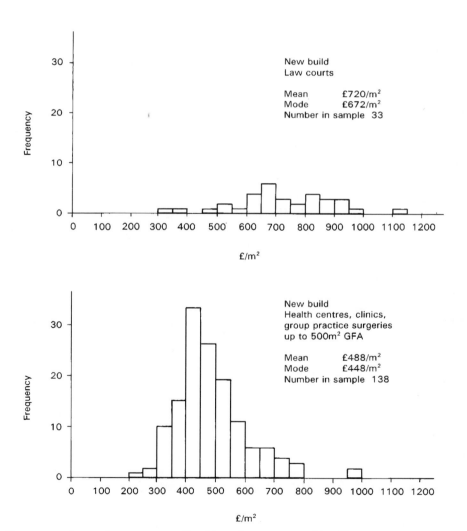

Figure 3.3   The range of costs for two types of building: law courts and health centres. *Source*: BCIS.

cost projects which results from the fact that there is for any building a more or less absolute minimum, but at the other end costs can be as high as someone is prepared to pay (or higher) and will depend mainly on the level of specification and the building's complexity.

It can be seen from those examples that an architect or cost adviser would be very ill-advised to draw conclusions on the likely cost of law courts from these data; but if asked to give an idea of the cost of a health centre, it would be reasonable to suggest that it is likely to be in the order of £400–500 per square metre (with adjustment for inflation and regional differences).

It is also important to recognize, when thinking in terms of cost per square metre, that the relationship between size and cost is not necessarily linear: a building twice the size of another may not cost twice as much even though they are both of similar design and perform a similar function. There are factors working both to increase the cost per sq. m. and to reduce it for large buildings. In one direction, for example, height often imposes extra cost, because of expensive foundations, lifts, services, fire escape requirements; on the other hand there are economies of scale in covering large volumes which may reduce relative costs. The effect of these factors can be seen clearly in other figures taken from the same BCIS information (see Table 3.2) (see also Chapter 10).

Furthermore, technologies are changing rapidly, in the constant search for cheaper and faster methods; and finally, costs depend very much on the stage of the building business cycle and the level of tenders. These factors

Table 3.2   Variation of cost per square metre with area or height. *Source:* BCIS.

Building type	Size range or height	Mean cost £/m²	Sample size No
Warehouses	up to 500 m²	317	29
	500–2000 m²	279	66
	over 2000 m²	233	102
Hypermarkets	up to 1000 m²	266	7
	1000–7000 m²	463	52
	7000–15 000 m²	380	9
	over 15 000 m²	259	2
Colleges	1–2 storey	446	29
	3–5 storey	534	13
	6+ storey	705	2
Offices	1–2 storey	481	238
	3–5 storey	610	218
	6+ storey	787	111

will be examined later, but are mentioned here as a precaution against too naive an approach to the figures.

Obviously many other building characteristics need to be considered before this kind of data can be used to produce serious estimates and these will be dealt with in Chapter 13. For now it is hoped that this discussion and the accompanying exercises will give some idea of the levels and range of costs for buildings in the mid-1990s.

Having some knowledge of the level of total costs for buildings of different types and sizes is a useful first stage but does not take us very far towards understanding why these costs are what they are. For that it is necessary to investigate both what those costs consist of and how they are generated. There are a number of ways of approaching the breakdown of these total costs. One, for example, is to consider the costs as generated by the amount of accommodation required for a buildings' main function, analysing a hospital's costs in terms of costs per bedspace or schools in terms of cost per pupil. This approach is useful and has recently been made easier by the publication of analyses based on this unit cost principle.

Here we will concentrate on the more common analysis by building 'element'.

3.4 The 'elements' of a building

The practice of analysing building costs by elements, that is by considering total cost as the sum of the costs of individual so-called elements such as walls, roofs, foundations, fixtures and fittings, stems from the development of methods of cost prediction. Since the 1950s quantity surveyors have based their predictions during the design stage on this technique because elements provide a useful and meaningful base of cost comparison between different projects. An element is defined as 'that part of a building which performs a specific function independently of quantity or quality'.

There are several different ways of dividing up a building into its separate elements and obviously it is possible to go into more or less detail. Table 3.3 gives examples of such analyses from the Building Cost Information Service. The figures are derived from bills of quantities at tender stage and are accompanied in the original tables by a considerable amount of detail about each project, including the type of accommodation provided, the main materials, the type of construction and the method of heating.

The figures are given not only as absolute amounts but as costs per square metre, that is per square metre of the building (not of the element). Using information of this sort, it is possible to derive reasonable estimates of likely cost for similar buildings by making adjustments of two main sorts. First, the necessary statistical adjustments need to be made. For example if

Table 3.3 Elemental cost analysis of five buildings.
Source: BCIS.

Elemental cost analysis at five buildings. Source : BCIS.

Element	Offices Cost of element £	Offices Cost per m²	Tax office Cost of element	Tax office Cost per m²	School Cost of element	School Cost per m²	Library Cost of element	Library Cost per m²	Factory Cost of element	Factory Cost per m²
Substructure	37 682	28.48	173 499	20.55	45 314	18.68	21 266	114.33	146 914	34.44
Frame	22 385	16.92	418 209	49.53	67 518	27.83	—	—	204 912	48.03
Upper floors	15 781	11.93	431 327	51.08	—	—	—	—	9 693	2.27
Roof	50 150	37.91	153 969	18.23	17 885	73.74	33 062	177.75	121 567	28.50
Stairs	19 126	14.46	113 498	13.44					6 412	1.50
External walls	55 024	41.59	315 923	37.41	26 985	11.12	109 861	59.06	111 376	26.11
Windows and external Doors	38 660	29.22	972 231	115.14	52 646	21.70	16 511	88.77	57 325	13.44
Internal walls and partitions	15 664	11.84	408 570	48.39	45 146	18.62	953	5.12	29 344	6.88
Internal doors	14 631	11.06	185 013	21.32	79 331	32.70	5 160	27.74	14 592	3.42
Superstructure	231 421	174.92	2 993 740	354.54	450 011	185.70	66 672	358.45	555 221	130.15
Wall finishes	11 464	8.67	168 349	19.94	28 437	11.72	2 608	14.02	5 297	1.24
Floor finishes	12 248	9.26	168 429	19.95	69 012	28.45	5 421	29.15	15 470	3.63
Ceiling finishes	15 571	11.77	218 535	25.88	39 132	16.38	1 276	6.86	5 371	1.26
Internal finishes	39 283	29.69	515 313	65.78	137 181	56.55	9 305	50.03	26 138	6.13
Fittings	520	0.38	22 326	2.64	71 207	29.35	6 762	36.35	—	—
Sanitary appliances	—	—	72 880	8.63	11 110	4.58	2 008	10.80	9 172	2.15
Space heating	—	—	767 160	90.85	157 160	65.78	13 000	69.89	62 243	14.59
Gas/electric installation	—	—	727 840	86.20	67 958	28.01	14 000	75.27	49 774	11.67
Other	—	—	224 995	36.65	10 492	4.32	2 265	12.18	23 494	5.51
Services	81 967	61.97	1 792 875	212.33	278 855	114.94	31 273	168.13	144 683	33.92
Buildings sub-total	390 873	295.44	5 537 753	655.82	983 068	405.22	135 278	727.30	872 956	204.63
External works	83 031	62.76	273 519	32.39	73 860	30.45	44 154	237.39	258 546	60.61
Preliminaries	56 192	42.47	481 620	57.04	82 729	34.10	20 466	110.03	65 833	15.43
Contract sum	530 096	400.68	6 292 892	745.25	1 139 657	469.77	199 898	1074.72	1 197 336	280.67

the building being used as a basis of comparison was built four years before the one for which an estimate is being prepared, an appropriate index (such as the tender price index described above) must be applied (see Appendix 1). Secondly, for each example analysed, BCIS gives an adjusted figure to show costs at the current average for the country as a whole; these can be used with the indices of regional variation to adjust for the fact that the buildings being compared may be in parts of the country with very different costs. (Simple examples are given in the exercises at the end of the chapter.) Thirdly, adjustments can be made for the different sizes or type of the different elements in the two compared buildings.

The other adjustment to be made is related to difference in specification; this is less straightforward, requiring qualitative assessment of their likely cost implications; this issue will not be pursued further at this point.

One thing that comes out very clearly from Table 3.3 is that building types not only differ in their overall costs per square metre as we have seen above, but that the distribution of those costs across the elements varies widely. The services element, for example, range from 12% of total cost in the case of the advanced factory to 28% for the Inland Revenue Office. The proportionate costs of the superstructure varies slightly less widely, from 33% to 46%. Figure 3.4 shows the variations in elemental cost distribution for a number of buildings recently completed.

These variations are perhaps not very surprising and reasons are easy to imagine. Obviously one important reason for difference between building types, such as the high level of servicing costs in some, is simply the difference in function. A modern office building necessarily contains a great deal of technical gadgetry, from computer installations to sophisticated lighting, heating, ventilation systems and lifts. It is not surprising therefore that this has become an increasingly important part of total costs. What may seem surprising is just how significant they can be and how relatively insignificant they can make other elements appear.

A second reason for the variation is the different types of materials and structural systems used. The development of relatively lightweight cladding and framing systems means that today large areas can be covered cheaply; but because of the economies of scale involved (a concept which will be discussed in detail later), such systems may not be economic for buildings of complex shape; though with the increasing use of computer-controlled manufacture of frame components even this is not necessarily true.

A third reason, linked to the first two, is variation in methods of building; for example where so-called fast-track techniques are used, they tend to be particularly effective in cutting down the costs of the building's structure and external envelope, leaving other elements as a higher proportion of costs.

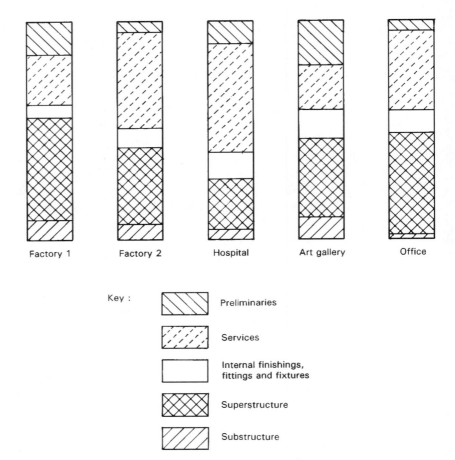

Factory 1   Factory 2   Hospital   Art gallery   Office

Key :

⬚ Preliminaries

⬚ Services

⬚ Internal finishings,
  fittings and fixtures

⬚ Superstructure

⬚ Substructure

Figure 3.4   The distribution of elemental costs (excludes external works) – selected recent buildings.
Source: various.

These last two points emphasize the need to be aware of how cost structures are changing over time, a process which has been happening for many years. The American historian Gregory Turner has produced a fascinating comparison of building costs across several centuries, using elemental analysis as a basis. Though obviously incorporating much informed guesswork, these comparisons illustrate dramatically how the technologies and the nature of building have changed. They also illustrate how the designer's function has changed in terms of the emphasis he or she tends to place on different elements (Turner, 1986) (Figures 3.5 and 3.6).

Though the changes illustrated by Turner have taken place over several hundreds of years, there seems little doubt that change has continued though perhaps with long periods of relative stability; the degree of variation

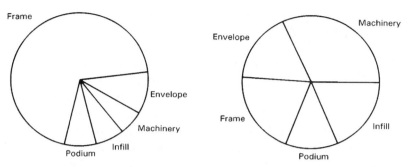

(a) Cost distribution in the ancient building   (b) Cost distribution in the modern building

Figure 3.5   Elemental distribution of costs – ancient and modern buildings.
Source: Turner (1986).

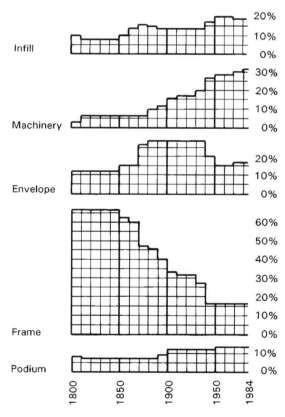

Figure 3.6   Historical progression of component cost percentages in non-residential buildings, 1800–1984, by decade.
Source: Turner (1986).

between buildings may well have become wider and be changing constantly. And that does mean that we have to be very careful in extrapolating from published data relating to buildings completed even quite recently.

Nevertheless, despite that caution, and the other sources of variation discussed above, it is useful for architects, their cost advisers and builders themselves to have a clear if approximate idea of where major costs are likely to be incurred. For the architect, such knowledge may give an indication of where it may be possible, for example, to achieve a desired result by trading off expensive finishes against savings in less aesthetically critical areas. The quantity surveyor will know that if it becomes necessary to achieve cost savings, these are more likely to be effective and less potentially damaging in some areas than others. And the builders themselves will have an idea about which parts of the construction process there are both dangers and opportunities in terms of achieving or failing to achieve cost targets.

What we have seen so far is that sensible use of published data can give a general sense of average costs of buildings and their separate elements; and that this knowledge can be of real use to architects, surveyors and builders in identifying and predicting approximately the levels of expenditure likely to be incurred in producing buildings of particular types and sizes. It can also help to indicate the likely cost consequences of important design decisions, such as the decision to use expensive materials on particular elements.

However, convenient and useful though it is, there are real dangers in relying on elemental data to reveal why a building costs a certain amount.

Although the total cost of a building is the sum of its elemental costs, to think of it solely in this way is to beg many questions. Most importantly it assumes that it is actually possible to cost each element separately. But buildings are neither designed or built as separate elements; the cost of walls or frame, for example, depends largely on the loads they are required to take; those loads are imposed by floors, roofs and other internal building elements. If a lightweight roof saves on the strength of frame required or the walls, it does not seem to be particularly logical to see the total building cost as lower because of the cheaper frame; it is lower because of the lighter roof.

It has long been recognized that there are serious shortcomings in the elemental analysis approach. One of the standard textbooks of the early 1960s put the problem in these terms:

> *We have seen that the so-called elemental cost which we obtain at present are not true costs at all, but are only a breakdown of a Bill of Quantities in which money may have been allocated to the various parts of the work in a quite capricious manner . . . it would therefore be dangerous to detach these 'costs' from the analysis and index them for the use of an architect as if they were scientific data like thermal insulation values* (Ferry, 1964, p. 45 (2nd edn)).

The high proportion of costs represented by 'prelims' in some analyses underlines the problem; if these are allocated across the elements in some arbitrary way, the real cost of each element is clearly not identifiable realistically.

To develop a better understanding of how costs are actually generated we need to look at them from a different perspective, seeing them as determined not by the elements of a building but by the resources that are required to construct it. Costs are actually incurred through the purchase of human skills and labour, materials, plant and tools.

3.5 Buildings as the conversion of resources

The fact that it is difficult or even logically impossible to identify separate elemental costs accurately is not a problem if we are interested merely in a rough estimate of how costs are distributed. But if we wish to understand why a building costs a certain amount, we need to know more about the resources which go into it. Some of the information required to assess resource costs – and the costs of materials and manpower for example – is exactly the same as that required for building up the costs of elements in a bill of quantities, but it needs to be looked at in a different way, with emphasis placed on the process by which these resources are converted into the final building rather than on their separate contribution to somewhat arbitrarily defined elements.

In fact, a contractor responsible for construction has to think in resource terms: the notional cost of a square metre of brick wall, for example, is less important than the requirements for the labour and materials required to build a wall at a particular stage in the whole construction programme. If bricklayers are hired specifically for that wall, this may be more expensive than if there is continuity of work from an earlier and to a later stage. Even the cost of the bricks may be very much influenced by the total number of bricks to be purchased for the complete building and the times of their delivery.

It is difficult at present to use a resource-based approach, as information is not published in this form. There is, as we have discussed earlier, the index of resource costs (Figure 3.1). And much detailed research has been carried out into resource requirements of different building types, but it is not updated or published in an operationally useful way. However resource-based cost models are being developed and will be discussed in some detail in Chapter 13.

Here we will simply stress that it is misleading to accept element-based analyses as indicating the real structure of building costs or giving any real insight into why buildings cost what they do.

Construction is in fact a process of resource conversion; materials are changed through the application of human and other forms of energy into parts of the final building. Sometimes that conversion process goes through many stages, the earliest of which takes place well before materials get to the building site; some arrive at the site in virtually their 'raw' state (sand and gravel, for example) and are converted as part of the building process.

This perspective on the building process can be illustrated by the following simple diagram (Figure 3.7), which, though it expresses no more than the obvious fact that building **is** a process of resource conversion, does imply a different set of questions about the relationship between design and cost than those discussed in the previous section. It suggests, for example, that instead of asking the question 'How much do roofs or walls cost per square metre?' we might ask the question 'How efficiently can our design allow resources to be converted into a building?'

The diagram can also help to illustrate an important fact of modern construction – the results of changes which have been continuing since at least the last century – that the process of conversion of basic materials into components of the building has moved increasingly away from the site; that more components are manufactured in factories and delivered complete and that therefore the process of construction is increasingly one of assembly. This means, for example, that the architect is now often selecting rather than designing part of the building, and that the builder's skills have

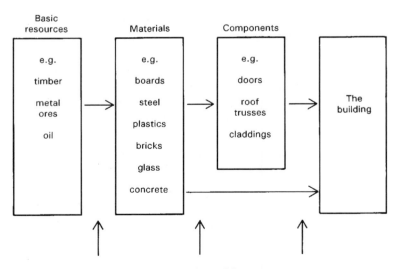

Application of plant machinery, labour, management

Figure 3.7   Building as the conversion of resources: at each stage there is further 'value added' through the use of capital and labour.

Table 3.4   Notional analysis of building costs by resources and by elements

Resources v	Foundations	Superstructure	Services	Finishes	Totals
Elements					
Materials	Mfo	Msu	Mse	Mfi	ΣM
Labour	LFo	Lsu	Lse	Lfi	ΣL
Plant	Pfo	Psu	Pse	Pfi	ΣP
Overheads	Ofo	Osu	Ose	Ofi	ΣO
Totals	Σfo	Σsu	Σse	Σfi	Total cost

where Mfo = materials in foundations, Msu = materials in superstructure etc.
Σfo = sum of foundation costs, Σsu = sum of superstructure costs etc.
Σm = sum of materials cost etc.

been redistributed with fewer of the traditional craftsmen such as carpenters and joiners and more semi-skilled workers trained to assemble. All this has highly significant implications for the way costs are generated, for the way designers have to think about cost and for the way contractors have to manage the building process for maximum efficiency.

Conceptually the two approaches to analysis we have considered might be combined in a matrix as in Table 3.4.

Whether costs are considered as the sum of the elements – that is summing each column and then adding those totals – or as the sum of the cost of resources – that is summing each row and then adding those results – we still arrive at the same total in the bottom right-hand corner; but whereas the contractor has to think horizontally (in terms of the diagram) – that is work out how resources are going to be distributed to produce the different parts of the building – elemental analysis works vertically and costs which cannot be attributed directly to each element have to be allocated in a rather arbitrary way.

3.6 Conclusion

In this chapter we have offered a simple working definition of building costs and looked at some of the major types of published data to gain some insight their general level. We have seen that it is possible to think of and analyse these costs in different ways and have suggested that the traditional approach, though giving us a good general idea of cost levels, does little to help us understand how costs are actually incurred; for this we need to consider resource inputs in more detail.

FOR FURTHER STUDY

1 Recommended further reading

Turner's book quoted in the text is well worth a look at; although mainly based on American examples, it gives considerable insight into the implications of changes in building construction techniques and building types for the distribution of costs.

The basic subjects of this chapter are covered from a different angle and in more detail in *Cost Planning of Buildings,* by Douglas Ferry and Peter Brandon, Chapter 3 and 12 and Ivan Seely's *Building Economics*, Chapter 6, 'Approximate estimating' and Chapter 8, 'Cost analyses, indices and data'.

2 Exercises

(Before attempting these exercises, it is essential that you read Appendix 1 if you are not sure how price or quantity indices work.)

a Describe carefully the meaning and implications of the graphs in Figure 3.1; explain carefully how it could happen that the two lines move apart and in different directions.

b Using the all-in tender price index in Appendix 1 or the most recent figures available, calculate the probable cost of a building similar to one built in 1989, on the basis of the following information:
1989 building: 1200 m^2; cost per m^2: £400
new building, 1450 m^2

c Using the most recent BCIS average building cost index calculate the cost of constructing a similar building at three points in time, 1985, 1991 and the current year. Make your own assumptions about the size and type of building.

d Study Table 3.1. List all the reasons you can think of which might account for the differences in average cost shown. How do you account for the wide range of figures for each building type?

3 Discussion questions

a Discuss the validity of the models of construction in Figures 3.7 and Table 3.4.

b Discuss the ways in which an elemental breakdown of a building's costs might and might not be useful to the contractor managing its construction.

4 Project

Consider either a recent building in your locality or (if an architectural student) the building you are currently designing. Use the published BCIS data on average costs (such as those in Table 3.1), together with an appropriate index to estimate its probable total cost.
(Set out your reasoning and the calculations used.)

The economic context: materials, labour and physical capital

4

Materials: markets and prices

Outline

- The vast range of building materials
- Importance of technical innovation
- Impact of economies of scale
- The nature and effect of competition in building materials
- The volatility of prices

4.1 Introduction

The SfB classification of building materials identifies 17 different main categories each of which is subdivided into between 7 and 9 subcategories; and some of those subcategories themselves encompass a further range of distinct materials; there are probably many more which in one form or another find their way into the fabric of a building. New materials as well as new uses for old materials are continually becoming available. This wealth of material gives architects a breadth of choice which their predecessors did not have, but it also brings many new problems: there are more comparisons to be made, new material characteristics to be investigated and understood, new risks involved.

Obviously, given the great number and variety of the materials used in construction it is not possible to discuss all their different economic characteristics in one short chapter. But materials represent some 50–60% of total building costs and all designers, surveyors and contractors need to understand at least a little about the underlying forces which determine their availability and their prices. It is particularly important to be aware of how and why relative prices change over time and also why prices can change very rapidly over short periods.

This chapter concentrates on some general aspects of building materials economics, factors which have affected and continue to affect production costs and prices. Issues of choice between different materials, which as we will see is never in fact a simple economic one and is always interrelated with other decisions, are left to Chapters 8 and 10.

Although there are so many materials and although each has its own specific economic characteristics, there are important features of modern production systems and markets which are relevant to all of them. This is true despite the fact, already referred to, that materials arrive on site at many different stages in their transformation from raw material to building element. At one extreme, for example, there are those used virtually as they come out of the ground, such as sand and aggregates; others are already formed in some way, into bricks, boards, beams, blocks, panels, pipes; a third group are those pre-manufactured into building components such as trusses, doors, window frames, staircases: a fourth group are finished interior fittings requiring fixing rather than building in as part of the fabric – kitchen units, for example. Then there are materials incorporated into the mechanical and electrical equipment which, as we saw in the last chapter, can represent a high proportion of total costs – lifts, boilers, air-conditioning systems. And today we are hearing increasingly of whole elements of a building such as bathrooms arriving complete on site.

This chapter considers three economic phenomena which are perfectly general yet help to explain in all these cases, though in different ways, price structures, costs and availability. The first of these is technical **innovation**; the second is the prevalence of **economies of scale**. These two are closely linked, but they are different phenomena and their economic consequences need to be understood. The third and highly significant factor which will be discussed is the nature of **competition** within the industry and particularly the fact that it is, for virtually all the main materials, 'oligopolistic'.

4.2 Technical innovation

'Technical progress is the single most important factor shaping the economy in which we live' (Jackson, 1982, p. 315).

In the building materials industry as in most others, the range, quality, characteristics, price and availability of products are continually changing as a result of technical development. The implications of this fact are considerable.

Given its importance, it is hardly surprising that the possible forms, economic causes and economic consequences of technical innovation have been the subject of much discussion, analysis and controversy. In the case of building materials, Marian Bowley's two studies published in the 1960s remain a major landmark (Bowley, 1960, 1966); in fact nothing of quite such thoroughness has been published since, though the processes of innovation she discussed have accelerated.

Bowley identified 12 logically and economically different types of innovations in building materials production but her arguments can be simplified without too much distortion. Essentially, technological innovation has two major effects. First it may improve the quality and range of materials – and this can happen through improvements in manufacturing techniques, changes in physical or chemical properties or the development of new materials altogether. Secondly it may have an effect on production costs and selling prices, reducing them absolutely or holding them below the level they would have reached without the innovation. The two effects – the quality and the price effect – may of course occur together.

There are very many examples; in fact technical innovation both in production and material characteristics is virtually continuous in the industry today, often following, as it has done historically, a pattern of major breakthrough followed by a succession of associated smaller developments.

Even in what is essentially a very simple process – known to societies 3000 years ago at least – the process of making bricks from clay, technical change has revolutionized methods and scales of production, range and quality during the last 150 years. But the progress was very slow to begin with. The introduction of the Hoffman continuous kiln, patented in 1858, increased the potential efficiency of the brick-making process, and hence potentially reduced costs. But in 1900, the Hoffman kiln was still less common than production by the slow intermittent kilns; by the 1940s it was the most common type. Today, most bricks are mass-produced in highly sophisticated computer-controlled plants, using tunnel kilns monitored sometimes by as few as five people and capable of producing a million wire-cut bricks a week.

As well as the major innovations in the methods of firing bricks, there were improvements in forming the bricks from the basic clays and in the use of a wider range of clays. The introduction of the semi-dry-pressed process, and particularly the development of the Fletton brick had dramatic effects. Although the method was first used in Lancashire (at Accrington) when applied by a local brick company at Fletton, Peterborough, from 1880, it proved so much cheaper than other bricks that it soon began to dominate the market. By 1889, it was claimed that 156 000 bricks a day were being dispatched from Fletton (p. 69) and by the 1930s 34% of all bricks produced were Flettons. The reasons for its relative cheapness were first that the clay contained enough combustible materials to reduce the fuel required for baking, that the process was relatively dry, thus again reducing fuel requirements, and that the bricks were relatively light, reducing handling and transport costs. It continued to retain these advantages. In the 1950s, calculations showed that the man hours requires to produce a thousand Flettons were under 10, as against an average for all bricks of over 15.

The early history of the Fletton brick and the development of kiln technologies showed the potentially enormous power of developments which were in essence technically simple. The development of glass was different, but again depended on a few significant breakthroughs (and suffered many false starts). The innovations came from all over Europe and the USA. During the nineteenth century the traditional crown glass was gradually replaced by improved forms of cylinder and plate glass. By the end of the century 'the introduction of gas as a fuel, of the tank furnace and finally of annealing lears, had revolutionized the methods of production and, once introduced, the equipment was constantly the object of improvement at the hands of the users' (Bowley, 1960, p. 102).

In the 1950s a really radical technical breakthrough came with the invention of float glass by Pilkingtons. The first provisional application for a patent was filed in 1953 but it was not available for general glazing until 1960 and not fully profitable until 1962. By 1967 it had completely replaced plate glass in Pilkington's output (Barker, 1977).

This long process of technical development had its parallel in the increasing and varied use of glass in building as architects and builders responded to its increasing availability, cheapness and versatility. From the Crystal Palace in 1851, the most dramatic early demonstration of the material's architectural potential, to the ubiquitous glass–clad skyscrapers of today, technical development has continued to widen the possibilities for constructional technique and architectural expression.

In both these cases, bricks and glass, research into the characteristics of the basic materials and developments in applications have led to greater variety, higher quality and wider availability. The manufacture of many construction materials has shown the same kind of development. Usually it has been from small-scale hand-production methods to the use of massive plant usually controlled today through computers. Concrete tiles and blocks are examples. For other materials the scale of production was always necessarily large but has become even larger and more automated; this is true of steel, of aluminium and plastics, though the fabrication of these into elements for building has often remained in the hands of relatively small concerns, particularly in the early stages.

Timber is a slightly different case in that the natural material is not transformed (as clay into brick) before use. The technical developments here have been in quality control, in mass storage, handling and transport; and most significantly of all, the development of mass-produced joinery and pre-formed elements such as roof trusses, largely replacing fabrication on site. In particular, the production of laminated timber beams, restoring some of the material's older structural functions, has also opened up new aesthetic possibilities.

A most significant – and relatively new – form of innovation is the adaptation of mass methods to the production of variety; this has been made possible through the use of computer- or robotically-controlled manufacturing techniques, allowing specification to be varied without disrupting production flows. Clay roof tiles, for example, can now be produced in virtually any colour and large manufacturers will produce specific colours for individual projects. Although 'hand-made' bricks are still produced by many small specialists the major manufacturers have also adapted their technology to produce a wide range of specials in many shapes and colours. Steel-frame manufacturers can now produce complex forms to order at little extra cost.

Finally, technical innovation has not only improved methods of production, quality and variety of standard materials but has led to the development of completely new materials, sometimes specifically developed for construction but more often adapted from original uses in other industries. Plastics are the most obvious case; there is now a vast range of plastic-based materials used in construction: glass-reinforced, unplasticized polyvinyl chloride, mastics, neoprene, plastic-coated steels, a range of roofing and insulation materials. New applications continue to be developed. Pultruded GRP (glass-reinforced plastic) was developed by the English Electric Company in the 1950s, but its first use as a structural material seems to have been only in 1993 (*Architects' Journal*, 1993a).

The driving force behind product innovation is the constant search by companies to retain or increase their market share, enabling them to grow – or survive – and to enhance profitability. To be successful they must produce something cheaper or better to offer an attractive combination of cost and quality compared with alternative materials. But it is not easy to assess the actual consequences on ultimate prices and qualities of so much change and innovation. What architects, surveyors and builders have to attempt is to keep up with innovations, constantly estimating their relative costs and values in particular uses. That is no easy task and requires a good information flow not only between manufacturers and the construction industry, but between the professionals in the industry themselves in the form of feedback from completed projects.

4.3 Economies of scale

The second general feature of modern production systems we identified as relevant and important to help us understand some aspects of building material economics was *economics of scale*. This phrase has come into common use to refer generally to the widely evident fact that the more of some product that is made, the cheaper it tends to be. But, strictly, as used in economics over the last hundred years or so, the term applies only to increases in the **scale** of production units, that is, raising their output capacity. For example, the increase of brick production from a particular location or group of kilns is not an increase in scale in this sense; but the development of a more efficient or simply larger manufacturing unit is such an increase. It is not always possible to maintain this distinction clearly, and indeed some economists have argued that it cannot logically be maintained anyway. But it is a useful distinction to draw as it helps to explain many characteristics of the building materials market.

Why do economies of scale exist? The reasons are sometimes purely physical and mathematical: it takes less steel per cubic volume to enclose large tanks than small ones for example. It is cheaper per gallon to transport oil in large than in small quantities, partly because of this but also because large ships don't require proportionately larger engine capacities or fuel consumption. The same basic principle applies to brick kilns though in practice other factors may have been more significant than simple increases in size of kilns. Again, delivering more bricks to larger sites using larger vehicles will reduce the cost of delivery per brick, simply because the cost of the driver's time and the cost of fuel remain relatively constant while the number of bricks delivered increases. The extra capital cost of the larger vehicles is unlikely to counteract this effect.

But the most significant generator of scale economies is the sort of technical innovation discussed in the previous section. New methods are often introduced precisely because they allow more output to be produced at a lower average cost. Complex and sophisticated machinery will cost more than the simpler early versions they replace; but their output capacity will be so much higher that capital costs per unit will fall.

Scale economies have been and still are significant in the production of all the main building materials; their existence helps to explain both the current structure of the industry and the behaviour of prices in the long and short term.

It is difficult to get precise data for these effects of scale economies on cost but there is plenty of evidence to indicate their importance. Marian Bowley was very cautious in her analysis of brick production in the 1930s. A massive increase in output between 1930 and 1935 – some 54% – was achieved with an increase of only 7% in the number of employees. But her general conclusion was that 'the growth of the London Brick Company did not result in major economies of scale – or if it did they were not passed on to customers (Bowley, 1960, p. 189).

However, a much later study by Massey and Meegan shows how the London Brick Company's policy of building new types of brickworks from 1968 reduced labour content to a third of the previous level. 'Before the old Kings Dyke works were demolished, 86 men produced 600,000 bricks a week. When the new plant was completed, 260 men will produce 3 million bricks, three times the labour force producing five times the number of bricks' (Massey and Megan, 1982).

An American study of glass manufacturing produced figures which showed that window glass produced by automatic machines in large factories required only 30% of the labour of traditional methods in the 1950s; again however there are no data on prices, which would also have to cover the additional cost of the automatic machines (Jackson, 1982, p. 292). With the invention of float glass, the large scale became the only feasible method of production.

But it is not only in the production of such bulk, standard commodities as bricks, cement and glass that economies of scale are significant. With modern techniques, as mentioned above, particularly computer-controlled machine tools, stock input and output, it is possible to produce a great variety of products in single large production units. The advertisement for Magnet joinery (Figure 4.1) shows this more dramatically than any statistical table.

4.4 The structure of the industry and the nature of competition

Technological development and economies of scale are clearly therefore important characteristics of building materials production. But what precisely are their effects? It is important to understand them because although this discussion may seem a bit remote from the question of prices as faced by designers, surveyors and contractors at the point of decision or purchase, they do help to explain much that may be puzzling at first sight, particularly the behaviour of prices.

One obvious effect, in fact almost part of the defining characteristics, of scale economies is that as the scale of production increases, and unit costs fall, prices will tend to be lower or profits higher than they would have been; prices may not actually fall, of course, because there may be general increases in the price of inputs. Nevertheless, we should therefore expect over the long term a general relative decline in prices (for a given quality) in those materials whose production is subject to such economies.

But perhaps the most important effect of the combination of technical innovation and scale economies is on the structure of the industry itself and through that on the nature of competition.

The need for expensive capital equipment to exploit the innovation and the existence of scale economies will tend to lead to production becoming increasingly dominated by large firms. Small producers may be neither able

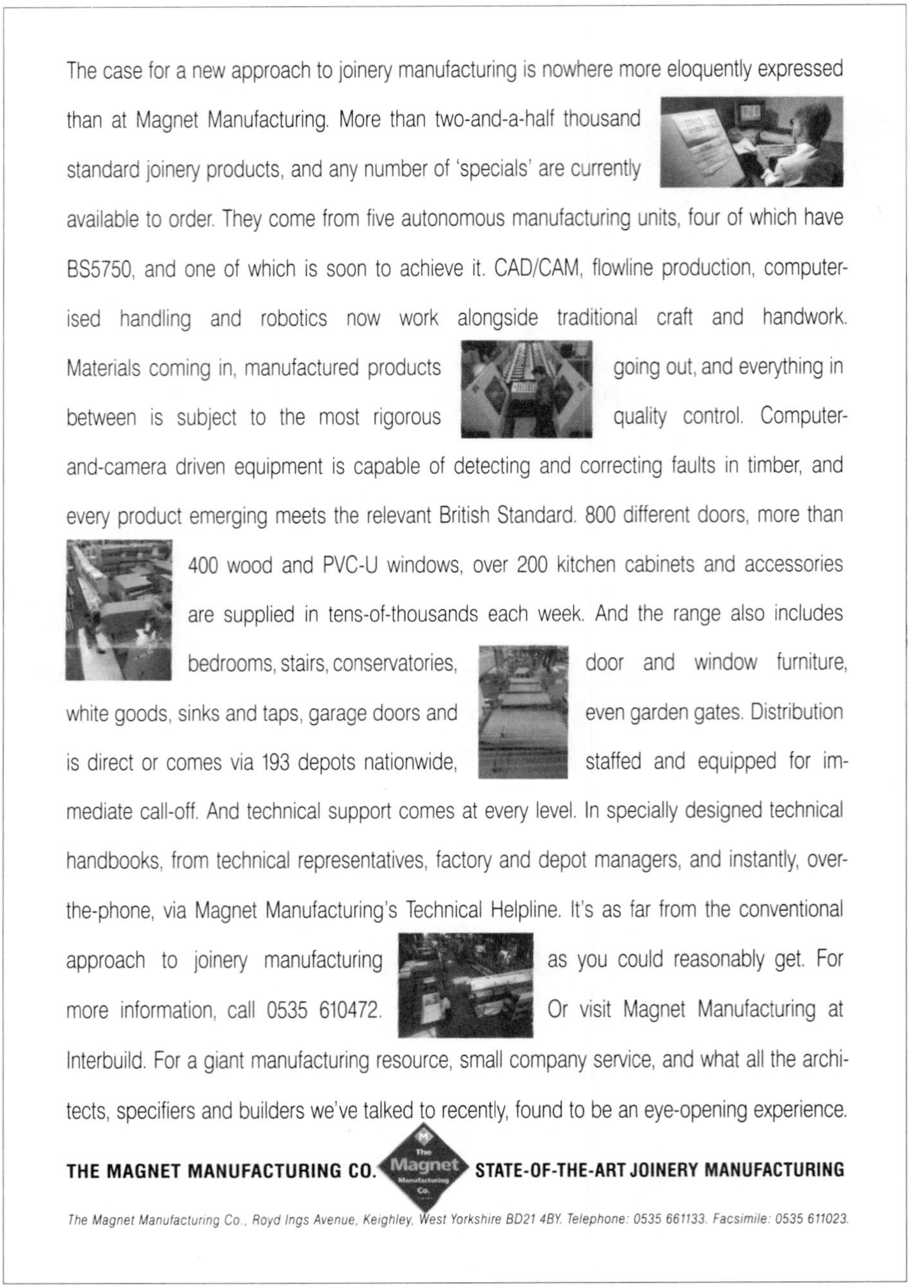

The case for a new approach to joinery manufacturing is nowhere more eloquently expressed than at Magnet Manufacturing. More than two-and-a-half thousand standard joinery products, and any number of 'specials' are currently available to order. They come from five autonomous manufacturing units, four of which have BS5750, and one of which is soon to achieve it. CAD/CAM, flowline production, computerised handling and robotics now work alongside traditional craft and handwork. Materials coming in, manufactured products going out, and everything in between is subject to the most rigorous quality control. Computer-and-camera driven equipment is capable of detecting and correcting faults in timber, and every product emerging meets the relevant British Standard. 800 different doors, more than 400 wood and PVC-U windows, over 200 kitchen cabinets and accessories are supplied in tens-of-thousands each week. And the range also includes bedrooms, stairs, conservatories, door and window furniture, white goods, sinks and taps, garage doors and even garden gates. Distribution is direct or comes via 193 depots nationwide, staffed and equipped for immediate call-off. And technical support comes at every level. In specially designed technical handbooks, from technical representatives, factory and depot managers, and instantly, over-the-phone, via Magnet Manufacturing's Technical Helpline. It's as far from the conventional approach to joinery manufacturing as you could reasonably get. For more information, call 0535 610472. Or visit Magnet Manufacturing at Interbuild. For a giant manufacturing resource, small company service, and what all the architects, specifiers and builders we've talked to recently, found to be an eye-opening experience.

THE MAGNET MANUFACTURING CO. ◆ **STATE-OF-THE-ART JOINERY MANUFACTURING**

The Magnet Manufacturing Co., Royd Ings Avenue, Keighley, West Yorkshire BD21 4BY. Telephone: 0535 661133. Facsimile: 0535 611023.

Figure 4.1   Advertisement for Magnet Manufacturing joinery, showing the scale of mass production and manufacturing technology in use.

to afford the new equipment or compete on price using traditional techniques. They may well be driven out of business or taken over by larger companies. This has happened throughout the building materials industry.

Brick and glass production again provide examples. In the early nineteenth century bricks were made by hundreds of small firms, often on specific sites adjacent to the building project in which they were to be used (Clarke, 1992a). Bowley could still refer to the 1930s as a period of 'large numbers of establishments and small average size in terms of output'. But by then the process of concentration, as large firms expanded and took over others, was well under way. By the 1950s Flettons were produced by only six companies but the output was dominated by the London Brick Company which by the late 1960s was the sole producer. There were, however, very many other companies making other types of brick. Further rounds of expansion and takeover have still left many small independent producers, but the market is now dominated by a very few. The top four firms, London Brick, Redland, Butterley and Ibstock, are responsible for nearly 60% of total brick output; and, furthermore, both Butterley and London Brick are now subsidiaries of the conglomerate Hanson Group, giving them considerable market power in both the Fletton and non-Fletton sectors.

In glass production the process of concentration was faster and more dramatic. Most small producers were unable to use and develop the new technologies introduced at the end of the nineteenth century, the numbers of makers of crown glass fell from about 19 in 1843 to 5 in 1858. Soon production of glass for windows was concentrated in the three firms, Pilkingtons, Chances and Hartleys. By the early twentieth century Pilkingtons controlled most of the market and when they took over Chances in 1934 their monopoly, in the UK, was virtually complete.

The same sort of process – at different speeds and to different levels of concentration – has taken place in the production of most of the major basic and formed materials.

In the production of prefabricated components, the story is less clear; partly because there is scope for a wide range of different products, and many relatively small firms can survive. But even here the process of concentration is evident – and tends to accelerate in times of recession. One well-known example, to which we have already referred, is the manufacture of joinery. The fact that some 170 steel fabricators went out of business between 1990 and 1993 implies a rapidly increasing concentration there too; because this is a business which has become more capital-intensive, it will be difficult for small firms to get back in or for new firms to enter.

Small-scale producers will continue to exist usually by differentiating their product in some way (hand–made brick specials from local clays for example), serving specialized markets or acting as distributors for the large firms; but as the larger operators continue to innovate in process and now in variety, and as they often have the financial resources to survive recessions, the task for the smaller companies becomes more and more difficult.

The size of firms and the scale of production (which are not the same thing, as a firm may own many plants) has increased not only or merely because of technical change in production methods. Throughout British industry we have seen an increase in acquisition and mergers as much for financial reasons as for technical reasons. This is especially true of the conglomerates – organizations owning firms and production capacity in many 'industries' such as the Hanson group referred to above. Sometimes mergers and takeovers have been across different functions within construction (the combination of materials producer and contractor and builders merchant such as Tarmac), sometimes it has been across totally unrelated industrial activities (shipping and contracting and building materials, such as Trafalgar House). Often mergers and takeovers have been on an international scale. This phenomenon of 'conglomeration' may also have implications for price and availability, as divisions in weak or highly competitive markets can be supported, for a short while, by the stronger sections of the organization.

4.5 Competition and prices

4.5.1 Oligopoly

The production of building materials has become, then, mainly the province of very large and powerful firms, a situation described by economists as 'oligopoly'. Such a clumsy word needs a little explanation.

Industrial structures have been classified in economics as a spectrum of degrees of competition. At one end of the spectrum, a perfectly competitive industry would be one where there are very large numbers of producers of a particular commodity (though this is not an absolute condition of the 'perfect' in this context). The essential characteristics are that no one producer is large enough to affect the general market price levels of their goods and all of them are seeking to maximize their profits. Under these conditions prices would tend to be determined by the strength of demand (how much purchasers are prepared to buy at given price levels) and the costs of the lowest cost producers. Perfect competition is more important as a theoretical concept and the basis for development of general theories than as a description of many real situations.

At the other extreme, there is monopoly – where one company produces all the output of a particular commodity. Prices, theory predicts, would tend to be higher than under perfect competition because monopolists have some degree of control over their market, cannot be undercut by competitors and can use price discrimination to maximize profits. But true monopoly is very rare, particularly in our international economy where even if one firm dominates in a specific country, there is competition from abroad. The example in materials which approaches most closely the economist's ideal case of monopoly is the production of glass – in fact it is one of the clearest examples of monopoly from any industry in the UK. But even Pilkingtons have to face competition from abroad and from other materials which can be substitutes in the sense that if glass prices are very high, builders may use smaller windows and more alternative material in the walls of a house.

In between these two theoretical extremes of perfect competition and monopoly there are many forms of 'imperfect competition' – the most usual position in the real world. The theoretical analysis of imperfect competition is dealt with at some level in all the standard economics textbooks and is too complex to be fully explored here. But, as we have suggested, one form of imperfect competition is particularly significant – so called 'oligopoly' (from the Greek word for few, *oligoi*), that is the competition in the production of one commodity between a few firms, each of which is large enough to affect the total market and each of which is aware of its competitors' activities.

If it is true, as we have suggested, that most construction materials are in fact produced under these circumstances, we should expect some help in understanding their price and output characteristics from the theory.

However there is unfortunately no simple theory of oligopolistic competition which can be used to predict firms' behaviour in any detail. Sometimes behaviour is analysed in terms of 'game theory'; outcomes depend on how skilfully the individual firms play the game. There is therefore no way of predicting specific outcomes from specific sets of economic conditions.

But there are features which are claimed to characterize oligopolistic markets and which do help to illuminate the materials business. Some of these arise fairly obviously from the fact that there are only a few large companies involved. Each is likely to be aware of and react to the behaviour (for example the pricing policies) of its rivals. Various forms of collusion – tacit or explicit agreement – may take place to prevent suicidal price wars. Or price leadership my develop, where weaker firms will follow the pricing policy of the more powerful. Firms will strive through advertising to differentiate their product from others – thus obscuring the price rivalry and possibly securing a particular market niche.

Examples of all these 'conventional' oligopolistic forms of behaviour are extremely common in the materials industry.

Co-operation between companies (called collusion when it is assumed to be harming someone's interests!) takes place at the same time as intense competition; there were attempts, for example, by brick producers to get some agreement to limit the rate of increase in stockpiles during 1991 and 1992 (Figure 4.2).

One has only to glance at the trade press, magazines such as the *Architects' Journal*, and *Building*, to see how prevalent is competition through advertising and particularly advertising the distinctive qualities that differentiate the advertiser's product from other similar ones (Figure 4.3).

But price competition remains important and in some sectors overwhelmingly so; it is the form this competition takes, particularly as the construction industry goes through periods of recession and boom, that is of particular interest. After all, customers – whether builders, architects,

City calls for cutbacks in brick production
Immediate factory closures needed to reduce massive oversupply. Adrian Barrick reports.

LEADING BRICK manufacturers and City analysts this week called for up to 20% cuts in production and more factory closures to tackle the massive oversupply in the industry – despite Tarmac's announcement last week that it was shutting down four plants.

Senior analyst Leslie Kent, of Carr Kitcat & Aitken, said manufacturers need immediately to cut by one-fifth the current production rate of 3.2 billion bricks a year – double the reduction proposed by the Brick Development Association.

Mike Roberts, managing director of Marley Building Materials, which has cut production by 50% since 1988, most within the past year, said the industry should slash output by 15–20%.

Last Friday, Tarmac announced the closure of four brick factories: Bothwell Park in Scotland; Campbell in Derbyshire; Kibblesworth in the North East; and Severn Valley in Avon. All were trading under the name of Tarmac Bricks.

The contractor also closed four Tarmac Topblock concrete block plants – at Nuneaton in the West Midlands, Morrinton in Scotland, and Fleet and Bracknell in southern England. The eight closures resulted in a total of 300 job losses.

Tarmac chief executive Neville Simms said in a statement he looked "to our competitors to follow this strong lead in reducing industry capacity in line with both current and foreseeable market demand. "

The loss of Tarmac's four brick factories, with a total production capacity of 100 million bricks a year, will make little difference to the market, as stockpiles are so large.

The BDA estimates these currently stand at 1.49 billion – seven to nine months' supply of bricks.

The BDA also calculates that stocks rose by 3% from January to July 1992, compared with the same period last year.

Brick prices have fallen by up to 40% since 1989, according to a leading manufacturer.

A Redland spokesman described the Tarmac cuts as "somewhat modest" in comparison with his own company's decision earlier this year to cut production by 170 million bricks a year.

"The industry continues to have chronic overcapacity. Other players in the industry need to do a lot more to help," he said.

Kent and fellow Carr Kitcat & Aitken analyst Lawrence Amboldt said that since overall construction output has fallen by about 20% in the past five years there should be a similar cut in the production of building materials such as bricks.

Figure 4.2   'City calls for cutbacks in brick production'.
Source: Building, Sept., 1992.

A 'well-studded' comparison between proprietary plasterboards and FERMACELL® gypsum-fibreboards

Or why you'll get more kick out of building with us

The better the equipment, the better the results. This is not only true in the sporting world. It's even more valid for the building field. Yesterday's products can only be second best. Tomorrow's product available today in building boards is FERMACELL gypsum-fibreboard. And it's not second to none. It's the number one. For the best builders. For better building.

 More fire-resistance. FERMACELL not only meets BS 476, Part 22, but also has longer built-in reserves than its direct competitors.

 The heavy-weight champion in load-bearing, 50 kilos can be hung on a screw fastened into FERMACELL with a wallplug. Equivalent plasterboards fall apart.

 FERMACELL ensures effective sound-proofing of up to R'w 57 dB. A very sound investment compared to plaster-boards of the same thickness.

 Easy and stable mounting. Nails, staples and screws can be driven within 10 mm of the outer edge of FERMACELL. A crumbling thought for the competition.

 Problem-free jointing. With FERMACELL, you don't have to fool with special tools. And there's no taping to be out of joint – as with plasterboards.

 There are no "wets" in our range. Even when splashed, FERMACELL retains its original stability once dry. Ideal for rooms with changing humidity.

The number one and only
Gypsum-Fibreboard
fermacell
Well Made in Germany

Figure 4.3   Advertisement for Fermacell: the emphasis on product difference is used as a competitive weapon. (Reproduced with permission from Walton Masters Advertising Agency, Ismaninger Strasse 67a, 81675 Munich, Germany.)

surveyors or clients – should not continue to be taken by surprise if pricing behaviour in these circumstances is to some extent predictable. Before looking at how prices have actually behaved, two further characteristics of the materials market need to be considered briefly – the significance of foreign competition and the role of the builders' merchants.

4.5.2 Competition from abroad

Building materials have been imported into the UK for a very long time: bricks were brought from Holland in the fifteenth century and timber from Russia and Sweden. Marble came from Italy; and, later, hardwoods came from South America, Asia and Africa. Today, imports represent over 90% of timber used in construction.

Improvements in packaging and transport, and the lowering of protective tariffs, have opened up the materials market to international competition on a very large scale. To some extent this is bound to put limits on the degree to which monopoly or oligopolistic producers in the UK can raise their prices (Figure 4.4).

Again, however, the consequences are never clear or certain; a foreign material may be cheaper than a home-produced equivalent at one time but be suddenly priced out of the market by changes in exchange rates. And the availability of foreign-made substitutes complicates yet further the problems of choice, particularly if quality standards are not applied (as was still the case in 1993 for uPVC window frames).

Foreign competition is certainly having a powerful effect on some sectors

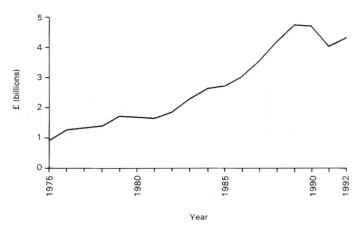

Figure 4.4   Imports of building materials, 1975–92.
Source: Housing and Construction Statistics.

of the home materials-producing industry. For example, one merchant has reported that in 1984 he sold two British slates for every one Spanish whereas by 1991 he was selling ten Spanish for every one British. Slates are now being imported from as far away as Brazil and China. At Canary Wharf, it was claimed, the costs of cladding the tower were brought down from 'an initial asking price of £800m^2 to £300m^2 . . . the advantage of having an international spectrum' (*Building*, 1991).

4.5.3 The builders' merchants

The role of the builders' merchants (like that of foreign competition) is a big enough subject for a section on its own and cannot be dealt with in detail here. The position is made complex in that they too, like the rest of construction, are going through a period of rapid evolution. There is still a very large number of local small firms, providing a channel from manufacturer (or large wholesale supplier) to the small and medium-sized contractors. But some merchants have themselves grown into very large organizations, operating on a regional or national level. Some have grown from specialist suppliers, some are subsidiaries of other large companies. And to make matters even more complicated, the supply of large quantities of material to the larger contractors is often direct from the manufacturers. The point to be understood is that by operating as middlemen, and having their own pressure for survival and maintenance of profit, they can and do (by the use of discounts, for example) determine the prices of materials as presented to final purchasers, often to the despair of the manufacturers. Again we look at some evidence in the next section where all these factors affecting prices and output are brought together with the evidence.

Indeed what happens in the materials market is not easily comprehensible in terms of oligopoly theory alone (though we have seen that helps to describe some characteristics). It is the outcome of all the factors we have described: continuous technical innovation, significant economies of scale, the particular structure of the market – its oligopolistic character, openness to foreign trade and its reliance on the building merchant system of distribution. The next section attempts a preliminary analysis of how these factors actually affect conditions in the materials market and looks at the evidence.

4.6 Secular change, short-term volatility

We will look at the effects on conditions in the materials markets across two rather vaguely defined time scales – the long term and the short term.

One long-term consequence of the phenomena we have described is on the choice of materials; the reduction in the number of producers and the

*Raising the image
('Brick is beautiful',
hoarding 1980s).*

large scale of production has not led as might be expected to excessive standardization, because it has been accompanied by technical innovation and competition through innovation. There are probably more shapes, colours and qualities of brick than there have ever been. There is certainly a wider range of glass available than ever and of course there are the new materials in abundance. And the cost of building materials relative to other costs has not increased.

A second long-term consequence of this combination of factors – large-scale, oligopoly, technical advance – has been the continuing battle between different materials which are possible substitutes – battles waged between giant firms or groups of firms acting together.

We have seen whole groups of large and powerful manufacturers competing against other similar large groups. Each will use the advantages of technical advance and scale economies to retain the market position of its own material. Over the last forty years particularly we have witnessed a fascinating game of attack and counter-attack as a new material is claimed as a satisfactory (and usually cheaper) substitute for another and then the traditional material is developed to meet the challenge. There are many examples: concrete tiles and slate; reinforced concrete versus steel frames; the development of laminated timber beams restoring the use of timber for large structural members; calculated brickwork; improvements in timber window frames in response to the advance of PVCu.

One important lesson to be learned from these long-term features of materials production is that architects, surveyors and contractors should never accept established advantages – either on price or quality – of one material over another as at all permanent. It is essential to keep abreast with developments both to ensure that one's preconceived notion of what is the most suitable material for a particular application has not become outdated and to take advantage of innovations as soon as possible.

To illustrate how circumstances can change and how mistaken prediction can be, the following quote is from a text of the 1970s:

It is possible that the peak of brick production was reached in 1965 – the highest output so far – and that the industry now faces a steady and permanent decline. Compared with other wall building components, a brick is very small and laying bricks demands a lot of what is now expensive labour. For most housing purposes, bricks and bricklayers are in the process of pricing themselves out of the market (Hudson, 1972).

What actually happened was that the brick industry, partly acting jointly through the Brick Development Association, improved its product, its prices, its delivery, its range of applications and, perhaps most important, mounted a large-scale, sustained and successful advertising campaign extolling the aesthetic qualities of brick. It almost certainly gained too from a general reaction in the UK (not replicated in most of the rest of Europe) against concrete. The consequences are that brick has regained much of its old market and some new ones too (brick paviours, for example).

A similar story could be told of other materials. In the early 1990s the timber producers, again partly acting jointly (through the Timber Research and Development Association) and the steel window frame manufacturers are mounting a counter-attack against the encroachment of PVCu into their markets (or getting into PVCu themselves by buying up production companies). The outcome of this particular battle is still not clear (for further discussion see Chapter 10).

If long-term features are mainly changes in range, choice and slow realignment of price advantages, the short-term implications of the factors we have discussed earlier in the chapter are the possibility of rapid price change and wide swings in availability (often measured by so-called lead times, the time it takes from order to delivery).

When the construction industry moves into recession, material prices would tend to fall whatever the competitive position among materials producers. But where materials are produced in large-scale units, firms will be extremely reluctant to cut back capacity. For the corollary of cheap, large-scale production – the reverse as it were of economies of scale, in that lower levels of production are extremely expensive – plant remains idle but has to be maintained and financed. Prices may remain high for a while as each producer tries to maintain profits, but as demand falls there will tend to be a wary price war; prices will fall as each producer attempts to retain a large share of a shrinking market but they will all be very much aware of their competitors' activities. No firms can survive for long at unprofitable price levels, but large firms, particularly those in conglomerate structures with large reserves, can survive longer than small ones. Their priorities will be to maintain output as high as possible even at the cost of unprofitable price levels, in the hope that once recovery begins they can quickly increase output and raise prices, thus recouping their losses. If the recession is prolonged and deep, factories will have to be closed – but each producer will keep a close eye on rivals hoping that they will give in first (Figure 4.2).

As soon, however, as recession ends or appears to be ending, firms, if they have survived, will want to recoup their losses, and prices will rise as fast as the market conditions allow. The nearer a firm is to a monopoly position, the easier it will be to raise prices as demand from contractors increases. If the recession has led to the closure of some large-scale capacity, then it is quite likely that demand will rise faster than firms can match; the result again will be rapidly rising prices and extended lead times.

So, although it is true that whatever an industry's structure, prices will tend to fall in a recession and rise as demand recovers, the effect is probably exaggerated by large-scale production and oligopolistic structure. Prices may fall, rather than production, in the short term, as demand slackens then rapidly increase as recovery begins. The effect may however be smoothed to some degree by the actions of the middlemen, the builders' merchants who will also be manipulating their retail prices – the prices charged to contractors, to maintain their own profits and market share.

The report from *Building* (Figure 4.2, p. 66) illustrates very clearly both the problems of recession when large-scale production is involved and also the acute sensitivity of producers to their rivals' policy. Attempts at agreed policies were made through the producers' association – but competitive pressures were clearly too strong.

By early 1993, as demand began to increase, producers moved quickly to raise prices as Fig. 4.5a shows. By June (Fig. 4.5b) the price rises were causing real alarm and by September further widespread increases were reported: ready mixed concrete, 7.5%; steel reinforcement bars, 12.5%; PVC drainage pipes, 15%; copper pipes and fittings, 23%. The reports from *Building* illustrate many of the points made above: the relative strength of the monopolies; the significance of imports; the difficulty in making price rises stick both because of competition and because of resistance from powerful purchasers. They show too how anxious the producers were to recoup losses incurred in the recession; despite their huge stocks, even the brick makers were managing to put up their prices.

The consequence of price rises of this order at a time when general inflation was at its lowest for twenty years were likely to be considerable, as Fig. 4.5b indicates; people responsible for estimating the costs of new building were likely to be caught by surprise, particularly as they had grown used to a period of very low prices and low tenders. Contractors and subcontractors become particularly vulnerable at such times because

Contractors face price hikes
Materials suppliers set for showdown. Alastair Stewart reports.

MAIN CONTRACTORS face a bruising showdown with material suppliers and subcontractors over attempts to raise materials prices.

Leading merchants and subcontractors this week told *Building* this time they are determined to pass on expected price rises in steel (up to 13%), glass (8%) and plasterboard (11–12%). It is also believed that aggregate producers will attempt a 6% rise in the spring.

A spokesman for one of Britain's top 10 contractors said "margins will be squeezed" on lengthy fixed-price contracts based on old materials prices. "We're now taking a realistic account of price rises, but only since the end of the year. "

Another top 10 contractor admitted its estimators had not assumed any significant rises in pricing its contracts.

Allan Collins, president of the British Constructional Steelwork Association and MD of Tetbury Structures, said steel subcontractors are determined to pass on the rises: "If main contractors don't price their jobs reasonably and think they can knock down the suppliers' prices they are going to be caught out."

City analyst Kevin Cammack of Smith New Court said that British Steel and Pilkington, in raising the prices of steel and glass, respectively, have the advantage that they are the only UK producers and competition from their European competitors has been reduced by the devaluation of sterling.

But Howard Proctor of Panmure Gordon, said: "None of the rises are likely to stick because contractors will go to other sources."

Figure 4.5a   'Contractors face Price Hikes' *Building* 22.1.93.

Materials hike chokes builders
City warns of squeeze on profits. Adrian Barrick reports.

MATERIALS PRICE rises of up to 13% are threatening contractors' profits, warns a report published by a leading City analyst this week.

In a 38-page report, analyst Panmure Gordon says "it is hard to see many companies making a profit on their contracting operations" over the next two years because of the steep rise in materials prices since April.

Contractors hit hardest, the report warns, will be those heavily committed to long-term fixed price contracts. On a £50m fixed price contract, an 8% rise in materials and labour costs could turn hopes of breaking even into a £4.9m loss.

"This will be all the worse for anyone who has deliberately taken on a loss-making contract in order to promote higher cash flow. This is the greatest problem the industry is going to have to face during the next couple of years," the report concludes.

To ease the impact on margins, contractors – including Mowlem and Costain – are responding by seeking fixed prices from materials producers, and buying as many materials as possible at the beginning of the contract.

Wob Gerretsen, Costain deputy chief executive, said: "We knew these rises were going to happen. It is now a case of giving ourselves sufficient protection. Within the group, we have said that any fixed price contract lasting more than 12 months needs board approval."

Ian Grice, managing director of Mowlem Europe, said: "We will not now take fixed price contracts of more than two years' duration."

According to builders merchants, recent rises from materials producers are beginning to stick. Steel is up 13%, plasterboard 11%. glass 8%, timber 7–8% and cement 2–3%.

London Brick also announced an average 1.1% rise in the price of some of its Fletton facing bricks last week, the company's first rise since January 1991. This followed Tarmac's announcement in April of a 7% rise in brick prices, which a spokesman said was now sticking.

Builders merchants predict more rises. Tony Travis, chairman of Northampton-based Travis Perkins, said a 5–6% rise in the price of roof tiles is expected in July, with building timber prices set to soar 15% over the next four months.

Figure 4.5b   'Materials hike chokes builders' *Building* 18.6.93.

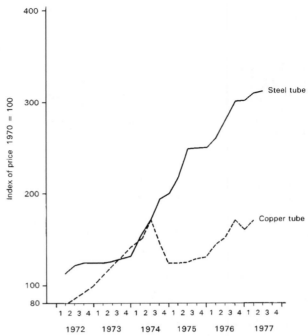

Figure 4.6   Indices of copper and steel prices in the early 1979s.
Source: Housing and Construction Statistics.

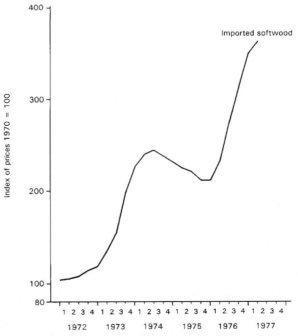

Figure 4.7   The steep rise in softwood prices, 1982–76.
Source: Housing and Construction Statistics.

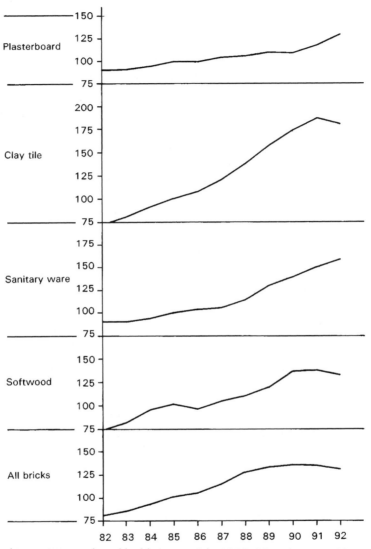

Figure 4.8 Differential price rises in selected building materials, 1982–92. Index nos 1985 = 100. *Source: Construction News.*

they may be working on fixed price contracts which they know to be only barely achievable without such increases in costs and indeed at the beginning of 1994 there were predictions of bankrupties on a very large scale. In fact neither the price rises nor the bankruptcies turned out to be as serious as predicted, as the recovery itself faltered.

The statistics for price changes both in the short term and the long term show that rapid changes are not unusual during periods when demand for construction is changing, and also show that relative prices, as a result of all the factors discussed in this chapter, can change quite significantly. Figure 4.6 for example shows what happened to relative prices of steel and copper tube during the period 1972–6 and Figure 4.7 the dramatic changes in softwood prices during the same period. Figure 4.8 shows the quite different courses of prices for a number of materials in the years from 1982 to 1992 and the particularly sharp rise in the price of clay tiles. To explain all these variations would require considerable detailed research; but the three diagrams themselves make an important point: it is never safe to rely on published prices unless they are very recent and it is never safe to assume that the relative cost of one material compared with possible substitutes is the same as it was some time ago.

4.7 Conclusion

The market for building materials is a highly volatile one; it is dominated by large-scale producers whose independent survival may not be assured, because competition from home and foreign manufacturers is fierce. In one sense this combination of high technology, scale economies and strong competition should be good for the British building industry as there are constant pressures on price; but on the other hand, there is often extreme uncertainty about price levels and availability and there are always questions to be asked, not entirely answered by the existence of Agrément and British Standard certification, about relative quality.

The aim of this chapter has been to give some insight into the building materials market and some understanding of some basic economic concepts – technological change, economies of scale and competition by demonstrating their impact on the materials industry rather than by theoretical exposition. In Chapter 8 we can address the questions of materials choice with an awareness that decisions are inevitably made in an environment of change and uncertainty, and that the information used to make these decisions has to be based on a realistic assessment of market movements.

FOR FURTHER STUDY

1 Recommended reading

For further understanding of the basic concepts discussed in this chapter consult a **recent** introductory economic text. Books relating the subjects specifically to construction include Manser (1994) and Raftery (1993a). A particularly good account of economies of scale and technological change is in Dudley Jackson *Introduction to Economics* (1982, Chs 7 and 8). Part 1 of Marian Bowley's *British Building Industry* (1960) and any of the case studies in her *Innovations in Building Materials* (1960) still make interesting reading. The construction press has to be the main source of information on current developments, specially the *Architects' Journal Focus* series and *Building's* regular *Materials* supplements.

2 Exercise

Using recent press reports (*Building*, *Construction Weekly*), establish whether materials prices are rising and at what rate. Explain the current situation in terms of the workload of the industry, and the supply and demand position for the various materials.

3 Discussion or essay questions

a Explain and discuss the meaning of 'economies of scale'. Why are economies of scale easier to achieve in the manufacture of building materials and components than in the process of building itself? What aspects of construction are subject to scale economies?

b What explains the survival of small businesses in the manufacture of: bricks; constructional steel; window frames?

c Does mass production necessarily lead to excessive standardization or lower quality? Consider the cases of bricks, glass, joinery and any other building material.

d Explain why 'monopolies' have been considered undesirable. Then consider the case of building materials: e.g. glass; are the disadvantages of monopoly outweighed by the advantage of scale? Bricks: could we finish up with one brick monopoly? Why has this not happened already? Would it be a bad thing?

4 Project

Visit a firm or firms manufacturing building materials or components on a large scale. Investigate the importance of scale economies, of modern technology and the nature of competition for the product. Try to establish the extent to which modern production methods are leading to the possibility of greater variety and individual specification within large-scale production systems.

5

Human resources for building

5.1 Introduction

It may be true that the task of the construction worker changed little over centuries. Shakespeare's Snug the joiner could no doubt have got along quite well with Robert Tressell's Ragged Trousered Philanthropists. Raymond Postgate in his now well-known 1923 comment; claimed an even longer immutability: 'If today a competent member of the National Association of Operative Plasterers were to meet the ancient Egyptian worker who used those tools, he might not understand the language, but he could work with him all day without suspecting that 4000 years lay between them' (Postgate, 1923).

Though there never was a typical building worker, the stereotypes are still recognizable; and it may still be true that a modern medieval bricklayer would find little different in the work of his modern successor. But the dominating image has changed; in hard yellow hat and boots, the construction worker drives a dumper truck or guides a concrete beam swinging from the jib of a giant tower crane.

The changed image reflects a changed reality. New skills have been developed to reflect new methods of working and the handling of new materials.

There is a general decline of craft skills associated with mixing, cutting, jointing, shaping and adapting materials on site. At the same time there is increasing emphasis in skills associated with positioning and alignment, measurement fitting and assembly. Traditional skills based upon rule of thumb are gradually being replaced by technical calculation (Gann, 1991).

The industry is still very labour-intensive, that is the ratio of labour to cost of capital is higher than manufacturing and other production industries. Most of the specific tasks involved in building still use very little mechanized equipment; the major exception is in the construction of high buildings where expensive cranes and concreting equipment are used but even there, the fixing and placing of beams, floor and all panels still use much manual labour. The costs of internal finishing, plastering, ceiling fixing joinery, floor laying, though all use small power tools, are still predominantly labour costs. In refurbishment projects the proportion of labour to equipment costs is even higher than in new building. The next chapter will consider some aspects of technology and its implications for productivity: this chapter concentrates on the workforce itself – its size, its changing composition and its costs. The full extent of the human resources needed to produce buildings is of course very difficult to estimate, for it includes not only the site operatives, but the administrative staff of the construction companies, the professional services of the architects, surveyors and engineers and all the other people inevitably involved in any construction project; however, we will concentrate here on the issues of the skilled and unskilled people who actually work on the site to put a building together.

5.2 A little history

The organization of construction labour has been very different from that of most other industries for much of the past 150 years. In fact its evolution has been through a virtually continuous tension between attempts to establish a permanent workforce with good working conditions – by both employers and unions – and the powerful market pressures leading to fragmentation of employment through casualization and labour only sub-contracting.

Buildings have usually not been, like most other goods, produced by people working as permanent employees of one organization; not like cars, for example, which are assembled in large factories by workers employed by the owners of the factory and the company – Nissan, Ford or whoever. Although component parts for cars come from dozens of different suppliers, these in turn employ a permanent workforce. The recent trend in

British industry generally to more part-time and short-term contracts has not yet radically altered that picture.

However in construction, although some major firms employ large permanent workforces and indeed the largest companies such as Wimpey and Tarmac have many thousands in their payroll, most of the work on most sites – the final assembly processes – is usually carried out by many different firms or individuals working on a subcontracted basis. For, although conditions have indeed changed and are changing rapidly, the relationship between building workers and building employers – the social relations of production as many writers usefully describe them – still shows remarkably strong traces of its medieval origins. In fact, as Graham Winch has argued, the Industrial Revolution, which changed the nature of work for most people from an 'independent' activity to factory labour, though it certainly did not leave construction unaffected (indeed it expanded the demand for construction dramatically and led to the creation of large employers of labour), did not undermine old construction craft divisions and the tradition of subcontracting.

The craft-based trade organization goes back to the medieval guilds; each craft, based on skills needed to work the different materials of building, developed its own ways of working, its own organizations and its own mechanisms of protection. As the guilds gradually disappeared under the pressures of the new contracting system of the early nineteenth century, some of their protective and training functions were taken over by the trade unions, but these remained until the relatively recent amalgamations, strictly craft-based.

Up to the beginning of the nineteenth century, a person requiring a building to be built would usually make separate agreements with individual groups of tradesmen, who would each be paid on the value of the work they did. The work itself might be co-ordinated by an architect, surveyor, one of the craftsmen or the building owner himself but none of them would be employers in the modern sense.

General contractors, employing men of all trades and contracting to take full responsibility for the whole building, became more significant towards the middle and end of the nineteenth century. Some of them ran very large organizations, employing up to a thousand men and owning their own joinery, stone-cutting and brick-making plants. They were in fact becoming more like the capitalist owners of the manufacturing industries which were expanding at the same period. The scale of operation of the larger contractors continued to expand during the twentieth century; through internal growth, and through takeovers of one firm by another the modern giant construction firms such as Tarmac, Laing, Wimpey came into being.

*Medieval
stonemasons at
work.*

But the practice remained of subcontracting parts of the operation to separate firms or individuals specializing in one aspect of work. This persistence of subcontracting is readily explained as a natural outcome of the discontinuity of building; there is never a guarantee that one major contract will follow another – and certainly no guarantee that it will require the same labour force or a sequence of trades which will allow continuity of employment from one job to the next. So from the main contractor's point of view it has always made sense to have a core of directly

*Modern
bricklayers: same
tools, new hats.*

employed people, then to take on extra on a short-term or subcontract basis as work required; this was common practice even in the mid-nineteenth century.

One important form of subcontracting (and it is only one of many forms) has been 'labour only' usually involving 'self-employed' workers, that is people hired to do a specific task or for a specific period of time, with materials and equipment supplied by the employer. Not all self-employed workers in the industry are subcontractors. Many, for example, particularly in domestic repair and maintenance, work directly for the building owners; and certainly not all labour-only subcontractors are self-employed, but the labour-only self-employed tradesman or labourer has become a significant and, as will be shown below, increasingly significant feature of the industry.

During the 1960s and 1970s, self-employed, labour-only subcontracting became the subject of bitter controversy. Known in its various guises as 'the lump' it was attacked both from left and right. The unions saw the practice as undermining the solidarity of the trades, weakening their bargaining power and undermining their considerable and successful efforts to establish national working agreements accepted by employers and unions alike. Eric Heffer, the Labour MP sponsored by the building union, UCATT, introduced a Bill in Parliament to have the practice outlawed in 1973. Ironically it was opposed on the far right and the far left, the 'Powellite' right (as it was then known) seeing the lump as an excellent example of a free untrammelled market in operation and the far left as the successful action of workers fighting capitalism – and its 'compliant' unions – with its own weapons (Lamb, 1974).

A special government inquiry (the Phelps Brown Committee) was set up mainly to investigate the extent and its implications of labour-only subcontracting (Phelps Brown, 1968). It came to the conclusion that better regulation was needed but that the practice should not be outlawed. Nevertheless it referred to 'the self employed form of labour only subcontracting which is officially condemned by both sides of industry', and said the evidence was that it had grown substantially.

Over many years unions and employers have attempted to establish a degree of stability mainly through the National Joint Council for the Building Industry (developed after the First World War and fully established in 1932) (Hilton, 1968). National agreements between employers and union representatives are set out each year in what is known as Working Rule Agreement (WRA). This, itself a frequent cause of dispute and hard negotiation, and quite possibly due to disappear shortly, defines conditions for building work in considerable detail. The 1994 edition runs to over 160 pages and is centred on 27 'rules' which define rates of pay, overtime, tool money, travel allowances, hours, holidays, sickness, retirement safety and much else.

The position of the unions in attempting to retain high levels of direct employment was undermined by many factors during the late 1970s and 1980s, particularly the sustained high level of unemployment. There was also the fact that new management methods were being introduced, that many of the new specialist subcontractors had little trade union tradition and most important of all government legislation was aimed at deregulation and the reduction of union influence.

Ironically even before the succession of Conservative government Acts aimed at reducing union influence, the Labour government Employment Protection Act of 1975 had, in the opinion of many employers at least, the perverse effect of encouraging a reduction in fully employed labour – as it increased the employers' obligations and costs. And when sections of Employment Protection Act were repealed, making national bargaining more difficult, the effect was reinforced. Self-employment was encouraged in government contracts; the Local Government Act 1988 made it unlawful for local authorities to impose conditions, such as requiring a proportion of directly employed workers, when appointing building contractors.

There is little doubt that the fragmented, casual character of employment grew more intense during the decade of the 1980s. But before analysing the issues in a little more detail we look first at some facts about the recent and current position – insofar as the reality can be deduced from the increasingly unsatisfactory statistics (several series have been suspended since 1991).

5.3 The construction workforce in the 1980s and 1990s

The problem is not simply a matter of limited and inconsistent statistics. It is quite difficult to get a clear picture of the overall size and structure of the workforce in the industry because not only does it vary with the stage of the building cycle, but there are also underlying secular changes taking place; the following paragraphs attempt nevertheless to assess the situation as it was at the beginning of the 1990s.

Total employment in the industry naturally reflects the level of work available; and construction has gone through two major cycles of slump and boom since 1972 with lesser ups and downs in between. A steep and sharp fall in orders in all sectors from 1972 to 1975 was followed by a relatively small rise and fall to 1980; there was then a long climb in sectors other than housing to a peak of activity in 1988 followed by a further steep fall going right through to 1993. Housing showed a smaller rise in the 1980s but shared the slump with other sectors at the end of the decade.

The number of people employed in the industry followed this pattern with a slight delay, falling from 1.7 million in 1975 to a low of 1.53 million in 1982; after a rise to 1.83 million in 1990, the numbers fell steeply to 1.4 million in 1993 (Figure 5.1).

However the most remarkable statistics are not the figures for overall employment but the way the composition of the workforce changed.

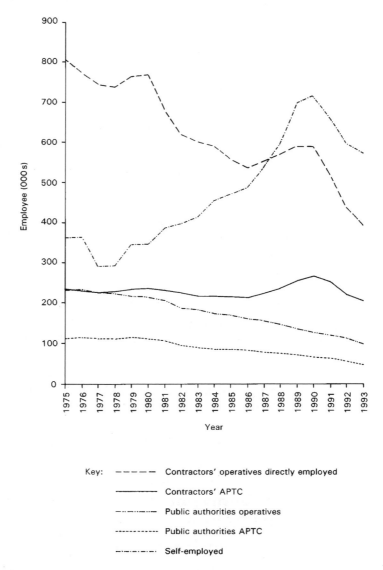

Key: – – – – –   Contractors' operatives directly employed

　　　　————————   Contractors' APTC

　　　　–··–····–··–   Public authorities operatives

　　　　-----------   Public authorities APTC

　　　　–··–··–··–   Self-employed

Figure 5.1   Number of employees in construction 1975–93, by category of employment. Source: Housing and Construction Statistics.

Employees are divided into two main categories in the published tables: operatives and APTC administrative, professional and technical grades; they are also divided into those working for contractors and those working for public authorities, those directly and those self-employed. Two major changes stand out. First, the drop over the decade in the number of direct employees in both sectors, by a third in the private (from 679 000 to 437 000 and by nearly a half in the public sector (from 205 000 to 112 000). The number of self-employed however increased from 385 000 to, at the peak year of 1990, 715 000; furthermore the group classed as 'employees not on the register', i.e. not working for registered companies, increased from 3000 to 94 000 over the whole period (Figure 5.1). Figure 5.2 shows the growth of self-employment more dramatically, from 27% of all operatives in 1977 to 60% by 1993.

This evidence of fragmentation of the labour force is underlined by other DoE statistics. Despite the recession, the number of very small firms was higher in 1992 than 1989 (though not as high as in 1990). In fact between 1982 and 1992, the numbers of firms employing over 24 people had dropped; but firms employing from 1 to 137 had increased from 126 000 to 193 000 (the range of firm sizes will be discussed further in Chapter 7. However the percentage of operatives employed by very large firms was as high in the early 1990s as in the 1980s (approximately 11%). Nevertheless to describe the industry as 'fragmented', and as increasingly so, seems to be reasonably well-justified by the figures. After all in 1992 over two-thirds of the operatives in the industry were employed in just over 200 000 different firms, each with less than 24 employees and most with considerably fewer. And when the figures are analysed by trade, the same kind of distribution is seen with only slight variations; 74 000 builders employ 12 100 operative; 21 700 electrical contractors employ 46 000 operatives. This is an average of only two in each firm, though in reality there is a wide distribution with some very large contractors and thousands of one-man ventures.

These bare facts and figures need filling out a little if we are to understand their implications and consequences at the side level and generally their implications for the costs and efficiency of the labour's contribution to construction.

5.4 Employment, self-employment and no employment

5.4.1 Cards in and subbies

The profusion of terms legal, formal and colloquial, used to describe conditions of employment in construction is formidably confusing. A

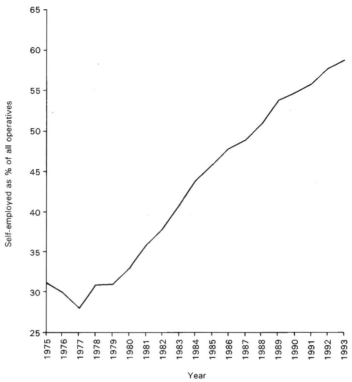

Figure 5.2   Self-employed as a percentage of all operatives, 1975–93.
Source: Housing and Construction Statistics.

building operative may, at one time or another have been described as 'on the lump' (less usual now), self-employed, 'cards in' (i.e. directly employed), a labour-only subbie, a 714, an SC60 – and no doubt a host of others, as the terms vary from region to region.

There are, however, fundamentally two types of contractual arrangements under which construction workers are employed – though there are many practices, widely recognized to exist which are on the borderline (or over) of illegality.

First a worker might be directly employed by a contracting firm, usually under the conditions of the Working Rule Agreement (WRA) referred to above (though there have been discussions on ending this system over the past few years). This, as was mentioned earlier, is a complex document, its very complexity seen as something of a disincentive to full employment by some contractors (especially smaller ones without personnel departments to handle it), but seen by the unions as providing the essential protection and guarantees needed in a volatile industry. Its requirements can be, as Figure 5.3 shows – part of the rule in tool allowances – extraordinarily detailed.

NWR 18—Tool and Clothing Allowances

(See Regional Rules on p. 102).

18.1 **Tool Allowances**

Tool allowances are paid in respect of the provision, maintenance and upkeep of tools provided by the operative and are NOT to be taken into account for the calculation of overtime, travelling time or of guaranteed minimum weekly earnings. Where employment starts after Monday, or is terminated in accordance with NWR 13 otherwise than on a Friday, the amount of tool allowance to be paid shall be the appropriate proportion of the weekly allowance for each day on which the operative was available for work in accordance with NWR 1.2.

Note—Tool allowances, although not forming part of an operative's basic rate, are liable to the deduction of tax and National Insurance contributions in the same way as other earnings.

Woodworkers providing and maintaining all necessary tools as and when required in connection with their work:

	per week
	194p

Carpenters and Joiners ....
Employers shall provide such special edged tools as may be necessary for use on Holoplast, Tufnol, or any similar plastic material.

Masons while manually working or fixing dressed stone with their own tools and producing on all necessary occasions for tools prescribed in the approved list.*

	per week:
Bankers Masons	152p
Masons Fixers	99p

Banker Masons are those engaged in shaping and finishing stones ready for fixing. Mason fixers are masons engaged in fixing dressed stone including jointing and cutting holes.

*See page 47

44

The Rule does not cover operatives using automatic or other tools supplied by the employer; nor does it cover machinists, wallers or paviors.

Plasterers. 99p per week to Plasterers while manually performing plastering work with their own tools and producing on all necessary occasions the tools prescribed in the approved list.* This Rule does not cover operatives using automatic or other tools supplied by the employer.

Bricklayers. 99p per week to Bricklayers while manually performing bricklayers' work with their own tools and producing on all necessary occasions the tools prescribed in the approved list.*

Painters. Overalls allowance .... 99p per week
To qualify for payment of this allowance the painter must provide himself with freshly laundered overalls at least once weekly.
Painters and decorators are not normally required to provide a kit of tools and, in consequence, they receive no tool allowance under this Rule. It is a recommendation of the National Joint Council that employers accept responsibility for the provision of tools which painters and decorators are required to use in the course of their normal employment.

Wall and Floor Tilers. 99p per week to Tilers whilst manually performing tiler's work with their own tools and producing on all necessary occasions tools prescribed in the approved list.*

Slaters. 99p per week to Slaters while manually performing slaters' work with their own tools and producing on all necessary occasions the tools prescribed in a list to be drawn up.

Woodcutting Machinists. Woodcutting machinists are not normally required to provide a kit of tools and, in consequence, they receive no tool allowance. It is a recommendation of the Council that employers accept responsibility for the cost of any necessary replacement of tapes and rules which the machinist has to use in the course of his work.

*See page 48

45

Figure 5.3   Extract from the 1994 edition of the Working Rule agreement. *Source:* WRA, 1994 edition.

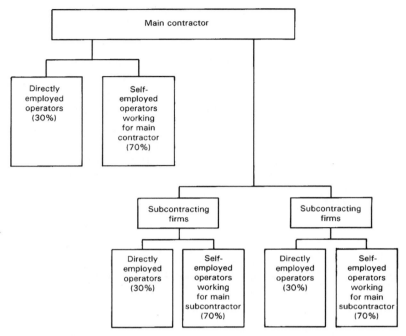

Figure 5.4   Possible organization of site employment (there will of course be normally many more than two subcontractors).

An employer is also responsible as in any other industry for the payment of the employer's share of national insurance, and of course for tax deductions under PAYE; they are naturally subject to the requirements of all the relevant employment Acts, health and safety regulations and a myriad others.

The second way of employing people is as subcontractors. Many of the subcontractors may be substantial firms which in turn employ workers directly. Some firms, especially in technical specialist areas, will also supply the materials; in which case the main contractor is only concerned with the total cost not the separate labour cost of a particular operation. However the main contractor may also subcontract to self-employed labour only subcontractors; these again may be groups of people working together or may be individuals. Furthermore the specialist subcontractors may also employ on a labour-only basis. Consequently the hierarchy of management and employment contracts on even a medium-sized scheme may become extremely complex.

Figure 5.4 is based on an actual – and relatively simple – example. The chain can be very much longer than this. Estimates from within the industry suggest that on an average site in the 1990s there will be about

30% directly employed, by main contractor or subcontracting firms and about 70% self-employed; some union sources put the proportion of directly employed as only 25% yet several major firms have said that only five to ten years ago the directly employed proportion could be up to 90% (including the directly employed staff of the subcontractors) – but this seems unlikely to have been general.

As if this system was not complicated enough, it is further confused by the fact that labour only subcontractors can be employed legally on two different bases. Self-employed subcontractors may be responsible for their own tax payment and national insurance, and of course make their own arrangements to holidays etc. To work in this the self-employed workers have to hold what is known as 714 certificates. These were introduced in 1975 (the Income Tax (subcontractors in the Construction Industry) Regulations) in an attempt to regularize the self-employment system and overcome the extensive tax evasion associated with it. A contractor employing workers on this basis is required to see the 714 (of which there are a number of variants – see Inland Revenue 1983) and employers have to certify to the Inland Revenue the gross payments made to each self-employed subcontractor. The Inland Revenue then calculates the tax liability each year.

The other basis on which self-employed subcontractors are taxed is the SC60 certificate; in this case, the employer deducts tax at the standard rate; the subcontractor then can reclaim any overpaid tax at the end of the year. Subcontractors do not like the system but have to accept it if for some reason they are ineligible for 714s.

There is considerable evidence, both anecdotal and documented through action by the Inland Revenue, that there are many ingenious ways in which the full tax liabilities are avoided and that much subcontracting is done on an unofficial basis. There is also evidence that not only the tax system but the social security system can be abused and manipulated, for example by employing labour-only subcontractors for very short periods at low rates, while they continue to claim benefits; a vigorous but, by its very nature obscure, black economy still undoubtedly exists.

One further twist to the complexity. The trade unions have successfully argued in many industrial tribunals that the so-called self-employed are in most senses of the word employed by the contractor; that the contractor still has a liability to provide them with proper site facilities, proper safety protection and many more of the Working Rule benefits.

Indeed National Working Rule 26 states

(employers shall undertake) . . . to take all reasonable and practical steps to ensure that all building trade operatives are in the direct employment of the

company and its sub-contractors and in either case are employed under the
terms and conditions laid down by the council, or if not directly employed, are
*holders of 714 certificates or engaged under SC60 arrangements and **are***
engaged under terms and conditions which, overall, are no less
favourable to the operative (authors' emphasis).

Many employers have fully or partly accepted this position and come to
local agreements with the unions on general policies to maximize security
of employment. Furthermore many of the self-employed are in fact former
employees of the contractor to whom they are now subcontractors; they
may have been forced into this position – made redundant and taken back
on a subcontract basis for particular projects; others appear to have chosen
the alternative, as overtime opportunities have reduced, to give themselves a
better chance of increasing incomes through extra work.

At the time of writing it seems that the Finance Bill of 1995 will make
major changes to the rules affecting 714s and SC60s, which some commentators have claimed will reverse the growth of labour-only subcontracting and
increase direct employment. The new provisions will not be fully in effect
until 1999, though will start to have an impact on the industry in 1996. The
long-term significance is hardly predictable at this stage.

NWR 26 is to be deleted from June 1995 and some of its provisions
incorporated into NWR 25. Agreement has been reached also to phase out
the current system of tool allowances illustrated in Figure 5.3.

5.4.2 An industry of casual labour?

The increase in labour-only subcontracting however is only one aspect,
though a very important one, of the way uncertainty has affected the nature
of employment. For many construction workers, even though directly
employed by major contractors, their jobs are very insecure; the industry is
still in many ways an industry of casual employment.

It is often claimed that this is an exaggeration; and much has indeed been
done to increase and improve the job security of workers over the last fifty
years. In its first paragraph the Phelps Brown Report rejected the adjective
'casual' but then immediately seemed to contradict itself.

> *It is misleading to describe construction simply as a casual industry. It is true*
> *that the levels of labour turnover and of unemployment are about twice as high*
> *as among workers generally* (Phelps Brown, 1968, p. 13).

The report argued that high rates of turnover affected only a minority.
However, a detailed study for the Construction Industry Manpower Board
in the late 1970s found evidence of extremely high employee turnover (that
is percentage of employees leaving a job per year) and a very low level of

stability of employment (measured by the average time men spent with a single employer) (Construction Industry Manpower Board, 1980).

The average 'labour turnover rate' was 70% in the year 1978–79 that is, by March 1979 70% of operatives had moved from the jobs they held in April 1978. Although when these figures were weighted to give an arguably more accurate figure they were slightly lower, the turnover was still remarkably high. The other measure used by the research group, stability of employment, also indicated a distinct lack of security. Although 'one year' rates were high (that is the percentage of workers remaining with one employer for a year), the three-year rates for general builders were just under 50%; in other words only half those employed by general builders stayed with the same firm for more than three years.

The general instability of employment must also be reinforced by the number of businesses failing altogether. Between 1989 and 1992, 12 000 self-employed construction workers went into bankruptcy and over 10 000 firms went into liquidation, some 15% of all liquidations in the UK.

To summarize, it is clear from the statistical as well as anecdotal evidence, that for the people who work in or would wish to work in it, construction is indeed an uncertain industry and that for many operatives, skilled as well as unskilled, it is an industry of casual and chance employment. One important point made by the Construction Industry Manpower board was that there was in fact no single group of 'construction employees' as people frequently moved in and out of the industry. In fact the report argued that the pool from which construction workers are drawn was something like a third greater than the actual number employed at one time; a situation which has probably changed little.

Two obvious questions arise. Why is it like this and what are the consequences? These are explored in the next sections.

5.5 Explanations and consequences

5.5.1 Causes

Many reasons have been given for the increase in the levels of sub-contracting and the continuing high level of casual employment in the industry. They include: the move by main contractors to manage increasing uncertainty and increasing risk; the wide range of more specialized work required, the pressure to cut costs in times of recession, the decline in the direct labour forces of the public authorities, the growth of small-scale maintenance work.

Curiously, and an indication perhaps that the phenomenon is not fully understood, both boom and recession has been blamed

> *Analysts of the sixties boom in labour-only subcontracting are unanimous in attributing the cause to the full employment and boom conditions of the time. . . . Price argues that the rise of labour-only in the 1890s was due to rising labour costs . . . this explanation will not hold for the 1980s* (Winch, 1985).

And during the early 1990s at a time of deep recession in the industry the phenomenon has continued to grow. Contractors interviewed recently by the authors are quite certain that the reason is simply the firms' inability to retain full-time staff when work is in short supply.

The advantages of labour-only subcontracting for the main contractors increased during recessions simply because it allowed them to cut costs. Their financial obligations to those working on site are considerably reduced; national insurance, sick pay and holidays are not their responsibility for example, despite NWR 26 quoted above. But more importantly, with work hard to come by and high unemployment among the trades, they can hold labour costs down more effectively by forcing competition among subcontractors.

However there are other explanations of the increase in labour-only work. Although this form of employment might seem to be a most unsatisfactory basis of employment for the workers themselves, there always seem to have been many who preferred things this way; again the reasons stretch back its history and the independence of the trades and the individual. Working on contract, especially at times of high activity, allowed a man to determine for whom and when he would work, to strike his own bargains. The more far-sighted in the unions have always known however that the main beneficiaries from such fragmentation would in the long run be the employers and the main losers the workers themselves; Helen Rainbird has described self-employment as

> *the self exploitation of self employed workers and their families, rather than the extraction of surplus value from other workers . . . Though in the short term they may obtain higher income than through direct employment, continuity of work is a major problem and considerable time and labour have to be invested in maintaining social contacts which may lead to work. This and the supportive family labour is not costed* (Rainbird, 1991).

Nevertheless there is no doubt that a very high proportion of the self-employed accept these disadvantages as the price of independence and well worth paying. On the other hand many have simply been forced into it. A recession, high unemployment among building craftsmen and the continued availability of repair and maintenance work would seem to have a fairly inevitable outcome, particularly as running a small maintenance business requires virtually no capital. Many will simply set up in business alone or with one or two others, and may occasionally subcontract to others when the opportunity arises.

5.5.2 Some consequences

Management issues. It has been argued that the kind of employment conditions existing in the industry are not only inevitable but are in fact an efficient response to uncertainty. It has also been argued that the last few years have seen great improvements in management efficiency which have counteracted and even exploited some of the effects of fragmentation. New forms of management have allowed the breakdown of old rigid trade demarcations, made it easier to dismiss unsatisfactory subcontractors (or select the most efficient), and given greater control to the project manager. The intensity of competition has led to reduced costs, allowing pressure to be put on subcontractors to perform to quite exacting standards and times.

However there is clearly a negative side as nearly all the official reports of the last fifty years have pointed out. It has been argued, for example, that the way construction workers are employed has reduced the level and availability of skills and made control of quality on sites and the allocation of responsibility more difficult. There is less commitment to either contractor, client or workmanship. Furthermore the breakdown of national agreements and the ubiquity of small subcontractors leads to free market in wages, which in turn has meant volatility in labour costs.

The Construction Manpower Board study cited earlier found over-whelming evidence among employers and employees of a preference for direct employment; the problems of instability were seen differently from each side, but were equally serious.

One example of the management problems the system creates is that men might be working side by side under different employment conditions and with contrasting attitudes to their work. The self-employed worker will be paid for a given task, his rates determined by the time normally taken to do that work (completing the tiling of a house roof for example); it is then in their interest to complete as quickly as possible – at least if they want to maximize their hourly earnings. The direct employee, however, paid at an hourly rate on the basis of a 39-hour week may not have the same incentive to complete specific tasks quickly. It is for this reason that all kinds of incentive and target schemes are common in the industry. They are even accepted as inevitable and necessary in the Working Rules, though relatively recently:

> *it shall be open to employers and operatives to agree an Incentive Scheme and/or Productivity Agreement . . .*
>
> *The objects of an incentive scheme or Productivity agreement are*

(a) *to increase productivity and reduce costs*

(b) *to enable operatives to increase their earnings by increased effort while maintaining a high standard of workmanship* . . . (NWR 1, 7).

But perhaps the major disadvantage of instability in employment is the effect it has on training and skills

5.5.3 Training and the level of skill

The question of levels and availability of skills is clearly important for our central theme of value for money and the possibility of translating design of high quality into building of high quality.

The acquisition of skill in construction was traditionally through a long apprenticeship; in more recent times this has often been combined with attendance on a day-release basis at a college. There has always been a problem of ensuring a steady flow of new skilled people into an industry; the problem has been particularly acute in construction because of chronic instability; many firms were not prepared or claimed that they could not afford the cost of training. Those that took their training obligations seriously resented the fact that others who did not could simply poach their skilled people; or that the newly skilled, once they obtained their qualifications, could go freelance as labour-only subcontractors at times of high demand.

The Construction Industry Training Board exists to overcome some of these problems; a compulsory levy on firms' finances, the Board's activities and the cost of the training course it runs. The levy remains controversial and came close to abolition in 1993. But its existence is probably critical to any chance of improving levels of skill and developing new skills (and combination of skills) required.

According to the IPRA study, the number of trainees registered with the CITB has fallen dramatically from 135 000 in the mid 1960s to under 50 000 in 1988. However, figures from the CITB's report of 1994 give a less pessimistic picture. Figure 5.5 shows the change in the number of apprentices and the changes in the number of youth trainees. Changes are fairly closely related to the construction business cycle (Gann, 1991).

At an anecdotal level it seems to be fairly commonly believed in the industry that the availability of skilled people has declined – though the quality of skills of those who are trained remains as high as ever.

The 1979 study for the Construction Manpower Board included a question on the levels of skill as perceived by the employers and already at that time there seemed to be an overwhelming view, particularly on the part of the larger firms, that the level of skill and the range of skills available had declined over the previous ten years. But the question was vaguely worded and obviously one to which highly subjective answers, coloured by vague memories of a golden age may have contributed.

As the industry appeared to be coming out of recession in the early 1990s, there were frequent reports of skills shortages and the threat of an explosion in wages. (See the extract from *Building*, Figure 5.6.)

However there are countervailing trends. Although the Construction Industry Training Board has had to struggle to survive, the combination of its efforts with the new government training initiatives, development of National Vocational Qualifications etc., has opened up new routes to skill acquisition; and there are centres of real excellence for training. The Board's report referred to above proposes a new industry training scheme offering many different routes to fully recognized qualifications in all skills (CITB, 1994).

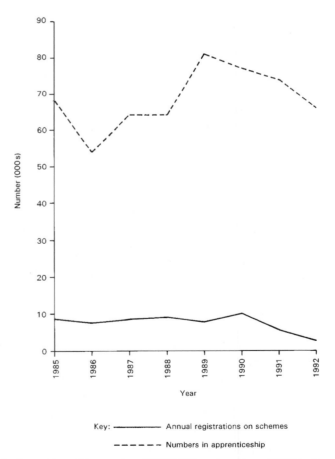

Key: ———— Annual registrations on schemes

– – – – – Numbers in apprenticeship

Figure 5.5   Change in the number of apprentices (1985–92) and number of CITB trainees (1976–92). *Source*: Construction Industry Training Board.

The fact remains that numbers of young people completing such training and then being able to develop their skills in continuous employment is too small; in 1993, the CITB's chief executive reckoned the need was 12 000 trainees a year against the actual 8500 that year (*Building*, 1993b). Whatever efforts are made, the very scale of self-employment remains an obstacle to upgrading skill across the industry. Helen Rainbird's research has shown that what one might suspect is indeed the case: the self-employed and the small subcontractors do not in general undertake training either for themselves or for their own employees.

5.6 Labour costs

The cost of labour as a component of the total costs of construction depends both on the money that is paid to employ workers and on their productivity. We look first at the basic costs of employment and then in the final section at productivity.

From the earlier discussion it will be clear that the cost of employing a building operative will depend on whether he or she is directly employed or not. And for the direct employees the total costs are of course, as in any

Skills gap threatens recovery
Survey shows supply trailing demand. Alastair Stewart reports.

SHORTAGES OF skilled labour are hitting some contractors and the majority are seeing material and subcontract prices rising, according to a survey of 300 contractors and consultants.

A quarter of all contractors questioned in September by market research organisation Gallup for *Building* and recruitment specialist Montrose said that supply of skilled labour did not meet demand. Another 38% said supply just met demand.

The findings cast doubt on whether the industry can cope with an upturn in workload. Dudley Barratt, Costain's group industrial relations adviser, said: "It only needs an upturn of 1.3% and there will be quite a problem. If it is 10% there will be real problems and you will see companies going over the fence for people, paying more to attract them from other firms."

Montrose director Les Dowson says shortages of bricklayers and carpenters are already hitting central London. He said the average number of replies to the agency's job adverts in the capital had fallen sharply in the past six months.

Dowson predicted wage inflation "could become an issue in the new year."

The findings are backed up in a survey of tender prices by QS Davis Langdon & Everest to be published in *Building* next week. The practice reports that the latest figure for direct and self-employed people working for contractors is 1.3 million. This is below the previous low of 1.4 million in 1986, when output was £15.5bn. The current figure is £17bn.

The Construction Industry Training Board has reported that the number of people completing building-related Youth Training schemes fell from 10 624 in 1990 to 6200 this year – a drop of 42%.

The survey also found that 56% of contractors reported rises in material and subcontractor prices.

The 300 firms said they planned to raise staff salaries by an average of 1.6%.

Figure 5.6   'Skills gap threatens recovery', *Building*, 1 Oct. 1993.

industry, considerably more than the wage rates. It includes the costs of insurance, pension scheme, tool money and much else. The all–in rates calculated for the purposes of cost estimation and published by Spon's and others incorporate all these extras. Figure 5.7 is an extract from Spon's Price Book showing how this all–in rate is derived. In theory this is the full cost of employing a craftsman, a figure from which the labour costs of a particular task can be estimated.

When self–employed workers are used rather than a firm's own direct

			Craft Operatives £		Labourers £
		£			
Wages at standard basic rate productive time.	44.30 wks	159.71	7074.93	136.11	6029.67
Lost time allowance.	0.90 wks	159.71	144.73	136.11	123.04
			----------		----------
			7219.30		6152.72
Extra payments under. National Working Rules 3, 17 and 18.	46.80 wks	2.05	95.94	4.11	192.35
Sick pay.	1 wk	-	-	-	-
CITB levy.	1 year	-	18.93	-	16.41
Public holiday pay.	1.60 wks	159.71	255.53	136.11	217.78
Employer's contributions to annual holiday pay, accidental injury, retirement and death cover scheme.	47 wks	18.85	885.95	18.85	885.95
National Insurance.	47.80 wks	13.62	651.04	9.06	433.07
Severance pay and sundry costs.	Plus	1.5%	136.90	1.5%	118.47
			------------		----------
			9263.59		8016.74
Employer's liability and third-party insurance.	Plus	2%	185.27	2%	160.33
			------------		----------
Total cost per annum.			9448.86		8177.07
			------------		----------
Total cost per hour.			5.47		4.73
			------------		----------

Figure 5.7   The composition of wage costs: typical build-up of all-in rates, 1993. Source: Spon's Price Book.

employees, the situation is less clear. In fact there seems to be considerable variety of practice. However, the agreed rates and conditions determined by the Working Rule Agreement set a level of wages recognized as a standard throughout the industry. Even though labour-only subcontractors will not be working under those conditions the rates they can charge will be determined on a reasonably realistic assessment of the time taken to do the work and the current going rate for that particular trade.

For example, trade union representatives advise on a reasonable rate as made up of the basic agreed NWR rate plus specific allowances for national insurance, travel, tools, sick pay and bank holidays. An example quoted to the authors was as follows (hourly rates)

Basic craft rate:	£4.81
National insurance (based on £200 p.a.)	£0.50
Holidays	£0.50
Sick pay etc.	£0.70
Travel	£0.50
Giving a total rate of	£6.21

But in all cases the actual rates paid depend on market conditions and on the conditions and terms agreed at an actual site. The variations can be wide from site to site and week to week. The realities of the situation in the trough of the slump in 1992 as experienced by one worker are brought out vividly in the article from *Building* (Figure 5.8) (*Building*, 1992).

Two years later there were reports of bricklayers keeping in touch with each other from one site to another by mobile phone as available wage rates rose rapidly. There was an immediate response of supply to demand in a perfect market response which few textbook examples could match. But this is a system which solves few problems except, in the short term, those of the lucky bricklayers who get the highly paid jobs; the shortage of skills and the instability remain.

5.7 Productivity

The word productivity is often used rather vaguely – particularly in construction where, whatever the definition adopted, it is difficult to measure with any accuracy. Sometimes it is used loosely to mean the general level of efficiency of an operation or an industry but, to be measurable at all, it needs more accurate definition. Productivity will be used here to indicate a measure of output per unit of input taken over a definite period of time; for example, the productivity of bricklayers could be measured as the number of bricks laid per man per day. An alternative is to measure the output in value terms – the value of work done per man per day.

Dispatches from the front

Twenty-three years after he came to London, the recession has thrust Irish carpenter Joe Neville back with the lot of the transient worker – no job security, no banking facilities and regular abuse by the employer. Alastair Stewart reports.

JOE NEVILLE, a self-employed carpenter, is not happy. Wages have nosedived, he has been thrown off several jobs and being Irish costs him money.

While most workers cash their pay cheques at a bank, Neville says he and many other Irishmen are forced to cash theirs at certain pubs in Kilburn, the centre of the Irish community in London. A publican's commission, though, can be somewhat higher than that of a high street bank.

"One charges £7. Others are worse. They can take 20% or 30%," says Neville, who has worked in mainland Britain since he left his native Antrim in 1969 to escape the troubles.

"Most contractors won't pay cash, and the majority of Irishmen don't have bank accounts. Banks are very reluctant to have them as customers."

The publican's commission (and the formality of a round of drinks at London's inflated prices before the transaction) is just another drain on resources. Married, with three children, he says: "Rent's up, everything's up, except the wages."

Two years ago he was earning up to £1000 a week working on some of the capital's biggest building projects, such as Chelsea Harbour. This entailed working seven-day weeks, at a daily basic rate of £95–100, with 12-hour shifts on double time at weekends.

But then the weekend shifts were halved. Next, the daily shifts started getting shorter, then the rates began dropping. "They started cutting back by £5 here, £5 there."

Now he is working six or seven days a week. "But I'm earning half what I was then."

For the past eight weeks Neville has been working for bricklaying subcontractor Vogue Developments on Bovis's Waterloo Channel Tunnel terminal, earning £60 a day. "Vogue are all right. Other companies would pay £50," he says.

Neville's experience of pittance rates includes one subcontractor who pays general labourers £30 for a 12-hour day. "And the men were not allowed to take a tea break in the afternoon." In contrast, labourers are paid £5.40 an hour by Vogue, says Neville.

Other more sinister stories suggest corrupt practices where subcontractors, for instance, pay cash in hand (and not very much of it) to workers in the knowledge that they are collecting unemployment benefit. Abuse of 714 and SC60 tax exemption certificates is rife among employers and workers alike, claims Neville.

Job security is elusive, he says. "I've lost countless jobs. The only regular work I've done lately has been at Waterloo. Firms can hire you and fire you at will." Often he has been on site for only a week before being kicked off.

Neville says sometimes he and other men have been told there is no work for them, but have subsequently found out they were replaced the next day by the same number of new hands.

Getting outstanding pay, let alone pay in lieu of notice, has become a labour, he says. It took countless phone calls over a period of 18 months and a trip to the Citizens' Advice Bureau before he received £475 for his final week's work on the Fulham & Westminster Hospital.

Wages and conditions for the self-employed are, in general, a disgrace, says Neville, who argues that self-employment's inherent problems are condoned by both employers and unions. The flexibility of using self-employed labour appeals to contractors, and the unions have been powerless to stop it. "I would love to be directly employed," he sighs.

Neville has been a member of both the recognised construction unions, UCATT and the TGWU, as well as the construction and building trades section of the electricians' union EETPU (now merged with the Amalgamated Engineering Union to become the AEEU).

He says he joined the EETPU because of disillusionment with the other two unions.

UCATT and the TGWU won a 2.5% increase in the national minimum wage at last month's annual bargaining round with the BEC and Federation of Civil Engineering Contractors. But Neville has nothing but contempt for the whole system of wages and conditions in this country, having seen German workers treated better while he worked there in the 1970s. "The pay increase doesn't relate to most building workers because they are self-employed. We have no conditions attached to our wages."

Figure 5.8   Wages – one man's experience in the recession. Source: *Building*.

Measures of productivity need not necessarily be restricted to labour but can be applied to other resource inputs such as cranes, or to a combination of inputs. However its most frequent application, for good economic reasons, is to the output of people, whether by manual or mental work, and that is how it is used in the next few pages.

In fact discussions of productivity in construction have generally been at one of several different levels – the productivity of individual gangs or groups of workers, the productivity on particular sites or projects and the productivity in the industry as a whole; but they are all essentially about the same thing – the output per worker over a given period of time.

In construction operations the level of productivity in this sense depends on a number of different conditions: three important ones are:

- the intensity of work;
- the type of work;
- the technology used.

5.7.1 Intensity of work

'Intensity' covers aspects of working such as speed and continuity and it in turn depends on different factors, skill, willingness to work hard but most importantly in construction, having the opportunity for continuous work. Productivity studies carried out for the NBS and BRE in the 1950s found that some skilled bricklayers could maintain high-quality work and yet do twice as much as some others; anecdotal evidence from sites today indicates that this is still the case.

Willingness to work hard is naturally a matter of individual motivation; this will be affected by general conditions on site, relationships between managers, supervisors and operatives but also by the terms of employment. Incentive schemes such as those briefly referred to above are quite clearly believed to be effective; and provided they combine a decent basic rate with bonuses do not any longer appear to be considered by the unions as necessarily exploitative

> *It seems generally accepted that subcontract labour is more productive labour . . . in part this is due to the fact that direct employees have to be paid for non productive time . . . but the main effect comes from the fact that subcontractors are usually paid by 'the lump' for specified pieces of work . . . this incentive attracts faster workers and encourages gangs to work effectively* (Winch, 1985).

Some reduction of the intensity and hence productivity of work on site is, to quote Bishop, 'related to individuals, walking time, casual conversation and deliberately incurred idle time such as card playing.' Some of this is inevitable, but keeping it under control without creating an atmosphere of oppression is clearly one function of sensitive management (and not always achieved).

However, the most significant cause of delay and idle time is the lack of continuity between tasks; achieving a smooth flow of work on site so that all trades can follow one another without interruption is a prime task of programming – Chapter 12 will examine this in more detail. But however good the programme, interruptions will almost inevitably occur through external factors such as bad weather, delays in the delivery of materials (or delivery of faulty materials) and delays in the delivery of equipment. Because so much in building involves a succession of stages, a hold-up at one point can have repercussions for the whole programme. In studies quoted by Bishop, idle time resulting from all these causes was found, in the worst examples, to mount to 80%!

Finally one very significant factor which affects the intensity of work – the speed with which activities can be completed – is the experience groups of operatives have had both in working together and in working on a particular form of construction – how far up their learning curve they are, as it is sometimes expressed. There is to a considerable degree a new learning curve for each project, but where a number of projects have the same characteristics and are carried out mainly by the same teams – such as on housing schemes – productivity can rise considerably (Bishop, 1975, p. 80; Phelps Brown, 1968, p. 173; CIOB, 1995).

It is, incidentally, the influence of all these factors on the intensity of work which partly accounts for the relatively small impact of the 'scientific management' approach through the study, control and intensification of individual activities. This has been the subject of exhaustive investigation and experiment particularly in bricklaying since the pioneering work of Frank Gilbreth at the turn of the century. (For a good account and bibliography see Steel and Cheetham, 1993.)

5.7.2 Type of work

The second major influence on labour productivity is the type of work involved, particularly whether it is mainly the assembly of prefabricated components, the repetition of similar operations or the individual fabrication and assembly of elements on site. There is something of all three types of work on all projects but some are very much more pre-assembled than others.

> *Designing a building as a relatively small number of components, whether in-situ or prefabricated, so that each is a substantial part of the whole building*

and can be completed by the work of one gang reduces the number of stages and leads to simplified management (Bishop, 1975).

Prefabrication can be expected to be a critical factor in measuring site productivity, for as most of the work is already done, although the final value added on the site will be lower, the apparent productivity of the building process will be higher; it will require fewer site man hours to produce the building.

However the position is not necessarily so straightforward. For example, problems of discontinuity do not disappear: new problems arise in the accurate fitting and jointing of components, particularly if they are not carefully made or tolerances are too low. Total costs, the outcome of the productivity of the system as a whole, are not inevitably reduced. The overall cost of a concrete panel delivered (expensively) to a site and erected with (expensive) cranes may well be higher than covering the same area with bricks laid by a skilled bricklaying gang.

There seems little doubt, nevertheless, particularly for large projects, that where the high fixed costs (discussed in the following chapter) of equipment can be justified, a building designed on a modular basis and assembled largely of standard components lends itself to higher productivity. This is certainly a view expressed in many reports on the industry including Latham.

5.7.3 Application of technology

Finally, labour productivity may be affected by the technology used – the plant, machines and tools. The next chapter is devoted entirely to this issue; but one of the conclusions may not be unexpected: unlike many other industries, technical advance, though significant, has not always been the major contributor to increasing site productivity.

5.7.4 The productivity of the industry as a whole

Measurements of the productivity of the whole industry, which are in any case very crude, based upon the **value** of overall output related to the size of the labour force seem to indicate that the critical influence is the stage of the building cycle (Figure 5.9). This is not surprising. As competitive pressures become severe managers, subcontractors and independent operatives are forced to produce more for less. One has to be very cautious in interpreting this as necessarily a good thing. There are questions of quality and the sustainability of the kind of high productivity induced by severe competitive pressures; firms are forced to cut corners and many are driven out of existence.

There can also be threats to quality at high levels of demand as everyone tries to obtain the maximum amount of work; skill shortages lead to higher costs and also to the use of less skilled people to do jobs for which they are not adequately trained.

Somewhere between severe slump and excess demand should be a level which can allow both high productivity and high quality to co-exist. A steady growth path (or even a stable state of demand) which would allow the stream of skilled people coming onto the industry to match the need for them, and which would allow firms to operate with confidence but maintain sufficient competitive pressure to keep them constantly aware of productivity and quality, would clearly be an ideal. It has never been achieved for long – and a discussion of the problems of achieving it would take us well beyond the subject of this chapter.

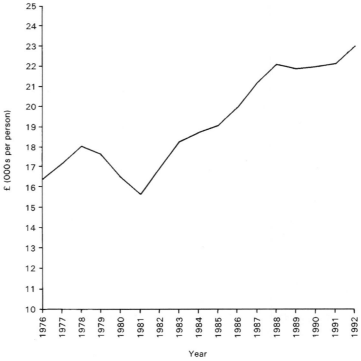

Figure 5.9   Productivity in construction: output per person, 1976–92.
Source: Construction Industry Training Board.

5.8 Conclusion

All of this might seem remote from the concerns of the architect and the quantity surveyor, if not from the building manager. All they can do, it might seem, is accept the sort of average costs published or discovered through their own market research and build these in to their own estimates. Yet there are issues which should be of great concern both in the consideration of the individual project design and at a more general level, in terms of the quality of building as a whole.

First at the project design level it is clear that labour requirements should be realistic in terms of the skills available and ways in which labour can be effectively employed. A project which offers continual employment for particular trades, rather than intermittent, will have several advantages: it will enable employing contractors to use workers more efficiently and therefore less expensively; it is more likely to generate a sense of commitment to the job from the people employed; shared pride in the work, which today may sound like a sentimental and nostalgic dream, has always been part of the best in construction and is still a powerful force for quality.

At a more general level, the whole fragmented system can be seen as a threat both to efficiency and quality. There are two different ways in which labour costs can be contained. First productivity can be increased through better management organization, better training, new construction techniques and possibly new technology. There are undoubtedly attempts being made to achieve these improvements.

But secondly, costs can be held down through pressure on payments from competitive forces and low tenders; these keep rates down and output up but often at the cost of quality. A system of massive self-employment does not as we have seen help to engender a climate of high-quality training and commitment to a project.

It may be, as Bishop argued, that the system is a natural and effective response to uncertainty and that uncertainty is endemic in the industry. There must be some good in the system; and there is certainly something quite impressive about the way the apparent chaos, dirt and noise of a building site is transformed into a new building or housing estate. It may be that there is a certain inevitability and some advantage from the employment patterns and methods the industry has clung to for so long.

Yet it is difficult not to believe that a more even flow of demand, and a more certain career structure for the industry's workforce, would go a long way to producing consistent high quality with reasonable cost.

FOR FURTHER STUDY

1 Recommended reading

On the general issues of the development of labour relations in the industry, the series of volumes produced by the Bartlett International Summer School contain many excellent analyses. See especially the many contributions by Linda Clarke, Jörn Janssen and Graham Winch.

Although now very dated, the Phelps Brown Report is still instructive and its analysis of labour only subcontracting still surprisingly relevant; the fact that it **is** still relevant itself says much about how intractable some of the industry's problems are. The same is true for Donald Bishop's essay on productivity in Turin, *Aspects of the Economics of the Construction Industry* – still essential reading; and much of what he had to say in his contribution to Phelps Brown still applies.

The study by Steel and Cheetham of the work of Frank Gilbreth gives an interesting historical insight into early efforts to increase the productivity of bricklayers both through 'intensification' and technology (Steel and Cheetham, 1993). An excellent recent summary and discussion of research on productivity is in *Effects of Accelerated Working, Delays and Disruption on Labour Productivity* (CIOB, 1975).

2 Discussion or essay questions

a Identify and discuss the advantages, disadvantages, causes and consequences of labour only subcontracting, from the point of view of the workers themselves, the employers and the architects. (This last group is hardly ever considered in this context.)
b Find out more about the application of so-called 'scientific management' to construction. Has the industry's attitude to management moved in line with modern thinking on management techniques?
c Define 'productivity' and explain (i) why it is difficult to measure in construction and (ii) why it is difficult to improve. What are the key elements in your view of high productivity levels?
d Have modern building methods and technology made the 'single craft' tradition outdated?

3 Project

a Play the Building Game (BRE, 1976) (this needs a large group, plenty of time and good organization; it is equally relevant to the following chapters).
b Try to discover and report on the incentive schemes, bonus payments and general wage structure operating within a particular firm or on a particular site.
c It is common to bemoan declining standards of craftsmanship in

construction. Yet some firms recently interviewed believe standards are actually improving, though the number of really skilled people is insufficient. Is there a 'skills crisis'? Explore the problem using evidence from the construction press and by talking to people in the industry.

Excavator and digger: basic technology of the small site; simple but flexible and efficient.

Tower crane: high technology.

6

Technology: from steampower to robots

Outline

- The myth of backwardness?
- A history of technical progress
- Technology on site: plant, tools, computers
- The impact of off-site technologies
- Basic economics of plant operation
- Robotics – the future?

6.1 Technological backwardness – myth or reality?

As total theatre it was an amazing spectacle . . . it was beautiful . . . it was impressive . . . Swinging a two ton block of stone hundreds of feet into the air before dropping it onto a cradle of its exact dimension looked dangerous and difficult to me, but the crane driver disdained to show any emotion. It was all magnificently orchestrated: . . . A minute adjustment to the chains, a nonchalant wave of the hand and up it went poised in one graceful movement . . . nobody applauded. Perhaps we should have done (from a description of the crane assembly for redevelopment at Lincoln College, Oxford, Gill, 1994).

The construction industry is, despite evidence to the contrary, still often described as technologically backward; it is an image the industry has lived with for a long time. Marian Bowley writing of the industry in the nineteenth century referred to the 'general failure of British architects to display interest in new methods of construction which were rapidly developing in other countries' and of the engineers who were by the end of the century 'quite as technically retarded as the architects' (Bowley, 1966, p. 33). A century has passed since the period to which Bowley refers and yet a report published for the Department of Employment in 1991 could refer to 'the failure to develop and take advantage of new techniques and methods of organisation in all but a few large construction projects (Gann, 1991, p. 8).

This view of the industry as technologically backward can be expected to have some foundation in fact if only on the principle that there is no smoke without fire – and it is certainly widely held. There is indeed a difference between the automated production line of most manufactured goods from cars to Kitkats (5 million of which are produced every day) and the apparent chaos of the building site. But the main reasons for the differences are not far to seek. As it is still the case that most buildings, except houses, are single unique objects, there is clearly not the same scope for production-line methods; where there is scope for repetition, as in housing, some of those methods can and have been applied; and where technologies have seemed to offer real advantages in productivity, they have been adopted. (The use of mobile phones by bricklayers and joiners mentioned in the last chapter, to keep a continuous check on going rates of pay on other building sites, may not help productivity but it shows a lively awareness of the possibilities of new technology!)

Nevertheless, it is certainly true that the level of capital per worker or per unit of output – the degree of capitalization – is lower in construction than in most other industries. Building is still, as shown in the previous chapter, highly labour-intensive. How then can the different images of construction be reconciled – the image of the new technology-driven industry which can create buildings such as the Hong Kong and Shanghai Bank building in Hong Kong and an industry where most of its constituent firms have no more equipment than a pick-up truck, ladders and a few hand tools? The fact is that of course these are two aspects of a very diverse industry which does adopt and has in the past adopted new technology where and when appropriate. There have undoubtedly been errors and missed opportunities; a climate of uncertainty tends to conservative attitudes, but the image of a completely backward industry is far from the reality.

6.2 Using available technology

6.2.1 Early developments

During the nineteenth century, as a recent study by Akira Satoh referred to in Chapter 5 has shown, the industry was as quick to take up new technologies as any, though, because of the nature of construction process, it was not possible to achieve the same gains in productivity. For example, the steam engine was applied at a very early stage in its development to lifting heavy items on site and to driving machinery in the manufacturing facilities often at that time owned by the large contractors. At St George's Hall in Liverpool a steam hoist was used by the local firm of Tomkinson Brothers (a firm which defied the uncertainties of construction for over 150 years, finally succumbing in 1993). 'The machine ran on a tramway laid parallel to the wall' and was said to accomplish its task 'with wonderful rapidity and precision' (Satoh, 1995) (Figure 6.1).

A host of devices for lifting, shifting and placing heavy components were devised in the middle of the century, gantry cranes, travelling cranes and a primitive form of tower crane (Figure 6.2). Machines were developed for excavating, for pile driving, for banking. New systems of scaffolding were developed and tried in a constant search for increasing erection speeds and greater safety, though collapsing scaffolding and falling from scaffolding continued and continues to be a major source of accident.

A concrete mixer was invented by Louis Cezanne in 1857 and there was one in use in the Birkenhead docks in 1870 – driven by a 5 horsepower steam engine; but the take-up generally seems to have been slow.

At the same time as these technical developments in construction itself were taking place, new techniques of forming materials were also being

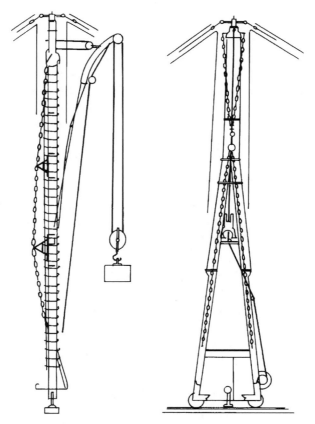

Figure 6.1   Steam-driven hoist used by Tomkinson of Liverpool at St George's Hall, 1803.
Source: Drawing by Paul Hodgkinson from nineteenth-century illustration in *The Builder*.

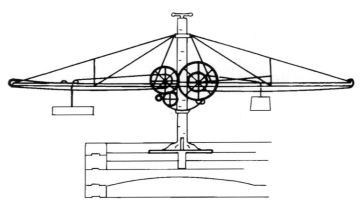

Figure 6.2   Early tower crane used in constructing the Melville Monument, Edinburgh in 1822. *Source*: Drawing by Paul Hodgkinson from nineteenth-century illustration in *The Builder*.

adopted by the larger contractors: planing machines, the circular saw, moulding machines for wood, stone cutting and moulding. Some of the largest general builders, such as William Cubitt in London, Messrs Holmes in Liverpool, Pauling in Manchester, set up considerable workshops with steam-driven machinery for every kind of timber and stone working.

That inventions were not only taking place but being adopted is indicated by the fierce opposition their use provoked from craftsmen who feared, often rightly, the reduction in demand for the traditional skills.

It is probably true, however, that during the first half of the twentieth century there was little major technical advance – at least in construction techniques in the UK and on conventional sites. But what the period did bring about was the capacity to build high; this of course was no mean technical achievement in itself. As Bowley demonstrated, however, the techniques – of using steel and reinforced concrete – were adopted very slowly in the UK compared with the USA. The problems of developing a successful pre-stressed concrete were solved in France but the material was used only intermittently in this country for a long while.

In a lecture to the Royal Society of Arts in 1959 (the fact that it was 'illustrated by lantern slides' tells us something about the general level of technology at the time) Dr G. Bonnell, the chief scientific officer at the Building Research Station (as it then was) listed the processes which had by then become mechanized or partly mechanized: joinery, plumbing (through prefabrication), the movement of materials, horizontally and vertically and the digging of trenches, and the mixing of large quantities of concrete (Bonnell, 1959). But he made no attempt to explain the slow adoption of the mobile or tower crane 'developed on the continent but a comparative newcomer to this country, the first of its kind having been imported by the Building Research Station in 1950. Similar cranes have been in use in France and Germany for more than 20 years' – though he identifies the first use as 1858. If not backward, the industry certainly appeared conservative.

A study published in the 1970s by J. F. Eden surveyed the state of the art at that time, identifying all the main forms of mechanization used commonly on sites in the UK (Eden, 1975). It did not show any major changes from Bonnell's list and a similar list today would not be very different: tower cranes; handling machines such as fork-lift trucks; concrete mixers and pups and a range of digging machines of every scale. Again the impression of slow, if any, change is difficult to avoid.

6.2.2 Versatility and variety

But some of the equipment used today is very versatile and can be used for several of these functions, such as the 'JCB'-type which can dig trenches, shovel earth, lift and carry quite heavy objects and also be used to compact earth to a limited degree. In fact so versatile is the JCB-type machine that on relatively small sites it may be virtually the only large piece of equipment in use; it is its very versatility which makes this sort of machinery cost-effective for the amount of idle time is obviously reduced to the degree it can be used on many different jobs. The same is true of the ubiquitous dumper truck, which can be seen carrying virtually anything around a site.

At the other extreme from the mobile versatile and relatively small items of construction plant is the tower crane; one of the very few pieces of machinery which was specially designed for building, this has become highly sophisticated. Two types were developed, one with a luffing jib, the other with counterbalanced horizontal jib and travelling trolley. Each became available as mobile cranes in tracks, as fixed cranes and as climbing cranes. As Eden says, 'the design of these cranes has been the subject of great ingenuity and skill to combine strength with light weight' (Eden, 1975, p. 107).

Certainly without them, the rapid construction of high buildings using large beams and panels would be far less efficient (though in fact they are not nearly so common on American sites). However, as a Danish researcher Elsebet Lyendal Pedersen has pointed out, after working with crane drivers on building sites in Denmark, there is still plenty of room for improvement in terms of comfort, safety and control mechanisms (Pedersen, 1990).

Other ingenious machines were in fact devised specifically for construction, such as the Humper, after studies by the Building Research Station 'combining the function of crane dumper and fork lift truck'.

Although the basic range of machines has changed little since Eden wrote, they have, like most vehicles and machinery, become considerably more sophisticated. And the range of products on the market is so great as to make selection of the best by any contractor quite problematic. Table 6.1 lists the main types of equipment in Spon's most recent Plant Guide and within each category there is wide range of options. For example there are 14 manufacturers of truck-mounted cranes, each producing up to ten different models. There are some twenty makes of hydraulic excavators and a total of nearly 150 different models. These figures mean little in themselves but do seem to indicate that if a job on site can be assisted by mechanical means there is likely to be a machine ideally suited for the purpose.

Power tools. One development which Eden only touches, though it is discussed earlier by Bonnell, and which may be less obvious but probably quite significant in terms of productivity, is the rapid growth in the use of electrically powered hand tools such as drills, saws, sanders, staplers, and hand-guided hydraulic tools.

Because of the scarcity or unavailability of the necessary data, it is difficult to identify the real significance of this revolution in small tools. An attempt was made to assess their impact on productivity by David Cheetham and Tony Hall, by relating an index of power tools output to an index of labour value productivity (Hall and Cheetham, 1987). Their results showed a clear relationship between the growth in the use of hand tools and increases in productivity, but as they were the first to admit, it was not possible to identify the precise productivity effect. Nevertheless, the figures they produced showing an increase in the sales of hand tools from £34 000 to £116 000 (at current prices), half of which were 'professional' sales, indicate that ways of working have changed considerably in recent years. Much work is easier, requires different skills and in the absence of some countervailing effect (such as for example that workers using power tools might relax more often) must be expected to have some impact on efficiency.

The use of construction plant and small electric tools is only a part of the total story of technical advances on site; the last few years have seen another minor revolution in the adoption of computers to very many tasks involved in construction – from computer-aided design, use of computers in estimating, project planning and now with hand-held computers to operations actually on site.

Table 6.1   Construction plant and equipment available in 1994
Source: Spon's *Plant and Equipment Price Guide*.

	Type of equipment	Approximate number of suppliers
Compressors	portable stationary mobile	10
Concreting	concrete mixers batching plants concrete transporters miscellaneous	14
Cranes	general purpose mobile truck mounted crawler	24
Dumpers	small rear dumpers tractor articulated	9
Excavators	crawler hydraulic hydraulic diggers backhoe mounted mini-excavators	34
Graders		10
Hoists and winches	passenger/goods materials twin cage builders'	6
Loading shovels	two wheel drive four wheel drive crawler loaders	11
Piling	piling hammers pile extractors pile frames and leaders earth boring equipment	6
Pumps	centrifugal diaphragm special	15
Rollers	(eight types)	19
Tractors	crawler wheeled motorized scrapers towed scrapers	10

*Lloyds Buildings,
London, during
construction*

*Lloyds completed
(angle of wall)
(architect: Richard
Rogers Associates).*

6.3 Information technology

Information technology has undoubtedly affected and is affecting the costs and efficiency of construction; again, though, it has been argued, for example by Graham Winch, that the adoption of computers at every stage of the building process from design to completion has been relatively slow compared with other industries (Winch, 1991). Quoting two surveys of the late 1980s he estimated that 62% of architectural practices and 71% of civil and structural engineering firms were using Computer Aided Design (CAD) but only 19% of medium and large building firms used Project Planning Systems. There were very few practical attempts to link design and drafting systems with either quantity surveying or project management software to form a fully fledged CAD/CAM type system. Winch suggests four reasons for the relatively slow development:

- organization of firms (design firms in particular) as partnerships, making access to capital difficult;
- contractors interested mainly in flexibility rather than cost reduction;
- most firms are small;
- the contracting system – in which the activities of the different actors are separated and all the groups do not necessarily share the same goals at the same time.

Interestingly Winch identified the advantage that such forms of construction as speculative housebuilding might be expected to have: 'many of the main transactions within the production information flow are brought within hierarchical rather than market governance . . . Speculative housebuilding firms take responsibility for all stages of the production information flow from design conception to the programming and control of site activities.' He went on to say, 'There does not however appear to be any evidence that such firms have made any greater progress within integrated CAD and PPS systems than firms within the contracting system.'

But only a few years later that evidence is clear: firms such as Laing Homes and Westbury are using integrated computer packages to streamline the management of the whole design and production process. Westbury's IT director has said: 'What we are really doing is turning this business into a manufacturing operation.' The claims made are impressive: 'QS measurement time per house as been cut from 25 man days to 15 minutes, the 51-day process to design, plan, cost and issue orders for a house cut to about 21 days; the exact amount of materials required is sent to site at exactly the right time, mimicking the just-in time system delivery systems of the Japanese car manufacturers' (*Building*, 1994b).

The same types of development are occurring rapidly in other countries perhaps more rapidly and more effectively. In France for example,

> *CAD is accompanied by the development of the rationalisation of production, essentially in response to the need to identify and to exert some control over realisation. Such an approach requires firms to multiply their collection of information direct from the site and to analyse it frequently . . . But this rationalisation is also extended to the later stages of the production cycle, to the study of the site timetable, schedule and methods. The aim here is to concentrate production combinations, taking the specific characteristics of each site into account and to identify the most appropriate form of organisation in order to take control over or even a reduction of costs and delay in a situation of variability.*

It is the large firms who are achieving this type of control (Campagnac, 1991).

Sten Bonke and Elsebet Fryendal Pederson of Denmark have investigated another and potentially highly significant aspect of the use of computers on site: that if it is to be successful it has to involve the site workers themselves, and in particular to enhance not threaten their sense of autonomy and control over their work (Bonke and Pedersen, 1991).

Indeed all the research seems to point to a central issue: if information technology is to be used to its maximum potential in construction, there has to be a greater degree of integration and involvement of all the parties concerned. Under the traditional contracting system in the UK this is inherently difficult. However, the implication is not necessarily that the traditional system must be abandoned, but merely that some traditional attitudes must be adjusted.

6.4 Prefabrication

We have discussed the use of mechanical, electrical and electronic equipment on site. But it is worth emphasizing again the significance of the removal of processes to the factory or workshop. As what happens on the site increasingly become the end of a process begun in the factory, there is not necessarily the need for highly complex operations on the site itself; indeed one of the motivations for using prefabricated components has been and is the reduced need for highly skilled labour for fixing (see the description below of the wiring looms in use in Japan). And the production of these components may incorporate the very latest technology.

For example a report in the *Architects' Journal* (*AJ*, 10 Nov. 1993, p. 31) described the Chicago Metallics new Belgian factory for making metal ceiling tiles, which using 'advanced manufacturing technology' converts steel coil into perforated panels of varying patterns and sizes on one

Hong Kong and Shanghai Bank, Hong Kong (architects Norman Foster Associates).

automatic machine. PVCu mouldings for widow frames are produced in vast quantities in completely automated plant such as that owned by Kommerling in Germany (a major exporter of PVCu mouldings to this country). The same type of production system exists for hundreds of components from door handles to cladding panels.

Today the list of components which arrive on site already manufactured is extremely long. It includes prefabricated panels, of concrete, of brickwork, of a range of cladding materials, of interior finished materials; pre-stressed reinforced concrete beams, roof trusses, a vast range of finished units for kitchens, bathrooms, restaurants, offices; and it now includes though not widely adopted yet in terms of the total building market, the complete room pods referred to in Chapter 3.

An example of the degree to which prefabricated materials have come to dominate the production processes can be gained from this brief account from a study in the mid-1980s by Linda Clarke where she observed materials in prefabricated form

from materials such as ready mix mortar, to simple components such as pitched fibre drainage or drylining, to more complex components as partitioning, suspended ceilings, floors, heating systems . . . the Kent firm made 100% use of prefabricated structures 70% precast concrete, 30% steel let out or wrapped up as supply and fix contracts . . . obviated the need for the firm to employ on site labour. [In other sites] precast concrete blocks, beams, columns, panels, lintels, widow sills, stairs, . . . The same was true for wood, from timber framed houses to trusses, doors, window frames, stairs. The effects of the prefabrication were nowhere more apparent than in the subcontracting on the commercial site: a total of 47 subcontracts, 10 labour only, 19 supply and fix, and 18 specialist supply and fix were to be found (Clarke, 1987).

Changes have often been slow – but what are apparently small developments can have quite significant effects on productivity. A very small scale study of the difference between two houses built in 1964 and 1974, showed that both used prefabricated roof trusses, in 1964, soon after they had first been introduced; they were only partly prefabricated, carried only part of the load and were used with traditional rafters. By 1974, they carried the full load and were completely prefabricated:

By using the totally prefabricated trussed rafters, considerable construction time was saved . . . the skilled job of the carpenter in roof construction was replaced by the negligible amount of skill needed by an 'erector' . . . the reduction in cost was of the order of 30% – the older form costing approximately £5.70 per m^2 and the newer £3.80 (Langridge, 1975).

In fact ideas for moving the whole building process forward to a system of assembly from complete standardized units as a way of 'industrializing' the industry has a long – and controversial – history. The prospects have excited architects, engineers and contractors, all perhaps with slightly different motivations, and the possibility of a highly capitalized industry, producing buildings of high quality and low costs developing exactly in the same way as has the manufacture of cars or computers, continually resurfaces. We will look at some examples and some explanations for disappointment in Chapter 10.

Certainly the widely held view that industrialized building in Britain 'failed' is too simple. The over-enthusiastic adoption of some systems – particularly load-bearing panel systems – without sufficient quality control on site led to problems and disasters, such as the one most often quoted, the collapse of Ronan Point in 1968.

But the basic principles of industrialized building, the assembly of units pre-manufactured in factories has, as the above quotation shows, continued to develop. The pre-manufactured components have become more sophisticated; the possibilities are no longer limited to the rather crude concrete panels that were the main form of the 1960s and 1970s. Many designers are now involved with manufacturers in the development of new construction technologies.

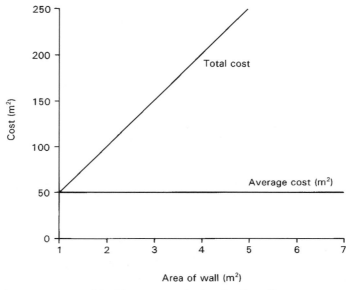

Figure 6.3   Total and average costs of building a straight, low brick wall.

The ideal – if it is an ideal – of the building completely assembled from factory-made units by automated machinery on a clean building site may one day be achieved in the UK. It does seem to be approached in the most advanced Japanese construction systems. There is not the space here to discuss the history of the ideas and the experiments, which are well documented elsewhere.

In parts of the world where politics and rapid population growth guaranteed sustained demand the industrialized systems were maintained and are still common. In some areas the results are nothing short of horrendous. But as the advocates of industrialization have often pointed out, it need not necessarily be so.

In summary the modern building system can be argued to be in so many ways technically advanced, and even the conventional modern house, as well as being in fact a mass-produced product itself, is the end-result of a long chain of technologically advanced processes, from the manufacture of plastic rainwater goods to the sophisticated gas central heating boiler.

6.5 Impact of mechanization on costs and design

The objectives of mechanizing building processes have essentially been to increase productivity and, consequently, to reduce costs and construction times. But the very existence of machinery has always had and continues to

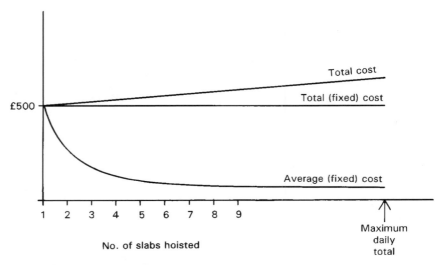

Figure 6.4 Total and average costs of using a crane.

have powerful impacts upon the design of buildings in two rather different ways. First, it opens up new design possibilities, making feasible new forms and the use of large components. But secondly, if machines are in fact to be used effectively, they impose requirements on designers to consider their use; an obvious example is the need to ensure as far as possible that expensive machines are not required only for short, widely separated periods; or that their designs can be put together with equipment known to be available at reasonable cost.

Table 6.2 Annual plant utilization rates, 1950s. *Source*: Stone, P.A. (1956) A survey of the annual costs of contractors' mechanical plant, *J. Ind. Econ.*, Feb.

Type of plant	Percentage of time on site	Percentage of time nominally working
Mixers	76	30
Mortar mills	86	60
Mobile cranes	76	50
Dumpers and powered barrows	80	66
Excavators	90	70
Tractors and shovels	86	66
Compressors	80	56
Independent compressors tools	36	10
Water pumps	56	26
Rollers (petrol and diesel)	80	56

Within the overall expenditure of even the smaller contractors, the small power tools discussed above are a very small item and little more needs to be said. It may be that the tendency to treat them as consumables is often overdone and represents a hidden and possibly substantial loss for firms which do not keep a close watch on what is happening, but nonetheless the overall cost is not great.

At the other end of the scale, the picture is very different. The larger items of plant are very costly indeed to buy. According to Spon's plant price guide, prices at the beginning of 1995 ranged from £50 000 to £300 000 for excavators, with a similar sort of range for mobile and truck-mounted cranes.

These are substantial sums: the small builder would not be in a position to finance such large amounts, and even for the larger builders there is little economic sense in actually owning anything other than standard items of equipment which are going to be regularly used. For these reasons, expensive plant is hired. The plant hire business is now a substantial sector of the industry. Some plant hire firms are in fact subsidiaries of the major contractors, who though they have the capital to finance the purchase of the machines and equipment, still find it advantageous to hire it out to others as well as to their own building divisions. Others are large national concerns, but most are local independent companies. In fact in 1993 there were over 360 such firms advertising in the *Contractors' Plant* journal.

The basic economics of plant use are easy to explain, using the standard cost concepts that we so cavalierly dismissed in Chapter 3, and particularly the distinction between fixed and variable cost, or as they are often described, indirect and direct costs (these two forms of nomenclature are often confusing to students but although they are not identical they refer to basically the same distinction). We will use fixed and variable here.

In activities such as building a low-level, straight brick wall, the costs are principally the cost of bricks, the cost of mortar and the cost of labour; all these will vary more or less with the area of wall to be built. That is, all the costs are variable and the relationship between total cost and amount built can be shown as a straight line (Figure 6.3). Average costs, which are simply average variable cost, the cost per square metre, are constant.

However for an activity using a crane such as the placing of concrete floor beams at second-storey level, the pattern of costs is quite different. There are still variable costs, particularly the labour required to place the beams; but the major cost will be that of the crane. If we assume the minimum hire period is one day (although in practice it might be much longer) and exclude the costs of setting up, the total cost of using the crane is fixed for the day however many slabs are hoisted. The average cost however will decrease depending on the number of slabs. If for example the cost of the crane was £500 for the day, the crane costs of hoisting only one slab in the day would also be £500, two slabs, £250 per slab, four slabs, £125 per day and so on. The average fixed costs curve steeply downwards as in Figure 6.4. There will of course be a physical limit on the number which can be hoisted in the day – and that will set the minimum average cost – the level of highest efficiency at which the crane can be used.

The key then to efficient use is the degree of utilization which can be achieved – and this is true of all forms of plant on site. Yet the evidence is that on many sites utilization is low and often difficult to improve. Although the figures are now very old, the table reproduced by P. F. Stone from an article written in 1956 is interesting (Table 6.2). The more efficient builders have undoubtedly improved on those rates, but as they were influenced by the actual nature of the building process, they may reflect the worst cases today. Casual observation of sites certainly seems to indicate much plant lying idle, probably inevitably, for long periods of time.

The simple economics of plant use however does carry an important lesson for designers: that any aspect of the design which allows continuous use of heavy plat rather than intermittent and repeated use is likely to have a considerable impact on costs.

It is the difficulty in achieving high levels of utilization that makes it so problematic to achieve improvements in productivity through mechanization alone; but the impact should not be underestimated. Plant is essentially a substitute for labour; it will bring about an increase in **labour** productivity, if it allows the same amount of work to be done by fewer operatives; it will bring about a gain in **overall** productivity only if the cost of labour saved is not outweighed by the cost of the machine; in some activities such as excavation the productivity gains have been very high. To use a very crude yardstick, the cost of digging a two metre deep pipe trench using mechanical excavation is something of the order of £16 per metre (according to Spon's Price Book), while the cost for hand excavation is approximately £33.

As pointed out in the previous chapter, productivity is notoriously difficult to measure (or even define) in construction but it is quite clear that there have been major gains through the use of mechanical equipment; that was the purpose of introducing the plant and otherwise it would not have received such wide acceptability. Eden, in the paper already cited above, compared a series of studies on housebuilding sites made from 1945 to 1970 that labour productivity had considerably increased over the period at the same time as there had been 'significant mechanization', measures as a change from the application of approximately 1.72 horsepower per man in 1945 to 9.9 horsepower per man in 1970. The slow rate of acceptance in

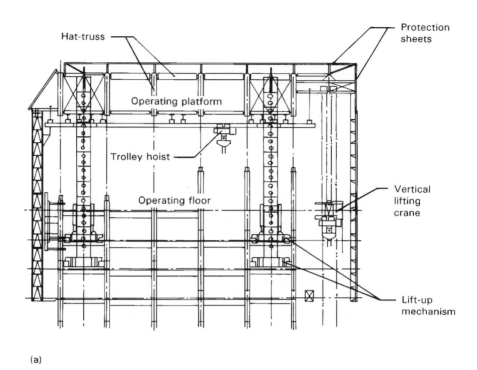

(a)

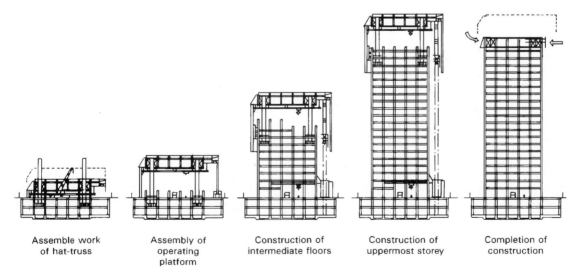

| Assemble work of hat-truss | Assembly of operating platform | Construction of intermediate floors | Construction of uppermost storey | Completion of construction |

(b)

Figure 6.5 Robot building: the SMART system. (a) Constitution of the SMART system; (b) the different stages of the automated construction procedure using the SMART system. *Source*: based on illustrations in the *Architects' Journal*.

the early days may have been due, however, to the fact that for traditional building methods, the productivity gains were not always dramatic or obvious; and as we saw earlier, the major determinants even of labour productivity on building sites may be factors other than mechanization.

6.6 The future – a robot takeover?

There is much discussion about the directions mechanization and automation will take and how far this is in fact the direction in which greater efficiency is to be sought in building production. Certainly there have been and continue to be rapid advances in the control technology for machines on site. Japanese robots currently in use have been described in a number of publications. Sidney Levy, in his book *Japanese Construction – an American Perspective*, gives a detailed account of some of them. They are mostly machines for very specific and limited tasks. And though they have the potential to save considerably on manpower for those tasks (and to increase safety), their contribution to total cost saving may be quite small.

One of these for example is a floor-finishing robot developed by three companies, Shimuzu, Kajima and Takenaka Komuten. It is described as 'a trackless self propelled trowelling machine on wheels that travels over newly poured concrete slabs, guided in its mission by a microcomputer, a gyrocompass, a travel distance sensor and a touch sensor to avoid columns and other obstructions'.

Other robots described by Levy include machines for bending and placing reinforcing bars, applying spray fireproofing to structural steel framework, testing the integrity of exterior tile and masonry walls and hoisting steel beams.

But more comprehensive building systems are already in use. Obayashi's automated robot controlled frame and cladding erection system was described in the *Architects' Journal* as follows:

> *Columns, beams, floors and external walling are placed by computer controlled cranes. Framing is robot welded, cladding is clip fixed. When a floor is completed the construction system climbs to the next floor. On reaching the top, the system is stripped out, leaving the top floor shell. Construction is monitored from a control room 500 m. away.*
>
> *The main innovation here is the integration of robots into a construction system. This shares the pragmatism of earlier single task robots in mixing man and machine where the machines are not yet clever enough. For example bolting of cross beams is done by hand as is the grouting between concrete floor beams (*Architects' Journal*, 1993d).*

The article takes two important points however. First the system can only work (as yet) with highly standardized design and components and secondly the cost-effectiveness of the system has not yet been demonstrated. The current state of the art is described in the papers of the Automation and Robotics in Construction Conference XI (Chamberlain, 1994 and Evans, 1994c). Figure 6.5 shows in outline the progress of building using the SMART system first used in Nagoya, Japan to construct an office block.

Gerd Syben has argued that it is organizational change rather than robots which holds the key to increased productivity in construction:

> *Technical solutions would have to involve the development of machines which equal or excel human abilities in a number of aspects. These include chronological and spatial co-ordination in directing material and tools, the ability to change direction and enlarge motions; the ability to control the radius of operation prediction and reliability. Speed of work and ability to react to environmental conditions . . . machinery must also continue to operate regardless of variations in dust, temperature, vibration and humidity. I suggest that the development of robots which are usable in this way under the conditions of building sites face special problems which are not comparable to those in fixed production processes found inside factories* (Syben, 1993).

This may however be once again to underestimate the potential of modern technology.

One further point might be made briefly on the range of technical advances in the industry. The amount and quality of technical research that has been dedicated to construction in the UK and throughout the world is vast. The BRE has worked steadily since its foundation in 1921 (as the Building Research Station) to improve understanding of the characteristics of materials, structural systems, construction methods. And as mentioned in the earlier chapter on materials, the materials companies themselves have dedicated huge resources to improvements in quality and range. In the field of structural engineering, knowledge has advanced to the point at which architects can talk seriously about buildings miles high (though why anyone should want such monsters is a different question).

6.7 Conclusion

In comparison with such modern manufacturing industry, there is clearly a sense in which construction is relatively unsophisticated; and there are many areas in which the use of higher levels of technology might improve efficiency. In particular, advances in robotics, greater standardization of components and the transfer of even more work from site to factory have been represented as essential elements in the transformation of construction into a truly modern 'high-tech' industry. However this chapter has argued that the industry has in fact adopted new methods where they were appropriate and where they yielded economic returns; it has been adept at using available technology in cost-efficient ways, as for example through the development of the plant hire system. It may be true that the structure of the industry and the cyclical, often erratic character of demand do tend to inhibit innovation; and the level of research and development spending in the industry may be inadequate. Nevertheless there is much being done and the achievements should not be underestimated.

There are certainly areas in which construction techniques still appear primitive; the modern trowel is no great advance on that used by the ancient Egyptians. But Foster's Hong Kong and Shanghai Bank, Hopkins' Inland Revenue Offices at Nottingham, Erskine's Ark, then new airport terminals at Stansted, Heathrow, Manchester, Paris and dozens of other cities throughout the world are not the products of a technologically backward industry.

FOR FURTHER STUDY

1 Recommended reading

On the development of technology in the industry see Akira Satoh's *Building in Britain* (1995) part II; Marian Bowley's *The British Building Industry* (1966). There is little easily available on the relationship between design and mechanization of the construction process; there seems to be no modern equivalent of Gardiner's 1978 text. Chapter 6, section 5 of Harper's *Building – The Process and the Product* (1990) is good but brief. However there is a growing literature on robotics; specific recommendations may quickly become outdated and the reader is advised to look at recent copies of the construction and architectural journals.

2 Exercise

Assume excavating equipment can be hired for a minimum period of a week. Explain carefully with the use of simple cost curves why the costs per m^3 of excavation will probably increase as the volume of material excavated per week decreases.

3 Discussion questions

a In view of the advances being reported in robotics, how valid is Gerd's argument quoted above?

b Is the relative under-capitalization of the construction industry a consequence of inherent characteristics of building, discontinuity of demand or sheer conservatism?

c 'The ruling factor in design should not be to enable the use of plant which the contractor has available' (Gardiner, 1979). Should the architect then simply ignore the issue of plant cost or availability and leave it to the contractor to sort any problems out?

d Give your views on the argument that if the building industry is to improve its efficiency, the construction of buildings should move more rapidly from site-based craft operations to the use of more industrialized processes.

e Identify construction processes which in principle could benefit from greater mechanization, automation or transfer to factory pre-manufacture. Why do labour-intensive methods – such as wet plastering and bricklaying – still play such an important part in construction?

7 Construction – a unique industry?

7.1 Introduction

The three previous chapters have surveyed some economic characteristics of the basic resources used in construction – materials, labour and technology – and have touched on the implications of those characteristics for the way buildings are designed and built. This chapter looks briefly at the industry as a whole, the network of firms which organize those resources to produce buildings.

Construction is, indeed, a very complex network and although in that particular respect it may be no different from many other industries, in terms of its modes of operation, the way its products are made and sold, it may well be unique. The next few pages attempt first to describe and to some extent explain the industry's structure and secondly to examine some features of its ways of working which help to explain both its problems and its successes.

7.2 The structure of the industry

7.2.1 The size of firms

Although there is an official definition of the industry (in the Standard Industrial Classification), in reality neither construction nor any other industry has clearly delineated boundaries. Some firms and some activities are unequivocally and wholly concerned with the activity of constructing buildings, but many construction companies engage in a wide range of non-construction activities and other companies predominantly involved in very different industries may have some construction subsidiaries; any firm in any industry owning extensive property, for example, is likely to have its own building maintenance department.

There is a question too of how far backward in the supply chain the definition should be extended. Are the building materials producers to be considered part of the construction industry? If the plant hire firms are obviously to be included, what about the plant manufacturers? At the other end of the process, many construction's clients could also be seen as part of the industry (unlike, say, the customers of the clothing industry who include everybody in the country). Property companies and public authorities have a very much closer and integrated relationship with construction than do customers with most other forms of production.

However, playing with definitions can be unproductive; one simply has to recognize that a concept such as 'the construction industry' is inevitably one with fuzzy edges. Figure 7.1, on which the following discussion is largely based, is just one way of setting out diagramatically its major components and their relationships. It is no accident of course that the diagram bears a strong likeness to Fig. 3.7 for these groups of firms are managing the production process illustrated there.

The standard division usually adopted in descriptions of the production sectors is between building and civil engineering; but a four-part division, distinguishing between civil engineering, speculative housebuilding, new build contracting and repair-maintenance, makes considerable sense in terms of the way the industry actually operates, as will be argued below.

Furthermore as the main focus of this book is on building, the discussion will concentrate on the building contractors, with some reference to housebuilders and the maintenance sector, saying no more about civil engineering as a separate sector. The diagram itself should be reasonably self-explanatory but there are a number of points which might clarify some of its possible obscurities.

First, the actual boxes drawn are rather ambiguous in that they include activities – types of operation – but also in some cases groups of firms. The

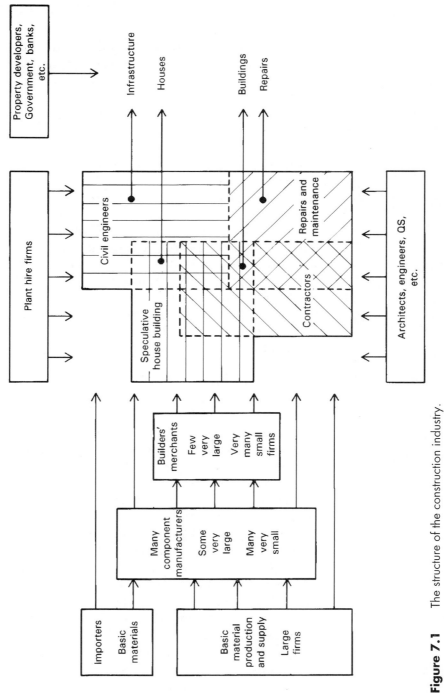

Figure 7.1 The structure of the construction industry.

central section of the diagram, however, does show the relationships between activities and firms. If each box is considered to represent all those organizations and parts of organizations involved in one activity, the overlapping sections show organizations involved in more than one. There is no attempt in the diagram to represent the actual relative scale of the overlaps. There is one section in which all types of activity converge which represents reasonably the actual position. Most of the larger companies are involved in all sectors though usually with a particular strength in one.

Plant hire is shown separately – though again many of the major and even smaller construction firms have plant hire divisions; the consultancy functions – design, engineering, surveying etc. are also to be found within the bigger companies, as is the production of materials but it is one of the enduring characteristics of construction that in general those functions are separately organized and managed.

This division of function is another aspect of the 'fragmentation' of the industry discussed in the last chapter: the very large number of small firms and individuals acting as self-employed subcontractors which carry out each different activity. It is possible to exaggerate the difference between construction and other industries; the use of outside consultants is widespread throughout all industry; and many industries have a similar structure of few large firms and many small. Nevertheless it may be true that the degree of separation of functions and disaggregation of operations in construction is extreme.

The statistics have often been commented on and analysed, and are easy to misinterpret, but the general picture is clear. Figure 7.2, based on the Department of the Environment' statistics, shows the numbers of firm in each of several size ranges, the sizes being defined in terms of the number of employees in 1992. Figure 7.3 shows the value of output by firms in each size group and gives a different impression; most of the industry's output comes from the medium-sized firms. As pointed out in Chapter 5 the structure changed considerably during the 1980s, as the number of large firms declined and the smaller grew relatively. Figure 7.4 shows the scale of these changes, particularly the expansion in one-man businesses and firms with fewer than eight employees.

This change in structure is obviously related to the growth in subcontracting and self-employment which was discussed in Chapter 5 and presents the same problems of interpretation. It is not at all clearly related to fluctuations in the industry's output and therefore explanations depending solely on the effects of recession and periods of high activity seem inadequate. There are apparently longer-term processes at work.

Obviously there are very considerable differences between the firms at the top of the size range and those at the bottom – so much so that it seems

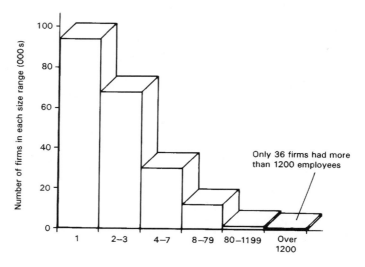

Figure 7.2   Distribution of firms by size (number of employees).
Source: Housing and Construction Statistics, 1992.

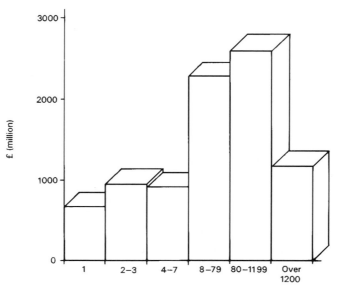

Figure 7.3   Value of output by size of firm.
Source: Housing and Construction Statistics, 1992.

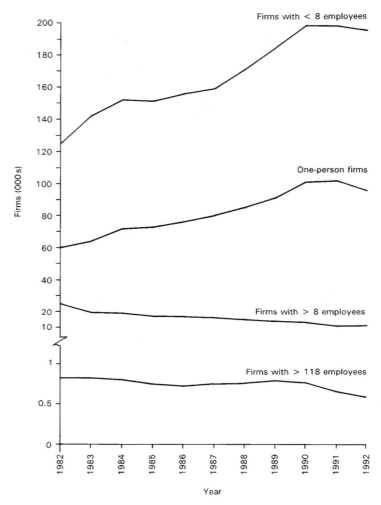

Figure 7.4   Change in the structure of the construction industry 1982–92.
Source: Housing and Construction Statistics.

almost absurd to consider them as part of the same industry; and yet the basic function they perform is of course the same – putting buildings together.

The giants at the top can themselves be divided into different groups. Of the ten largest (in terms of turnover) in 1993 (Table 7.1) three, P&O, Trafalgar House and BICC, are conglomerates with major construction divisions or subsidiaries, the first two having their origins in shipping and the third in cable-making. The other seven out of the top ten are mainly civil engineers and contractors, most with housebuilding divisions. Figure 7.5 outlines the structure of two of the largest contractors.

Table 7.1

The 'Top Ten' contractors by turnover (in £ million), 1993. *Source: Building* 10 May, 1994.

Tarmac	2699
Amec	2184
P&O (Bovis)	1642
BICC	1641
Wimpey	1587
Mowlem	1342
Laing	1264
Taylor Woodrow	1150
Costain	1143
Trafalgar House	1116

If we treat housebuilders as forming a separate sector and list the top ten by volume of house production – figures which incidentally are very approximate and subject to considerable variation from year to year (Table 7.2) – some of the same top ten contractors appear in the list but there are others such as Barratt and Redrow which, though both in fact starting in civil engineering, are now almost entirely housebuilders; even these firms however have a wide range of other activities, including property and contracting.

The same kinds of mixture – of some firms active in several sectors and others more specialized – is apparent further down the scale of firm size; but the smaller they become the more likely they are to be specialized in one field or another. Yet at every size range, from the top to the bottom are firms which describe themselves as 'general builders'.

Many of the smaller firms, however, are involved in only one small part

Table 7.2

The 'Top Ten' housebuilders in 1993 by number of houses built (approximate figures). *Source: Building*, 10 May 1994.

Wimpey	8140
Tarmac	7340
Barratt	5300
Beazer	4800
Wilson Connolly	3840
Bryant	3140
Persimmon	3000
Bellway	2700
Trafalgar House	2545
Laing	2430

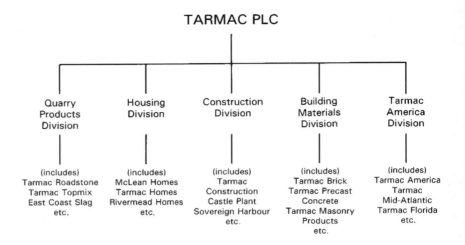

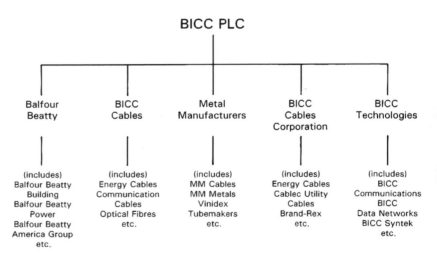

Figure 7.5   The structure of two major companies showing the spread of interests in and beyond construction. These charts give a very limited idea of the total scope of activities – for example, Tarmac has over 700 subsidiary and associated companies.
Source: Company accounts.

of the construction process as specialist subcontractors – engineers, plumbers, plasterers etc. In fact each of these specialist trades shows a similar structure to that of the whole industry, with a few large firms and very many small ones; the main difference is that the largest are nowhere near the size of the major contractors (see Table 7.3). There appear to be no firms of plumbers, joiners, or plasterers with more than about 100

Table 7.3   Number of specialist construction firms, by size of firm (i.e. by number of employees in each firm). *Source*: Housing and Construction Statistics 1982–92, Table 3.6

Trade	Number of firms in each size group			
	Very small 1–13	Medium 14–114	Large 100–1199	Very large >1200
Plumbers	14480	167	—	—
Carpenters	14137	160	—	—
Painters	10662	312	14	—
Roofers	7267	248	9	—
Plasterers	3800	86	—	—
Glaziers	6700	279	9	—
Demolition contractors	653	64	—	—
Scaffolders	1682	88	9	—
H & V engineers	9250	418	9	<5
Electrical contractors	20968	763	18	—
Plant hirers	5364	231	24	—
Constructional engineers	2558	138	19	—
Flooring contractors	2206	74	<7	—
Insulating specialists	1168	90	<7	—
Suspended ceiling contractors	1714	36	<7	—
Tilers	1491	30	<7	—
Ashphalters	1157	97	9	—

employees and most are very much smaller 1–3 men businesses. On the other hand there are some very large electrical contractors and painting businesses.

The same kind of pattern is repeated among the consultants and the plant hire firms, though here the number of large firms is even smaller.

Housebuilding appears to show to some degree the same kind of spread in size as contracting; there are big firms, medium-sized ones and small ones; and some of the biggest are also major contractors – Wimpey, Tarmac. However, detailed research on this sector in the 1970s indicated that scale economies were much more significant (Ball, 1981; Morton 1982). The volume builders as they have come to be called, use standard house designs and their purchasing power to keep prices low. They operate much more like a manufacturing firm going for high turnover rather than high unit profits, spreading their overheads. Small firms can only survive because they acquire small plots of land in which the large firms are not interested and they can usually only compete at the top end of the market. But what distinguished the activity of speculative housebuilding from contracting is that it involves making a product, then selling it (though often in times of high demand, the sale can be made before the product is finished). The products may be customized but they are essentially one of a number of standard designs. Chapter 16 discussed some of these issues in more detail.

The research also showed housebuilding to be constantly changing within an apparently fixed structure. At the top were long-surviving and stable firms; but every now and then they were joined by others which grew very rapidly; some of the newcomers reached considerably size (Northern Developments for example) then disappeared just as rapidly. Others survived and then spread their activities into contracting. There was also a stable middle group, some growing slowly, others virtually static, producing more or less the same number of houses each year, usually at the higher end of the price range. At the bottom end were many small builders who moved in and out of contracting and housebuilding as the market allowed, sometimes buying the odd plot of land for only one or two houses. The picture has probably not changed a great deal since then except that there appear now to be far fewer opportunities for the smaller builders, virtually none in some areas. And many of the regional builders of the 1970s have been taken over by or merged into the larger contracting and conglomerate organizations. But it still seems to be an industrial sector where opportunities can be seized and reap rapid success – as the recent dramatic success of Redrow shows (*Building*, 1994a).

It may well be the case – and more detailed research is necessary to confirm it – that the structure of housebuilding has become more concentrated recently. However there is one interesting feature which it is not feasible to discuss any further here and that is that there seems to be a limit to the total output of individual companies. Although at the time when local authority housing was a major source of demand, firms such as Wimpey reached combined outputs, private and public sector, of nearly 20 000 houses a year, the maximum sustainable level by any one firm seems to have been in the order of 10 000.

Housebuilding is then a different sort of operation from contracting and has to be thought of as a different sector, though many companies are involved in both; many individual employees may shift from one to the other, and subcontractors operating in both fields will be working on identical activities. Having made this point, however, we will say little more about housebuilding specifically until Chapter 15, and concentrate on the structure and market mechanisms of the contracting business.

7.2.2 Why so fragmented an industry?

There are many questions raised by the peculiar structure of the contracting side of the industry. Is fragmentation an inevitable consequence of the nature of construction itself? Why has the process of concentration into fewer hands, so common in other industries including, as we have seen, materials production, apparently not taken place to the same extent in contracting? Indeed why does the industry appear to be moving in the opposite direction? The forces of technological change and economies of scale seem to have been less significant.

One explanation of the wide range of firm sizes and the persistence of very small ones is the structure of the demand; although it is the big scheme or building – the Channel Tunnel, the National Library, the new Glyndebourne Opera House – which claim the headlines in both the general and the specialist press, the vast majority of construction projects are small. In fact the range of firm sizes seems almost to match that of projects sizes.

Large firms, of course, can and often do complete small projects; they can probably do so as efficiently as the smaller and they are far more able to carry the risks. However, any competitive advantages they have are often outweighed by the disadvantages – primarily the high overheads any big firm carries. Directors of large firms have said that smaller projects do not yield the cash flow they require and though having many small projects spreads risk, it is expensive in administrative and organizational terms.

Small firms on the other hand do not have the resources to manage big schemes. The market is therefore layered, with groups of companies of one scale competing for a range of projects of a suitable size. Again of course there is much overlap, particularly in the middle range where companies such as Tarmac and Wimpey, organized into regional divisions, compete with regionally based medium-sized independent firms.

The very large number of very small 'general builders' is again largely accounted for by the nature of demand. Repairs and maintenance accounts for over half of the work of the industry. Although some of this work is on a major scale – particularly the refurbishment of commercial buildings – most is very small. There is no need to labour the point: it is obvious that a firm like Wimpey is unlikely to be interested in fixing the casement windows at 25 Acacia Avenue.

The small firms which are not classified as general builders are for the most part again working in the repairs and maintenance sector or as subcontractors to the builders. Some of the characteristics and reasons for the prevalence of subcontracting have already been discussed in Chapter 5; perhaps the most important of these are the discontinuity of work and the variation in scale between one project and another. However, two further points might be made here, before going on to look at the contracting system as a whole. First, the increasing number of specialisms, a part of the technological change in the industry, discussed earlier, towards greater prefabrication, has produced many new special subcontracting firms, some of which are quite small. Any new product – such as PVCu windows, suspended ceilings – generates a new group of specialists. Concomitantly, the range of specialisms required on modern construction projects is so wide – and different from project to project – that it makes obvious sense for the main contractors to subcontract rather than attempt to incorporate every skill within their own organization. In fact on large projects that would be virtually impossible; at Canary Wharf there were 700 major trades and 2000 subtrades. Over 400 separate participating companies were listed in *Building's* special report on the project (*Building*, Special Supplement, 1991).

The second point, to be expanded later, is that subcontracting is a way of spreading risk; to subcontract a portion of work to someone else is at least partly to put the risk of failure on to them. In an inherently risky business, the development of a subcontracting culture might be seen as a natural kind of response.

To summarize this section, the division of the industry into many small firms can be seen at least partly to stem from the nature and structure of demand which is itself fragmented, differentiated and erratic; there are not the powerful economies of scale generated by mass production and technologies in other industries, because the individual nature of the project makes that difficult to achieve, except, as indicated above, in housebuilding.

7.2.3 The division of control functions

Although it is possible to go some way to explain the multi-firm structure and the prevalence of subcontracting in terms of the nature of demand and of the construction process, the separation of architectural design, structural engineering and construction into generally discrete and very different management organizations is not so obviously logical. The divisions are not so deep in other countries, though they do exist. The reasons are partly historical. From the eighteenth century at least there were strong social class distinctions between architects and clients on the one hand and the craftsmen and labourers on the other (with of course many finer distinctions in between). The development of civil engineering and the strengthening of the surveying professions in the nineteenth century involved a struggle to establish these activities as professions on a par with the architects. The American architectural historian, Marston Fitch, described a similar evolution in the United States:

> As contrasted with the architect, the engineer's assignment from the industrialist was the simpler: to build quickly, cheaply and efficiently and to hell with the looks . . . as a system of formal education in engineering began to evolve, the neglect of the 'artistic' of building began to solidify into programmatic contempt (Fitch, 1973, p. 126).

That perhaps is putting it a little strongly but there is no doubt that the development of separate educational and training systems and the maintenance of distinction (even social distinction) through the formation of the professional bodies reinforced the historical tendencies to a compartmentalized industry (Morton, 1990).

However, the real differences in the activities should not, as they often are in current discussions, be underestimated. We have indicated some of these in Chapter 2 and suggest further references at the end of this chapter. The newer forms of procurement arrangements discussed in Chapter 13 attempt to resolve some of the problems that result – but as will be argued there, may not provide the answers.

However the fact that there are large multidisciplinary practices, and that these have often been exceptionally successful in being the prime movers and managers of high-quality building, indicate that closer relationships can work; it does not necessarily prove that any problems arising from traditional divisions between design and construction may not be overcome in many different ways.

Figure 7.6 shows in outline the organization of a leading Japanese construction company; it is put in without further comment to provoke thought and discussion.

7.3 Modes of operation

7.3.1 The contracting system

As suggested above the structure of the contracting industry may not itself be unique. What is so different from general manufacturing is precisely the contracting system itself. This has been widely analysed, discussed and criticized for over a century since the basis of the modern system came into being (see particularly Bowley, 1966 and Ball, 1988). The particular way in which the contracting system developed was intimately related to the developing relationship between clients, designers and builders; the different forms it takes today – the systems of procurement discussed in Chapter 13 – still powerfully influence that relationship and particularly the division of risk and responsibility.

The contracting system in its present forms exists for the following reasons.

■ Each building is unique; it is provided for a specific client (unlike most furniture, clothes, shoes and all cabbages and chocolate bars).
■ Partly because of its uniqueness, its costs are difficult to predict.
■ The level of risk is high for all the parties involved, **including the client**. The last point is significant: when purchasing most things the

customer can see them knows their qualities, knows their value. If they are not what they seem the consumer has protection in law. Buying a car – or even a bar of chocolate – may never be totally risk-free but the risks in procuring a building are of a totally different order.

■ Competition between firms cannot take place in the same way as in other industries – for example equivalent products cannot be put on the market at lower prices. The tendering system is the mechanism through which competition occurs.

Chapter 13 will examine the different forms the system can take and the implications each has for the design–cost relationship; all of them have developed essentially to reduce or reallocate the risk, to establish firm costs at an early stage and to secure the maximum benefits of competition while minimizing its dangers. In the rest of this section the issues are analysed at a general level – as they are relevant to all forms of procurement and dominate the industry's way of working.

The Building Construction Division of the Ohbayashi Corporation

Design
Sub departments
Interior design: special projects: proposals
Local area development; education, research etc. buildings, office buildings
Commercial buildings, sports facilities, office buildings
Welfare facilities, high density housing, office buildings
Factories, warehouses, nuclear power facilities
Developing working drawings and new technology
Design Administration
Facilities design
design and construction inspection

Planning
Project planning,
development projects,
presentation

Sales
Sales promotion
sales administration
tenant search

Construction Administration Department

Satety Administration

Estimates Preparation

Construction
Six departments for all construction jobs in the division

Site support
etc.

Figure 7.6   Subdivisions of the Building Section of the Japanese company Obayashi.

7.3.2 Risk

It was suggested above that the risks in construction are high and are widely distributed. They are also very varied and have been classified in numerous ways for different purposes. One distinction often made is between risk and uncertainty. To quote Patricia Hillebrandt: 'Risk arises when the assessment of a certain event is statistically possible; risk is insurable. Uncertainty arises when the probability of the occurrence of an event is indeterminate; uncertainty is not insurable' (Hillebrandt, 1974, p. 163). But, as Hillebrandt goes on to say, 'there is no hard and fast line between risk and uncertainty'. Another distinction, which incidentally ignores completely the risk/uncertainty distinction is into four types: fundamental (such as war damage); pure (fire or storm damage); particular (collapse subsidence); speculative (ground conditions, inflation, weather). This categorization from the Shorter Form of Building Contract (Clamp, 1993) is also used by Latham.

But these classifications are not really very revealing. It is perhaps clearer to consider the actual risks incurred by the parties involved in any building project; some of these can be shifted onto other people, some reduced, some better managed. Hardly any of them can be avoided completely:

The client:

- escalating cost;
- construction times exceeded;
- quality standards not met;
- third part liabilities incurred.

The architect. Professional liability for building failures (can be sued at any time during the building's life, if failures can be attributed to design or other architect responsibilities under a particular contract).

The contractor. Here the list seems almost endless; Hillebrandt outlines ten different risks and uncertainties, which attend virtually every contract. The following is only a brief summary:

- labour – poor workmanship, shortages of skills, rise in cost;
- materials – unavailability, quality problems, price rises;
- subcontracting – poor performance;
- bill of quantity items – errors, variations;
- soil conditions;
- management failures;
- weather;

■ designer created uncertainties: architects' and engineers' drawings not available in time, not detailed, inaccurate;
■ catastrophes – natural or unnatural;
■ time overruns – leading to penalties.

It is because these risks are so prevalent and inevitable that the building contract has become so important in the system – and so controversial. Attempts to standardize forms of contract so that everybody understood exactly what obligations each party was undertaking have in a way been remarkably successful (one or other version of the JCT form is now used in 80% of contracts including the very large number of small works contracts), but they have not succeeded in eliminating ambiguity and consequently, conflict. Efforts are made to adapt, to change, to revise – resulting in constant proliferation of new clauses and new interpretations.

Beyond the contract itself, the risks and the costs of carrying them may be shifted; firms acting as subcontractors have become particularly vulnerable for example from main contractors adopting a 'pay when paid' policy; this is supposed to have been outlawed in government contracts and the Latham Report suggests it should be outlawed generally. What has been happening is that main contractors have been refusing to pay the subcontractors until they are paid by the client (or employer); subcontractors may then refuse to pay their sub-subcontractors until they are paid and so on down the line – each pushing the risk of non-payment further down.

The risks outlined above are only the risks involved once the project is undertaken; the major risks to the contractor are, in fact, the risk of not getting work at all and the risk of failing to maintain a positive cash flow or make profits over a period of time and over a series of projects. To obtain work they have to put in a successful tender; this is another difference between construction and other industries; it is the construction **client** who determines the conditions – including the extent of competition – on which the product is to be bought. The tendering system is therefore another critical and specific component of the market context in which the builders have to operate.

7.3.3 Competition and tenders

The actual process of tendering for work is of course not restricted to construction – but again it seems to have become a particularly contentious and complex issue. The tendering system itself is fraught with risk – to clients and builders; it is open to abuse and can be used to restrict as well as to encourage competition.

From the client's point of view it might seem that the more open a tender is — that is the more builders who tender for a particular project — the higher the chance of getting the best price. But there are problems; not all builders are equally capable of producing the same quality; not all are equally able to guarantee completion on time. Many firms have gone into liquidation during a contract creating serious problems for everybody — so the client needs to be as confident as possible that the contractor is financially strong. It therefore makes sense for a client, advised usually by consultants, architects and quantity surveyors, to limit the tender list to contractors whose capacities are known.

From the contractor's point of view also, there are disadvantages in long tender lists. Preparing a tender is expensive. The contractor has to be as sure as possible that the price will enable him to make a profit; yet the price has to be low enough for him to have a chance of winning the tender. Furthermore the system encourages phoney tendering — that is contractors will put in bids at very high prices, with no intention of winning, but in order to be retained on future tender lists. Finally, the system encourages, especially in times of recession, fierce and ultimately counter-productive levels of price competition. Builders desperate for work put in unrealistically low bids, perhaps hoping to make up profits from variations during the contract; in fact they may then be forced to cut corners — trying to reduce specifications for example. They may ultimately be unable to meet the price except at a heavy loss or at the very worst be driven into liquidation.

The Latham report brings out some of these problems very clearly. It gives examples of what seem totally unreasonable tender lists — 28 tenders for the installation of heating and 38 firms on the 'short list' for a school project. The report also details (in its table 10) the costs of tendering — comparing Design and Build with traditional methods, a point taken up again here in Chapter 13.

To be successful — that is to survive and make a profit — in this system, firms may develop complex tendering strategies; they will decide which type of contracts to bid for, considering the scale of the projects and the type of work involved in relation to their own capacity and skills. They may calculate the probabilities of winning and the risks of losing and therefore how much effort to put into the preparation of each sort of tender, how many tenders to submit.

The larger firms will have separate estimating departments and specialized staff to work on all these issues. The smaller, however, do not have the staff or the skills to make these kinds of assessments; they are more likely just to keep on submitting tenders where they get the chance, making their best guess at a realistic and profitable price. If they make a mistake, it can be terminal. Many contractors are ruined by a single project

– maybe through their own misjudgement but just as often through the actions and misjudgements of others.

7.4 Survival and growth

As we suggested earlier, there is some danger of overestimating the degree of difference between construction and other economic activities; but it should be clear from the last two sections that the degree of risk to contractors is exceptionally high and that the form competition takes is not at all the same as in, say, manufacturing or retailing. Contractors do not know their competitors' prices (unless there has been collusion); they may not even know who their rivals are; they cannot test the prices and profitability of their products in the market over long production runs.

It is perhaps therefore not at all surprising that construction has such a bad record of business failures (see Chapter 5). The bare statistics however tell only part of the story. For many firms in the industry do survive and have done so over very long periods of time. This applies at every level. At the top end Wimpey and Laing have survived and – with major ups and downs – prospered for nearly a century. Other well-known names of the past may have disappeared, but this is often because the firms have become merged in larger groups and in some cases still exists as virtually separate divisions. One of the most well-known of the nineteenth-century contractors, William Cubitt (brother of the even better known Thomas Cubitt), was absorbed into Holland Hannen and Cubitt at the end of the century and its name still survived until very recently as a subsidiary of Tarmac.

At the lower end there are regional firms with very long histories; the Liverpool firm of Tomkinson has already been referred to in Chapter 6; it existed from the beginning of the nineteenth century but unfortunately went into liquidation only a few years ago. A detailed study in the 1970s of small firms in the Merseyside region, though concerned mainly with housebuilders, found many surprisingly old businesses, the origins of some being lost in the last century. But death rates were high and very few of the firms examined then have survived the last few recessions.

As Patricia Hillbrandt argued in her 1974 study (the problem of growing from a small to a medium and then to large contractor is itself fraught with special difficulties): 'it is considered by persons in the industry that there is a major point of crisis in a firm's growth when it is too big for the directors to control every project without further expertise and too small to afford this expertise' (Hillebrandt, 1974, p. 117). In fact there is probably not just one point, but many points where this dilemma occurs. As a firm tries to move

Construction site.

Completed estate. From apparent chaos to final order: the underestimated skills of construction.

up the scale, taking on not only more but bigger projects, it faces extra risks and even when the step is taken onto a higher level of operation there are no guarantees that the new size can be maintained. Nevertheless if they do manage to climb the ladder cautiously – without overextending their capacity at any one time, they undoubtedly can, as the success stories of many regional firms have recently shown, increase their strength and their security.

Among the most critical problems any construction firm faces – whether small, growing or large – is the adequacy and sustainability of its working capital, that is the money needed to finance its continuing operation. All types of business have the same problem, but it is exacerbated in construction by the fact that production is not a continuous process. A manufacturer turning over regular output of consumer goods will of course be affected by slumps in his or her market but in normal times there is a steady flow of cash from sales to finance the continuing operation. The well-managed (and fortunate) construction firm can reach more or less the same position if it has a sufficient number of good contracts overlapping in time. But frequently in the course of each project there will be long gaps between income and the need for expenditure; if a major new contract is won, the initial funding will usually be far higher than can be financed from the firm's own resources. Borrowing is inevitable – usually from the banks; as long as the level of borrowing is thought to be reasonable and interest can be paid from current cash flows, there need be no problem. But with slow payments from clients, delays in the project from whatever cause or simply misjudgement by the firm, borrowing can become excessive; a business becomes too 'highly geared'. The fate of many a company is decided in the end by the banks and, as Figure 7.7 shows, the threat is very real even for the big firms.

Contractors put on danger list
Upturn worst time for contracting failures. Alastair Stewart reports.

A LEADING subcontractors' watchdog body this week revealed that it classes 20 building companies, with turnovers up to "several hundred million pounds" to be at "extreme risk" of receivership.

John Huxtable, chief executive of the Confederation of Specialist Subcontractors, said the 20 companies have "five star" ratings in its list of those believed to be at risk. Roughly three quarters of the list – kept to advise members of potential bad debtors – are in the £50m–100m turnover range.

Huxtable said building companies of this size are most in danger of receivership as the industry starts to recover: "We are expecting a major wave of insolvencies as and when we ease out of the recession."

Contractors, which had reduced overheads and built up debts, could fail once new orders start.

Neil Burton, the insolvency partner for London-based property consultants Grimley JR Eve, backed up Huxtable's warning. Most of the large companies going into receivership at the start of the recession had major property portfolios, which were hit by the rise in interest rates, he said. But then contractors had two to three years of work load, which has now almost dried up. "1992 will be the year in which the construction sector suffers the effects to the same degree that professionals and developers have for the past two years," he said.

Banks which had refrained from calling in the receivers to many loss-making companies during the worst of the recession see more interest from potential buyers in an upturn, he added.

(a)

One-fifth of firms set to vanish

Accountant predicts heavy casualties. Peter Cooper reports.

ONE FIFTH of construction firms are likely to vanish over the next 18 months, according to a report from accountant Price Waterhouse and a poll of 200 top builders which found two fifths admitted to buying work.

At the BEC annual conference in London this week, 84% of the delegates polled by Price Waterhouse said they did not believe the shake-out was going to happen. Yet 40% admitted to taking on loss-making contracts and 62% did not see a recovery in the construction market until 1995.

The report predicts a huge upheaval involving a number of forced mergers, hostile takeovers and receiverships. "We estimate that up to 20% of companies currently independent might no longer remain so," said Price Waterhouse partner Colin McKay. "The companies that suffer most will be those with the highest borrowings."

The accountant highlights four reasons why the industry is in this situation: 30% overcapacity means there are more companies than the market can support, intense cash flow pressure has led to companies taking on work at below cost; increased competition from recession-hit European contractors; and the fact that 40% of companies have stockmarket valuations below what they are worth, leaving them vulnerable to takeover.

Pressure on contractors' cash flow is set to increase as the industry emerges from recession, because subcontractor and material prices will rise on contracts won at low margins.

"Contractors can manage their businesses for cash rather than profit for some considerable time," said McKay. "But it is going to catch up with them."

The report states: "Many contractors have been forced to take certain actions which in a recovery environment does not leave them in an ideal position." It accuses contractors of making unrealistic assumptions about prices that can be achieved from subcontractors, raiding the construction claims bank, and taking an over-optimistic view about land values.

"Companies need to take steps to protect themselves now. We see clear niche opportunities for contractors in the UK and in central and eastern Europe, the Far East and South America," says Price Waterhouse.

(b)

Construction firms still lead business failure league

MORE CONSTRUCTION companies failed than in any other sector during 1993 – despite a 17% drop in insolvencies, according to figures published by the Department of Trade and Industry this week.

According to the DTI's Insolvency Service 1993 annual report, 3189 construction companies failed last year, compared with a peak of 3830 in 1992. But construction still tops the league table for company failures, ahead of the business services and retailing sectors.

Self-employed people in the construction industry fared less well than companies. The number of individual bankruptcies in 1993 remained virtually unchanged at 4300.

Overall, the total number of company failures throughout all sectors fell by 15% last year, from 24 425 to 20 825. But despite the drop in insolvencies, the number of directors disqualified rose from 409 to 419.

There was a 13% rise in the number of directors investigated by the DTI following reports from the official receiver.

(c)

Figure 7.7   The vulnerability of construction companies.
Source: Building.

Chapter 12 looks in a little more detail at the cash-flow problem itself and the implication it has for the way the design programme is developed. The wider problems of managing the small and medium-sized construction company are dealt with well in the recommended texts at the end of this chapter. They will be read in any case by construction management students, but should be looked at by architects and quantity surveyors to give some insight into the problems with which even the best-run firm has to cope.

7.5 Conclusion

We have seen in this chapter that the construction industry consists of thousands of firms from the smallest possible – the single proprietors – to the giant conglomerates, some specializing in one aspect of business, others involved in everything. Any generalizations made about such a diverse industry are likely to be misleading; yet there are features of the construction process itself which present all these firms with some common problems: the problems of achieving continuity of operation; the unique nature of each project (with exceptions such as housebuilding), the historical legacy of separation between the central functions of design and building; a contractual minefield; a high level of financial risk for all involved.

The fragmentation of the industry – particularly its subcontract culture – has been seen by some as a relatively efficient response to these problems and to the market conditions in which it has to work; others, however, have seen fragmentation as a large part of the industry's fundamental problem.

The most recent major report on the industry by Sir Michael Latham proposes many reforms and at the time of writing it seems as though some action will indeed follow; but perhaps we should not expect dramatic change. An understanding of the nature of the industry in which one works or intends to work is perhaps more useful than the belief that somehow it is all soon going to be very different. In 1851 a writer of a pamphlet entitled *In Contracting with Builders and Others Beware!* reported on his enquiries into the fate of some local builders: 'I find that out of seventeen builders . . . seven have been ruined only and entirely from taking contracts too low and trying to cut each other out by competition. Of the remaining ten, six have very nearly shared the same fate and are now very much lower both in position and character than they ought to have been and the others are in a small way of business' (quoted in Satoh, 1995).

It sounds very familiar.

FOR FURTHER STUDY

1 Recommended reading

For a rigorous general analysis of the nature of the industry, there is still nothing to match Michael Ball's *Rebuilding Construction* (1988). *The Modern Construction Firm* by Patricia Hillebrandt and Jacqueline Cannon examines the character, management and policy of construction firms. Hillebrandt's report on small firms (Hillebrandt, 1971) is now quite old but it is doubtful whether things have changed very much in that sector. The more recent book by Roger Harvey and Alan Ashworth, *The Construction Industry in Great Britain* is a useful synoptic survey. For regular reviews of the industry and individual companies, the weekly journals – *Building, Construction News* etc. – are essential. These days, too, companies' reports and accounts can make surprisingly interesting reading. The Latham Report (1994) examines critically and in some detail the current modes of working.

2 Discussion and essay questions

a Is the construction industry as different from others as is usually claimed? Identify the ways in which it is and is not like the others.

b Is the separation between the different professions in the industry an inevitable result of different functions – or the result of historical accident and the current education system?

c What are the reasons for the high rate of failure among construction firms? Are they mainly to do with insufficient management skills, business cycles, awkward clients or the nature of the contracting system itself?

d What are the advantage and disadvantages of the practice of subcontracting work to specialist firms?

3 Projects

Consider the list of departments in the firm Ohbayashi in Figure 7.6. Could this inclusion of every aspect of design and construction within the same firm eliminate the problems of conflict which seem to trouble the British industry? Find out more about the practice in Japan and other countries in comparison with your own. (The series of booklets by CIRIA on the industries of European Community construction industries is a good starting point.)

Economic aspects of design decisions

8 Costs and choices – the short-term and the long-term

Outline

- The problem of choice
- Methods of selection
- Initial costs and quality – an example
- Long-term cost: techniques of assessment:
  - the present value approach
  - other methods
- Problems and opportunities

8.1 Introduction

Designing buildings is very much about opening up possibilities, a creative process of imagining and defining many possible forms through which a client's requirements might be met and his or her objectives expressed. But design is also about making straight choices from existing options – selecting a form of flooring material, for example, from those which are actually available, deciding what type of roof or wall cladding to use. Some decisions required will be major strategic ones – the basic form of the building and the type of structure; others will be in one sense minor (though if, as Mies van der Rohe insisted, God is in the details, just as important for the quality of design), such as the type of door handles or light switches. Whatever the level of decision, major or minor, choices will have to be made using different criteria appropriate to the particular problem. But two overriding factors will recur: quality, and cost. Achieving the best possible quality within the budget must be a major objective.

Quality, however, is a word which encapsulates many different characteristics. A flooring material may be judged on its appearance, its resistance to wear, the ease with which it can be cleaned, its acoustic and heat insulation properties, its feel – rough or soft; these may be described as its aesthetic and functional properties. Some of those same properties will apply to many components; but for items such as doors, door handles or taps, other qualities will include how well they actually operate to perform their function.

These different dimensions of quality – aesthetics, efficiency, durability – may conflict, though there is usually a positive relationship between, say, the quality of workmanship, the efficiency of operation and the perceived aesthetic quality of something such as a door handle or a tap. But high quality will very often be difficult to achieve at low cost, making some sort of compromise inevitable in the face of limited budgets. One can imagine an ideal situation where the different criteria were carefully considered, weighed in relation to others and a decision reached which in some sense was 'optimal'. Architects usually think like that in a very rough and ready way; but they have neither the time nor the information to work scientifically through a very wide range of possibilities. And of course all the criteria are not in any case commensurable; there is no 'scientific' way to assess aesthetic value against cost.

Two economic aspects of this problem are discussed in this chapter – first, making selections on the basis of relative prices (related of course to quality) and, second, attempting to take explicit and formal account of total costs in use – or life-cycle costs – of a material or component.

First, however, we consider briefly some evidence on the ways architects actually do make these decisions. A research group at the Institute of Advanced Architectural Studies at York identified nine methods used by the practices (small and large) which they studied (Mackinder, 1980). These were:

1. subjective selection;
2. selection based on the availability of test information;
3. selection based on functional analysis;
4. selection based on feedback;
5. selection based on study of user requirements (user participation);
6. selection based on habit and experience;
7. standard specification;
8. performance specification;
9. computer-aided design.

For a full analysis of these the reader is referred to the original report, but from our present point of view, several of the report's comments are of particular interest. First, subjective selection was extremely common. This might include systematic listing of criteria, but depended on final choices made on the basis of an individual's or group's knowledge and experience; intuition and inspiration were referred to frequently.

Secondly, though formal accreditation, by for example Agrément certificates and BS standards, was seen as extremely important they by no means provided all the answers to the problems of establishing quality. This is not surprising: (a) not every individual batch or item may in fact meet the standard; (b) there are for many products still no agreed standards; (c) the designer may be looking for something above the basic requirements with performance characteristics that have not yet been tested; and (d) some products which have not received accreditation may in fact be perfectly adequate for the purpose.

Thirdly, formal feedback tended to be difficult to obtain and difficult to communicate; in fact 'feedback' tended to be negative, even restricted to real problems; when something went badly wrong, architects were sure to know about it.

The use of standard specifications (such as the National Building Specification) was common in some large but not in small offices. 'Architects' attitudes were ambivalent; they agreed that for items which were not visually important . . . there were advantages. . . . Many seemed slightly suspicious of the way components had been chosen. There was a general feeling that cheapness was too often the dominant criterion' (Mackinder, 1980, p. 123).

Fourthly, 'previous use and experience were found to influence selection more than any other factor . . . there was a strong tendency in all offices to develop a vocabulary of favourite products'. The advantages and dangers of relying on experience and 'subjective selection' are obvious. It saves time, it is relatively safe but it does mean that better alternatives may be missed, and changing relative prices may not be given sufficient attention.

There is, however, no simple answer to the problems of choice; and whatever the method of decision, some common elements will exist. In the next section we look at these with the help of a very simple example. We will make no attempt to delve deeply into the aesthetic issues here as it is impossible in a brief chapter to talk sensibly about a topic with 2500 years of philosophical debate behind it. The focus will therefore be on functional suitability and cost, taking the aesthetic dimension as being important of course but unanalysed at this stage.

8.2 The initial costs of alternative materials and components

8.2.1 Costs and quality

It is natural that in choosing materials or components for a specific element or function in a building, designers will always be trying to balance aesthetics, functional characteristics and cost. The difficulty is in striking the right balance; often there may not **be** a best or correct answer; even more certainly, there will not be the time of the information to discover what the best answer might be. There is often today a bewildering range of possibilities, not only in terms of different materials which can perform similar functions, but from the many different manufacturers of each material or component all claiming advantages, often both in cost **and** quality, for their own product.

One element of any analysis of possibilities must of course be a comparison of current prices for materials or components which meet the performance requirements – for example the costs of different floor materials for a bathroom, where resistance to wet and ease of cleaning will be prime considerations. But often it is not simply the price of the material itself that is significant; that may indeed be a relatively small percentage of the cost of incorporating that material in the building. In the case of brickwork for example, what is significant is not simply the cost per unit of material (a brick) multiplied by the number of units, but the cost of actually building walls in a particular place. This will include the cost of transport, the cost of labour, any equipment used. Furthermore the full costs of using a particular material may depend on the ramifications for the use of others. As a simple example of this last point, in designing new offices and studio for Channel Four Television in London, Richard Rogers and Partners were reported to have chosen a concrete frame because it reduced ceiling heights and consequently the area of expensive cladding required. The cost of concrete itself, that is of the actual material about which the decision was being made, as opposed to alternatives such as steel, played a relatively small part.

Because of this sort of problem and the great complexity and range of possibilities, this section is limited to one relatively simple example – the choice of floor covering – problems of complex interactions and choice between whole elements are left to later.

8.2.2 An example: the selection of floor covering

Taking as our example the selection of the best material to cover a floor, the possibilities appear to be bewilderingly wide. There are a very large number of ways of doing the job and many materials – hundreds of manufacturers and thousands of suppliers. However when the decision process is set out formally but simply, the problem is less intimidating. Table 8.1 shows in abbreviated form the range of prices based on a recent *Architects' Journal* study.

Two features seem to stand out from Table 8.1. One is the fact that there is a wide range of cost within each category; the difference between carpeting 2000 m^2 of offices with a cheap carpet and an expensive one could be based on these figures, about £50 000 – a substantial sum. The second is that each floor type has a similar price range, with the exception of the extremely expensive marble and Portland stone.

Table 8.1   Types and costs of floor coverings (London prices, late 1994) *Source: AJ Focus/Davis Langdon and Everest, Oct. 1994*

Material	Price range £/m^2
Carpet	
80% polypropylene	6–8
80% wool medium duty	15–18
heavy duty	33–8
Carpet tiles	
80% polypropylene	10–12
nylon	19–24
antron	31–5
Flexible flooring	
Cork	21–3
Linoleum	13–14
PVC tiles	7–30
Thermoplastic	6–7
Hard surface	
Marble	100–25
Slate	30–5
Ceramic tiles	27–47
Terrazzo tile	40–5
Quarry tiles	14–23
Mosaic tiles	35–45
Portland stone	100–20
York stone	70–80
Wood floors	
Softwood	8–12
Hardwood	30–50
Chipboard	5–7
In situ jointless	
Cementbased	6–10
Asphalt	8–9
Epoxy resin	25–40
Terrazzo	35–55
Latex	3–5

The first stage of the decision-making will be a rapid narrowing down of the possibilities on grounds of suitability, durability and approximate budget levels. We can consider each of these in turn.

Some surfaces will clearly not be suitable for some uses such as plastic tiles in the boardroom or carpets in the railway station washrooms (though there will always be exceptions and designers willing to try anything!). The choice will therefore in most cases be limited to a few particular types on suitability, that is on functional and aesthetic grounds.

Secondly some general idea of where cost levels will be pitched may already exist at this stage. The actual determination of cost limits and budget levels is examined in Part III of this book, but it is obvious that there are at one extreme some 'prestigious' projects and at the other extreme projects where the budgets allow only minimum specification in every respect. The designers will have a good idea as to whether they are dealing with an expensive item (carpet in the boardroom of a large company) or relatively cheap (carpet for a small guest-house lounge?).

Nevertheless, the choice is still wide; for example with the improvements in the durability of the carpet, it is now possible and usual for carpet to be specified for an area subject to very heavy wear indeed. For example, Pier 4 at Heathrow Airport, designed by Nicholas Grimshaw and Partners, is carpeted throughout with Collins and Aikman's Symphony carpet, although areas which carry the heaviest traffic in airports are usually surfaced with a harder material, such as the Silician granite at Stansted. Though at Stansted too the waiting areas in the departure lounge are carpeted. Richard Rogers also specified carpet to be used throughout the extension to the airport at Marseilles.

Even when the basic decision has been, perhaps tentatively, made, the specific material (make and quality) still has to be determined. Some relationship has to be established between cost and quality, because, whatever the budget level, designers will want to give best value for the money available.

For many materials and components it might be safe to assume a simple direct relationship: the more expensive, the higher the quality, and that price increases roughly in proportion to quality. But this is by no means always the case. Again the different dimensions of 'quality' need to be separated out and designers need to be aware of continuing changes in relative cost and qualities for different materials resulting from the kinds of technological advance discussed in Chapter 4.

For example, there are two major types of material for carpets – wool and man-made fibre; each has different 'quality' characteristics. Wool retains its appearance, its luxuriousness and springiness and is relatively easy to clean. Man-made fibres are inherently tougher but can become compressed, matted and hard. Each fibre has different levels of resistance to damage such as cigarette burns; earlier man-made types were easily damaged in this way but some are now fire-retardant. The best man-made carpet, however, which matches more closely the excellent characteristics of good-quality wool carpet, is becoming much less price-competitive.

All these factors need to be taken into account – for all the types of suitable flooring – before a final decision is reached; and one might suggest a decision process roughly as follows:

- a basic decision will be taken on the general type of finish required – a decision taken on aesthetic and functional grounds;
- the different ranges of material of the preferred type will be surveyed using several sources of information: the practice's own resources, both formal and informal; manufacturers' and suppliers' literature; durability will be a major criterion;
- cost information will be gathered at a general level via cost consultant or directly from sources such as price books;
- check will be made with suppliers on current availability and prices;
- decisions will be adjusted, confirmed or revised according to the result of these investigations.

This schematic outline seems to tally with the description of actual practice in another of the York studies, *Design Decision Making in Architectural Practice*. But there is one characteristic of the actual decisions they examined which does imply that the process can often be improved:

> *The implications of cost constraints were continually present in all the designs (studied) but did not overtly manifest themselves until detailed decisions were being made. Then cost was stated as being the prime influence over decisions. Cost trimming during the design was found to be a common cause of 'backtracking' either because the client decided to retract his intentions or because the architect's ideas exceeded the cost budget* (Mackinder and Marvin, 1982, p. 65).

Furthermore they found that too much time could be spent attempting to save money when the amounts involved were trivial:

> *Time spent on individual items was quite often disproportionate to their actual cost; for example a small area of floor finish might involve a day or so of research and reference to all sorts of information sources in order that a special requirement might be fulfilled, while its monetary value might be no more than £100 in a project costing £30 000.*

The cost of design time has clearly to be taken into account as well as the cost of material and this may often imply not defining optimal solutions but getting a good one quickly. Unless budgets are very tight indeed, there seems little reason for not aiming always for the highest quality for relatively insignificant elements within a reasonable range of costs. Of course if all the small elements are treated in this way they do become significant; the designer has to make these judgements in each particular case.

8.2.3 Other considerations

This general description of the incorporation of first cost considerations into design decisions on floor covering will apply to many similar decisions at the detailed design stage. For example, internal doors: there is a range of possible qualities, materials and finishes; there are some special considerations (such as need for fire protection, ease of opening and size for people with disabilities); but in general there will be a positive relationship between cost and quality, and the decisions will be made according to the same principles outlined for floors. In many situations building and planning requirements will impose severe constraints on choice such as window types and exterior finishes in conservation areas — but cost comparisons will still be required between alternatives.

Where special difficulties do arise is in the case of new materials which appear to offer superior performance at the same or relatively lower cost. It is in this situation that the various objective standard systems become invaluable. In theory if a new component or a material is approved to a particular British Standard or has an Agrément Certificate, it should at least meet a predetermined performance standard but, as the York researchers found, all the problems are not removed. For a description of the British Agrément and British standard see *Architects' Journal* (1993b).

However even at the most detailed level BS standards give guidance in specification and making some decisions are therefore more a matter of cost. BS 7352 was described as a 'shot in the arm for British hinge manufacturers' which 'for too long had been overawed by continental suppliers and seduced by the low prices of the Far East, which often came with quality to match'. What this means is that specifiers can identify defined quality clearly with a particular price range, though of course it might still be the case that the 'Far East' products may produce higher quality at lower cost.

Even when the design decision has been made, the issue is not necessarily resolved however. The contractor or the quantity surveyor may suggest alternatives; this is so common indeed that it has been given a name — 'specification substitution'. What needs to be established is both the motivation and the knowledge base on which the alternatives are recommended. If the suggestions are by the contractor they may be based on a better knowledge of current market conditions, of particular problems in installation which will raise costs, or they may simply be an attempt to save the contractor money. In an article in the *Architects' Journal*, Max Hutchinson, former president of the RIBA wrote,

> *It is one thing to enshrine a specification choice in a bill of quantities . . . it is another to ensure the choice is implemented, that the time spent poring over*

catalogues and samples . . . turns into precisely the right application for the job . . . The contractor can use considerable pressure, particularly in the later stages of a contract to suggest cheaper alternatives to save money (Hutchinson, 1993).

And his advice to designers is to 'hold firm'. On the other hand, it is clearly incumbent on the architect to check that the original decision was indeed the right one and not automatically to respond in a negative way to any alternative proposed. Where good relationships are established between architect, QS and contractor – and even more where the collaboration has taken place from the early design stage, this is less likely to be a problem. But there it can develop into real conflict.

Conclusion to first part. This discussion of the way initial costs influence design decisions at the detail level has been concerned with the relationship between cost and quality. One aspect of quality is always 'durability'; but durability can only be defined in terms of time and so far we have not looked at the problems of incorporating time into decisions, in a formal way. The second half of this chapter is devoted to that issue.

8.3 Costs and the life of buildings

8.3.1 Considering the future

It has become increasingly accepted over the past few years that such decisions should explicitly take time – and particularly the expected lifetime of a building and its many parts – into account. They always have done so in a very general way; the assessment of the 'durability' of a material, for example, implies a consideration of time, of its length of life. But it has not been usual – and in practice still is unusual except in a very limited number of situations – to make an accurate assessment of the time dimension of costs.

The example used above is an interesting case in point. Flooring does seem to be an obvious example of where long-term costs need some careful attention. It is true that in choosing a higher-quality, higher-price product, one has already taken length of life and resistance to wear into consideration. However there is seldom any attempt to calculate alternatives, or to persuade a client for example that a more expensive finish might be worth while in the long run using actual figures.

There are three major long-run costs to be considered: cleaning and maintenance and replacement. The cost at Marseilles are clearly going to be considerable; according to a report in the *Architects' Journal*, the following procedures are going to be required:

> *Airport maintenance staff were trained directly by the manufacturer to follow a four point cleaning method:*
>   *Effective protection at entrance areas . . . the mats are vacuumed daily and cleaned every nine days*
>   *Regular vacuuming with a rotating brush*
>   *Stain removal . . . constant checking for individual stains*
>   *Periodic deep cleaning (AJ* Focus, April 1993, p. 14).

On top of that it is expected that areas will have to be taken up and replaced quite often.

Whether the airports authority costed this as against maintenance cost of a hard floor is not known; it would certainly be a question which a client might wish to consider. In the case of airports, of course, the carpet cleaning may be such a trivial part of the cost of the whole operation that such considerations are irrelevant. In this particular case it was the client that decided.

Yet as many studies have shown the running costs of buildings over their lifetimes – the costs to owners and users – are probably higher than their initial costs. And this is true of individual parts or components. More is spent on fuel than on the installation of a heating system; and as we saw above the cleaning costs of a heavily used floor may amount to much more than its original costs.

One estimate of the scale of such 'life-cycle costs', or costs in use as they are sometimes called, is shown in Figure 8.1. Figure 8.2 gives a more detailed breakdown of the user costs for different types of building.

Though the importance of considering lifetime costs or costs in use has been pointed out by writers on building economics for many years and is now widely recognized by architects, surveyors, contractors and clients, there are still considerable practical difficulties in applying the well-established decision principles. This section examines at a general level those principles themselves and the problem associated with putting them into practice, using some of the examples as in the first half of the chapter. The application of these ideas in the more complex, strategic design decisions such as the determination of basic plan and structure and environmental control systems are considered in following chapters.

8.3.2 The present value (PV) approach

The general idea underlying life-cycle costing or costs in use is that in choosing a particular material, a particular heating system, a particular building component or indeed in making any choices, we should be aware of and if possible calculate both the immediate and future costs; only by doing that can the relative merits of different alternatives be assessed.

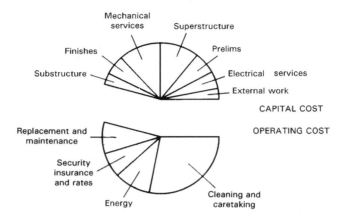

Notes:

(a)   size of each segment is in relation to the cost of each item;
(b)   data relate to the full expected life of the building of 50 years;
(c)   operating costs are discounted by 2% net of inflation;
(d)   site cost and design fees not included;
(e)   fixtures and fittings included with superstructure.

Figure 8.1   Comparison of the capital (initial) cost of a building with the present value of its running costs.

In a single section we can only outline some basic principles and point out some practical issues. For more detailed understanding, readers should explore the recommended sources at the end of the chapter. However, although the treatment here is relatively superficial we cannot stress too strongly the importance of understanding the central issue at this level; in fact because of the practical difficulties in full life-cycle cost assessment, we would argue that it is more important for architects and surveyors to understand the principle than the details of the calculation methods in order that their often quick and sometimes subconscious choices may be informed by an understanding of these issues.

The objective is to relate the short-term to the long-term costs – that is, in the context of building, the capital costs of construction with the running costs over the building's useful life. As this is just a special case of a general economic problem – relating expenditures or incomes in the future to expenditures or incomes in the present – there are well-established solutions.

In trying to make comparisons of this sort (whether of expenditures or incomes, receipts or payments), the difficulty arises because it is not sensible in a modern economy to treat future and immediate costs (or receipts) as equivalent. There is a considerable difference between knowing one has to

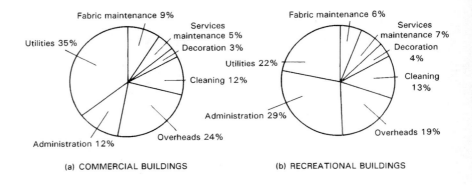

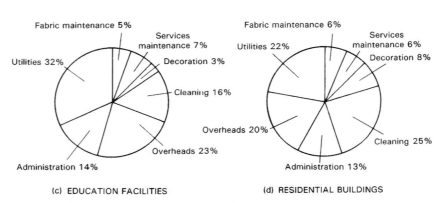

Figure 8.2   Distribution of running costs for a number of different building types.

spend £1000 tomorrow and knowing one has to spend £1000 in a year's time; or between knowing one is going to receive money tomorrow or the same amount in a year's time.

The difference arises because of the disadvantages and risk attached to not having one's money immediately available. These disadvantages are recognized by the payment or receipt of interest on money lent or borrowed for a period of time. There is also an element of compensation for inflation in interest payments, as interest rates tend to be higher in times of rapidly rising prices, but conceptually it is important to keep the notion of interest rates as payments for waiting and risk separate from the idea of inflation; even if inflation is zero, interest payments will still be made or received.

How then can future and present payments be compared? To take a simple example, comparing money received at different times. Consider the following possibility: you have received a legacy which includes a non-interest-bearing bond maturing in five years' time; this is in fact a promise to pay £1000 in five years' time. However, you want the money now. You can sell the bond – but not for £1000. Anyone who paid you £1000 would clearly be extremely foolish; if he or she wants £1000 in five years' time, and of course that is all the bond is worth, he or she could put much less than that in a building society account and let it accumulate interest. How much less depends on the rate of interest. If we assume for the sake of argument that an account can be found guaranteeing a fixed rate of interest of 5% the amount will be £784. In other words if someone put £784 away now he will have £1000 in five years' time. One way of describing this is to say £1000 in five years is **worth** only £784 today or the 'present value' (PV) of £1000 at a discount rate of 5% is £784.

The same principle applies in the case of costs. If you know for certain that £1000 is to be spent in five years' time, you could, using the same interest rate of 5% as in the last paragraph, ensure you have that money available by putting away £784 today. There is a very simple formula for relating single future payments of this sort to their present values:

> where PV is the present value
> i is the discount (interest) rate
> n is the number of years (or intervals between payments)
> Cn is the cost incurred n years from the present
> then: $\mathrm{PV} = Cn/1+i^{n}$ or $Cn(1+i)^{-n}$

Values for PV of £1 can be found in published tables (Present value of £1 table, extracts from which are given in Table 8.2a) or worked out quickly on a financial calculator. The derivation of the formula is shown in Figure 8.3; you should be sure you understand this.

The principle of comparing future costs (or incomes) with present costs (or incomes) can be extended to consider streams of future payments. For example one might wish to calculate the present value of future heating bills or maintenance costs (as in Chapter 11 below) or future rents (discussed in Chapter 17).

One way of doing this is simply to add up the individual present values of the future payments. For example, if heating bills are expected to be £1500 per year for the next five years (and we make the simplifying assumption that the bills are paid at the end of each year) and we wish to calculate the present value of that total, then we could simply make the following calculation (again using an interest rate of 5%):

	Payment	*Present value at 5%*
Year 1	£1500	£1428.45
Year 2	£1500	£1360.53

Year 3	£1500	£1295.75
Year 4	£1500	£1234.05
Year 5	£1500	£1175.28

Total present value: £6494.06

If the above calculation was made using a discount rate of 10% the total would be £6532. And if we simply multiplied £1500 by 5, that is not discounting at all, the total would be £7500, a considerable difference.

Table 8.2a   Present value of £1: receivable or payable after a number of years, for selected interest (discount) rates for selected years

Year	2%	5%	8%	10%
1	0.98039	0.95238	0.92592	0.90909
2	0.96116	0.90702	0.85733	0.82644
3	0.94232	0.86383	0.79383	0.75131
4	0.92384	0.82270	0.73502	0.68301
5	0.90573	0.78352	0.68058	0.62092
10	0.82034	0.61391	0.46319	0.38554
15	0.74301	0.48101	0.31524	0.23939
20	0.67297	0.37688	0.21454	0.14864
25	0.60953	0.29530	0.14601	0.09220
30	0.55207	0.23137	0.09937	0.05730
50	0.37152	0.08720	0.02132	0.00851
100	0.13803	0.00760	0.00045	0.00007

Table 8.2b   Present value of £1 per annum: at selected interest (discount) rates for selected periods of time ('years purchase' table)

Year	2%	5%	8%	10%
1	0.9803	0.9523	0.9259	0.9090
2	1.9415	1.8594	1.7832	1.7355
3	2.8838	2.7232	2.5770	2.4868
4	3.8077	3.5459	3.3121	3.1698
5	4.7134	4.3294	3.9927	3.7907
10	8.9825	7.7217	6.7100	6.1445
15	12.8492	10.3796	8.5594	7.6060
20	16.3514	12.4622	9.8181	8.5135
25	19.5234	14.0939	10.6747	9.0770
30	22.3964	15.3724	11.2577	9.4269
50	31.4236	18.2559	12.2334	9.9148
100	43.0983	19.8749	12.4943	9.9992

Provided all the future payments are the same and made at the same intervals, there is a simpler way of deriving the results above, again by using a formula or looking up the values in tables. The formula and its derivation are given in Figure 8.4 and the relevant table headed 'Present value of £1 per annum' (Table 8.2b). Use the table to check the above result. If payments were different or made at different intervals the separate values will have to be added as in the example.

By in effect converting future payments to their present values we can compare them with current payments. We can then treat immediate

If you put £P in an account paying (i x100)% interest compounded yearly (for example, if the interest is 5% , i = .05), then at the end of year 1, the sum in the account will be A where

$$A = P + iP$$

(if the interest is 5% and P =£200, then A will be 200 +(.05 x 200)= £210)

at the end of the second year

$$A = (P+ip) + i(P+iP)$$

(in the example A will now be £210+ 5% 0f 210 = £220.5)

This can be written as:

$$A = P(1+i) +iP(1+i)$$
Or
$$A = P(1+i)(1+i)$$
=
$$A = P(1+i)^2$$

At the end of the third year, the amount will be the value at the end of the second year (i.e. $P(1+r)^2$) plus 5% 0f that value that is

$$P(1+i)^2 + iP(1+i)^2$$

which is equal to

$$P(1+i)^3$$

In fact each year one is multiplying by $(1+i)$

So for n years the general formula when A is the amount to which P accumulates over n years at (i.100)% interest is

$$A = P(1+i)^n$$

But if $A = P(1+i)^n$, then obviously

$$P = A/(1+i)^n$$

i.e. the present value of an amount A receivable or payable after n years, discounted at (i x100)%

is equal to $A/(1+i)^n$ or $A(1+i)^{-n}$

Published tables give the present values for £1 at different rates for different years.. Therefore to find the value for any given amount, simply multiply that amount by the factor derived form the tables.

Figure 8.3   Derivation of the formula calculating the present value of a single amount receivable or payable in the future

If the the amount A is to be received at the end of each year.

The PV of the first Amount is A/1+i

The PV of the amount received after 2 years is $A/(1+i)^2$

The sum of present values for any number of years is therefore

$A/1+i + a/(1+i)^2 + A/(1+i)^3......+A/(1+i)^n$

This is a geometrical series of the form $V + Vr + Vr^2 + Vr^3...... Vr^n$

the sum of which is $V(1-r^n)/1-r$

substituting $A(1+i)^{-1}$ for V and $(1+i)^{-1}$ for r in that formula gives

$$\frac{A(1+i)^{-1}(1-(1+i))^{-n)}}{1-(1+i)^{-1}}$$

which after some manipulation reduces to $A(1-(1+i)^{-n})/i$

ie. the present value of £1 per annum receivable for n years discounted at (ix100) %

p.a.is

$$\frac{A(1-(1+i)^{-n})}{i}$$

As $(1-i)^{-n}$ is the formula derived above for the PV of £1 (single amount) this formula is

sometimes simplified to **A (1-PV)/ i**

(There are also other versions of the formular used which are mathematically equivalent)

Figure 8.4   Derivation of formula for the present value of a future stream of income or expenditure

expenditures and future expenditures together. We could for example add them. If we wished to compare the total costs of two heating systems, A and B, one way of doing this would be to add the initial cost of A with the present values of the heating bills for say the next ten years and compare that with the cost of system B plus its heating bills for the next ten years. The system giving the lower total costs (present plus discounted future costs) would be the most economic over the ten years.

Or to return to the floor-covering example, we could add up the initial cost, the maintenance, cleaning and replacement costs of each proposed material over the total life of the building (about which some assumptions would have to be made). In reality there is not much point in trying to look too far ahead; no-one knows what is going to happen in 20 years' time; and the effect of discounting means that there is little difference between assuming a life of, say, 30 and 60 years (study Figure 8.5). Assuming a life of 30 years, the calculation could be set up as in Figure 8.6

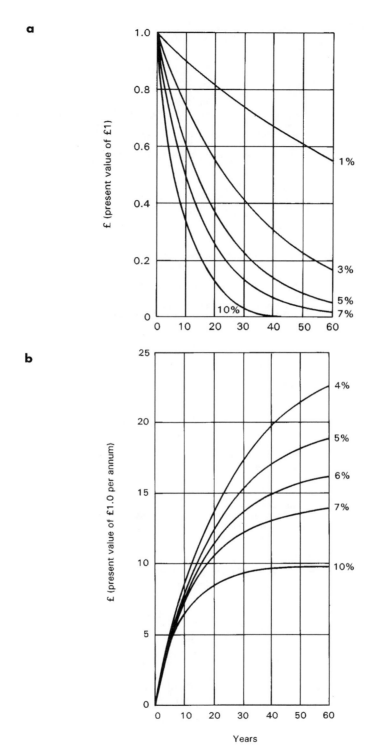

Figure 8.5   Effect of discounting using different rates

<u>*Assumptions:*</u>

Building Life: 50year
vynil tiles   initial cost : **£19** per m^2.   replacement required after **15** years
carpet tiles   initial cost : **£17** per m^2 replacement required after **10** years
Cleaning cost of vyni   £3 m^2 per year
Cleaning cost of carpet   £1 m^2 per year
Discount rate **5**%
Assume (for simplicity) costs of cleaning incurred at the end of each year

<u>*Initial Calculations*</u>

1. Cleaning costs,

Using the "present value of £1 per annum" table at 5% for 50 years, showing pv of £1 per year=18.2559

the pvs of cleaning costs are: Vynil: 18.26 x £3   =**£54.78**
                                Carpet 18.26 x £1   =**£18.26**

2 Replacement costs

The present value of the replacement costs will be: (using the pv of £1 table)
Carpet: 1st Replacement £17 discounted at 5% over 10 yrs:
                =£17 x .613= **£10.42**
                2nd Replacement £17 discounted at 5% over 20yrs:
                =£17 x .377= **£6.41**
                (3rd and 4th replacements come to **£3.9** and **£2.4** respectively
        Total pv of replacement costs = £23.13

Vynil: 1st replacement: £19 discounted for 15 yrs
                =£19 x .481 = **£9.14**
                2nd replacement: £19 after 30years
                =£19 x .231 = **£4.39**
        Total pv of replacement costs = £13.53

<u>*Total lifetime cost comparison*</u>
(figures rounded)

	Vynil Tiles	Carpet tiles
Initial costs (per m^2)	£19.00	£17.00
Costs of maintenance	£54.78	£18.26
Cost of replacement	£13.53	£23.13
Total Lifetime cost	£87.31 m^2	£58.39 m^2

Figure 8.6   Example of a cost in use calculation for two alternative floor coverings.

basing calculations on Table 8.1. Before moving to the next section, you should work through that example carefully; it should raise a few questions in sceptical minds! On the assumptions described an apparently small advantage for the carpet tiles is converted into a major one when the full lives are taken into account, but this may be a good example of how unrealistic such calculations are in relation to actual decision-making. It is used merely to demonstrate the method in a simple way.

8.3.3 Other methods of comparison

However there are other ways of comparing present with future costs. Most of them are not strictly 'correct' in that they do not fully take account of the significance of different time-scales or the impact of interest rates, but they are often easier to use and for some purposes perfectly adequate.

One alternative is to express an initial capital cost of an item such as a heating boiler in terms of its financing cost over future years; that is, instead of converting future costs to present values, one spreads the present cost over the future, as happens in any case if an item was bought on hire purchase or through a loan repaid in instalments. So if a house owner were to install double glazing, financed through a ten-year loan repaid by equal instalments, the cost could be compared with the savings on the annual fuel bills. In this case one is not explicitly comparing the relative costs of two systems, but calculating whether the investment in the double glazing is worth while, which it would be if the annual loan costs were lower than the savings in fuel. However, the savings would continue after the loan was paid off, so the comparison would not take account of all the savings to be achieved over the full life of the glazing. The problem could be solved by amortizing the costs over the full presumed life of the glazing system.

This approach is particularly appropriate where a capital expense is expected to make a direct measurable contribution to income and the client is interested in a relatively short time horizon. So an extension to a hotel will be expected to yield extra income from guests; from that income will have to be deducted the extra expenses incurred to give a net income. This can then be compared with the annual finance cost of the extension.

A second alternative, and very straightforward, approach, frequently used as we will see in Chapter 12 in discussions of energy costs and savings, is the 'simple payback method'. This may or may not incorporate an element of discounting. Using this approach, one simply works out how long a capital item takes to 'pay for itself' through the extra incomes or savings it generates. So, taking the same hotel extension example as above, assuming the cost of the extension was £100 000 and the extra net income was £10 000 a year, the extension would pay for itself in ten years; ten years is said to be the payback period. An element of discounting can easily be incorporated by reducing the future payments to their present values and then again calculating the number of years needed to pay off the capital costs. Obviously, the number will be higher than the simple payback, but it will more accurately reflect the real values.

8.3.4 Life-cycle costs and design: problems and opportunities

Despite the simplicity of the principles and calculations described in the last section there are many problems in applying them in practice. One set of problems stems from the simple fact that however sophisticated we make our methods – incorporating risk analysis and probabilities – we can still not know the future; these we can call problems of prediction. The second sort of problem is the lack or unavailability of necessary data problems of data availability – though often this can also be the result of not knowing the future. Thirdly, there is the problem of identifying the discount rate to use; and finally, there is a set of problems connected with scepticism – by clients, contractors and architects themselves and with the way present and future costs impinge on different groups. Even when the architect or quantity surveyor is convinced that a client might be better selecting one option with high initial but low running costs, the client's own priorities may be very short-term cost. This section examines each of these sorts of problem in turn.

1. Unpredictability. In attempting to incorporate life-cycle approaches in design decision-making, we have to make judgements about the future course of events; about how long the building is going to last, how it will be used; how each of its parts will be maintained; how quickly some elements will become obsolete or simply out of fashion; about what will happen to interest rates and inflation; about possible changes in technology which might affect the activities within and outside the building; about government policies . . . and so on.

Some of these things simply cannot be predicted and we can do little but ignore them; it would have been impossible for anyone to predict that the Government would impose Value Added Tax on domestic fuel in 1994; estimates made of the value of fuel saving systems in, say, 1990 would have been underestimates.

Other changes seem to be aspects of trends or cycles about which we can make intelligent guesses; but there are no certainties. The course of interest rates and inflation was extremely erratic from 1979 to 1994 as Figure 8.7 shows and the range in that period extreme. Even short-term forecasts could be quite inaccurate and over the long term extremely unreliable.

To take another example of dubious prediction, there seems some certainty that the pace of innovation in office technologies will be maintained but no-one predicted the rate at which word processing was to replace typing; and current predictions of widespread 'distance working' through terminals and a consequent reduction in office space needs could be wrong; or there could be a major revolution just round the corner. Consider this extract from a report in *Building* in 1993:

The first wave of a new technology that will change office design and cut costs by millions hit the market last week. NET, from computer giant Olivetti is a method of networking personal computers by radio wave instead of cabling. The development is seen as significant . . . because it promises to make raised floors redundant . . . more people do not want raised floors; they immediately add 4% to the cost and then there is the extra height which bumps up the cost of cladding. However Stephen Hill of Oscar Faber said . . . 'I don't think it will have any significant effect on the market for 10–20 years' (Building, 11 June 1993).

But who knows? Predicting future office redesign and refurbishment costs seems fraught indeed.

2. Inadequate information. Three sets of data are needed for making life-cycle cost calculations. First, figures are required for the initial costs of items for which the assessment is being made. There is usually little difficulty in identifying these; if we wish to compare the long-term costs of two different roofing materials, the basic initial cost will be obtainable from suppliers or merchants; but as we have seen even at this level change can take place quickly and variations can be considerable depending on the size of the contract and the contractor.

The second type of information required is data on the life expectancies

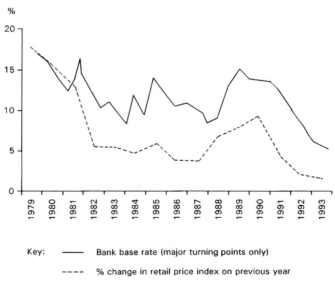

Key: ———   Bank base rate (major turning points only)

          ----   % change in retail price index on previous year

Figure 8.7   Interest rates and inflation, 1979–83.
Source: *Annual Abstract of Statistics.*

of the different materials or components; and linked to this, the assumptions to be made about frequency and costs of maintenance. A highly efficient boiler may save energy, but overall costs will depend on how often the boiler needs replacing and how expensive it is to maintain.

By its very nature (involving again assumptions about the unknowable future) such information when available at all is bound to be suspect. As new materials and products come on the market, estimates of their useful lives are made by manufacturers, but the truth will not be known until the time has actually elapsed. And even then there will be a wide range of different results, with some failing before others, possibly due to neglect of maintenance, possibly due to random differences in original quality. The fact that one can see the odd beautifully maintained 1927 Austin 7 on the roads in the 1990s and many a neglected and disintegrating five-year-old car does not mean that predictions cannot be made about the lives of cars and their costs of maintenance. Such predictions and analyses are of course widely published.

The problem with building components and materials is that there has not until fairly recently been the same attention paid to such analysis partly because of the difficulty of gathering the information, the enormous variety of relevant materials and products and the very different conditions under which they are used.

However, serious attempts have been made to produce usable data by organizations such as the Building Maintenance Cost Information Service and the former PSA. The third edition of PSA's *Costs in Use Tables* was published in 1991 and this gives estimated total costs in use for a range of different alternative specifications for all the major building elements (see extract, Figure 8.8). There is a British Standard BS7543: 1992 (BSI, 1992; Chevin, 1992), which not only lists design lives for components but indicates reasons for premature deterioration.

The third type of information required is about the client or users of the buildings concerned; what kind of priorities do they have in terms of capital and running costs? This may be affected by their financial and tax position. This information cannot of course only be discovered and assessed in discussions between architect and client. The important thing is to know what sort of information is required and how it can be used.

3. Choosing the discount rate. If it is decided to use a present value approach or to convert capital costs into equivalent future annual payments, the results will be critically affected by the interest or discount rate chosen.

Figure 8.5 showed the effect of a range of different rates on the present value of £100 receivable or payable in a given number of years. The dramatic difference between using 10% or 5% over a long period can quite easily be seen.

There is no 'right' discount rate to use, and there has been much discussion on what is most appropriate. Official and professional bodies such as the Treasury and the RICS make recommendations at different times.

A sensible practice is to use a rate which reflects the sort of interest available on loans at the time the decisions are being made. The rationale of this is easy to see. Assume that the cost in ten years' time of a replacement boiler will be, say £5000. If the owner can earn 5% on his money, he could fund that replacement by putting aside £3070 at 5% compound. The present value to him of the £5000 is £3070 (check these figures using the tables of formula; you will find slight discrepancies due to rounding).

Unfortunately for this argument, interest rates, as we have seen, change and there is no way of knowing what they will be in five years' time and then perhaps using an average rate to make the calculations.

One way of getting over the difficulty simply is to carry out what is sometimes rather grandly called a 'sensitivity analysis', that is to test the results of a present-value calculation at a range of different rates. If, for example, we wished to compare one roofing material with another over the life of a building, we could calculate the respective present values using a range of rates; it might be that under any reasonably likely rate, one system comes out more cheaply than the other; the decision is then clear. If, however, the result turns out to be sensitive to different rates then some judgement has to be made as to which are the more probable; or it might be concluded that there is no significant lifetime cost difference between the two alternatives, given the uncertainty of the future trend of rates, and that the decision will be made on other criteria. There are other approaches such as using the 'internal rate of return' which will not be discussed here.

4. Persuading the client. The last set of problems in applying life-cycle approaches which will be considered here are the problems involved in actually persuading clients or sometimes contractors to adopt what appears to be the best solutions. There are a number of reasons for this difficulty. First clients themselves might have very short-term objectives. A developer who intends to sell a building on completion to let to tenants on a full repairing and maintenance basis may not be unduly concerned about long-term costs; he or she may simply want the lowest possible initial cost. Secondly, clients may simply not be convinced that the life-cycle approach is a valid one; long-run issues are always more difficult to think about than immediate concerns and clients may believe it is as well to leave future events to occur as they will rather than try, on what seems to be very shaky evidence, to incorporate them into their initial cost calculations.

3   INTERNAL FINISHES

3.B   Floor finishes—*continued*

No	Description	Capital	Cleaning	Cyclical	Repairs	Total
1	FLOORS — *continued* m²					
m	Marble 20, Italian; cement and sand screed; 50 total	184.47	50.10	–	1.01	235.58
n	Hardwood blocks, Iroko, 275 × 75 × 25, t&g, bedded in mastic, to pattern; cement and sand screed; 50 total; sanded, sealed, wax polished	51.29	50.10	27.15	0.14	128.68
p	Hardwood block slips, felt backing 5, up to 100 × 50, bedded in adhesive; cement and sand screed; 50 total	32.41	50.10	31.60	0.10	114.21
q	Linoleum sheet 3, fixed with adhesive; cement and sand screed; 50 total	20.56	50.10	9.87	0.31	80.84
r	Vinyl tiles 2, fixed with adhesive; cement and sand screed; 50 total	18.06	50.10	8.21	0.28	76.65
s	Vinyl sheet 2.5, fixed with adhesive, seamed joints; cement and sand screed; 50 total	19.93	50.10	9.45	0.31	79.79
t	Thermoplastic tiles 2, fixed with adhesive; cement and sand screed; 50 total	13.92	50.10	5.46	0.24	69.72
u	Rubber safety floor, studded, 4, fixed with adhesive; cement and sand screed; 50 total	34.30	61.57	11.70	0.50	108.07
v	Cork tiles 4, fixed with adhesive; cement and sand screed; 50 total; sealed	18.80	230.46	16.01	0.30	265.57

Figure 8.8   Extract from PSA, *Costs in Use Tables.*

Cleaning			Cyclical			Repairs					
Annual Cost	Frequency No	Yr	Work	Cost	Cycle in Years	Cause/ Action	Cost (£) and Risk	Occurs in Years	kg/m²	R value	No
											1
Sweep 2.38 Scrub/ wash 0.72	250 50	1 1	–	–	–	Loosened/ damaged tiles	187 2%	1–60	47	0.07	m
As above 2.38 0.72	250 50	1 1	Wax polish Sand, seal, wax polish	1.65 2.77	1 30	Loosened blocks, surface wear	51 1%	1–60	57	0.21	n
As above 2.38 0.72	250 50	1 1	Wax polish Replace entirely	1.65 28.37	1 30	Loosened slips, surface wear	36 1%	1–60	70	0.11	p
As above 2.38 0.72	250 50	1 1	Replace lino, patch screed	14.86	15	Patch lino, patch screed	23 5%	1–60	77	0.10	q
As above 2.38 0.72	250 50	1 1	Replace tiles, patch screed	12.36	15	Patch tiles, patch screed	21 5%	1–60	76	0.09	r
As above 2.38 0.72	250 50	1 1	Replace sheet, patch screed	14.23	15	Patch sheet, patch screed	23 5%	1–60	78	0.10	s
As above 2.38 0.72	250 50	1 1	Replace tiles, patch screed	8.22	15	Patch tiles, patch screed	18 5%	1–60	77	0.10	t
Wash 3.81	250	1	Replace sheet, patch screed	28.60	20	Patch sheet, patch screed	37 5%	1–60	79	0.10	u
Sweep 2.38 Scrub/ wash 11.88	250 12	1 1	Replace tiles, patch screed	13.39	10	Patch tiles, patch screed	27 5%	1–60	75	0.14	v

Nevertheless, although these are real obstacles, the increasing awareness of the significance of running costs, particularly among business and government clients, means that there **is** more readiness to consider arguments based on the long term if they are convincing enough. A potential tenant for an office building will today be very much concerned with the likely heating and maintenance costs, and the original developer might well be able to recoup the extra expenditure involved in, for example, low-maintenance floor finishes, in the rent he or she can charge.

Public-sector buildings sometimes present a different kind of problem. Total budgets may be set in such a way that minimum specification is inevitable. The fact that this might lead (and as was seen in much housing built in the 1950s probably will lead) to more rapid deterioration and increasing expense for future taxpayers is frequently ignored. One very important consequence of a thorough understanding of the issues discussed in this chapter is that the professionals in the building industry should be in a strong position to argue against the long-term irrationality of specifying the lowest quality to save on immediate expenditure.

8.4 Conclusion

The purpose of this chapter has been to establish an understanding of the way costs can be and are incorporated into design choices, first considering initial cost only and then taking into account the longer term. Despite the difficulties of applying the life-cycle approach discussed in the last few paragraphs, it is well worth while thoroughly understanding the simple mathematics of comparing present with future costs (and we will be looking at other important applications of the same basic calculation in the chapters on value). The following chapters examine the economics of design choices for different elements of buildings and it will be seen that there are circumstances in which calculations of future costs can be made and can help to determine design decisions.

FOR FURTHER STUDY

1 Recommended reading

For a good analysis of the application of a range of selection criteria to many different building materials and a discussion of performance specification see Chapter 6 of Harper's *Building, The Process and the Product* (1990 edition). There is a clear brief description of the Agrément process, British Standards and the new European codes in an *Architects' Journal* Special Report, 12 May 1993 – and no doubt there will be updated versions from time to time.

There are explanations of life-cycle cost analysis in most construction economics and quantity surveying texts (e.g. Seeley, 1972, Chapter 11). Despite its age, P.A. Stone's *Building Design Evaluation – Costs in Use* (1967) is still one of the most clear and comprehensive discussions. The College of Estate Management produced a design manual, *Life Cycle Costing for Architects* in the 1970s and a good modern text is Flanagan, Meadows and Robinson's *Life Cycle Costing* (1989) Ruegg and Marshall's *Building Economics* (1990) and Thorbjoen Mann's *Building Economics for Architects* (1992) are perhaps the most thorough explorations of investment-appraisal techniques in the context of building design.

2 Exercises

a Using the same basic data as in Table 8.4, recalculate using discount rates of 2% and 10%. What difference does this make to the relative advantage of the carpet tile?

b A choice needs to be made of kitchen units for a housing development. The following data are available:

type A: proprietary blackboard, painted
    requires repainting every 5 years at a cost of £90 and replacing after 15 years;
    Initial cost: £603.9

type B: best-quality hardwood
    requires replacing after 25 years; initial cost £1059

Assuming a building life of 50 years and using interest rates of 8% which is the most cost-effective choice? For whom? What effect does discounting at 2% or 10% have on the result?

3 Discussion or essay questions

a To what extent should the internal finishing and fittings of an office building, a local authority day centre for elderly people and a housing association block of flats be determined by the architects? (There are all the issues of user participation as well as the role of interior designers and component manufacturers to be explored here).

b Given all the uncertainties attached to life-cycle cost analysis in the context of buildings, is it simply a waste of time attempting to apply the techniques – or can they make a real contribution to sensible decision-making?

4 Project

Using data from any convenient source, identify some alternatives and their relative costs (first cost only) for internal partition walls and ceilings in a small office building. (Suggested data sources: *Architects' Journal*, Focus; *Building*, Materials Supplements; Spons or other price books; BCIS.)

9 Concept, shape, plan: morphology and cost

'Form follows Profit is the essential aesthetic principle of our time'
(Sir Richard Rogers).

9.1 Introduction

Many of the world's greatest buildings are extremely complex in their external form, their internal plans, the variety of spaces they enclose, their materials, their decoration. The façades alone of cathedrals such as Chartres or Notre Dame astonish us by their wealth of detail; and though the basic plan of the great Gothic churches was relatively simple, the profusion of small chapels, the great traceries of the windows and roof, the host of buttresses and pinnacles externally gave enormous variety of space and form. The major buildings of the Italian Renaissance, tightly controlled though they were by the rules of classical proportion, both in plan and elevation, enclosed spaces rich in interest and surprise. The exuberant decoration of the baroque seems sometimes to overwhelm the basic forms of the buildings.

*Casa Mila,
Barcelona by
Antonio Gaudi.*

Yet underlying all this there was usually a guiding principle of organization – religious or secular. Rational planning has been known and practised at least since the ancient Greeks and often underlies the apparent confusion of even the most richly decorated building; indeed Pugin himself, master of Victorian Gothic has been described, and described himself, as a 'rationalist'. But it is only in the twentieth century that a powerful and positive ideology of simplicity developed, becoming almost a religion with a host of prophets preaching their own versions – from Adolf Loos's credo that 'decoration is crime', Mies Van der Rohe with his aphorism 'less is more' to the many variants of (often confused) functionalism and rationalist design philosophies.

But architects and public alike have continued to seek and to see interest in complexity of form and intricacy of detail.

'Architecture' wrote Robert Venturi, 'is necessarily complex and contradictory in its very inclusion of the traditional Vitruvian elements of commodity, firmness and delight. And today, the needs of program, structure, mechanical equipment and expression even in simple buildings in simple contexts are diverse in ways previously unimaginable'. His answer to Mies van der Rohe was 'less is a bore' (Venturi, 1966, p. 22).

Other architects have, throughout the twentieth century, also resisted the pressures towards stark functionality. To expressionist architects such as

Antonio Gaudi and Eric Mendelsohn, straight lines were almost anathema; Gaudi's extraordinary Mila house in Barcelona exhibits curves and bulges along its street façade like, as one critic has said, the skirts of a Spanish dancer. His plans for the Church at Santa Colona would defy the bravest cost analyst (Figure 9.1)! Recently the Cuban architect, Ricardo Porro, who has designed a school in Paris which seems to have echoes of Mendelsohn, Le Corbusier's Ronchamp and Gaudi, has commented that 'modern architecture conveys no sense of ecstasy, which is what I want my architecture to do'.

Yet all the textbooks tell us that simple forms are cheapest; we live in an age when clients of almost every sort, public and private, seek buildings at minimum capital costs even though in reality over their lives they may not well provide the best value for money. So are we then condemned to cheap boxes with the occasional exercise in high-technology fantasy? Or is there a more subtle and complex relationship between the morphology of buildings, their quality and their cost, which allows variety and interest to be achieved with economy?

In this chapter we look at the basic implications of form for cost and cost for form, recognizing that this is only one aspect of the possible answers to those questions, but a highly significant one.

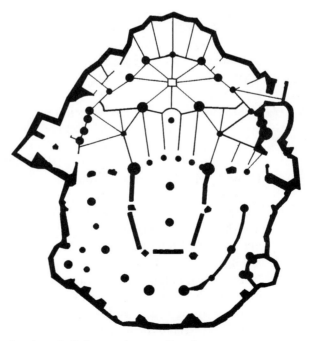

Figure 9.1   Plan of the church at St Colona – Antonio Gaudi.

9.2 Plan shape and cost

We consider first the simple mathematics of the relationship between the shape of a building and the probable costs of its major elements such as walls and roofs.

9.2.1 Areas, perimeters and the costs of walls

It is obvious that the perimeter of a building of a given area will be a different length depending on the plan shape; and consequently the cost of those elements which are directly related to perimeter length such as walls will also vary with plan shape. These relationships are very simple but they are worth spelling out as a basis for discussion later in the chapter (and indeed are also relevant for later chapters).

Consider some possible shapes for a building of 2500 m^2 as shown in Figure 9.2. Because they have the same floor area, they could all potentially provide the same amount of physical accommodation, though different arrangements of the geometry will be desirable or indeed necessary to satisfy the functional needs of the building (an issue to which we will return). The shapes illustrated do however have very different perimeter lengths, and as the costs of many building elements are directly related to the length of the perimeter, these costs will rise as the length increases.

The cost of walls is the most obvious and probably most important. It is clear from the figure that if our sole objective were to minimize the length of wall needed to enclose a given space, we would design circular buildings. That of course creates problems, particularly problems of internal planning, fixtures and fittings. In a circular house fitting standard kitchen and bathroom units is hardly a possibility without wasting considerable space; even hanging pictures on the wall becomes a challenge.

Yet some of the finest buildings throughout the history of architecture have been circular. The remarkable Pantheon in Rome, built for the Emperor Hadrian in the second century AD, has been imitated many times through later centuries. And circular buildings come in every size and at all levels of sophistication. Bramante's small Tempietto in Rome has been described as 'perfect' and in Britain we have among others fine buildings like the Radcliffe Library at Oxford and the Albert Hall and also the humbler ones such as the railway building now housing the Round House Theatre in London. In most of these cases the reason for the circular form may have had little to do with cost or minimum use of material – though in the case of many castles built from the time of the crusades, circular fortresses exploited another of the circle's physical characteristics – its greater resistance to impact.

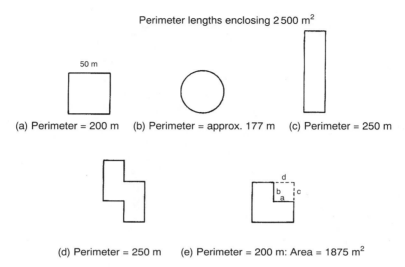

Figure 9.2   Plan shapes of similar area.

The traditional houses in many societies have been circular again not necessarily to save cost, though the saving in material may well have been one factor in their development (Rapoport, 1969).

However Buckminster Fuller's Dymaxion house and its later development the Wichita house (Figure 9.3) were designed in hexagonal and circular form specifically to minimize the costs of production and fulfil Fuller's fundamental aim to produce buildings at minimum total energy cost, including the energy content of materials. The fact that heat loss was also minimized, as wind resistance was reduced by the hemispherical form, was equally important. And the planning could work: Fuller himself lived for a while in a house built on these principles (McHale, 1962).

Nevertheless, despite the virtues of the hexagon and the circle, square corners and straight walls have obvious advantages and in terms of perimeter costs alone, square buildings should be cheaper than rectangular ones. As a rectangle becomes longer and thinner (less square or deep) the percentage increase in perimeter is quite rapid, as the curve in Figure 9.4 shows. Furthermore it is likely that more window area will be required in the longer walls and the provision of windows can cost up to three times that of equivalent area of the wall material. Assume a simple factory building could be built on either the square or rectangular plan represented by the two extremes of Figure 9.4; using PVF2 coated aluminium on steel rails, insulated, for the walls, with steel, single-glazed, galvanized and painted windows, and making realistic assumptions about height and fenestration, the costs would be approximately £41 250 for the square and £61 000 for the rectangle.

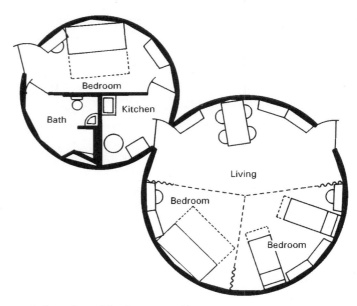

Figure 9.3   Buckminster Fuller: plan of the Dymaxion House.

This of course represents capital costs only. There is also a clear relationship between wall length on the one hand and long-term running and maintenance costs on the other. For example heat losses and gains will increase, as will the costs of cleaning and external painting. The relationship between shape and energy flows is mentioned in section 9.2.3 below and taken up again in Chapter 11.

It is worth noting from the examples in Figures 9.2 and 9.4 that in considering perimeter length alone, it is not necessarily complexity but 'depth' that determines efficiency (in this limited sense). If you take a given rectangle and turn it 90°, even several times, the wall perimeter is the same (Figure 9.2d). However as Figure 9.2c illustrates it is still the case that an L shape is very much less efficient than the square; by shifting the two interior angled walls out to form a square you could enclose an extra 625 m^2 with the same walling material.

The costs of external walls, even of a constant height, are not determined only by their length. Both materials and labour costs will tend to vary directly with the length but labour is obviously more susceptible to the influence of other factors, such as the number of openings and the number of corners. A study reported in a paper to a CIB Symposium in 1993 found that the productivity of bricklayers was directly related to the number of openings in a wall and the number of corners; not surprisingly, long, straight areas of wall were built faster. What seems surprising is the

Le Corbusier: Villa Savoie. Elegance from simple geometrics.

Le Corbusier: the chapel at Ronchamp: drama from complex forms.

size of the effect: output could drop from a little over 2 m^2 per hour to only just about 1 m^2 per hour. The same effect – increasing cost with the **complexity** of the structure – would apply with systems other than brick, as corners must always imply extra work (Horner and Ab-Hamid, 1993).

External walls of course are not the only elements which vary with the length of the building's perimeter. It is also likely that distribution systems, such as water supply, waste disposal, electrical wiring, will also increase as the shape moves away from square. This is because the number of points needed to be served by such systems will increase, thus extending the lengths of these essentially linear systems.

If there are strip foundations the costs of these too will show the same sort of relationship with shape as the costs of walls.

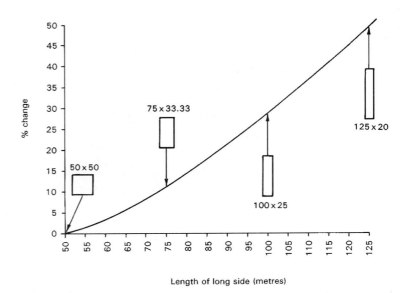

Figure 9.4   Increase in perimeter length with change in shape of a rectangular building of fixed area.

9.2.2 Roofs

The question of roofs is more complex. Thinking still in terms of a fixed floor area, we might expect the costs of a roof to depend mainly on the area to be covered, with relatively little variation with shape. But things are not quite so simple. Roofs comprise three integrated but distinct parts: the structure, the covering and the perimeter. Considering each in turn it can be seen that shape will have a significant but different influence on the possible structural solution and its cost.

The single most critical factor in terms of cost is span. The less the span, the greater variety of potential solutions, including for example, timber, steel, in-situ concrete and pre-cast concrete; and, particularly significant for cost, the shorter the span, the less cross-sectional area of beams or trusses (for a given material and design) will be required. As span increases, some solutions will be eliminated (timber, for example, without intermediate support or use of gulam and composite systems); more reinforcement will be needed in concrete and greater thickness of steel for structural steel solutions.

Thus shapes which facilitate smaller spans per unit of gross floor area provided will prove more economic roof support – and in the case of relatively small buildings such shapes are likely to be rectangular rather than square. This argument applies not only to roofs but equally to the intermediate floors in multi-storey buildings, whose costs (per m^2) will also increase with the distance to be spanned.

It may be quite straightforward, of course, to provide interior supports in the form of load-bearing walls or columns and to do so in ways which are compatible with the internal planning. This will keep the cost of the roof structure itself down; but load-bearing internal walls will necessarily be more expensive than ones which are not load-bearing, and the costs of columns when they are used solely as roof supports serving no other internal functions, can be considered simply as a further cost of roofing a wide space.

In larger buildings where internal support is likely to be necessary, whatever the plan form, the difference between square and rectangle may less important than the relationship between the spans and the optimum or standard available lengths for the material used. To some extent the courtyard form, or the 'square doughnut' produces the benefits of both square and rectangular buildings. It has been used in many recent buildings for that reason. For example, a police station recently built in Haywards Heath Sussex (Figure 9.5) is essentially a square with a small, central courtyard roofed at first-floor level. The structure is reinforced concrete frame, with main beams spanning 9 m from outside walls to courtyard. This gives a basically economic structure, but in this case the roof forms themselves are complex, making a quite expensive element. Part of the mid Kent Oncology centre, designed by Powell Moya Partnership (Figure 9.6) also adopts the same basic structural plan, but using steel roof structure and an open courtyard.

Where large spaces are covered using columns as supports for the roof, the columns themselves may also serve many internal functions, supporting lightweight partitioning, intermediate floors and staircases. Architecturally, columns themselves become or can become in the hands of good designers powerful elements of interior form – as they have been for well over 2000 years. Egyptians, Greeks, Romans and the Gothic cathedral builders were forced to use often veritable forests of columns because of the limited distance that could be spanned with the only materials available – timber, stone, brick and, to the Romans, a form of concrete – but in responding to these physical constraints they developed what became, through constant revivals and renewals, the dominant architectural languages of the Western world. And as architects and engineers such as Nervi have demonstrated, the internal column can still offer new modes of expression.

Internal load-bearing walls are also more than simply supports for roofs; if the plan requires division into many internal spaces with good sound insulation between them, the extra costs of full load-bearing walls may be relatively small.

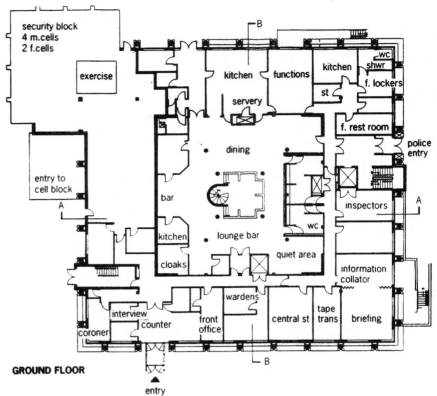

Figure 9.5   Plan of Police Station at Haywards Heath, Mid Sussex Divisional Police HQ, Sussex Police Authority Architects.

Then there are many ways of covering quite large spans without internal supports. The builders of classical Greece and Rome and the early architects of the Islamic countries knew how to cover large, open spaces, circular, rectangular or square with domes and arches which at the same time increased the spans they could cover and provided another source of interest and expression in design. The concrete dome of the Pantheon has a span of 43.2 m (more than that of St Peter's built 1400 years later). The church of Hagia Sophia, built in Constantinople under Justinian as a celebration of victory, covers a vast open, virtually square, space of 71 × 77 m with a central dome 32 m in diameter supported on a series of semi-domes and four massive piers.

Economy of construction was not a design criterion for Hagia Sophia, which has been claimed to be 'the largest, most lavish and most expensive building of all time' (Watkin, 1986). Grandeur, mystery and magnificence were the objectives, achieved through sheer size, simplicity of form and richness of decoration.

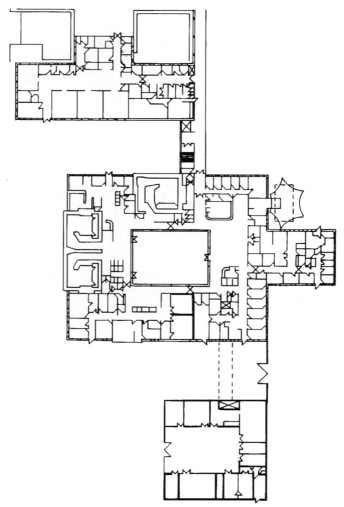

Figure 9.6   Oncology Centre, Kent, by Powell Moya.

But in the nineteenth century the need to cover large space at relatively low cost for factories and railway stations was met through the development of arched iron and later steel roof trusses.

However the elimination or the reduction of columns and interior walls by the use of arches and domes does not reduce cost proportionately; for the powerful lateral forces of wide spanned arches have to be contained. The dome of the pantheon referred to above was supported on 20 ft thick walls, in what David Watkin calls a 'structurally unimaginative way', while the load of the roof of the Hagia Sofia was taken, through a whole series of

Bond centre, Hong Kong – desperate determination to avoid orthogonal simplicity?

Bond centre, Hong Kong – desperate determination to avoid orthogonal simplicity?

arches, semi-domes, columns and piers (ibid. pp. 55 and 78). By the beginning of the twentieth century it was possible to span enormous spaces; the Centennial Hall at Breslau built in 1911–12 to the designs of Max Berg has a reinforced concrete dome spanning 67 m.

At a much more humble level, a delightful modern example of the use of the single-span arch system is the railway museum at Hollywood in County Down; it is built on the same highly economic principle as the army Nissan hut – a simple rectangle with barrel-vaulted roof, made from aluminium panels supported on steeled trussed arches and troughs; the lateral forces are contained by reinforced concrete buttresses. The overall cost of the building is low at something like £500 per m² of gross floor area, but the costs of the structure itself come to nearly 50% of this.

So to summarize the argument on roofs so far, the costs of the structures required to support roofs will tend to be cheaper, the shorter the spans. This may favour a rectangular form, but where internal supports have multiple purposes there is likely to be little difference between deep, even square, and narrow plans. The key factors are almost certainly simplicity and rationality and the co-ordination of internal planning with supporting structures, whether they be walls or columns.

In whatever way large spaces are spanned, the basic cost principle will remain that simple geometries will be more cost-effective.

Span, however, is not the only issue; the overall complexity of the geometry, including the pitch or pitches is also important. Pitched, domed and highly articulated roofs will tend to be more expensive than flat roofs as the structural requirements are more complicated. But for any roof type, the greater the complexity of the building plan, the higher is likely to be the cost of the roof structure.

The cost of the roof covering itself will be relatively insensitive to the building's plan shape, as it will be related primarily to area; but again although the total amount of material required will be roughly a function of area, labour costs will also be more a function of complexity of plan form. Complexity may also increase the quantity of material wasted as the amount of cutting required increases with the number of junctions and boundaries.

The costs of roofing perimeter components on the other hand is determined largely by plan shape. Such elements as fascias, eaves, gutters, kerbs, parapets, rainwater pipes and the like will all increase with perimeter length of the building. This can be an expensive part of the whole roof structure; it often involves a variety of different trades to do relatively small, distinct operations, something which is bound to lead to low productivity and hence high labour cost. If the perimeter of the roof is not only long but complex, it will require more joints, ends and corners, which will further increase the cost.

9.2.3 Plan shape and building life

Most buildings, historically, have in fact been either rectangular or based on systems of rectangle conjoined perhaps with limited curved elements. To see the truth of this simply scan through a well illustrated history of architecture, then think of the usual shape of the most common building type of all – the house – which throughout Europe and America, though less so in the Middle East and Africa, has been predominantly a basic rectangle. The reasons are not only to do with simplicity and costs of wall or roof structures; there are other factors.

Perhaps the most important is that the longer wall area has itself major advantages. It allows more windows and provides more internal wall space. So in cellular buildings, which most buildings are, more of the smaller spaces into which the building is divided can have access to natural light and ventilation. In urban areas, the influence of street layout and relationships to other buildings has been important; for example narrow frontage houses have had advantages for speculative building developers; wide frontages have advantages for shops.

These factors have not – in the past and in the West generally – been outweighed by the countervailing disadvantages such as lower wall costs and the greater heat loss from buildings with more wall area.

Such considerations raise again the issue of long-term, life-cycle costs. Where does the balance lie between the advantages and disadvantages of the thin, rectangular shape and the square or fatter rectangle? There seem to have been few attempts to assess this in total – and the problem is made more complex today by the development of more effective forms of insulation, natural ventilation, air-conditioning and heating which make any generalizations likely to become quickly out of date.

However, an attempt was made to make precisely this calculation in an interesting study carried out by the Laboratories Investigation Unit in 1970. Costs in use as well as capital costs were calculated for two simple three-storey building plans. The two examples used are shown in Figure 9.7 and the result of the analysis shown in Table 9.1.

Even though the cost figures are now very much out of date and relative costs may have changed (double glazing, for example, is relatively cheaper now) the results are revealing. Not only do they show that when everything is considered, a longer, thinner building may be cheaper than one of deep plan (and same area) but that even the capital costs may be lower. It can be seen from the table that the main reason for this result is that although the external envelope (total of walls, windows, external doors and roofs) are much higher for the thin building, this is outweighed, by the high costs of services in the square building. As we will see in Chapter 11, such a relationship does not necessarily hold if buildings are designed to make maximum use of passive energy and natural ventilation.

9.2.4 Site considerations

All these arguments discussed so far on the relative cost efficiency of circles, rectangles and squares are very general. The actual shape of a particular building will in fact be greatly influenced, perhaps almost determined, by two other major factors and their effect on the costs of a particular shape: first is the nature of the site and secondly the internal planning requirements of the building. We look at each in turn briefly.

At the most obvious level, the site may virtually impose a shape on the designer. This is particularly likely to be the case in heavily built-up areas of course. A recent example in London illustrates the problem and how it can be overcome to advantage; the designers of the nursing home for the frail elderly built at Hazlebourne Road (Figure 9.8) were faced with a tightly constrained and almost rectangular site; the building itself is basically a rectangle, given some variety and form by cranking it slightly in the centre. The positive advantage of the shape was that it allowed all the residential

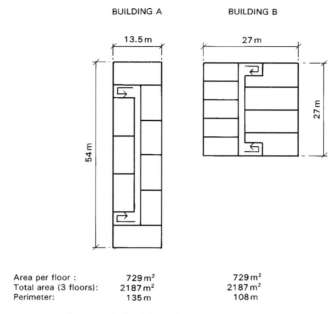

	BUILDING A	BUILDING B
Area per floor :	729 m²	729 m²
Total area (3 floors):	2187 m²	2187 m²
Perimeter:	135 m	108 m

Figure 9.7   Long, narrow versus short, wide building: the LIU experiment.

rooms to face south, with service rooms at the rear, north side.

If not actually determined by the site, the possible positions and forms of a building may be restricted by adjacent buildings or by landscape features such as slopes, trees to be retained, water courses, rock outcrops (which can be moved but at great expense).

Even when there is some choice as to shape and position, physical features will influence potential costs. If for example the site slopes, a longer thin building will probably have lower foundation costs because of the reduced amount of cut and fill required; even a complex shape using the land contours may be cheaper than a simple one which requires, say, the removal of rock. There may be culverts, old cellars, changes in ground conditions which may demand expensive foundations but which might to some extent be avoided by altering the building's plan. Whether such a strategy is cost-effective will need to be calculated in each case.

It is also likely that there will be planning constraints on the use of the site, not only in terms of the type of the building and its general order of specification (for example, natural stone elevations in a national park), but also the maximum number of storeys allowed. The plot ratio, determined by the planning authorities, will dictate the size of the building in relation to the overall size of the site and of course the relationship of ground-floor area of the building to the total site area will affect the cost of external

Table 9.1   Costs relating to Figure 9.7
(a) Comparative capital cost of alternative schemes.

Element	Building A Single-glazed £	Double-glazed £	Building B Single-glazed £	Double-glazed £
Foundations	659	659	595	595
Frame	16019	16019	15890	15890
External walls	2886	2886	4389	4389
Windows and external doors	13973	18174	4738	5973
Roof	792	792	634	634
Partitions	5407	5407	4932	4932
Blinds	1407	1407	454	454
Heating	14750	12550 }	24700 }	23140
Ventilation	1590	1590 }		
Lighting	5436	5436	6654	6654
Extra plant room	—	—	1575	1575

Notes: All elemental costs are inclusive of preliminaries and the services element costs are, in addition, inclusive of builder's work and main contractor's profit and attendance.

(b) Comparative annual costs through life arising from variations in Table 9.1(a)

10% compound interest untaxed	Building A Single-glazed		Double-glazed		Building B Single-glazed		Double-glazed	
	30 years	60 years	30 years	60 years	30 years	60 years	30 years	60 years
Amortized capital costs from Table 9.1(a) above	6674	6312	6886	6513	6848	6478	6814	6444
Window cleaning	235	235	235	235	79	79	79	79
Redecoration	275	283	275	283	164	169	164	169
Fuel oil	288	288	225	225	113	113	93	93
Electricity	174	174	174	174	900	900	900	900
Tube replacement	22	24	22	24	80	82	80	82
Mechanical services renewals	67	110	67	110	80	176	80	176
Electrical services renewals	—	31	—	31	—	38	—	38
Annual cost totals	7735	7457	7884	7595	8264	8035	8210	7981

For comparison, the total annual costs assuming 7% compound interest untaxed are given below:

| | 6150 | 5707 | 6248 | 5787 | 6634 | 6260 | 6588 | 6217 |

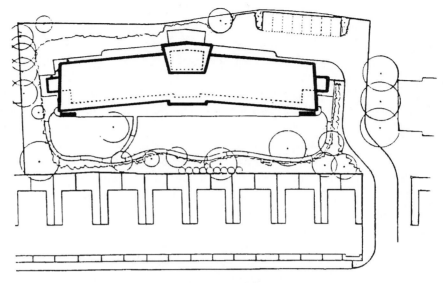

Figure 9.8   Use of a restricted site: Minnie Kydd House, Hazlebourne Road, London (architects: Greenhill Jenner Architects).

works, also a significant element of total building costs. The smaller the footprint of the building on the site, the higher will be the costs of land-scaping and paving.

The physical characteristics of the site may not be too restrictive, but nevertheless designers, clients and planners will want a building to respond to its particular location. Sometimes this will mean reflecting or incorpora-ting features of the site such as in perhaps the most famous example, Frank Lloyd Wright's house, Falling Water. Or the response might be quite the opposite – rejecting or contrasting with the surroundings like Ralph Erskine's London Ark referred to in Chapter 2, deliberately turning its back on the unpleasant and noisy surrounding environment.

Whole books could be written on this relationship of building to site; the point here is just to emphasize that the cost advantages of simple shapes may be overriden by the benefits of a particular design responding to a particular site, either in terms of cost or in less quantifiable ways.

9.3 Internal plan and outer form

Similarly, internal planning requirements might have implications for overall shape which outweigh advantages of simple rectangular or square forms. A major objective for any design is to provide internal spaces that allow a build-ing's function to be fulfilled efficiently. For some industrial and commercial buildings these may restrict the planning possibilities considerably, for example where a factory requires long production lines. But for most buildings, there will be very many ways of meeting clients' and users' needs. Yet for complex buildings an optimal solution, optimal in the sense that it meets a range of different requirements as closely as possible, may well be very difficult to produce within an obviously economic plan.

Solving these problems is one of the designer's essential skills and occupies much of the time and thought that goes into every project whether in the university design studios or the practice office. Here we can merely indicate some of the considerations which have a direct impact on costs both in the short term and the long.

One important planning objective will be to eliminate unnecessary space and this may conflict with or reinforce the cost efficiency of particular forms. Internal spaces can for many buildings be divided into those areas in which the functions of the building take place – the offices, the factory floor, the hospital wards, the classrooms – and the circulation areas, or other ancillary area such as plant rooms, store rooms. Both forms of space are of course equally necessary for a building to work; but there are obvious cost advantages in reducing the circulation areas, for example, to a minimum consistent with ease of movement. It means that the actual functions of the building can be provided in a smaller and therefore generally cheaper building, for any given quality.

In commercial buildings where parts are let to different clients, the distinction between the different types of space becomes one between total area and 'net lettable area'. Clients renting offices on the tenth floor of an office block **need** lifts and stairs of course, but their main concern is the office itself for which they will pay a rent based on its size (the actual rent level will depend on other factors as well – such as location, quality, services available, but for any given level of these factors, rent will vary with size). The building owner wants to maximize the rent received and therefore ensure that as much as possible is lettable. The efficiency of the planning in that sense becomes a dominant factor for large commercial developments where calculations of economic viability may be very finely balanced. It is the need to minimize lettable space, to keep capital costs low and to provide daylight to offices, together with high land costs discussed below, that has produced the vast number of rectangular slabs of offices that dominate the centres of cities.

There are, however, circumstances where the circulation areas are themselves performing dual purposes and are as usable or rentable as the rooms. Corridors may be exhibition galleries or viewing areas; commercial organizations might want large and impressive entrances; separate organizations may wish to use the landing on their own floor as foyer and reception. The fashion for atrium buildings is perhaps an extreme example; the obvious loss of lettable space is compensated for by the dramatic internal environment created, particularly attractive to corporate clients interested in prestige as well as in working space.

The opportunities for flexible use may be considerable. The 'mall' in the Swanlea Secondary School built in 1992 (Figure 9.10, p. 206) is a high proportion of the total area but it acts, in the architect's words, as 'the centre and focus of the school' and of course allows for the easy movement between classrooms of large numbers of pupils, as well as being, with its striking curved roof a delightful environment far removed from the concept of the traditional school corridor (*Architects' Journal*).

ABN Amro Bank, Amsterdam. Complex in every dimension – yet efficient (see Figure 9.19).

9.4 Size, height and costs

9.4.1 Size

The absolute size of a building and its height both have effects on the costs per m^2 of floor area. In the example used to discuss the effect of plan shape (Figure 9.5) we compared buildings of the same area but different shapes. If we compare buildings of the same shape but different areas and volume we can see other important geometrical relationships. See Figure 9.9.

Buildings are three-dimensional objects and storey height is an important influence on cost. One way which used to be popular for making quick estimates (the cubic method) used volume as the basic comparator. However relating the area of wall to the total area of the floor – to produce a **wall to floor ratio** – has proved a simpler and reasonable way of assessing a building's cost efficiency. The wall to floor ratio is calculated by dividing the external wall **area** of a building by the total gross floor area. The gross floor area is defined as the total internal floor areas of all floors up to the internal faces of the external walls.

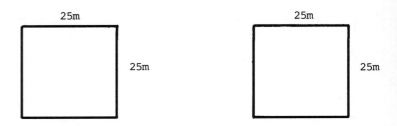

A: Area of each building =   625m²
           Total area   =   1250m²
           Length of Perimeters =   200m

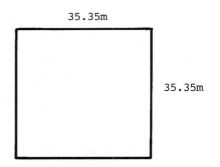

B.   Floor area   =   1250m²
           Length of perimeter.   =   141.2m

Wall to floor ratios

If storey height is 2.8m wall to floor ratios ¿

           A: (200 x 2.8)/1250   =.448
           B: (141.2 x 2.8)/1250   =.316

If storey height is 3.4m, wall to floor ratios

           A: (200 x 3.4)/1250   =.544
           B: (141.2 x 3.4)/1250   =.384

Figure 9.9   Comparison between one large building and two smaller buildings of the same total gross floor area, showing the differences in wall to floor ratios at two storey heights.

If we increase the floor area of a simple single-storey building without changing its plan form or its storey height, the wall to floor area decreases. A large square building will have less wall per m^2 of floor than a small square building. Obviously if the storey height is increased there will be a higher wall to floor ratio in both buildings. The effect of two alternative ways of enclosing a given area, either with one large or with two small square buildings of two possible storey heights, is shown in Figure 9.9. In terms of total wall area for given floor area the larger building will be less expensive, whatever the storey height.

An education authority might wish to have separate buildings on a site, perhaps linked by walkways, but this would be very much more expensive in terms of wall costs alone than putting the accommodation together, even if the larger single building was slightly higher. Although the area of roof would be the same in both cases, the total roofing costs would almost certainly be higher for the separate units; how great that difference would be must depend on the type of roof and the actual sizes involved. There would be extra costs involved in the single building if the spans required intermediate support, either with load-bearing walls or with columns.

However it is very important not to jump to conclusions or over-generalize and also not to ignore the important trade-off between on the one hand cost effectiveness of shape and size and on the other hand the myriad different factors that affect cost. For example two of the three educational projects shown in Figure 9.10 appear to have shapes which are highly uneconomic – many separate or almost separate units and exterior perimeters of considerable complexity. But the advantages of these designs for their purpose clearly outweighed in the designer's and client's view any extra costs the shape implied. The internal functions are reflected clearly by the plan; and although there are separate components each is in itself highly cost-efficient and to the extent that they share walls that efficiency is increased. The QS for the Swansea School project put the point neatly if bluntly:

> *Although the curved roofs of glass and aluminium look and are expensive, the rest of the building is based on very economic materials and detailing . . . The classrooms are just a lot of square boxes with no fancy bits. They are made of plain concrete blockwork with simple plaster finishes. The contractor was not tied to particular products and found it a doddle to build* (Building, 24 Sept. 1993).

In fact the costs of external walls for the University College, Stockton on Tees and the Swansea School were both just over 6% of total costs though the costs at Stockton per m^2 of gross floor area were higher, at £53 compared with £40 at Swanlea. Wall costs at Aylward were in the middle at £46.41, though a lower proportion of total costs (4.6%).

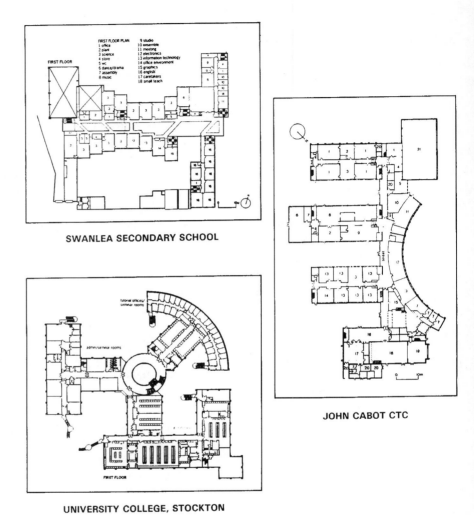

SWANLEA SECONDARY SCHOOL

JOHN CABOT CTC

UNIVERSITY COLLEGE, STOCKTON

Figure 9.10   Three educational projects.

These examples demonstrate quite clearly that though efficient planning is vital, it is simplistic to assume that large, simple rectangular or square buildings necessarily offer the most cost-effective solutions when all other costs elements are considered.

9.4.2 Height and cost

Whatever the ground plan of the building, its costs per square metre of floor area will increase with height, certainly after three or four storeys.

The reasons are straightforward but need to be understood clearly.

In fact there are, as was pointed out in Chapter 2, some factors which increase and some factors which decrease the cost per square metre as height increases and furthermore the significance of these factors changes at different heights. Figure 9.11 tabulates the probable effects of height on different elemental costs of a building.

One extremely important factor that is not apparent from Figure 9.11 is the impact of height on the ratio of net to gross floor areas. The greater the height of a building, the more people will be using it in total; there will need to be more and bigger lifts and stairways. But these will affect every floor and therefore increase the ratio of circulation to usable space. For example, five offices on the second floor of a two-storey building will be served by one small staircase; the same five offices on the second floor of a 15-storey building will have to share the space with perhaps three to four lift shafts and one or two wide stairways.

The effect is shown clearly in two examples from the analyses in Duffy, Cave and Worthington's book *Planning Office Space* (Duffy, Cave, Worthington, 1976) already referred to (Figure 9.12). The building shown in Figure 9.12a is two storeys high and has a net floor area which is 80% of the gross. In the taller building (10 storeys) the net figure is only 60% of the gross. The same effect is shown by the graph in Figure 9.13 derived from the conclusions of a study published in the *Architects' Journal* in 1974 (*AJ* p. 974).

Although there are therefore a range of different effects, the overall result is that high buildings cost more per unit of usable floor area than low ones. Earlier P.A. Stone estimated a rise in costs in use for factory buildings of 43% as the number of storeys increased from 1 to 10 and the study in the

Learning resource centre, Liverpool: economic form with elegance (Architects: Austin Smith Lord).

Comparison between two different design solutions for an air-conditioned office development each of identical specification and floor area.

BCIS[1] Elements	Two 6 storey blocks	One 12 storey block
1. Substructure	Double the quantity of column bases, ground bases and slabs needed.	Half quantity needed but probably more expensive piled foundations needed.
2. Superstructure 2a Frame	May be no need for frame as load bearing walls possible. Otherwise two sets of frames needed but smaller columns required. Less vertical lifting.	Larger columns needed to support heavier loads. Increased vertical lifting. More expensive solution.
2b Upper floors	One less upper floor needed - less expensive.	One more upper floor needed. Increased vertical lifting.
2c Roof	Twice roof area needed.	Half roof area needed but some additional expense due to increased vertical lifting.
2d Stairs	One less flight of stairs needed - less expensive solution.	One more flight needed. Stairs probably need to be wider because of means of escape. Increased vertical lifting costs.
2e External Walls	Less vertical lifting required.	Increased lifting required. May need stronger cladding to withstand greater wind pressures.
2f Windows and External Doors	Slight advantage due to less vertical lifting. Twice as many external doors needed.	Increased vertical lifting needed. Possible need for thicker glass to upper floors to withstand greater wind pressures.
2g Internal Walls and Partitions	Probable saving due to less vertical lifting.	More vertical lifting needed.
2h Internal Doors	As above.	As above.

Figure 9.11   Effect of height on different building elements.

BCIS[1] Elements	Two 6 storey blocks	One 12 storey block
3. Internal Finishes		
3a Wall Finishes	Little significant difference.	Little significant difference - possible higher costs as more vertical lifting.
3b Floor Finishes	As above.	As above.
3c Ceiling Finishes	As above.	As above.
4. Fittings & Furnishings	As above.	As above.
5. Services		
5a Sanitary appliances	As above.	As above.

5b Services equipment]
5c Disposal installations]
5d Water installations]
5e Heat source]
5f Space heating and air]
  treatment]
5g Ventilating system]
5h Electrical installations]
5i Gas installations]
5j Lift and conveyor]
  installations]
5k Protective installations]
5l Communication installations]
5m Special installations]
5n Builder's work in connection]
  with services]
5o Builder's profit and]
  attendance on services]
	More expensive as two separate systems required.	Will be less expensive but slightly offset by greater vertical lifting, need for larger sized distribution systems (pipes, cables and fittings). Faster and more expensive lifts will be needed.

6 External Works		
6a Site Works	Likely to be les expensive as smaller site area available for landscaping etc.	More expensive as greater area of site available for developing.
6b Drainage	More extensive and expensive system will be required.	Some economies in length of pipe runs and numbers of manholes.
6c External Services	As above.	As above.
7 Preliminaries	Two tower frames will be required if blocks to be built simultaneously.	Larger capacity tower crane will be needed.
	Site likely to be more congested for contractor to work in.	Site likely to be less congested - more space for contractor to work in.
	Possible saving in preliminaries as overall construction time likely to be less as blocks can be built simultaneously.	Overall construction time may be longer.

[1] Standard Form of Cost Analysis. The Building Cost Information Service of the Royal Institution of Chartered Surveyors, December 1989 (reprinted December 1987).

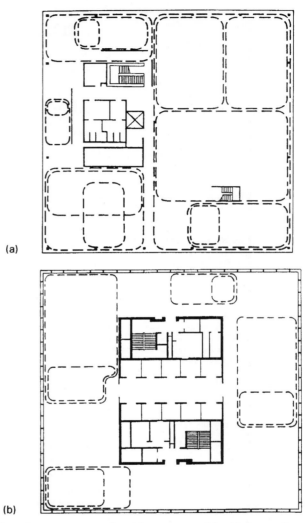

Figure 9.12   Effect of lift and stair space on lettable area in tall building: (a) floor of low building showing area available for offices; (b) floor in high building showing high proportion of space required for lifts and stairs.
Source: Duffy *et al.* (1976).

Architects' Journal, November 1972 showed a rise in the cost per m^2 of usable space in office buildings to be almost 100% for increases from 1 to 20 storeys (Figure 9.14).

The question then arises why tall buildings are built at all and though the answer is apparently simple – that land is in some areas in short supply and therefore very expensive – there are a number of complex issues involved.

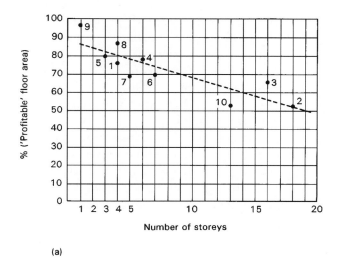

(a)

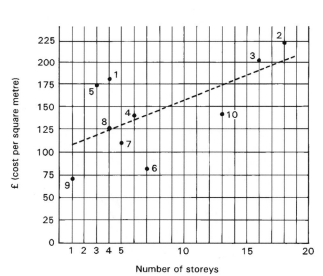

Figure 9.13   Relationship between height, usable space and cost. (a) Relationship between number of storeys (including basements) and proportion of 'useful' internal floor area not occupied by circulation and services. Numbers relate to different office buildings; (b) effective cost per m^2 of 'profitable' or 'useful' floor area.
Source: Architects' Journal, 27 Mar. 1974.

The value of land is itself determined by the amount of rent that can be earned on the buildings erected on it; it is therefore partly determined by the height of buildings which can be erected. So where there is an intense demand for accommodation, commercial or residential in a restricted area, such as near the centre of a prosperous city, the very possibility of building high, and therefore accommodating more people in a smaller space, itself pushes up land prices. This in turn means that tall building becomes cost-effective, as the high cost of the land is distributed over a greater lettable floor area of building.

A rather less obvious reason for high building, particularly in rapidly developing countries and even where land is abundant, is the saving in the costs of infrastructure compared to a widespread low-rise development. When the area already serviced by roads, gas, water and electricity is limited, building will tend to be confined at least initially to those areas – a quite significant factor in some rapidly developing countries.

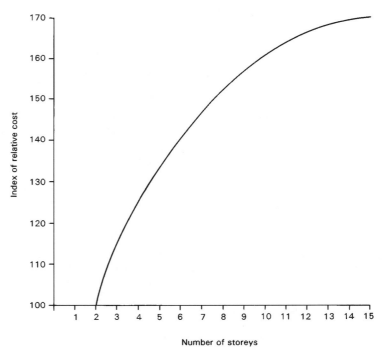

Figure 9.14   Increase of cost with height: office buildings.
Source: base on *Architects' Journal* Information Library, Nov. 1972.

9.5 Taking everything into account . . .

The evidence and arguments above have suggested that simple, square – or rectangular – shaped buildings will tend to be less expensive in terms of some important cost elements, that large buildings tend to be less expensive per square metre of floorspace than small ones and that high buildings cost more than low ones. It has also shown that the form of a building might be determined by many other factors than the relative costs of these elements. In this section a few very simple examples are examined to illustrate the interrelationship of some of these cost and morphological characteristics of buildings.

The first example takes the form of a study made originally for the *Architects' Journal* and republished in *Planning Office space* (Duffy *et al.*, op cit. pp. 105–7). It examines the relative costs of three simple possible office shapes for a commercial office block of a total of 5000 m^2 (see Figure 9.15).

The study was based on one real building and two possible alternatives with different shapes but as far as feasible, the same specifications. Two sets of comparison were made, one assuming air conditioning only in the square building where it was essential, the other assuming similar air conditioning in all the buildings. On the first set of comparisons the square, 5-storey alternative is the most expensive, the 9-storey rectangle, the second most expensive and the 5-storey L-shaped building the cheapest. As expected, the wall costs for the square are low but this is entirely outweighed by the cost of services; the higher rectangular building is more expensive than the lower L-shape mainly because of frame and upper floor costs.

However if it is assumed that all three buildings are fully air-conditioned, the square building becomes the least expensive by a considerable margin.

Floor area : 5000 m²

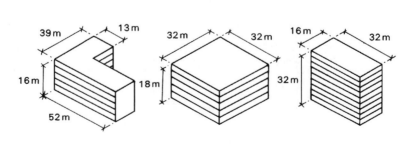

Perimeter floor area 0.59   Perimeter floor area 0.46   Perimeter floor area 0.61

Figure 9.15   Three simple office blocks.
Source: Duffy *et al.*, (1976).

As another brief case study, we compare the relative costs and shapes of some recently completed buildings reported by the Building Cost Information Service (Figure 9.16) which shows the plans of four buildings. The first is included for contrast and is a simple and cheap warehouse. The other three are all hospital units, two serving the same function (genito-urinary units) and the third a maternity and gynaecological unit.

As can be seen from the selected information given in Table 9.2, all three medical units had very similar overall costs, despite the variety of their form; this is hardly surprising as they will have been built under similar

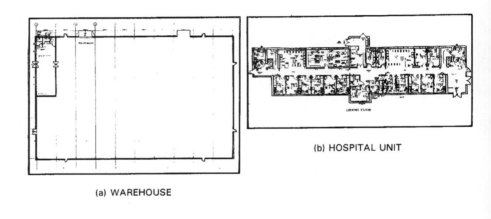

(b) HOSPITAL UNIT

(a) WAREHOUSE

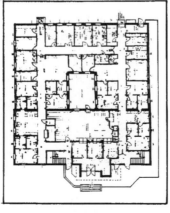

(c) HOSPITAL UNIT

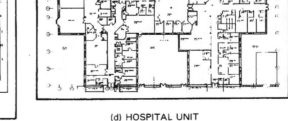

(d) HOSPITAL UNIT

Figure 9.16   Four plans from BCIS analyses.

budgetary controls. The point is that designers have achieved the results in different plan forms. One obvious reason why this was possible is of course that the cost of those elements directly related to perimeter is a very small proportion of total costs. Walls, for example, are 5% in the case of B and C and less than 3% for building D. The cost of services, in each case, is nearly one half of the total. By contrast the cost of the warehouse walls (A) was

Table 9.2   Cost comparison for the four plans (Figure 9.16)

Building	Gross floor area	Cost per m²	Wall to floor ratio	Cost to walls £/m²	Cost to roof £/m²	Cost of services £/m²
A	2325	205.6	0.61	23.46	22.37	7.13
B	646	862.4	0.70	41.62	48.00	279.27
C	935	836.9	0.65	36.82	75.99	297.14
D	4467	893.9	0.42	22.38	40.66	403.80

Note: These figures, for buildings constructed in 1990 to 1992 are not adjusted for regional cost variation or specific construction date. The figures for total costs per m² adjusted to a base date and a mean location are:

A: £165.58   B: £786.6   C: £777.5   D: £776.31

The figure for the wall to floor ratio of building B is estimated, as data were not available for the area of doors and windows.

Cricket Pavilion, Birkenhead: simple but striking (Architect: Carl Thompson).

about 20% of the total and services, only 3.5%. Furthermore, the functions of the warehouse are almost certainly more efficiently performed in the rectangular shed; it is clear that any complex shape would be unjustifiable on any grounds. In the case of the hospitals, on the other hand, the need for daylight to the wards, the acceptability (and in some cases the necessity) of artificial environments in treatment rooms etc. has allowed rational planning with basically economic shapes; the square building has a central courtyard allowing natural light and ventilation at the core.

The effects of absolute size are also evident: the lowest wall to floor ratio of the hospitals is the one with the longest and most complex perimeter; but it is a very much larger building than either of the other two, nearly 4500 m^2 compared with 650 m^2 and 930 m^2; in fact its 'efficiency' in terms of wall costs is greater than that of the cheap warehouse (the walls of which are of course, higher).

All these buildings however have a simple and rational structural grid – and it is that which makes them cost-effective and buildable structures.

9.6 Conclusion

What remains to be explained is why architects may nevertheless design buildings with complex and apparently expensive forms; are there for example compensating advantages or are these sort of designs only feasible where clients' budgets are generous?

All the examples used in this chapter tend to demonstrate that the pressures of economics have forced many of our new buildings to be, if not simple boxes, highly rectilinear in their basic form. We make three points in conclusion.

First it does not follow from the inevitable pressures for simple forms that buildings have to be dull and unimaginative; however, to create elegant solutions within the constraints of economic form requires a high quality of design – and a high quality of detail.

Secondly, there will be ways in which the basic simplicity of structure may be allowed to yield complex forms; this has become perhaps easier today with the availability of new roofing and cladding materials.

Thirdly some clients will wish for and be able to pay for more complex and even inefficient forms of building; perhaps by trading off that shape against lower levels of specification, perhaps by simply being willing to spend for reasons of prestige or display.

Three final examples may make these points visually (Figures 9.17 – 9.19).

The first is a very recently completed building by the practice of Austin Smith Lord for the Liverpool John Moores University (for a full report see

Architects' Journal, 13 Apr. 1994) which demonstrates beautifully the possibility of applying principles of rational planning to produce a building of interest and excitement which serves its function well and was built within a tight budget limit.

The second is a small cricket pavilion in Birkenhead Park by Carl Thompson, where what is essentially a simple brick box is lifted to an original if small-scale piece of architecture by the use of a white-tented membrane roof (*Architects' Journal*, 26 Jan. 1994).

Finally as a prelude to the discussion in Chapter 11, consider the plan of the NMB Bank Headquarters in Amsterdam. This was built for a commercial client on a constrained urban site and has been claimed as the most energy-efficient building yet built. It is not known whether anyone has attempted to calculate the wall to floor ratio or what it would tell us if they did!

This chapter has been concerned with morphology and cost; it has not been the aim to claim that there are always high-quality, cheap solutions; there clearly are budget levels below which the use of the simple shapes and cheapest materials and forms of procurement, which do not allow sufficient design skills to be applied, would become necessary; quality and economy can then and frequently do become incompatible. The point is rather than by understanding and identifying those aspects of form which can be achieved with economy, architects give themselves a better chance of achieving quality within limited budgets.

FOR FURTHER STUDY

1 Recommended reading

Many architectural students will already have studied the mathematics of building morphology and the very wide literature on systems of harmony and proportion. There is often though very little specific reference to cost; books which do discuss shape–cost relationships tend to take a very simplistic view of the architectural dimension. However most of the cost planning and building economics books referred to earlier have sections on shape and cost (see for example Ferry and Brandon, ch. 16 and Seeley, *Building Economics*, ch. 2). There is a brief article in *Architects' Journal*, 9 Sept. 1994 ('Plan shape and building costs').

2 Exercise

Calculate the 'wall to floor ratios' for each of the building configurations in Figure 9.2 assuming a two-storey building, 5 metres high; then recalculate the ratios using the same plan shapes, but twice the area. Examine the results and explain why wall to floor ratios cannot in isolation be used as a measure of plan efficiency.

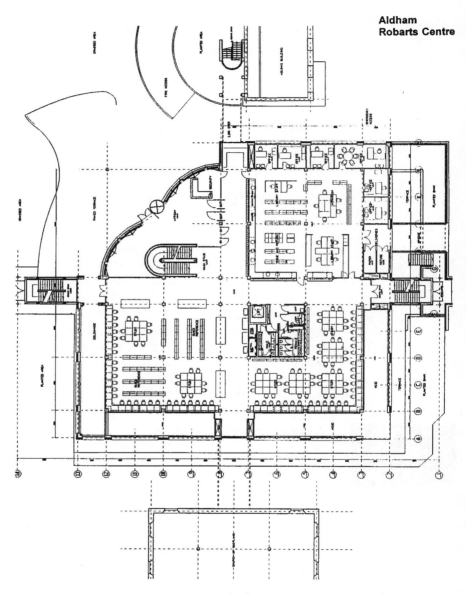

Aldham Robarts Centre

Figure 9.17   JMU: Learning Resource Centre, Liverpool John Moores University (architects: Austin Smith Lord).

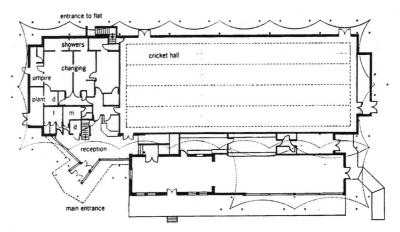

Figure 9.18   Plan of Cricket Pavilion: Birkenhead Park (architect: Carl Thompson).

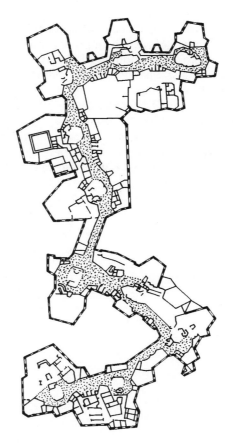

Figure 9.19   ABN Bank Headquarters, Amsterdam. See photograph p. 203.

3 Discussion questions

One of the *AJ*/Bovis awards for Architectural Design in 1994 was to Daniel Libeskind's Jewish Museum in Berlin. It was described as dealing 'with extraordinary imagination, with the most thankless of subject matters for any building – the Final Solution . . . the architecture is without a single orthogonal or cartesian reference point; its disturbing and fractured plan form reminiscent perhaps of the SS lightning symbol' (*Architects' Journal*, 25 May 1994). A correspondent later expressed outrage that such an 'irrational' building should be held up as fine architecture. Discuss the issues.

4 Projects

a Study the plans of any recently published buildings, together with the cost commentaries and discuss each of the following questions. How far has the design attempted to be cost efficient? Where there are obviously inefficient shapes, what seem to have been the design intentions behind them? Have the apparent inefficiencies been offset in some other way (e.g. by modular planning, lower cost construction forms, improved accessibility and better internal planning)?

b (For architecture students) Consider your own recent or current scheme. Would it be criticized on the grounds of 'inefficiency' by the quantity surveyor? How would you respond to the criticism?

(For construction and surveying students) Consider the plans of recent or current schemes developed by architectural student colleagues. Discuss their apparent cost efficiencies with the designers.

10 | Structure and envelope

10.1 Introduction

The selection of the structural system and outer skin of a building are so frequently interdependent in cost as well as design terms, that we deal with them here together in one chapter. In most smaller buildings today, and in the great stone structures of the past, there is in any case no clear distinction between the two; load-bearing walls are both structure and envelope.

Though a distinction between 'low' and 'high' is inevitably vague, the choices of structural system can be divided usefully into those for low buildings, that is systems which are commonly used up to about three-storeys or four-storeys and those which are feasible for tall buildings. There is clearly considerable overlap; steel and concrete frames can be used at any height from one-storey upwards; and as long ago as 1891, the Chicago architects Burnham and Root built their 16-storey Monadnock Building without a frame, 'pushing the load-bearing wall to its uttermost limits' (Fitch 1973, p. 200). Now, with new techniques even brick can be used as load-bearing material up to a considerable height. Though timber frame is used mainly for low structures, what has been claimed as the first five-storey modern timber-framed building in Britain was built in 1993 at the Quayside is Swansea (Midlands Builder, 1994). For our present purposes here, however, the distinction between low and high will be convenient.

10.2 Houses and other small buildings

In one sense the range of choice for an architect designing relatively conventional small buildings has already been limited by the pressures of economics, building regulations and public taste. So houses in the UK have come, at the beginning of the 1990s, to be built almost entirely of brick and blockwork load-bearing walls or frames with brick exterior panels and interior walls of blockwork. For low office buildings and special-purpose buildings (surgeries, day centres, nurseries, clubs) the use of frame and a cladding system opens up a much wider range, but again in practice, partly because of planning restrictions and public taste, the exterior façades of smaller buildings are very frequently in brick. The senior official of a large local authority responsible for the schools building programme recently said that he insists the materials 'must be traditional' (that is, brick and timber) an attitude not uncommon among clients, public and private.

The case which is the most common Western European building type, the brick house, is worth looking at in some detail first. Time and again during this century particularly, cost-conscious politicians, builders and architects have thought it odd that we are still building houses with a technique used thousands of years ago, laboriously piling one small clay object on top of another. On the face of it, the process seems primitive, slow and uneconomic; it seems obviously possible to devise more efficient ways of building small buildings.

There are certainly plenty of alternatives; and since the 1920s, so many different systems have been tried even in the UK alone that it would be difficult to list them comprehensively, still less analyse them; the same process of experiment and innovation has gone on in the USA, in Europe and on an international scale. Experiments have tended to incorporate several different approaches to increasing efficiency: the use of cheaper materials and less labour – that is using fewer resources for each house; secondly attempting to take advantages of economies of scale in reproducing identical or similar units; thirdly more efficient planning of individual houses.

In the period after the First World War in the UK when subsidized housing was first built on a big scale, the governments of the day encouraged local authorities to use experimental approaches. A 'Standardization and New Methods of Construction Committee' was appointed and some authorities took up its recommendations with enthusiasm. Liverpool, for example, tried the Dorman Long steel-frame system, among others such as Duo slab, Steelcrete, and Unit. A local firm, Messrs Boot and Sons, developed a concrete pier and panel system and Costain used a timber-frame; but ultimately the City decided that none of these could compete with traditional methods (Pratt, 1975).

After the Second World War there were more sustained attempts at non-traditional building. By 1955, thousands of houses had been built using steel frame, timber frames and concrete in many forms, large slabs, pier and panel and in situ systems such as Laing's Easiform and Wimpey's No Fines which saved on labour and formwork basically because it was mixed relatively dry and therefore light.

In a remarkable table calculated from the 1953 National Building Studies report on new methods of house construction, Marian Bowley showed how and why 'except for two of the systems using in–situ concrete, the total costs for the non traditional systems exceed those of the traditional, (Bowley, 1966). The main reason was the much higher cost of the materials used in the walls (see Table 10.1).

In 1970 P.A. Stone came to the conclusion that

> It seems clear that it is by no means easy to develop systems of factory built construction which are more economic of resources than traditional forms of construction. For example, in spite of hundreds of systems which have been developed in the last fifty years, especially for housing, none appears, at best other than marginally cheaper than traditional forms (Stone, 1970, p. 226).

But he makes a different point from Bowley's:

> The difficulty in achieving economy by the use of factory prefabrication and other non-traditional forms of building lies in the small proportion of the costs of a dwelling in which economies can be achieved in this way (ibid, p. 228).

Table 10.1   Comparisons made in the 1940s of relative costs of different forms of housebuilding. (The comparisons are made with a traditional house for which the labour costs were £442 and the materials cost in the walls alone were £150, the total cost of the traditional version (unbelievable though it seems today) was £1015). *Source*: Bowley (1960).

Type of construction	Variation in labour cost	Variation in cost of materials in walls	Variation in total cost
	£	£	%
Precast concrete			
site 1	+26	+136	+16.0
site 2	−52	+254	+19.9
site 3	−90	+128	+3.7
In situ concrete			
site 1	nil	−49	−4.8
site 2	−49	−28	−7.6
site 3	+118	−11	+10.5
Steel frames			
site 1	−19	+147	+12.6
site 2	−39	+102	+4.2
wooden frame			
site 1	−70	+138	+6.7

The actual structure and envelope in fact only represented just over a quarter of the total costs of a house at that time, the rest being land, curtilage works, and internal fittings and finishes. As Stone pointed out in another book,

attempts to rationalise the design of buildings have taken as their aim the reduction of labour requirements, in particular the reduction of skilled site labour. The accepted solution has been to increase the size of building units, to eliminate finishing trades and to prefabricate off site. The use of large units requires dimensional accuracy and materials which remain free from distortion. Such materials tend to be expensive . . . an increase in the cost of materials by a sixth roughly needs a reduction of a third in the costs of labour (Stone, 1966, p. 75).

The same point was illustrated when speculative developers turned to timber frame as a low-cost solution in the late 1970s and 1980s. The savings they achieved came not from any economies in the costs of construction itself but from the speed with which the houses were erected. At a time of high demand this enabled the builders to reduce the time between land purchase and house sales considerably, saving mainly on finance. Indeed one builder claimed the rapid turnover enabled him to sell most houses before they were built. Timber frame became unpopular with the public and, more importantly, with the building societies after some bad publicity which confused particular cases of poor quality with the basic characteristics of the system itself.

The fact that non-traditional systems did not prove economic does not mean of course that no changes took place; the traditional house of today is in fact a very different building than its predecessors. Economies of scale have been achieved in many facets of the construction operation; we have already discussed their impact on the basic materials such as bricks and glass (Chapter 4) and the use of computers in design, programming, stock control and the ordering of materials. It is partly because the improvements in productivity have taken place in areas other than the actual structure of the building that the traditional methods − or at least a traditional appearance − has survived, almost. One has only to consider the houses being built in the UK today to see just how many new components they incorporate: plastic rainwater and waste pipes, PVCu window frames, concrete roof tiles, to name a few; and in the parts unseen there are probably more relatively recent components: prefabricated roof trusses, concrete floor slabs, PVC electric cable, glass fibre and other insulation materials.

The process of change has not taken the same course in other countries, often because brick is not so cheap and the resistance to concrete not so strong; or as in Sweden timber has remained the main housebuilding material and the construction system become highly sophisticated.

We have already referred to Buckminster Fuller's design for the Dymaxion and Wychita houses in the USA; these were intended for mass production and mass delivery on exactly the same model as the motor car or the aeroplane. The cost of the Wychita (1945/6) was expected to be reduced from $6500 to $3500 as full volume production of 500000 a year was reached, but the project was never fully realized as finance to develop the production lines was not available. However William Levitt, a man with little architectural knowledge but considerable business acumen, did approach a mass-production process with his houses at Levittown in Long Island and Pennsylvania. Yet it was not by shifting work to the factory.

> *Instead of having a moving assembly line he had a moving work crew . . . the Levitts cuts the cost in every way they could; by slipping lumber pre-cut from their own mill in California, they mounted a smooth daily flow of materials to the building site, where swarms of non-union workers moved from one site to the next, performing their own specialized tasks.*

Levitt himself, who was quite explicit about his imitation of Ford, said 'the only difference [from a car production system] is that at Ford the products move to the men; in my system the men move along the production line' (*Newsday*, 1994).

Although the results horrified the critic Lewis Mumford with what he saw as their appalling uniformity – little boxes set in regimented though curved rows on a flat plain – the design was cleverly flexible and today, set deep in mature trees and extended in every direction, the Levittown houses appear a remarkable success.

In the UK, however, the brick house remains apparently unchallengeable; apart from the features described above, it does have characteristics which are perhaps making it even more successful, particularly that, in an energy-conscious world, the heat insulation and retention characteristics of a heavy two-skin system either with concrete block inside, an insulated cavity and brick outside, is difficult to beat.

The main housing application in Britain of industrialized and prefabricated systems was of course for the high-rise developments of the late 1950s and '60s; they are not strictly relevant to this section and have in any case become a subject for extensive study. A brief reference is made to them in various other parts of the book but for fuller accounts the reader is referred to the recommended reading at the end of the chapter, particularly the recent history by Glendinning and Muthesius (1994).

The reasons for the continued predominance of brick building in housing apply also to a degree to other low non-industrial buildings; one can demonstrate the simple economics of this today by comparing the notional alternative costs of a very simple two-storey rectangular building. Table 10.2 shows the basic all-in costs for a small building on some very simplifying assumptions.

The exception – and it is a very significant one, having altered the appearance of much of the industrial urban landscape in some areas, particularly in the ubiquitous industrial and commercial parks – is the steel or reinforced concrete-framed shed, using cladding most often of profiled steel or aluminium. One significant difference between these types of buildings and the small office or public building is that the costs of the envelope and structure are likely to be potentially a higher proportion of the total, making it particularly cost-effective to use cheap-walling methods. They may have large expanses of unbroken wall, allowing fast construction with large panels.

10.3 High buildings

10.3.1 The frame

Although there are again many variations in the form and detail, the essential choice for tall buildings today is between reinforced concrete and some form of steel frame. It is a little surprising in fact that there is still a choice as one might have expected that, different in material as they are, after many years of use one or the other would have emerged with a clear cost advantage (rather as the brick and block combination seems to have done for the ordinary house in the UK). In fact this appeared to be happening in the 1950s. As often, Marion Bowley's work provides the examples and some explanations:

> . . . in the case of comparisons between reinforced concrete and steel frames encased in concrete to comply with fire prevention regulations, there has been sufficient experience gathered to remove all real dispute about the existence of a cost differential in favour of the former. There is no serious disagreement among builders or engineers about the conclusion that the former is normally cheaper than the latter for multi-storey buildings.
>
> The reasons for the relative cheapness of a reinforced concrete frame are obvious. It requires only about one third of the amount of steel that a steel frame requires and this saving cannot be offset by the greater amount of concrete required. The very important item of shuttering the labour required for manipulating it are not substantially different in cost for the two types of frames (Bowley, 1966, p. 41).

This is another example, perhaps, of the dangers of dogmatic assertion and prediction in construction economics. The fact is that cost differences

Table 10.2   Consider a rectangular building 30 m × 15 m on plan 2 storeys in height (a total of 6 m).

Assume an external envelope is 75% solid walls and 25% windows and doors. Total external walls are (90 × 6) × 75% = 405 m².

Possible solutions:

Description	Cost per m² £	Area m²	Total cost £
1. Sofwood stud wall, vapour barrier and plasterboard inner lining decorated with PVC weatherboard outer skin*	69.00	405	27 945
2. As above but tile hanging on battens*	74.00	405	29 970
3. PVF2 coated galvanized steel profiled cladding on steel rails insulated, full height insulating block inner skin, plaster and emulsion*	94.00	405	38 070
4. Precast concrete panels including insulation, lining and fixings with:			
standard panels*	127.00	405	51 435
brick clad panels*	209.00	405	84 645
natural stone*	495.00	405	200 475
5. Composite cavity wall with facing brick outer skin, block inner skin, 50mm cavity insulation, plaster and emulsion	84.00	405	34 020

*Need for frame to provide structural support.
Costs based on Spon's Price Book, 1993.

today are remarkably small, not identifiable with accuracy, and highly dependent on concomitant costs implied by a particular design or particular circumstances; such as a requirement for exceptional floor to ceiling heights, the choice of cladding, the design of service runs, the configuration of the building as a whole.

In 1993 two important reports were published on the relative costs of steel and concrete framed buildings, one by C.H. Goodchild for the Reinforced Concrete Association (RCA) and one by R.M. Lawson for the Steel Construction Institute (SCI). Both are very careful and detailed analyses of specific buildings and specific building types and both stress their

Component building: timber-framed houses under construction, early 1980s.

independence and impartiality; the first (for the concrete producers) came to the conclusion that the concrete frame was generally the cheaper and the second (for the steel producers) that the advantage lay with steel! A careful reading of the original reports is necessary for a full understanding of the issues but we can make some general points here (Goodchild, 1993; Lawson, R.M., 1993).

The Concrete Council's report looked at two building types, one for a seven-storey and one for a three-storey commercial building. For each height two basic designs in two supposed locations were compared, a square air-conditioned building with curtain walling on the M4 corridor and a rectangular naturally ventilated building with brickwork cladding on the M62, that is eight different variants in all.

The report's conclusions were:

- In terms of the overall construction cost, the seven-storey steel-framed building was found to be 5.5% more expensive than the concrete equivalent on the M62 and 2.6% more expensive on the M4 site.
- The three-storey steel-framed building was found to cost 5.2% more for the rectangular M62 building and 2.6% more for the square M62 building.
- The steel buildings had between 0.3 and 1.48% less net lettable area

*35 years on –
houses at Levittown,
Long Island, USA;
photographed
1982.*

The differences in cost are greater if net floor area is considered rather than gross.

■ With regard to overall speed of construction, the study found little to choose between the two materials.

The conclusions from the second study are less unequivocal. A different method for comparison was adopted. Two buildings were 'fully designed', one a standard commercial specification and one for a prestige development. Costs were calculated for 13 different structural systems divided into two categories, short-span and long-span and including different steel, concrete and composite options. The general conclusion was that the cheapest options in terms of structure alone were composite slab and beam, reinforced concrete flat slab and for the prestige building the parallel beam system. However, when 'variable costs due to cladding and foundations are included, the slim floor, (steel) options are equivalent to the reinforced concrete in terms of total building cost.'

It is also claimed that all the steel options gain a further 0.5–1.5% as a result of time-related savings due to speed of construction, a conclusion which flatly contradicts that of the other study.

The report's final conclusion is that the differences between the three cheapest systems is 'within the margin of error of the study'. When one considers that the calculated total building costs per square metre of gross floor area ranged only from £554 to £564 per m², this seems to be putting it generously. For it has to be stressed that neither of the studies were the buildings actually built and the range of other factors to be considered in a real situation could easily reverse such small differentials.

However it also needs to be remembered that both studies were undertaken using the best expertise available and that considerable care was taken to incorporate as many conditions as feasible. So, for instance, construction techniques, probable construction programmes and hence construction times were all modelled carefully.

One general conclusion one might draw from the comparisons is that in practical cost terms it does not matter very much which system is used, provided it is rationally designed to maximize the benefit of that system and is one which meets specific requirement of the brief most effectively. For example, where column free space is particularly important, long-span systems have a clear advantage, and as we have mentioned earlier the choice of structural system may well be made on the basis of the cladding, less of which is needed for the concrete frame. An interesting example of the exploitation of concrete's advantage in requiring lower floor to ceiling heights is its use in Washington USA. There is a planning requirement that no building in the central area should be higher than the Capitol. Therefore although steel frame is the normal method of construction in the USA, concrete frames allowing two-way spans are used in Washington and make it possible to create an additional storey within the overall height limitation.

However there are other specific advantages and disadvantages in each form of construction and despite the narrowness of the cost differentials brought out by the two reports discussed above, it is worth analysing their data in a little more detail as it helps to identify where these might be.

The advantage of concrete claimed in the Concrete Council study arises mainly from the cost of the superstructure itself, which is between 32% and 24% less than for the steel-framed versions. This, however, is balanced to some extent by much higher costs for the foundations in the concrete systems (between 27% and 47% more than for steel) due of course to the considerably greater weight of the concrete frame. But the concrete-framed designs show further savings in cladding and internal partition costs. In the case of cladding the savings arise from the fact that storey heights have to be increased for steel versions 'to accommodate increased allowances for constructional zones'. The claimed savings in internal partitioning are considerable – up to 63% – and stem from the dual use of concrete core walls as both structural elements and internal walls.

One result which directly contradicts that of the other study is that the savings in terms of net lettable area are greater for concrete than steel – partly as a result of space lost for steel bracing. The steel study, however, claims that longer spans allow more relative internal space and increase steel's advantage in maximizing lettable space.

The Steel Construction Institute's report also analyses elemental cost implications of each of the 13 systems studied. Perhaps the most surprising contrast is very much smaller differentiation identified between the actual structure costs of the systems than in CSA study. Both agree on the cheaper substructure required for steel. The SCI study gives figures for steel options £17 per m^2 of floor area as against a maximum of £24 for concrete, a similar differential to that in the CSA. But although it shows a maximum range from £54 per m^2 (cheapest concrete system) to £64 (most expensive steel system) for the superstructure costs of one building type, some of the steel-based systems (composite beam) are shown to yield lower costs for superstructure alone than the best concrete version. For the second building type (their Building B) the composite-beam system works out consistently cheaper than reinforced concrete.

There are even differences between the two reports on the implied costs of cladding. Whereas the BCA is unequivocal about concrete's advantages because of lower-storey heights BSI claims that with appropriate design cladding costs can in fact be cheaper with the steel options.

Both reports agree that the choice of structural system has very little if any effect on the costs of services, floor, wall and ceiling finishes or the costs of doors and windows. But they disagree on the relative building times of the two systems and the consequential savings in finance costs and earlier earning potential.

10.3.2 The external envelope

The external envelope of a building consists of many different parts – the walls, roofs, the doors, and windows; where there are non-load bearing walls, the essential function of all these is to act as barriers and filters: keeping heat in, allowing light through but filtering out glare and excessive solar gain; keeping out rain and wind, but allowing ventilation and the escape of excessive moisture. The choice of particular forms of envelope is therefore largely dominated by their efficiency in performing these filter and barrier functions as well as their appearance. But again cost inevitably plays an important part. We have already looked at the implications of the size and shape of a building for the general level of roof and wall costs in Chapter 9, but not the relative costs of different materials.

The range today is so wide that it is not in fact easy – or rather it could be quite misleading given the speed with which, say, cladding systems are developing – to make any attempt at definitive cost comparison. But some general indication of the sort of current differentials in prices might be helpful.

Table 10.3, derived from information published in *Building*, gives an indication of the range of costs to be expected for different roofing materials. The original data also included estimates of the risks of damage to each roof type and the likely costs of repairs, thus giving enough information to make a rough calculation of full life-cycle cost comparisons (*Building*, Roofing Supplement, 1992a).

Table 10.3   Comparative costs of various roofing materials. *Source*: Adapted from *Building, Roofing Supplement 28 Feb. 1992.*

Description	Initial costs £/m²	Durability/ life cycle years
Built-up roofing		
Bituminous felt, BS747 three layer, type 2B bonded	11–13	15–20
High performance, glass fibre polyester bituminous 1.8 kg/m², two layer, bonded	9–12	15–20
Elastometric, polyester based bituminous, one layer 1.8 kg/m², one layer 4 kg/m², bonded	11–13	20–5
Elastometric, polyester/glass fibre based bituminous, base layer, one layer 1.8 kg/m², bonded	17–19	30+
Laminated bitumen/fibre semi-rigid steels, single layer 2.45 kg/m², jointing strips, bonded	13–15	25–30
Metal roofing – fully supported		
Lead – Code 5	54–74	90–120
Copper – 0.61 m	45–74	30–80
Zinc – 0.81 m	38–57	20–60
Aluminium – 0.9 mm	29–67	20–60
Profiled metal sheeting		
Steel profiled, PVC colour coated, 0.7 mm	16-18	30 average
Aluminium profiled, pre-coated, 0.7 mm	18–21	25–40
GRP profiled, 1.6 mm	16–18	15–20
Tiles, slates and shingles		
Clay tiles, plain, double lap, machine made	31–42	50+
Clay tiles, single lap (interlocking – 2 edges)	17–29	50+
Clay tiles, single lap (interlocking – 4 edges)	28–42	60+
Concrete tiles, plain, double lap	28–40	50+
Concrete tiles, single lap, profiled interlocking	12–16	50+

It can be seen that the range of costs is very wide, but the data are a little deceptive in that not all forms of roofing would be suitable for particular applications. The actual range of choice for a particular building might be much narrower but still with a considerable differential. Concrete tiles came to replace clay for standard low-rise roofs basically because of price and the figures in Table 10.3 confirm its continuing advantage.

It also brings out clearly the appeal of the profiled sheets in various materials – steel, aluminium and GRP. What it does not show is the relative costs of the various forms of glass and acrylic roofing systems which have become more practical and widely used as the technology has improved and bulk production brings costs down.

The Swanley School at Whitechapel, designed by the Percy Thomas Partnership and already referred to in the previous chapter, uses a system called Okasolar. At Chur railway station in Switzerland, Ove Arup used a system of steel trusses with laminated-glass panels to produce a high curved roof.

The economics of wall-cladding systems are particularly difficult to analyse at present because of their range and rapid development; doubts on the longevity and impermeability of some types such as thin stone facings have been expressed, research continues on the development of improved versions, on sealants and modes of fixing; so actual and relative costs are bound to change. Nevertheless, for high buildings, particularly, the variety of finish they now admit and the speed with which they can be assembled makes them an attractive solution for every kind of building.

In his 1983 study of cladding systems, Alan Brookes classified them as follows (Brookes, 1983):

■ precast concrete cladding
■ glass reinforced polyester (GRP)
■ glass fibre reinforced cement (GRC)
■ profiled metal and asbestos
■ sheet metal cladding panels
■ curtain walling

Relative costs of a selection of particular types were published in the *Architects' Journal* in 1987 for a single-storey warehouse; however the same relationships would not necessarily apply for taller buildings, nor have they been necessarily maintained since then (Figure 10.1). The impact of recession and developing technologies have both tended to reduce prices but there is no way of distinguishing one effect from the other. In 1992, for example, a manufacturer of aluminium claimed that a standard vertical curtain wall system using glass and panels would have cost £250 per m^2 in 1989 but the price of the same system had been driven down to £180. It is not possible to tell whether the 1989 price was too high, though the 1991

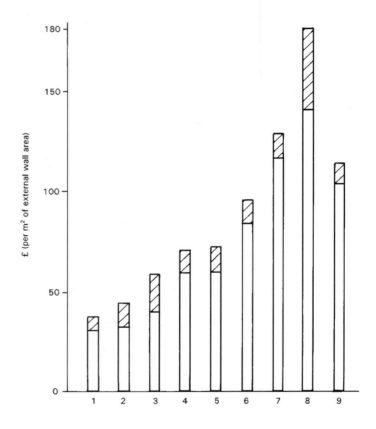

1 - Insulated PVC coated steel cladding with inner lining
2 - Insulated coloured aluminium cladding with inner lining
3 - Facing brick and blockwork cavity wall
4 - Precast concrete panels
5 - High-quality coloured aluminium sandwich cladding
6 - Single-skin GRP panels and back-up wall
7 - Double-skin GRP panels and back-up wall
8 - Single glazed curtain walling with back-up wall
9 - PVF coated metal sandwich panel on steel purlins with lining tray

Figure 10.1   Relative costs of cladding materials. 1987.

price was almost certainly too low in the sense that it could not be sustained if manufacturers were to remain profitable.

The following quote (*AJ* Focus, Sept. 1993) gives a flavour of the current rate of technological change in one material alone – glass:

> *It is now possible to specify double glazed units which have low E coatings on surfaces 2 and 3 with a gas-filled cavity between to achieve a U value of 1.1W/m2K. Pilkington and BASF have together been carrying out research into a granular aerogel which provides a transparent insulation layer . . . Photovoltaic glass, recently only an experimental technique, is rapidly becoming a cost-effective option . . .*

On major projects, the cladding systems may be designed – or certainly adapted and manufactured specifically for a particular building. For Channel 4 Headquarters by the Richard Rogers Partnership, a total system of cladding curtain walling and internal metal partitions was designed by Permastela (*AJ*, 1994b). Such bespoke work is inevitably expensive and involves long lead times; but if as we have seen in this case that expense can be compensated for elsewhere, the opportunities it opens up to the architect seem boundless.

To conclude this brief discussion on cladding, it is clear that there are few generalizations to be made about cost; straightforward coated steel panels are probably always economic for simple geometries but for more complex schemes, using some of the more advanced systems, each will have to be investigated individually and costs are going to be very difficult to predict until the manufacturer has been chosen and probably negotiated with.

Davis Langdon and Everest figures for 1993 (*Architects' Journal*, Focus, 1993d) show a range of costs for curtain walling from £170 per m^2 for an economical double-glazed panel system to one-hour fire-resistant curtain walling at over £650 per m^2, price for all types, doubling if curved. The most expensive glass alone is shown as nearly eight times the cost of the least expensive.

10.3.3 Windows

Although the major cost of the envelope of any building is the wall itself, the windows and doors are a not insignificant part of the whole. The range of possibilities for doors is vast and no simple summary could give a reasonable account of the alternatives in economic terms. But it is feasible to discuss the major alternatives for window frames both meaningfully and briefly.

There are of course many different possible shapes and sizes of widow and furthermore the major decisions may be about the total fenestration required and its relationship to the total wall area; increasing window sizes as a proportion of the wall usually increases the overall cost of the two together, particularly if the windows are double- or triple-glazed.

In theory the decision should be a very carefully calculated one which takes into account the life-cycle and energy implications as well – the heat loss, the solar gain, the daylight characteristics, cleaning and maintenance costs. Current computer programs and CAD systems generally allow the energy calculations to be made but rarely incorporate the facilities to make full life-cycle cost assessment for specific window types. Figure 2.1 indicated some of the considerations that ought to be taken into account. The theoretical principles on which the optimized window design might be calculated were defined by Tom Markus many years ago in an article which is still worth studying if only to show what happens when you try to take everything into account (Markus, 1967). His method involved estimating the trade-offs between heat loss and gain, noise, and cost over time.

However in reality, as is so frequently the case, the decisions are actually going to be made on the basis of aesthetic characteristics and initial cost with some very general assessment of life-cycle and energy implications, ensuring at the least that current building regulations for heat loss through the building fabric as a whole are met.

For example in a recent housing scheme by a housing association in the north-west, the association committee wanted painted softwood windows in preference to PVCu; the staff of the association tended to favour the PVCu on the grounds of its lower long-term maintenance costs. Some time was spent with manufacturers in trying to discover a PVC design which matched the character of wood – without success. In the end the much lower capital cost of the PVC combined with its expected long-run savings on maintenance persuaded the committee to accept it.

An assessment of the relative costs of the main alternatives for frames was published in *Building* in April 1993 (Essex, 1993). The life-cycle cost element seems to have been calculated without any reference to the need

Table 10.4   Comparative costs of windows. *Source*: Building, Doors and Windows Supplement, 30 Apr. 1994.

	Softwood £	Hardwood £	Aluminium £	PVCu £
Installation (100 m²)	16 000	21 000	19 000	18 000
Occupancy costs	37 750	43 750	38 550	27 750
Total cost in use (excl. replacement)	53 750	64 750	57 550	47 750
LIfe expectancy	35 yrs	40 yrs	50 yrs	40 yrs
Replacement cost over 50 years	22 850	26 250	19 000	22 500
Total of cost-in-use and replacement cost (£)	76 000	91 000	76 550	68 500

for discounting future expenditure and this could distort the results; nevertheless the figures seem to be the most recently published to make some assessment of this kind and the results are interesting. They show the initial cost advantage of softwood outweighed by the longer term advantages of PVCu and matched by aluminium. Hardwood is expensive both in terms of initial and long-run costs. These results do need to be treated with caution; apart from the assumptions built in to the figures (explained in the original article), changes in assumed lifetimes, a reduction

The new shed aesthetic? Liverpool Freeport, 1984.

in the relevant time horizon from 50 years to 20 and discounting at a reasonably high interest rate would erode if not eliminate the advantage of PVCu. And furthermore as has been continually stressed, the relative prices of all the materials might change. Belfield and Everest's comparative figures published in October 1993 also include steel windows and gives figures for initial costs only. There is no doubt at present of the popularity of the PVCu systems and the rapidly developing industry: 'In 1980 . . . specifiers could choose between one British and seven imported systems; eight years later the count was 36 imported systems competing against home grown' (Osborne, 1991).

10.4 Conclusion

The number of possible ways to combine feasible forms of structure with different forms of covering a building must verge on the infinite. Realistic choices are constrained to a degree by what is actually available, by tradition and current practice and by cost. Yet even within those constraints the opportunities for innovative and exciting design are wide because the basic structural technologies are highly flexible. Virtually any shape can be made from steel or concrete frame (it is often not realized that Corbusier's chapel at Ronchamp is a concrete-framed building). The possibilities of brick have been known and exploited for centuries; and the more modern forms of cladding and roofing can be curved and swept into expressive forms as in Nicholas Grimshaw's roof for the new international terminal at Waterloo Station in London. Now, with more collaboration between manufacturers and designers, the possibilities are continually being extended.

Of course, cost always imposes limitations and may ultimately force specific decisions from a limited range of choices; it may and frequently does make the full realization of client's and architect's ambitions unrealizable but we have enough examples in the last ten years to show that it is not always an acceptable excuse for drabness and banality in design.

FOR FURTHER STUDY

1 Recommended reading

Marian Bowley's *The British Building Industry: Four Studies in Response and Resistance to Change* (1966) is still very worth while reading as an analysis of both the development of frame systems and the experimental houses. E. R. Scoffham *The Shape of British Housing* (1984) looks at the different structural forms of housing designed from the 1950s to the late 1970s. Chapter 8 of Harper's *Building – The Process and the Product* (1990) is particularly relevant and the two reports referred to above should be studied.

Alan Brookes has written a great deal on cladding and is involved in research into cladding systems – but there seems to be little on relative costs published at present. The *Architects' Journal* in its technology series and its Focus supplements, and *Building* in its Building Materials supplements produce information on current developments in all the areas discussed in this chapter. See for example the special report on 'Building with steel', *Architects' Journal*, 14 Sept. 1994.

2 Exercises

a Make an approximate estimate of the structure and envelope costs of a small building using alternative methods; architectural students could do this with a building they are currently designing. An alternative would be for QS or building students to make estimates of the cost of architectural student designs and discuss the results with the designers. Use Spon's 'all in' rates or similar as basic source of cost information.

b Read the two reports referred to and identify exactly where the differences in cost arise, what different assumptions are made in the two. Try to establish why some of their results seem contradictory. Find and discuss other evidence on steel versus concrete frame.

3 Discussion and essay questions

a Why have houses not changed in appearance as much as factories in the last half century? Is it, for example, to do with costs, fashion or the technology of production?

b High-rise buildings not only tend to cost more per gross floor area than comparable low buildings but tend to provide less usable space. Explain why this is so and why, nevertheless, tall buildings are the normal form in city centres.

4 Projects

a Consider any multi-storey construction taking place or recently completed in your area; identify what sort of structural system was used and attempt to assess (by, for example, asking the architects) on what grounds the choice was made. A good class exercise would be for different groups of students to investigate one building each and then compare notes.

b Undertake the same project as above but for claddings. It could be done at the same time and for the same buildings.

11 **Energy and services**

11.1 Introduction

As figures quoted in earlier chapters have shown, the costs of the equipment needed to provide heating, lighting, ventilation, water and power supply are today a very significant part of total initial costs of a building; in the case of highly serviced buildings such as the hospital units referred to at the end of Chapter 9, they can amount to almost half the total costs of the project. Furthermore, the energy needed to ensure a comfortable environment for the building's occupiers and to enable a building's functions to be carried out effectively is likely as we saw in Chapter 8 (Figures 8.1 and 2) to account for a high proportion of a building's total running costs. The long-term costs of using a heating system will certainly outweigh its initial costs. Perhaps more than for any other element, it is necessary to consider the costs of building services in life-cycle terms if we are to make any realistic assessment of the relative benefits of different systems.

Designers and building owners are increasingly concerned with total energy use and the important interrelationships between all the different forms in which it is delivered, so 'services' have come to be considered as part of a total integrated system of environmental control and energy delivery. Rather, therefore, than consider the separate costs of different heating systems, lighting and air conditioning, this chapter looks at the evidence on the overall cost efficiency of different ways of controlling internal environments. It begins with an examination of some basic principles and a definition of the objectives designers should be trying to meet; it then examines in turn the economics of passive and active systems and concludes with a look at some recent examples of integrated approaches.

11.2 Energy use: global and individual objectives

The primary objective which designers and those responsible for the management of building are continually being exhorted to achieve is to minimize the use of energy in buildings. But setting such an objective raises a number of questions. Is the minimum possible use of energy in buildings an overriding priority? How does that aim relate to other aspects of building economically? How is it compatible with the need for comfort and efficiency? What are the priorities and whose priorities are they? Is it more important – and more cost-effective – to save some forms of energy than others?

There are two different levels at which these questions can be addressed and in current discussions the distinction is often not clearly made. For simplicity we will call them the global level and the individual level. Ultimately these cannot be kept separate, of course, for whatever affects the whole earth affects all the individuals who live on it; but it will be useful to retain the distinction through most of this chapter, bringing the two aspects together at the end.

11.2.1 The global issues

The global consequences of excessive and wasteful energy use are now well-known and the need for action to avoid or limit those consequences is widely recognized; there are many good accounts of the problems and possibilities now available, but it is worth summarizing the main issues here briefly.

The major threat posed by excessive use of fossil fuel energy is that of global warming through the production of the so-called greenhouse gases, the most significant of which is carbon dioxide (CO_2); 80% of carbon dioxide is produced through the burning of fossil fuels such as coal and oil and 18% produced through the burning of wood (including forest fires).

Secondly, the generation of power and direct burning of fuels produces a whole range of other pollutants, the ultimate effects of which are not known, but include the increased incidence of serious illnesses such as cancer and the production of 'acid rain' with consequent damage to forests, fish and agriculture – and indeed the whole human food chain.

Thirdly, there has been concern expressed about the limited stocks of fuel available; this seems less of an issue than it has sometimes been made out to be for, although there is probably enough to last the world 1000 years, there is no possibility of consuming that fuel without disastrous consequences through the release of CO_2.

Fourth, methods of generating and delivering and using useful energy absorb resources which could be used in alternative ways. In purely economic terms therefore, and particularly in terms of the distribution of world resources, the present vastly wasteful use of energy in the developed countries can be seen as wholly unjustifiable.

For all these reasons there is now consensus among scientists, politicians and a large proportion of the public (though some remain unconvinced) that reducing energy use is an important national and world objective in its own right. Whether there is yet the political will to take the action required still appears to be doubtful. Agreements were reached on a number of targets at the Rio de Janeiro conference in 1993 (including reduction of 10 million tonnes of carbon emissions by 2000) but there still seems some doubt about the willingness and ability of many governments to take the serious action required. Although the UK government has issued a policy document (HMSO, 1994d) on a strategy for sustainable development which incorporates policies to reduce CO_2 emissions, the proposed requirements for insulation standards in buildings are, according to many critics, far too weak to enable the objectives to be met. For example, Arthur Quarmby, an architect who has specialized in 'green' issues, has argued that targets can only be met if required U values are 'drastically reduced' (*AJ*, 1992a, 1993c). Yet the current proposals leave some of the standards untouched. On the other hand the establishment of the DoE Energy Office and the work of BRECSU – the Building Research Energy Conservation Support Unit – have had a considerable impact already on improving the construction industry's appreciation of the importance and possibilities of achieving high levels of energy efficiency in new and existing buildings.

The production and use of buildings is responsible for somewhere around 50% of total energy use in the UK and therefore around 50% of CO_2 emissions. An accurate figure is difficult to obtain; many different estimates are available and depend largely on what assumptions are made; whether for example they include or exclude the energy required to make building materials. The DoE Energy Office estimate for 1993 was 43% for 'use of energy in buildings' (BRECSU, 1992).

However, if we accept that a reduction in energy use is essential we have also to recognize that there are costs attached and economic factors to be taken into account.

We could perhaps define one objective for the construction industry – clients, designers and builders alike – as being able to produce buildings in which energy use was at a minimum compatible with the reasonable comfort of building users and the efficiency of activities for which the buildings exist. But the costs of achieving this may be considerable; many measures which in themselves save energy or reduce CO_2 emissions impose other costs, both financial and environmental, which may make their adoption questionable. The controversy over the development of 'wind farms' illustrates the possible environmental conflict well; many people living near the new experimental farms have objected strongly both to their visual impact and their noise.

Nevertheless, if one recognizes the seriousness of the global threats and accepts the part that might be played in diminishing those threats by reducing the use of energy in buildings, then clearly architects and contractors have a heavy responsibility to play their part in meeting these global objectives. Indeed the 'sustainability' provisions of the Maastricht Treaty have been interpreted as placing a legal duty on architects to design and specify 'in a benign environmental fashion' (Edwards, 1993). But architects have also a responsibility to satisfy the needs and requirements of individual users and owners of buildings.

11.2.2 The individual perspective

Owners and users of buildings are interested in being warm and comfortable; in being able to operate machinery efficiently, in having adequate lighting and hot water. But they are also interested in costs. It is expecting too much of human nature to imagine that (at least until the threat appears more imminent) people are going to make major financial sacrifices to reduce global warming or global pollution. If they are responsible for paying the bills and are therefore keenly interested in the cost of energy to them. Here again there are many different issues involved. Often (as with some tenanted houses and offices) the interests of owners and users might conflict or at least reflect different priorities; indeed quite recently developers have argued that the costs imposed by suggested restrictions on air conditioning would be unacceptable and the Housebuilders Federation has been quoted as asking for a delay in the imposition of new building regulations as 'it all costs money'; on the other hand many individual housebuilders have been raising the energy efficiency of their houses, recognizing that it can in fact be a selling point.

The critical questions at the individual level are whether the measures taken to save energy can actually be afforded and financed and whether they can be shown to be economically worth while **for those incurring the costs**.

Fortunately, the answer to these questions will often be 'yes', partly as a result of the extremely inefficient systems currently in use. And the scope for reducing energy consumption cost effectively is particularly great when the right decisions are taken at the design stage, that is when buildings are actually designed with energy efficiency as a prime consideration.

If this is correct then there may be, in many situations, no fundamental conflict between pursuing the 'global' objective of minimizing energy use and the individual objective of cost-effective energy use. But there are very many different ways of achieving these objectives and they have different cost and benefit implications. We will concentrate in this chapter on the issues for the owners and users, not because the global issues are unimportant but because they have been widely discussed and we can take them as given overall objectives with which the individual objectives need to be reconciled.

11.3 Comparing costs and benefits

The conditions under which an energy-saving features of design is economically worth while for an individual building owner can be set out very simply. On the one hand there are the extra costs involved in providing features which save energy and on the other are the savings resulting from the lower energy use and other benefits such as increased comfort. It might be helpful for the following discussion to set the conditions out in the form of a very simple equation (or rather an inequality), where C = the costs of energy saving measures and B = the benefits derived from it.

An energy-saving measure is worth while, then, if

$C < B$ (C is less than B)

But C consists of:

■ the capital costs of the measure (for example the cost of insulation, or a more efficient boiler);
■ the costs of maintenance;
■ the costs of replacement;
■ any associated costs (e.g. loss of rentable space, increased cost of energy management).

B consists of:

- the saving in the costs of fuel;
- increased levels of comfort;
- other benefits (e.g. lower levels of sickness in offices, fewer tenant complaints in rented homes).

When the issue is set out like this, it should be immediately obvious that there are some problems in making an accurate assessment of the economic advantage of any specific improvement.

The first set of problems is simply identifying and evaluating the costs and the benefits. Take the capital or initial costs first. Sometimes there will be no difficulty; for example, a domestic condensing boiler is almost twice as expensive as a non-condensing boiler of the same output. If a decision is made to use such a boiler instead of a cheaper one, the cost of that decision is clear; it is the difference between the two prices (adjusted for any difference in installation costs should they occur). Or if insulation is installed in an existing building, again the costs will be easily measurable – they will be the contract sum for the job plus perhaps the cost of disturbance, if for example work has to be suspended in an office while the job is done.

But in other situations it may not be so obvious what should be included. If a design incorporates a combination of such features as higher insulation standards than required by building regulations, use of materials for their energy efficiency, cool ceilings, natural ventilation, then it might be extremely difficult to measure the extra costs of these things over some alternative design which might have been developed but was not.

The long-term costs – maintenance and eventual replacement – can only be approximately estimated; though again with modern efficient boiler systems regularly serviced reasonably accurate prediction of future costs is feasible.

The benefits are more difficult to assess and to predict accurately. The most obvious is the saving from lower energy use; this will depend very considerably on the way the building is used and managed, but that is not totally within the control of the designer; it will also be affected by the actual costs of energy to the user. The imposition of VAT on domestic fuel in 1994 has already been referred to in Chapter 8; this changed at one stroke the advantages to be gained from low-energy systems so any calculations made before that legislative change was known about would have underestimated those savings considerably; a change in the tariff structure for gas currently being discussed may well also change relative cost and benefits.

Some benefits may not be measurable at all: the increased comfort of a building's users, the increase in work efficiency which might result, the better use of space possible, reduction in sickness, greater satisfaction of tenants; some of these will, it is true, have financial consequences for commercial building owners, but they will be extremely difficult to measure.

A further problem is that it is often not possible to isolate the effects of a particular measure or the reasons for a particular level of saving if a design is developed as a total energy-saving package; it may in other words not be possible to isolate the elements of B or C above separately from other general costs and benefits of acquiring and using a building.

Even if realistic figures are available, they will include initial capital costs and a flow of cost and benefits occurring over a long period of time in the future. So there still remains the problem of relating future to present costs. The techniques for doing this have already been discussed in Chapter 8. Applying the basic principle discussed there to our criteria for establishing the economic rationale of energy-saving measures means redefining C and B above as follows:

C = the cost of the improvement plus the discounted future costs of maintenance and repair;

B = the discounted value of the future savings in fuel and any other quantifiable benefits (i.e. their net present value).

The expenditure is still, as before, worth while if B is greater than C. The non-quantifiable benefits simply have to be considered as a separate but highly relevant issue. For example if on the basis of this sort of net present value calculation, a heating system appears to be only barely worthwhile but it is expected to increase the level of comfort considerably, then this could sway the decision in favour of making the expenditure.★

In fact, largely because of the difficulties in using present value discussed in Chapter 8 most of the case studies published are assessed in the simpler method of payback, that is estimating how long it will take to recoup the costs. This is as we have seen a relatively crude and inaccurate approach because it ignores the total lifetime of the improvement and the benefit it yields; but it gives a rough indication of the order of magnitude of any financial commitment. Some publications by BRECSU give a much more detailed assessment using present value methods, assuming certain interest and inflation rates, but most keep to the payback method because, they

★BRE has used a different formulation of the decision criterion but it amounts to the same thing; they define NPV as the net present value of the benefits **less** the capital cost of the improvement (*k*). The investment is then worthwhile if NPV/K is greater than 1. Unfortunately in some of the BRECSU publications a different definition is used and the criterion incorrectly stated.

claim, it is more easily and widely understood.

In spite of all the difficulties, estimates of costs and benefits of low-energy systems have been made in many case studies, chiefly by BRECSU over the past 15 years. It sometimes turns out that the benefits are clearly so large that inaccuracies in the calculations are unlikely to make a difference to a decision; but there **are** cases where there does seem to be a possible financial loss or doubtful gain to owners or users; cases, that is, where the global objective of reducing energy use in buildings may indeed conflict with the narrower financial interests of individuals. It is in those situations that the building professionals have perhaps their greatest responsibility.

We explore some of these issues under two basic heads: first the costs and benefits in general of reducing energy consumption in buildings by **passive** energy conservation measures; secondly, we consider **active** methods of controlling the environment through heating, lighting and ventilation, discussing the different fuel sources and ways of using them to deliver energy.

11.4 Passive paths to energy saving

By passive methods of control will be meant here the use of the building's form and materials to provide optimum comfort with a minimum use of fossil-manufactured fuels such as coal, electricity, gas and oil – a wider definition than often used. In practice it may not always be possible to identify active from passive but the distinction will serve to structure the argument.

The methods can be classified as:

- high levels of insulation;
- reduction of unwanted air flows – in or out, by draught-proofing for example;
- use of the building's thermal capacity to retain or absorb heat and thus provide warmth or cooling as required;
- use of glazing, shutters, shades etc., to optimize the balance between heat loss and heat gain, adequate natural light and glare;
- use of the building **orientation** to optimize heat and light conditions for the occupants;
- use of building **form** to maximize use of natural light and natural ventilation and to maintain reasonably constant, comfortable temperatures.

The economic attractions of passive energy-saving design appear superficially to be overwhelming; in effect most of the environmental control is provided without using expensive fuels, the sources of heat, light and cooling are free – simply the sun and fresh air. So the negative effects of fossil fuel use are avoided.

But there are always costs to be incurred in harnessing or disposing of energy: the TANSTAAFL principle, as one of the early writers on environmental economics called it − 'there ain't no such thing as a free lunch' − a principle which, as he pointed out, bears some resemblance to the second law of thermodynamics (Dolan, 1971).

The costs are of two sorts, the first of which is obvious and well recognized, the second sometimes ignored. First, much of the actual material needed to improve energy efficiency by passive design methods will almost certainly involve cost over and above what would be incurred in a conventional building, such as extra insulation, the use of denser materials, double and triple glazing, extra shutters, blinds and canopies, and possibly electronically controlled energy management systems.

But perhaps an even more significant cost − and this is a point which becomes very apparent from a study of buildings completed over the last few years − is the high cost of the design process itself. Making the best use of orientation and form requires careful design tailored to each specific site; even with the computer models now available, this is not a trivial task and effects are not yet fully predictable:

> *The engineering of buildings to provide an acceptable environment for occupants, to a price . . . needs to be precise; this requires dependable modelling especially for passive cooling; if the engineering of a cooling services system is wrong first time it may be relatively easy to resize a fan or pump or tweak controls. If the form and fabric of a passive building is wrong, resizing may be impossible . . . liability is a real issue here* (Evans, 1992).

Design expertise of that order has to be paid for. It may well be worth while for it should be outweighed by the benefits both in energy saving *per se* and in terms of lower costs in use for users and owners; but it is a cost which cannot be ignored or skimped.

Insulation − the costs and benefits. The costs and benefits of high levels of insulation are now well documented; so clear are the benefits − at both the global and individual level − that the building regulations or equivalent codes in most Western countries can now require rigorous standards to be met, without much opposition. It may indeed seem that architects, QS and contractor, need not be over concerned with the **economics** of providing the level of insulation required − it simply has to be achieved. However there are a number of points to be considered.

First, and most importantly, it is widely felt that the UK standards are still very much lower than they should be and that designers should be aiming to achieve much higher levels of insulation than currently required.

Secondly, there are many different ways of achieving the standards, which are expressed as U values for different building elements, and the different techniques will have different cost implications.

Thirdly, even the level of insulation required by current building regulations and *a fortiori*, any higher standards, does impose a cost which might be seen by some developers or building owners as an 'extra', to be compensated for by savings elsewhere.

There is still a considerable difference between the required U value of walls in Britain (0.45) and in other European countries where they range from 0.18 to 0.4. Current proposals for change (at the time of writing (*AJ*, 12 Aug. 1994) do not include higher standards for walls but do suggest better floor and ceiling insulation levels for domestic buildings) have been received with disappointment by people keen to see the UK move quickly to the standards already met elsewhere; the new regulations, they claim, will not go nearly far enough; it is an interesting example of the apparent lack of political will to take the issues seriously. But if this view of the inadequacy of current British and similar standards is accepted, then, for the general environmental benefits it will bring, architects should be persuading clients to accept higher levels. This is precisely what organizations such as BRECSU actually recommend them to do but in order to succeed they will need to demonstrate the economic benefits to the clients themselves.

Whether there will be in fact tangible benefits depends on the costs of the insulation used and the consequent savings in energy costs.

To take first the cost of the insulation itself. There are two basic ways of ensuring low levels of heat loss: first, the building envelope itself may be made or partly made of material with low U values – such as lightweight concrete blocks, various cladding materials; secondly, special insulating material can be added, internally, externally or in cavity walls. There is a wide range of such materials and, on economic grounds alone, the best choice will be the one with the lowest installed cost for its insulation value.

In a study published by the *Architects' Journal* in January 1994, Davis Langdon and Everest identified the costs of some twenty different ways of achieving the currently required U value for exposed walls in dwellings of $0.45\text{W/m}^2\text{K}$. Their study shows that there is very little difference in cost between the three main systems, full cavity fill, partial cavity fill and internal insulation; but quite a wide range between different specific methods in each group. Table 11.1 tabulates their results (*AJ*, Focus, Jan. 1994).

All the assumptions on which these calculations were based are not stated, so there may be circumstances where the relationships alter and there may be reasons for using the more expensive systems, but what the calculations do show is that there is not a necessarily direct relationship

Table 11.1 Cost of insulation. *Source: Architects Journal*, Focus, Jan. 1994.

FULL CAVITY FILL

outer leaf	cavity	blockwork inner leaf	inner finish	U-value W/m²K	£/m²
Clay facing bricks (1700kg/m³) £275/1000	70mm blown fibre	125mm dense, (1950kg/m³)	13mm lightweight plaster with bonding undercoat	0.45	52.70
ditto	50mm blown fibre	100mm aerated, (650kg/m³)	13mm lightweight plaster	0.44	49.45
ditto	65mm mineral fibre slabs	140mm dense, (1950kg/m³)	13mm lightweight plaster with bonding undercoat	0.44	57.00
ditto	50mm mineral fibre slabs	100mm aerated, (650kg/m³)	13mm lightweight plaster	0.40	52.30
ditto	65mm mineral fibre slabs	100mm lightweight aggregate, (1100kg/m³)	ditto	0.40	53.90
ditto	50mm mineral fibre slabs	125mm aerated, (650kg/m³)	ditto	0.38	54.35
ditto	ditto	100mm aerated, (480kg/m³)	ditto	0.36	52.80

PARTIAL CAVITY FILL

outer leaf	cavity	blockwork inner leaf	inner finish	U-value W/m²K	£/m²
ditto	40mm extruded polystyrene foam 25mm clear cavity	100mm dense, (1950kg/m³)	13mm lightweight plaster with bonding undercoat	0.45	57.15
ditto	30mm foil-faced rigid urethane foam insulation board 50mm clear cavity	100mm medium density, (1350kg/m³)	ditto	0.44	53.05
ditto	40mm mineral fibre slab, 25mm clear cavity	100mm aerated (650kg/m³)	13mm lightweight plaster	0.42	51.55
ditto	30mm extruded polystyrene foam, 25mm clear cavity	ditto	ditto	0..42	55.25
ditto	30mm foil-faced rigid urethane foam board, 50mm clear cavity	140mm medium density, (1350kg/m³)	13mm lightweight plaster with bonding undercoat	0.42	55.95
ditto	25mm foil-faced rigid urethane foam board, 50mm clear cavity	100mm aerated, (650kg/m³)	13mm lightweight plaster	0.41	54.15
ditto	30mm foil-faced rigid urethane foam board, 50mm clear cavity	ditto	ditto	0.37	54.75
ditto	50mm expanded polystyrene board (standard duty), t&g edges 50mm clear cavity	100mm aerated, (480kg/m³)	ditto	0.36	53.10

INTERNAL INSULATION

outer leaf	cavity	blockwork inner leaf	inner finish	U-value W/m²K	£/m²
ditto	clear	100mm medium density, (1350kg/m³)	39.5mm plasterboard laminate (30mm urethane board bonded to 9.5mm plasterboard)	0.43	53.95
ditto	clear	125mm aerated, (650kg/m³)	29.5mm plasterboard laminate (20mm urethane board bonded to 9.5mm plasterboard)	0.42	54.35
ditto	clear	140mm medium density, (1350kg/m³)	39.5mm plasterboard laminate (see 1 above)	0.41	54.20
ditto	clear	100mm aerated, (480kg/m³)	29.5mm plasterboard laminate (see 2 above)	0.40	52.30
ditto	clear	ditto	ditto	0.38	56.80

Key
1 facing brick
2 block inner leaf
3 plaster
4 cavity insulation
5 unfilled cavity
6 insulating plasterboard

between cost and the effectiveness of insulation; high levels can be achieved with little or no extra expenditure.

BRECSU's 'Energy Efficiency in Housing' sets target levels of 0.36W/m² for walls, and floors, 0.23 for roofs and 2.92 for windows, and argues that the costs are virtually no more then for buildings just meeting the 1990 Building regulation standards (see Tables 1 and 2 of that publication).

There are of course much more expensive ways of achieving desired levels — and these should clearly be avoided unless there is some overwhelming reason to adopt them. The other factor to be considered is the 'greenness' of the material itself — for example, does it contain CFC gases, did its manufacture involve large amounts of energy? On these grounds, both recycled paper and cellular glass score highly, but paper has some serious disadvantages and glass insulation is expensive.

The gains to users of extra levels of insulation are usually very high. The BRECSU 'Good Practice Case Studies', of which there are now over 200, consistently show short payback periods — usually in terms of fuel cost savings. They include projects where insulation has been added to existing buildings and where it has been incorporated from the beginning. Although, as we have seen, the payback period is not the most accurate mode of assessment, comparisons of different case studies do give some indications of what can be achieved and what feature may be questionable in purely economic terms. However, whereas many of the case studies of housing schemes incorporating energy efficient measures give payback periods of from 4 to 9 years, others seem very difficult to justify. In one for example (Case study 91), which incorporated heat-reflective roller blinds and some solar-heated water systems, the payback period worked out at 45 years.

Some of the studies of housing association and local authority schemes try to quantify both tenant and landlord benefits and compare them with the capital costs. Study 155 is particularly interesting in that it does use 'correct' discounting methods for evaluation. The capital cost of the scheme was approximately £1400 per house; the benefits to tenants alone in terms of the present value of their fuel cost savings, calculated with an 8% discount rate and assuming a 25-year building life, were estimated at approximately £1300. But when savings to the landlord were included — savings rising from lower voids (and therefore higher income from rents) and reduced repair costs, the estimated full value of the savings was nearly £3000 — twice the initial expenditure. Some of the calculations and assumptions may be questionable but they do seem to indicate that the potential returns on simple energy-saving measures, when considered using sound investment criteria, can be very high.

There can be very few circumstances where the incorporation of high insulation and other simple measures at design stage are not cost-effective for housing; and the benefits to users over the life-cycle are considerable. There is now enough evidence for architects and QSs to be able to persuade the most sceptical client, unless that client genuinely has no interest in the longer life of his or her building. Even in those cases, however, the general realization of these benefits by the users (tenants of commercial buildings, house purchasers etc.) means that they will eventually incorporate them into their assessment of the rent or price they are prepared to pay.

There will come a point however at which increasing levels of insulation ceases to be cost-effective; there are bound to be diminishing returns at some stage, that is there will come a point at which extra expenditure on insulation will have less and less extra benefit. And it is certainly the case that as higher and higher levels are aimed for, there is a greater need for very careful design and site practice; otherwise purported gains from the insulation will be lost through cold bridging and air leakage throughout the construction.

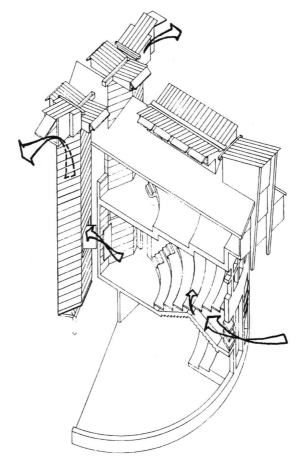

Figure 11.1   The 'most extensive use of stack ventilation in the UK' – Laboratories, de Montfort University, Leicester.

Other forms of passive control. The other forms of passive energy-saving design need to be considered together as they are usually integrated in a total system, which will of course include the high insulation levels discussed above.

Some of these methods of ensuring control have been used for centuries in various vernacular architectures – 'stack ventilation' for example – using natural convection currents to draw cool air into a building at the appropriate times – and exploiting the thermal capacity of the building material to retain heat energy and to provide cooling by absorbing heat from inside a building.

Most of the 'energy-conscious' designs actually built over the last ten years in the UK and elsewhere have tried to incorporate these ideas and integrate them with other active, but low-energy, techniques – such as the district heating in the Nottingham Tax Office referred to below. A number of projects have been analysed in the architectural journals and in special articles by the staff of BRECSU (see list of case studies at the end of the chapter).

Although there are now many examples of buildings designed to passive energy-saving design, it is difficult to find any assessments of the costs and benefits to the users, though their advantages in terms of reduction in energy use are clear. Discussion is generally in terms of the low-energy usage compared with conventional buildings. In most cases, the clients themselves have been convinced advocates of energy-use reduction, have been keen to experiment and have been willing to take some risks. Some of the buildings were clearly quite expensive for their type and time; others were achieved within overall budgets set on conventional assumptions and must therefore be assumed to have been cost-effective.

The Inland Revenue building in Nottingham designed by Michael Hopkins and Ove Arup – the first building to achieve the maximum score in the BREAM environmental assessment – cost £50m, approximately £1500 per square metre. It harnesses the stack effect, with some fan assistance in drawing air through floor vents, uses heat from the district heating scheme and has very high levels of insulation. The costs were presumably within Treasury guidelines.

In the case of the National Association for Consumer Research's office at Milton Keynes, capital cost savings were claimed as well as considerable energy savings from using stack ventilation, again with mechanical assistance, rather than full air conditioning, and making use of high thermal mass.

The School of Engineering, de Montfort University, which Dean Hawkes has described as having 'the most extensive use of stack ventilation effect in the UK since the 19th century' (Hawkes, 1994) is an extremely complex and original building and perhaps illustrates the point made above that it would be very difficult to judge the costs of its energy-saving characteristics independently – they are so much a part of the overall design. But again it has been built, and to an approved budget, which would not, one assumes, have allowed wildly expensive solutions.

Cost pressures in the commercial sector, however, can force designers to fall back on less than optimal solutions; for example, inter-plane blinds for Peter Foggo's office buildings at Leeds proved too expensive and had to be substituted by less effective but cheaper internal blinds (Evans, 1994a).

Until we have more detailed research demonstrating the cost-effectiveness of the different methods perhaps all that can be said is that some of the techniques must obviously be worth while and others may have to be subject to careful cost appraisal. For example, there should be little or no extra costs for a building which is oriented and fenestrated to minimize and maximize solar gain as required at different times of the day or year. But a building which incorporates underfloor ventilation, sophisticated Building Energy Management Systems windows with internal blinds, controllable shutters, light shelves etc. must incur extra costs. By modelling the expected savings, using the computer programs now becoming available for commercial buildings, some attempts can be made to estimate the energy benefits but it is not clear that we are yet in a position to make full cost-benefit appraisals in economic terms from the point of view of users and owners.

11.5 Active control of the environment: the input of energy

A building designed using all the possible means of passive environmental control discussed above might well (and in some climates definitely would) need no active intervention. It might not, however, be a cost-effective solution either for the clients or in terms of its contribution to global energy reduction; the costs, including the energy cost incorporated into the materials, might be higher than using some energy input in the form of electric power, gas or other fuels. In any case some positive energy input is still going to be necessary in most circumstances, for powering equipment obviously but also for some environmental control purposes.

There are therefore again economic choices to be made, taking into consideration the individual as well as global costs and benefits. Two main types of decision are to be taken, one on the type of energy source to be used and another on equipment required to deliver the energy usefully. The decisions are not independent because whether one selected electricity instead of gas, for example, will be affected by the available installations or fitments.

Fuel costs. For some uses there are no serious alternatives; electricity is essential for lighting, the running of machinery and electronic equipment. There are of course still questions as to how electricity can be most economically used for those purposes. For other uses, and particularly space heating which absorbs most energy used in buildings, there are alternatives – oil, gas, solid fuel and electricity.

All these fuels are processed in one way or another before finally delivering energy as heat into the space of a building and their costs depend on the efficiency and cost of those conversion processes. It is possible to measure or estimate those 'costs' in different ways. One way which is relevant to the economics of a system for the building users is simply to use the market price of the fuel and calculate how much heat is delivered per £. Another way, which gets closer to measuring the true social and environmental costs of the various fuels, is to estimate the amount of primary energy required to deliver a given amount of usable energy. When this is done, electricity turns out, in the UK at least, to be an extremely expensive fuel to use for space heating; most of the energy contained in the primary fuels is dissipated in waste heat or distribution losses. These are so great that even though electricity can itself be converted to useful heat with 100% efficiency, this cannot compensate for the losses in the process of generation and distribution. The other major disadvantage to electricity is that its generation normally releases large quantities of CO_2 into the atmosphere.

In a perfectly working market system, where prices reflected true opportunity costs, these disadvantages would be fully reflected in price differentials; but there are no markets that are perfect in this sense and in the case of fuels, markets are particularly 'distorted' by monopolistic elements, by differential taxation and subsidies. The arguments for and against these distortions are complex but an interesting example of the difficulty of assessing actual prices against true costs is the availability of cheap, off-peak electricity. As Figure 11.2 shows, this brings the cost of electric heating using storage heaters to a reasonable level compared with alternatives. And it is easy to see why it is possible for electricity companies to charge these low prices: generation capacity must be adequate to meet demand at busy times of the day; at other times, the capacity is under used; but the costs of distributing power from capacity already in existence is low. As long as the prices charged cover these 'marginal' costs, the companies do not lose. However it could be argued that from the point of view of global energy efficiency, it would be preferable to reduce peak loads and peak capacity requirements – though realistically it is difficult to see this happening.

The variability of fuel prices poses more problems. Oil problems doubled in 1974, making it one of the most expensive fuels for heating; by the early

1990s prices had declined so far that it was once again the cheapest as Figure 11.2 shows. However there is no reason to believe that the current prices reflect any more accurately than at any other time the true long-term costs of oil extraction and delivery.

Clearly, in these circumstances the best the designers and their clients can do is to keep abreast with changing prices, use the best forecasts available and make decisions on heating systems which give the best chance of minimizing total costs to users and making the maximum contribution to global energy reduction targets.

The specific circumstances and priorities of particular clients have to be considered. There may, for example, be advantages in the use of electric systems such as low installation costs and less space used; and the relative advantages or disadvantages of electricity would be very different, particularly in terms of the release of CO_2, where hydro-electricity is easily available or if new 'green' forms of generation, such as wind, wave or solar power, become economic.

Even accepting that gas and oil are currently the cheapest fuels in the UK, there are of course more and less efficient and economic ways of using them. If electricity or other fuels are preferred or necessary for some reason (because for example no gas supply is available) there are still decisions to be made about the most economic systems to use.

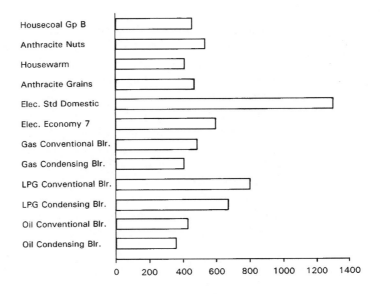

Figure 11.2   Comparative costs of fuels.
Source: Sutherland's Comparative Domestic Heating Cost Tables.

Appliances for heating. Fortunately, and partly because of greater awareness of environmental issues and the competition between equipment manufacturers to respond, we are seeing much more efficient technologies being used which without doubt can deliver usable energy at lower costs. The difficulty is still, however, that capital costs of more effective equipment may be high and there is still then the problem which has recurred in all our discussions of life-cycle costs, of persuading clients that the extra expense is worth while.

We will look at just one example, but a very significant one, the gas-fired condensing boiler.

> *Condensing boilers offer high energy efficiencies by recovering heat from the flue gases; this is done by increasing the heat exchanger surface area which recovers extra sensible heat whenever the boiler fires. They become even more efficient when system water temperatures are low because the extra heat exchange promotes condensation, allowing much of the latent heat to be recaptured* (BRECSU Digest 339).

Although the capital costs of installation can be up to twice the cost of conventional boilers, the savings in energy costs are enough to make the expense worth while in a wide range of applications including housing, schools, hospitals, public houses, and offices.

But despite the arguments and the many documented case studies many clients and architects still seem reluctant to adopt the system and the reason usually given is the extra capital cost involved.

That reluctance can be overcome but needs a little confidence. In a recent housing association consortium scheme in the Merseyside area, only one of the associations insisted on the use of condensing gas boilers. The extra cost involved was only $435 per house (about 1% of the contract sum). The savings in energy costs to the tenant however were reckoned to be £75 per year (giving a simple payback of 6 years). There are some interesting features of this case: first it was the client not the architect who made the decision; secondly other associations saw the extra cost as unjustifiable (or were unaware of the possibility) and third if the architect and other associations had agreed to incorporate the condensing boilers from the beginning the actual addition to the contract sum would probably have been less.

Air conditioning. Apart from heating, the other main 'active' method of environmental control are air conditioning and ventilation. As awareness of the possibilities of natural, passive technologies has grown, a debate has developed on whether full air conditioning is required at all and considerable pressure developed to limit its use. In response, the industry is developing new forms of air quality control which are part way between active and passive, using for example stack ventilation, chilled ceilings, and heat exchangers (for a discussion of the current state of the art see *Building*, Special Feature Heating and Ventilation, Nov. 1993).

Here again there is potential conflict between the individual client's search for cost effectiveness and the global requirement for both energy reduction and reduction in CFC emissions: some engineers and quantity surveyors have claimed some alternative, energy-efficient systems are up to 36% more expensive in installation costs than conventional systems, while others have argued that costs can be competitive.

The conflict is clear from the response of the Property Federation to proposed government restrictions on the use of air conditioning in the draft 1994 Building Regulations: interestingly the proposals seem to have been temporarily abandoned. The rate of change in attitudes, knowledge, available systems and costs seem so rapid at present in this area that it would be very rash indeed to predict what will be seen as the most economic and environmentally acceptable systems within the next few years. The only firm prediction that might be made is that the move away from comprehensive air conditioning to maximizing the use of natural methods will continue and will itself bring down the cost of new approaches.

11.6 Energy-efficient design – some conclusions

All of the methods of energy-efficient design, whose economics we have examined briefly, can and often have been brought together in single buildings. It is obviously very difficult to assess whether or not such designs have been economically successful – in terms of either of the two main criteria we have used – global saving of energy or cost effectiveness for clients. To begin with it is not usually possible to isolate the energy-saving features in terms of costs – that is to identify what the building might have been; the more totally integrated the energy-saving features are, the less meaningful it is to talk about what the building might have been without them. Secondly, actual energy savings data are difficult to obtain – and in some cases unobtainable in principle. Thirdly for some of the key energy-saving designs built in the last twenty years, there are not even basic reliable cost data accessible.

However, the evidence from the many case studies published by the journals and by BRECSU leads overwhelmingly to the following conclusions:

■ very high levels of the most straightforward forms of insulation are invariably worth while;

■ double and triple glazing may still be difficult to justify in purely economic terms when incorporated in existing individual buildings, but as part of an overall design strategy to achieve highly energy-efficient building, they are essential;

■ passive energy design can be achieved within overall budgets – but as yet not easily and not without very careful and expensive design; some features – orientation, the best use of fenestration and the thermal capacity of buildings – imply little extra construction costs; other features (photovoltaic glass for example) are still extremely expensive.

The objective of producing buildings using minimal amounts of energy remains of the highest importance – but it has to be approached with some realistic appreciation of its associated costs. In a report on the Third European Conference on Solar Energy and Urban Planning held in Florence in 1993, Martin Pawley wrote

> *while speaker after speaker promoted solar architecture as nature's way, the intermediate steps between the energetically costly glass buildings of today and the promised free solar energy architecture of tomorrow seemed painfully absent: . . . to achieve what solar architecture wants to achieve to live off the income energy of the sun as opposed to its fossil fuel capital, is no less intractable a task [than putting men on the moon]* (Pawley, 1993).

Which implies first that it needs large resources dedicated to it and secondly that it can be done. And we do not know what major developments are round the corner; dramatic breakthroughs in the technology and cost of photovoltaic cells have recently been reported from Australia (where there is plenty of sun to use!) and we may yet see this become a major source of usable energy.

FOR FURTHER STUDY

1 Recommended reading

Brenda and Robert Vale's *Green Architecture, Design for a Sustainable Future and Toward a Green Architecture* (six detailed case studies including the NMB Bank in Amsterdam) are both essential. However neither of the books goes into any detail on costs.

John Pezzey's *An Economic Assessment of Energy Conservation Measures in Housing and Other Buildings* (Buildings Research Establishment, 1984) is not for the faint hearted, but is the most thorough analysis available of the economic issues and forms the basis for the principles on which the BRECSU case study material is assessed.

BRECSU Case Studies in the *Best Practice Programme* series: there are now very many of these published for all types of buildings. Some are more useful for managers and owners; others are aimed specifically at designers. Each is only a few pages long.

Some other case studies:.

Association for Consumer Research Offices, Milton Keynes (John Outram), *Architects' Journal*, 5 May 1993.

School of Engineering, De Montfort University (Short Ford and Partners; Max Fordham & Partners), *Architects Journal*, 9 March 1993.

Office Park Buildings, Leeds (Peter Foggo Associates), *Architects' Journal*, 6 April 1994.

The Malta Brewery (Simon Farson Cisk), *Architects' Journal*, 10 February 1993.

Inland Revenue Office, Nottingham (Michael Hopkins, Ove Arup), *Building* 23 Apr. 1994 and *Architects' Journal*, 16 June 1993.

Two documents produced by the Commission of the European Communities (1986, 1991) contain many case studies of solar architecture with economic assessments, though the section on cost benefit analysis in the first one is not very helpful. There have been many articles recently on solar architecture, photovoltaic cells, chilled ceilings, stack ventilation; search the indexes of the main construction and design journals under these and similar subject headings.

2 Exercises

a Using any of the available BRECSU case studies, examine carefully the claims for energy and cost savings. Where the information is given calculate approximate present values of savings compared with capital costs. Compare the result with figures given in the case studies of simple payback periods.

b Prepare a written argument, with calculations of costs and benefits to persuade a reluctant public house owner that his new heating system should be based on an oil-fired condensing boiler, even though it is more expensive than others available (see Energy Efficiency in Public Houses series by BRECSU, Gas Fired Non-domestic Condensing Boilers Information Leaflet 18 and BRE Digest 339, Condensing Boilers).

3 Discussion and essay questions

a Why should the problems of global warming and pollution be particular concerns of architects and builders? Should this concern extend to the selection of all materials as well as the system of environmental control?

c Are traditional air-conditioning methods becoming rapidly outmoded? Consider all the objections to and advantages of air conditioning and examine the alternatives. What evidence is there for relative cost effectiveness and energy-saving characteristics of alternatives?

Relating design choices to building and its management

12 Programme, cash flow and buildability

12.1 Introduction

The economic criteria for design choices discussed in the last section have involved mainly the comparison of one alternative with others in terms of the costs of the resources incorporated into the building, particularly labour and materials; we also considered the long-term economics from the point of view of users, particularly in the last chapter on energy use.

However one extremely significant aspect of the link between design and cost has only been briefly touched on: that is the influence of design on the actual process of production. The drawings produced by the design team are essentially descriptions of the final product itself – the building. Even the so-called 'working drawings' of details are of representations of what will be there when the assembly is finished. Design drawings themselves do not indicate the procedures by which the building is to be built – the process.

This in itself is not necessarily a bad thing; indeed it could be argued that the separate functions of the designer and the constructor are accurately reflected in this inevitable distinction between product and process. It is the architect's job to show what is to be built; it is the builder's job to work out how to build it. However if the divide between the two is too great the consequences may well be serious – and costly. A design which is developed without sufficient consideration for the construction process may simply pose the builder with unnecessary problems. The builder may well be able to cope with them but at a cost; or they may prove insuperable, with the result that he or she has to go back to the designer to ask for some revision of the design or alternatively, in order to make the building process easier, may well make adjustments which compromise the designer's intentions.

This is often referred to as the problem of 'buildability' but we suggest here that the issue is much wider than the buildability of particular details (which is how the word is often interpreted). It includes the failure of designers occasionally to appreciate fully the complexities of managing a building programme, particularly a large one; and it includes lack of appreciation by builders in some circumstances of what the designer's intentions are and of why particular design decisions have been made. It can indeed happen that the architect has designed or specified an element which is unnecessarily difficult or expensive to construct or produced a design which makes it very difficult for labour and plant to be used efficiently. It may on the other hand be that the builder has failed to understand the design requirements and created inefficiencies unnecessarily. Both do occur and both can often be avoided through more effective communication and understanding. Some techniques for improving the flow of information are discussed in Chapter 13; this chapter concentrates on the problems facing the contractor in converting the information he or she has into a programme of work.

The problems are not universal and are not insoluble. On many small schemes architects work closely with builders with whom they have worked before; a working relationship is established through which each can discuss the others problems and solutions can be reached. Even in major schemes high levels of co-operation and understanding are frequently achieved. For example during the construction of the new Glyndebourne Opera House, the close collaboration of architects, engineers, management contractor and subcontractors, allied with a shared understanding of objectives, led not, of course, to a project free of argument, but to a conclusion which seems to have pleased client, architect and contractor alike. The structural system of the Inland Revenue Office at Nottingham was refined and developed co-operatively by the architects Michael Hopkins & Partners, engineers Ove Arup, contractors Trent Concrete and the many specialist subcontractors (Evans, 1993b).

Nevertheless problems rising from mutual misunderstanding, if not universal, are extremely common. In this chapter we look at three aspects of the construction programme – the problems of overall programming, the problems of organizing specific resources and the problem of maintaining a positive cash flow. One object is to point out that the contractor's task is formidable enough even when the design is relatively straightforward to build and that designers need to bear that in mind, if they wish the construction to be as trouble-free, as efficient and therefore as economic as possible.

The first section of the chapter describes the construction programme itself, which is derived directly from the design requirements. The second section examines in more detail the problems of managing particular resources and the third shows how the programme of work is translated (or not) into cash flow for the contractor. Finally we take a brief look at the more conventionally defined issue of 'buildability'.

12.2 The construction programme

Every project, from a domestic kitchen extension to the likes of Canary Wharf needs a programme, a plan identifying the resources, time and cost implications of the project. However a plan alone is insufficient; there has to be a project control mechanism to review how well the project is progressing and allow managers to judge whether the original plan is still realistic or not, and what adjustments are necessary. Almost inevitably the plan **will** need correcting, probably for one of three main reasons: changes due to alterations or omissions in the design; changes in the contractor's available resources, unavailability of plant etc. and third, problems created by external factor such as bad weather and the unavailability of materials.

For the smallest scale projects the programming is often not done in any great detail, either because it is not thought necessary or because the smaller contractor involved doesn't work that way; but some planning is nonetheless necessary if a strict budget and time scale is to be met. For the larger scale projects detailed planning has to take place for the project to work at all; the complexities and potential for disaster are so great that as little as possible can be left to chance; chance will anyway do its worst.

It is often the case, under certain procurement strategies (which will be described in Chapter 14), even on larger projects that construction planning is not given the attention it needs at the vital tendering stage. This happens because of the shortage of time and the non-recoverable costs associated with what is a highly complex task needing considerable experience.

There are many techniques used and advocated for planning and controlling construction effectively; they range from simply setting out on paper the sequences of operations and their probable time spans, to complex computer-based systems such as PERT and Superproject; from simple bar charts to the use of complex network analysis.

These techniques have been developed to help builders to organize the flow of construction work so as to complete the job in the optimum time and to deploy the various resources most effectively. The activities which are part of the building process have different characteristics and different relationships to other activities. Some, for example, cannot take place until others have been completed, some require time to elapse between them (for the setting of concrete for example), some can be carried on simultaneously with others. Integrating all these activities with their different characteristics can be a formidable task. Whatever the techniques used, the aims are the same and require four sets of decisions to be made:

1. identification of the various activities needed to carry out the project;
2. determination of the sequence of activities;
3. determination of the duration of each activity;
4. allocation of resources to each activity.

To arrive at his optimum programme the contractor will have to go through these planning stages several times, as each affects the others.

Identifying the activities. The content and scope of activities depends very much on the size and complexity of the project and the organization of the building firm concerned. A useful definition proposed by Skoyles and Forbes is that an activity is work that can be carried out by one gang without interruption by another: the carrying out of work of one kind requiring certain resources and time (Forbes and Skoyles, 1963). The contractor's planning department will examine the project documentation and decide on the activities needed to complete the work.

Examples of 'activities' include:

■ excavation work for foundations (Activity A);
■ cast concrete foundations (Activity B);
■ build external brick walls to first floor (Activity C).

The sequence of activities. To decide on the sequence of the activities defined. In a simple project the sequence will be very obvious and straightforward. For example the sequence of the ones described above would be Activity A → Activity B → Activity C.

In complex projects there will be many activities and probably a number of options for their sequence. It is also likely that some activities can be carried out simultaneously (in parallel) rather than one after the other (sequentially).

Duration of activities and the critical path. Having identified the activities and their relationship the next stage is to work out the duration of each. This is normally identified in weeks and days, often with probabilities attached showing most likely, optimistic and pessimistic time scales. Most computer programs incorporate the facility to reflect those three conditions by weighting them like this: most likely four times; optimistic and pessimistic, once each.

Once the durations and sequences have been assigned, it is possible to determine the 'critical path' which is defined as the longest route through the project. This is 'critical' because if any activity on that path is delayed, the whole project will be delayed; it is the longest path but it represents the shortest time in which the project can be completed. If for example a whole project had six sequential activities which took one week each and none could start before the previous one was completed, the project could not be finished under six weeks. But if one of the activities could be carried on at the same time as the others, the project could be done in five weeks; the activity carried out in parallel with others would not be on the critical path.

Allocating the resources. In allocating resources to each activity, the contractors will have to meet certain conditions.

First they have to see that there are no 'upper limit violations' of each resource. To put it simply, if they have 25 men on their labour force and 30 are required, according to a proposed programme on a particular day, then the duration assigned to that activity cannot be satisfied (Figure 12.1).

Secondly they have to see that the resource utilization is as smooth as possible; a programme which required 5 labourers on Monday, 25 on Tuesday and 15 on Wednesday would be highly inefficient.

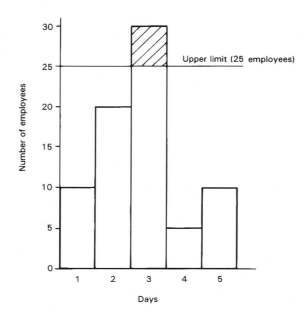

NB   Upper limit violation on day 3 – impossible to carry out
      activities unless an extra 5 employees are hired on day 3.

Figure 12.1   'Upper limit violation'.

To alleviate this sort of problem the contractor will look closely at all the activities but especially those which are carried out in parallel. Some of these activities will be not only 'non-critical' but will have 'float' attached to them; that is they will take less time than some of the critical activities going on at the same time – so their exact timing or duration can be adjusted to make the best use of labour and plant. Of course there are limits; if fewer resources are allocated to an activity so that it now takes longer than others going on in parallel, it may itself become critical.

12.3 Programming techniques

Bar or Gantt charts (so-called after their inventor Henry Lawrence Gantt one of the pioneers, with Frank Gilbreth and Frederick Taylor of 'scientific management' at the beginning of the century) are often used to carry out this planning process as they are easy to understand. They show clearly the tasks or activities to be performed, when each task can be performed and how long each takes. Figure 12.3 on page 274 shows a typical chart of the series of activities involved in building a floor slab and even before we describe its derivation, it will be immediately comprehensible.

However for complex programmes, bar charts on their own have serious limitations. To begin with it is not easy to identify specific or necessary relationships of one activity to another, whether for example they could be run in parallel or whether they must be sequential. Linked bar charts are often used to help overcome this limitation by indicating links between preceding and succeeding activities.

A further limitation is that it is difficult to manipulate the information a bar chart contains. It does not, therefore, lend itself to the use of iteration in the search for a best solution; this becomes particularly problematic at the control stage if changes occur in the construction programme as the whole bar chart will need updating.

Because of these limitations more sophisticated methods such as network analysis are often used. Network analysis is a generic term for a number of techniques such as precedence diagrams and critical path analysis, which show time relationships between activities. In its simplest form it can be done on paper, but is most effective when carried out using the now standard computer programs. The critical path method (CPM) was developed by DuPont engineering for use with their chemical plans and the PERT program (program evaluation review technique) by the US Navy for use with the Flett Ballistic Missile Weapon development program. The advantages of these and similar computer-based systems is that they allow many iterations to be made quickly and once the plan is established and the work in progress, allow control, monitoring and adjustment to take place in the most effective way.

The key to using critical path methods is the preparation of a network diagram where each line or arrow shows the activities to be performed (step 1 above – identifying the activities) and their relationship with each other, expressed by the linking nodes or circles (step 2 above – the sequence of activities).

A network diagram for the construction of a typical floor slab is shown in Figure 12.2.

Once steps 1 and 2 have been completed, step 3 can now be carried out by assigning durations to each activity; these will be assessed on the basis of the contractor's experience and possibly careful work study of similar operations on previous projects. The duration, in days allocated to each activity, is shown on the diagram and referenced in the list. The activities crossed with small double lines are on the critical path; some activities have 'float', that is they could start sooner or later. The dotted lines (so-called 'dummies') are required to complete the logic. Take activities Q and R for example (air conditioning units and false ceilings). The diagram shows that Q takes 4 days and R 5. Both have to be completed before S can start. Because R takes longer than Q at this point it is on the critical path; and we are told that Q has a one-day float – it could start up to a day after R. The node 13 is just a way of representing separately the end of activity R, which is then linked by a dummy line to 16, the end of activities Q and U.

Once this is all worked out, step 4 can be carried out and the resources allocated to provide the construction plan for the complete project.

The diagram also shows the so-called 'hammock activities' – supervision and site facilities, which are required throughout; they are often called 'indirect activities' as their costs are time-related not directly proportional to the amount of work performed in each of the direct activities.

The network diagram shown in Figure 12.2 is an 'activity on the arrow' diagram. An alternative way of representing the same information, favoured by some construction planners, is the 'precedence diagram' where activities are represented by boxes rather than lines or arrows; the boxes are then linked by lines to show their relationship to each other. However as mentioned earlier, these techniques will now almost certainly involve the use of one of the standard computer programs, which have the enormous advantage of allowing numerous iterations to be made quickly in helping the contractor to establish the best programme.

In complex projects it is likely that a number of these techniques will be used together. For example a network analysis may be used for identifying and optimizing, usually with the aid of a computer, the critical path, the resource inputs required and their costs; bar charts will then be produced as a means of effective communication of what is to be done when, especially in the site office. It is important to stress that the bar chart should

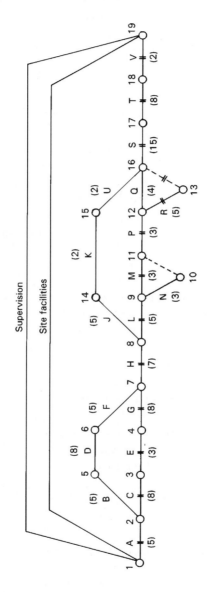

Note: 20 activities — critical path 72 days

ACTIVITY	DURATION (days)	ACTIVITY	DURATION (days)
A - Prepare slab	5	L - Internal walls	5
B - Prepare shaft and stairs	5	M - Timber frames and openings	3
C - Concrete slab	8	N - Plumbing works	3
D - Concrete shaft and stairs	8	P - Service ducts	3
E - Prepare external walls	3	Q - Air-conditioning units	4
F - Brick and block shaft	5	R - False ceilings	5
G - Concrete external walls	8	S - Plaster and paint	15
H - Brick and block ext. walls	7	T - Complete fittings	8
J - External facade	5	U - External painting	2
K - Glazing	2	V - Carpet tiles	2

Key: Critical path   ⊢——⊩➤

        Logic   2 ➤
                       ○

        Activity with
        duration (days)   (5) ——➤

        Dummy   – – – ➤

NB: 1 - A dummy is added to prove the logic
      2 - Float on activity Q = 1 day
      3 - Float on activities J, K, and L = 7 days
      4 - Hammock activities required for 72 days
         (supervision and site facilities)

Figure 12.2 Network diagram: construction of concrete floor slab.

be derived from the network analysis – not the other way round.

Bar charts alone are often used at the tender stage when the contractor has limited time to prepare his bid – perhaps up to only six weeks for a large complex project. During this stage, the contractor will prepare a 'method statement' which sets out how the project will be constructed. It will also define the main resources needed, which work is to be subcontracted and the sources of supply for the principal materials. Such a method statement will generally be established from a bar chart showing the relationships of the major activities. One of the problems of lump sum tendering is that the more sophisticated techniques such as network analysis are not used until after the contractor has been appointed. This means that the programme on which the contract is based may not represent the optimum solution and may at worst be quite inaccurate. The tender bid derived from it will then be an unsatisfactory basis on which to manage the project financially. No amount of sophistication applied too late can rectify inherently wrong initial assumptions.

The photograph of a multi-storey building under construction (not in the UK) illustrates dramatically the problems and dilemmas of programming an effective sequence of activities. Had the concrete floor slabs been designed to sustain greater dead loads, then repetitive use of expensive formwork could have been achieved by stripping as each floor level was completed and re-erecting on the completed floor slab, ready to receive the casting of the floor above. However, by keeping the formwork in place as shown in the photograph, it was probably possible to complete the building structure more quickly, as casting floor slabs will be on the critical path and less delay would be encountered waiting for concrete to achieve sufficient strength to support the casting of the floor above.

Multi-storey formwork.

MULTI-STOREY OFFICE BLOCK - BAR CHART - TYPICAL FLOOR SLAB																
Activity Description	Time (days)															Remarks
	05	10	15	20	25	30	35	40	45	50	55	60	65	70	75	
A - Prepare slabs	▨															
B - Prepare shaft and stairs		▨														
C - Concrete slab		▨▨														
D - Concrete shaft and stairs			▨▨													
E - Prepare external walls			▨													
F - Brick and block shaft walls				▨												
G - Concrete external walls				▨▨												
H - Brick and block ext. walls					▨▨											
J - External facade								▨								
K - Glazing								▨								
L - Block internal walls								▨								
M - Timber frames and openings								▨								
N - Plumbing works								▨								
P - Service ducts									▨							
Q - Air conditioning units										▨						
R - Suspended ceilings										▨						
S - Plaster and paint											▨▨▨▨					
T - Complete fittings														▨▨		
U - External painting								▨								
V - Carpet tiles															▨	
Supervision	▨▨▨▨▨▨▨▨▨▨▨▨▨▨▨▨														▨	Hammock
Site facilities	▨▨▨▨▨▨▨▨▨▨▨▨▨▨▨▨														▨	Hammock

Figure 12.3   Bar chart for floor construction.

However, as the picture shows, this option prevented the builder carrying out any work on any floor as all the space was occupied by the formwork props. This could well have led to the overall programme taking longer.

The detailed techniques of programming are dealt with in all texts on project management; architects can benefit from studying these as they are equally applicable and useful in managing the design process itself. There is no reason at all of course why architects should try to pre-empt or predict the contractor's programme. But the point to be made here is that one of the designer's priorities should be to make that programming easier not more difficult. The more complex a design is to programme, the more expensive the work is likely to be, because it may take longer, because there are more opportunities for mistakes and because it is difficult to make the best use of resources. Designing to reduce these potential problems is one aspect of buildability; the next three sections examine how the most efficient use of each of the three major types of resource can be inhibited by a failure to appreciate the specific links between the design and the construction programme.

12.4 Specific resource problems

12.4.1 The sequence of trades

If contractors were themselves to employ directly all the people with the skills needed to product a building – a situation which as we saw in Chapter 5 has rarely been normal practice in construction – and were therefore paying them on a weekly or monthly basis, they would obviously try to keep employees occupied in productive work as continuously as possible. This would be difficult if they had only one contract; carpenters may be needed to make formwork at the beginning but not again until brickwork is finished; plasterers and painters are not needed until towards the end. There will be gaps between the first fix (of electrical services, for example, the cable runs) and the second and final fixes (switches and fittings).

Although almost all contractors do in fact subcontract most work, the more employees of their own they have the more likely they are to run into the problems of providing continuity of employment and possibly paying workers for much idle time. If there are several projects, it may be possible to organize them so that each one is employing different trades at a given time and if a single project is very large, there will for a long period be continuity of work. House-builders for example, building a number of houses, can sequence the work very effectively for all trades; this is made very much easier when there are a number of houses of basically similar design on one site and the starts and finishes can be phased. But for medium-sized building firms working on a number of different sites on different types of building, each with a fixed handover date, the problems can be formidable. Contractors usually manage by juggling one scheme's timetable against another, often making decisions about deployment of their men from day to day. Even with the best planned operations some *ad hoc* decisions of this sort are inevitable; when the whole programme becomes *ad hoc* however, trouble looms.

For very large projects, the problems are of a different scale and more sophisticated means of overcoming them are needed, including the computer-based scheduling systems referred to above.

These problems of maintaining continuity of work are of course one of the reasons for the prevalence of subcontracting in the industry and hence for one of the forms of 'fragmentation' discussed earlier. By subcontracting for a fixed price particular stages or particular activities, the main contractor avoids the problems of having temporarily under-employed staff who have to be paid (and for whom he or she has legal obligations in terms of insurance, sick pay, terms of redundancy). However, the problems of co-ordination are by no means eliminated. Subcontractors may be engaged to start on specific dates, but if the programme lags behind schedule or parts of it get out of phase, it may be necessary to postpone a stage; if the subcontractor has other subsequent commitments this will create further problems and cost.

Furthermore, subcontracting raises problems of its own. The main contractor has not the same control over performance and quality as he or she might have with their own employees; there can be disagreement over specification of exactly what was required by a contract; it is not unknown for subcontracted gangs, particularly self-employed labour-only sub-contractors, to walk off a site on the offer of a better contract elsewhere.

And the basic problem of co-ordination remains; it is obviously easier for everyone concerned that subcontractors are employed for a continuous period; to employ for several separate periods, expecting them to find other work to fit in between simply pushes the problem of continuity down to the subcontractors themselves.

Designers cannot of course take all these factors into account as they develop their proposals; they may not know which contractor will be building the project or even what sort of organization the contractor might have. But designers can certainly keep in mind the potential cost implications of a design which ignores the need for logical sequencing of trades, for continuity of activities. This means that they continually need to ask themselves the question, as the design develops, 'How and by which trades is this going to be built?'

12.4.2 Plant

Many of the points made about continuity of employment of labour apply equally to the continuity of plant utilization. And the circumstances that lead to widespread subcontracting are similar to those that lead to contractors hiring rather than buying most forms of large-scale equipment. A plant hire firm in busy times might be able to keep its equipment busy for quite a high percentage of its useful life by hiring it out for short periods to many different contractors. A builder who might only be able to use a particular piece of equipment intermittently would not find its purchase economically worth while as we saw in Chapter 6. In fact the labour and plant issues are directly linked. A large contractor in the north-west of England, which owns a considerable amount of equipment, is finding at present (mid 1990s) that it can hire plant, with operators, more cheaply than it can use its own plant with its own employees; this is because the accounting for 'own resources' must incorporate the overheads, while an outsider might be prepared to cut prices to virtually direct cost (or even less) to get the business.

There is, as in the case of labour, no question of a designer being able or expected to predict the exact deployment of machinery or equipment that is going to be required to construct the design. That is essentially the contractor's or project manager's task. But consideration given at the design stage to the probable equipment requirements can help the contractor use plant efficiently.

Much standard machinery, as already described in Chapter 6, is versatile and will be used at all stages of the programme; this is true for example of dumper trucks, fork-lift trucks, concrete mixers, and all the small hand tools. Some, however, is highly specialized and may be used at only one time; there is probably going to be no problem in hiring such equipment as required. Some large-scale plant however may be expensive to hire, can be hired only for fixed periods (in days, weeks or months), takes time to deliver and install and may be difficult to locate on site. The cost penalty for using this sort of plant inefficiently (for example by operating it for relatively short periods separated by long gaps), may be very high indeed.

One simple example of the sort of cost implications is given by Ian Ferguson in his book *Buildability in Practice:* a house designed with a rendered finish to the walls at first-floor level will need scaffolding to be left erected long after it has been finished with for the brickwork. The decision to use render may still be taken but it should be taken in the knowledge of the extra cost implied not only by the rendering work itself but the 'unemployed' time of the scaffolding.

A more complex and more significant problem is ensuring that the best use can be made of any necessary cranes, particularly if they are the large tower types. The problems are fairly self-evident – but need to be borne in mind at the design stage; they include:

1. ensuring access to the appropriate part of the site is possible – and possible at the right time;
2. ensuring that the crane can cope with maximum reaches and heights required as well as be used for lower levels and shorter reaches;
3. ensuring minimum number of moves on site;
4. ensuring maximum possible continuity of use;
5. ensuring it is required for the minimum possible time.

12.4.3 Organizing the materials

The materials, components and pre-assembled parts of the building have to be acquired, delivered to site, possibly stored, formed or mixed and then incorporated appropriately into the building. So much is obvious. What is not so obvious is how complex and fraught with problems this process can be.

If all the materials could simply be acquired at the beginning and used when needed the whole building project would lose many of its difficulties. But that is not usually possible for a number of reasons. First, there is simply not room on many sites to store the materials required (and leave space for the building operation to take place efficiently). Secondly, some materials will deteriorate if left exposed to the weather. Thirdly, all materials are vulnerable to theft and vandalism, even when security arrangements are made. (It is a problem on some sites even when materials are built in; at a site in the north-west known to the authors whole kitchens were removed overnight after they had been installed.) Fourthly, there is a financing problem. Though some suppliers, including building merchants, will allow periods of free credit, they may also allow discounts for prompt payment. (The credit is therefore not in reality free at all; it costs the difference between the full price and the discounted price.)

Contractors will have to use their own funds or borrow money to buy most materials; they will not be paid until the work incorporating the material has been completed and payment can be quite a long time, even without buying earlier than necessary. The consequent cash flow problems are discussed in more detail below.

Because therefore materials cannot be simply acquired at the beginning and stored, their purchase and delivery has to be matched with the building's progress. For some materials this presents little problem; ready-mixed concrete can be ordered almost instantaneously; cement is readily available; brick commons can be supplied from stock as can any size of the commoner softwoods except at the highest peaks of the building cycle.

But for others there are varying 'lead times', that is periods required between order and delivery; these are now reported in the professional journals, but the reports only give averages and show the situation at one point in time (Figure 12.4). The position can change quite rapidly. And for specially designed components the lead times may be very long indeed.

Further materials may not be easily or cheaply available at all in the form that the designers request. One of the very common complaints that the authors heard from builders when discussing these issues is that architects are unrealistic in their expectations and often have little idea of what is available and in what form. One very obviously helpful decision for the designer to take is to use standard sizes wherever possible. On the other hand manufacturers are often keen to work with architects to produce particular components for particular functions or even to develop new materials as was the case with the Nottingham Tax Office referred to above

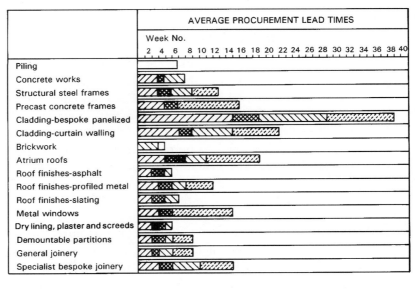

Figure 12.4 Lead times for various materials and compoments, mid 1994.
Sources: *Building*.

where the load-bearing brick piers were prefabricated to the architects' design. At Glyndebourne, similarly, the brickwork arches were specifically researched and made to Hopkins' design by brickmakers, Irvine Whitlock (*Architects' Journal*, 13 April 1994). But for this sort of collaboration to be successful it is necessary to allow a longer time than is normally available between the initial conception and the building stage when the component is required.

Architects need therefore to be aware of the likely supply position for the materials they specify; builders and surveyors need to be alert to warn architects of possible problems so that alternative solutions may if necessary be designed at an early stage. Otherwise, there will be delays (which of course will affect not just the particular stage but all subsequent stages), there will be waste and there may be unsatisfactory results. All these imply higher costs than necessary and sometimes considerably so.

As in the case of plant and labour, it is not always possible or desirable for the architect to predict in precise detail the programming implications of the design; but all designs can be checked against the information available to ensure that miracles are not expected (or not too many at least) from the contractor.

12.5 Cash flow

So far, the argument of this chapter has been that one source of unnecessary cost, the mismatch between the design's requirements and the actual possible deployment of men, machines and materials, can be reduced if these issues are considered at the design stage. But there is another aspect of the contractor's programme that the architect and quantity surveyor need to appreciate, if only to understand that a contractor's hostile response to requests for changes may not simply be the result of cussedness, but the consequence of the fact that often they can seriously affect his or her cash position, even if in the end he or she will be fully compensated.

Contractors are usually paid on the basis of monthly certification of the value of work completed (a tradition which the Latham Report recommends should change). They themselves however are incurring expenditure continually. Contracting firms, particularly the smaller and medium-sized, which are the majority, generally do not have substantial cash reserves, or working capital. They are seldom in a position to finance a great deal of work from their own resources until they receive payment from the building owner or client. They have instead frequently to rely on some form of credit, loans, overdrafts, credit from builders' merchants and materials suppliers. If they are continually spending more than they are receiving, that is their cash flow is negative, they will be incurring interest charges on top of the actual cost of paying for materials, labour and plant.

And if they are forced into deep and continuous debt, the survival of the business can soon be threatened; more contractors fail through high levels of current debt than through inability to achieve a profit.

'Cash-flow' can be defined as the net difference between the construction expenditure and income relating to the project at any point in time during the construction.

The build-up of costs **incurred** by a contractor during a project can be represented by a simple graph (expenditure against time) such as those shown in Figure 12.5a. The curve is shown as S-shaped because the value of work completed tends to be relatively small during the first stages, then work accumulates much more quickly as more tasks can be performed simultaneously; finally there is a tapering off towards the end.

However the curve may be steep or shallow, depending on whether the contractor starts all the non-critical activities as soon as possible or as late as possible; the two extremes are shown in Fig. 12.5a as forming an 'envelope'; provided the contractor keeps within the two, the project will be completed on time and within total budget; he will select a particular profile as the basis of his plan. For the sake of the present discussion assume the relevant curve is C1.

The rate at which contractors actually **spend** may not follow the same profile as the rate at which they **incur** costs. For example labour will be paid weekly in arrears, supervisory staff, monthly; material and plant usually 14 days in arrears or maybe more. A second S curve can therefore be drawn representing the accumulation of actual expenditure. In Figure 12.5b, curve C1 is reproduced from 12.5a (representing the costs incurred) and curve E represents the contractor's expenditure.

To complicate matters further, two more S curves can be drawn representing the build up of 'value' of the work completed; one represents the full cost of the work including overheads and profit (curve V1); the difference between the costs curve and this value curve represents the contractor's mark-up; at the end of the contract V1 will be equal to the contract price. However there is another definition of value during the contract, the valuation made monthly by the client's QS, which is based on the contract bill of quantities (V2 in Figure 12.5d). This is particularly important, for on it are based the stage payments made to the contractor. As will be explained further in Chapter 13, the bill does not represent accurately the cost of real resources used over time; contractors well aware of this may have 'front-loaded' the bill, that is claimed that early stages cost more than they actually do, to ensure they get their money as soon as possible. There will therefore be a discrepancy between the actual value of the work done and the value as represented by the bill, during construction.

There are therefore four possible S curves which show the build-up of costs, value of work done and contractor's expenditure. As **payments** to the contractor are made in monthly stages, these can be shown on a cumulative graph as a stepped line, Y in Figure 12.5d.

Putting all the curves on one graph leads to confusion so Figure 12.5e includes only three:

■ V2 – the S curve representing **cumulative values** as derived from the bill; this is the basis on which payments to the contractor are calculated;

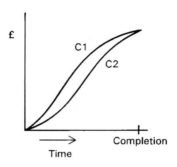

Curve C1 : Costs incurred if all activities
　　　　　 started at earliest possible time
Curve C2 : Costs incurred if all activities
　　　　　 started at latest possible time

(a) Costs incurred 'S' curve envelope

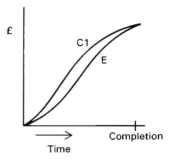

Curve C1 : Costs incurred
Curve E　 : Contractors' expenditure

(b) Costs incurred and contractors'
　　expenditure 'S' curves

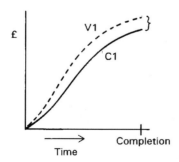

Curve V1 : Value of work completed
Curve C1 : Costs incurred

(c) Value of work completed and
　　cost incurred 'S' curves

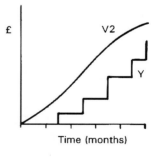

V2 : Valuation based on contract
　　 bill of quantities
Y : Actual payments to contractor
　　 from contract bill of quantities

(d) Value profile based on contract
　　bill of quantities, early stage only

Figure 12.5

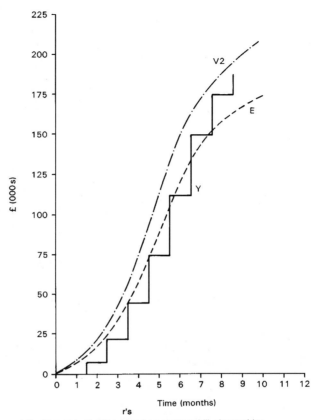

V2 : Forecast valuation based on contract bill of quantities
E : Forecast contractor's expenditure
Y : Forecast actual payments to contractor from contract bill of quantities
    (based on a 2-week delay and deduction of retention after monthly valuation)

(e) Value profiles based on contract bill of quantities together with contractor's
    expenditure

Figure 12.5

- ■ E – the S curve representing the **actual expenditure** by the contractor;
- ■ Y – the stepped line shows the actual **payments made to** the contractor.

The figure on the vertical axis assumes a contract worth £210 000, completed over 10 months. (Fig. 12.5f shows an enlarged section of 12.5e.) So after 4 months for example, the estimated value of the work done is approximately £75 000, the contractor has spent £60 000, but he has received only £45 000 (which represents the amount of work completed earlier as valued according to the BQ). He therefore has received £15 000

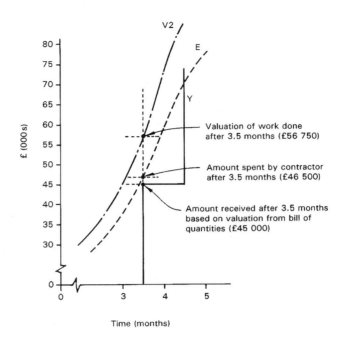

Valuation of work done
after 3.5 months (£56 750)

Amount spent by contractor
after 3.5 months (£46 500)

Amount received after 3.5 months
based on valuation from bill of
quantities (£45 000)

Time (months)

(f) Enlarged section of Figure 12.5(e)

Figure 12.5   Cost value and expenditure curves.

less than he has spent; this money, his working capital, has to be found from his own resources or borrowed.

Now consider the graph as a whole (Figure 12.5e) it can be seen that the contractor remains in this position right through to month 8; throughout the whole period his cash flow is negative; and if he has had to borrow, he is also incurring interest charges (even if using his own resources, there is an opportunity cost – the cost of interest he could have been earning).

What is striking is that even if everything goes well and no unforeseen expenditure is incurred, the contractor is continually in the red (or more formally has a negative cash flow) – until the end of the project and this is through no fault of his own; it is the consequence of the way payments are made in the industry. If clients fail to pay on time, the contractor's position can rapidly become serious. This constant pressure on the contractor is something which quantity surveyors and architects need to understand and have some sympathy with; they are employed as consultants to act in the client's interest, which may appear to be to delay payment as long as possible. But if this leads to or contributes to a contractor's financial failure, everybody loses; and the ultimate cost of the project will almost certainly escalate.

Contractors of course have strategies for mitigating the problems caused by this system. The main one as mentioned above is to 'front-load' the costs. Contractors can increase their unit rates for work carried out early in the project such as excavation and foundation work, decreasing unit rates for work occurring later in the construction process, such as finishes and fittings. Therefore it may not always be clear whether the contractor's view of the build-up of costs is in fact a more realistic one that is implied by the bill, or whether it represents some degree of manipulation.

Another strategy adopted by contractors is 'pay when paid', that is, pay subcontractors only when contractors have received payment from the employer; in terms of Figure 12.4e, this in effect means they shift their expenditure curve as far to the right as possible, or at the extreme convert it into a stepped line following their own income pattern. This practice of course simply puts the problem onto someone else; it does not eliminate it. The practice is now banned in government contracts (*Building*, 30 July 1994, p. 10) and the Latham recommends it be outlawed generally.

Although such strategies as front-loading enable contractors to keep their own costs down and hence able to make more competitive bids, there are dangers in the practice for the building owner. Should the contractor go into liquidation during the construction process it is possible that substantial over-payments will have been made.

Throughout the construction, the builder will be observing very closely the project plan and the selected S curve to establish whether the work is ahead or behind schedule and is over or under budget compared with the income he or she has received from the building owner. If major variances occur then the contractor should be able to adjust the plan to enable the project programme to be put back on course or if not at least the consequences of the deviations will be known.

It is changes in and interruptions to the original project programme that cause most contractual disputes and claims in the building industry. That is because frequently the contractor will claim that the design team has created the necessity for such changes, through design variations and delays in providing information. The designers on the other hand may argue that it is the contractor's own inefficiency that caused the difficulties. Many of these problems can be alienated by very simple measures – which are obvious but ignored with remarkable frequency. For example, if contractors produce a clear programme of what is to be done before they commence on site and if clear records are kept on bad weather, breakdowns of plant, delayed information from the architect, disputes might be more quickly resolved and less frequently incurred. But that is probably a counsel of perfection.

However, it is inevitable that the design solution will have a major influence on the cash flow and how much the contractor will have to borrow in order to finance the project. The contractor is bound to try to create a positive cash flow as early as possible so that the project becomes self-funding. The designers and quantity surveyors are doing their client no real service by making this difficult to achieve.

So, for cash-flow reasons as well as elimination of unnecessary extra costs, the design team should aim to produce a design which commits a gradual build-up of producing a maximum resource commitment over the middle two-thirds of the project construction phase and a gradual reduction of resources towards the end of the project. The design should not demand intermittent resource utilization and should try to facilitate continuous rather than intermittent use of subcontractors, especially those selected by the design team. This is particularly so with subcontractors concerned with mechanical and electrical services. Intermittent use of such specialist subcontractors complicates the programming and makes cash-flow control much more difficult for the main contractor.

12.6 Conclusion: buildability as a general issue

An awareness of and response to the problems of effective deployment of resources and the problems of cash-flow management are themselves only part of that sensitivity to the contractor's operational programme which can help to ensure the buildability of a design. Architects also need to consider the technicalities of constructing individual elements of a building and, often a critical area of failure, of the junctions and interfaces between elements and sub-assemblies. It is true that this kind of knowledge about traditional building methods is part of the architect's stock in trade and that the development of a thorough understanding of basic construction technology is a fundamental part of the architectural student's training. But nevertheless the complaints from builders that the realities of detailed construction are often misunderstood are too common to be ignored.

It is particularly when new methods are being tried, when new designs are developed, that difficulties arise. The problems come from two directions; the architect, while believing fully in the feasibility of a particular design feature, and having in fact designed it to be buildable, may not have fully appreciated the range of skills needed for its effective execution and in particular may not have matched the design requirement with the capacity of the particular contractor to supply the necessary skills. The contractor on the other hand may not be sufficiently flexible to adapt his or her approach to the requirements of the design. The only way around this is of course better consultation at the early design stage.

Unfortunately, the competitive tender system as it is operated in many contexts today not only discourages but does not even allow the necessary fertilization of ideas at an early stage. This is one of the reasons for adopting a procurement method which brings a designer and contractor together before the design has been determined in detail.

But failing this still all too rare collaboration at the beginning between designer and builder, there are many ways in which architects can help to check and reinforce their own awareness of the production implications of each level of their design decision-making.

In his *Practical Buildability*, based on the work done for the CIRIA report, *Buildability: an Assessment*, Stewart Adams suggests a check-list of 'buildability factors' and gives examples illustrating each one and their combination in various circumstances. Many of these points have been discussed above, but his list is an excellent summary and *aide mémoire*.

1. Investigate thoroughly – site and other conditions which might affect progress
2. Consider access at the design stage
3. Consider storage at the design stage
4. Design for minimum time below ground
5. Design for early enclosure
6. Use suitable materials
7. Design for the skills available
8. Design for simple assembly
9. Plan for maximum repetition/standardization
10. Maximize the use of plant
11. Allow for sensible tolerances
12. Allow a practical sequence of operations
13. Avoid return visits by trades
14. Plan to avoid damage to work by subsequent operations
15. Design for safe construction
16. Communicate clearly

(Quoted with permission from Adams (1989) *Practical Buildability*).

FOR FURTHER STUDY

1 Recommended reading

The 3-volume teaching package *Designing for Production* (including slides, lecturers' notes and many worked examples) published by the Building Research Establishment (1994) is probably the best source of specific examples other than lecturers' own experience.

Stewart Adams book, quoted above, also gives some detailed case studies. However these and other books on buildability concentrate on the design and construction of buildable details rather than the relationship between the design and the building process as a whole. Harper, *Building: the Process and the Product* (1990), Chapters 5 and 6 however does look at these general issues. Other books on project management which give insights into different aspects include: Harris and McCaffer's *Modern Construction Management*, Fryer's *The Practice of Construction Management* (1990), Walker's *Project Management in Construction* (1989) and Cooke's *Construction Planning Case Studies* (1985).

2 Exercises

a Using the example in the chapter or any other set of reasonable assumptions work through the monthly cash flow situation of a contractor, calculating the maximum working capital (or loan) he will require.
b Why might the S curves of cost be likely to have different shapes for different types of building?

3 Discussion or essay questions

a Why does the Latham Report recommend the outlawing of a 'pay when paid' policy?
b Discuss the major buildability issues to be considered in the design of a multi-storey office block with air conditioning to be erected on city centre site.
c Buildability is the concern of the builder not the designer. Discuss.
d Why should S cost curves vary in shape for different types of construction project?
e Explain why interim valuations based on the bill of quantities may not give an accurate profile of the work carried out by the contractor.

4 Project

Identify the major stages and their probable durations for the construction of a two-storey, detached, three-bedroom house. Prepare a network diagram for the construction; explain why it is necessary to match the rate of working of the various gangs involved.

<table>
<tr><td>

13

</td><td>

Cost prediction – science or guesswork?

</td></tr>
</table>

13.1 Introduction

Chapter 3 outlined a simple and conventional way of analysing a building's cost and showed that there are different, but equally valid, ways of defining the total cost of a building, depending on the perspective from which the problem is being viewed (for example that of the contractor or the client). It was also argued there that the analysis of costs by element, based on bills of quantities, cannot reflect truly the ways costs are actually incurred or generated, mainly because it ignored the interaction of one element with another and take insufficient account of the actual **process** of construction, which consists of bringing resources together under particular conditions.

In Part II, the economic factors affecting the prices and availability of the major resources were examined. Part III explored how design decisions take account of the relative costs of different ways of combining those resources in determining the materials to be specified, the form of the building, the structural system to be used and the way the internal environment is to be controlled.

In the last chapter it has been argued that if design intentions are to be realized effectively, designers need to take account of the process of production and contractors need to programme and control that process successfully.

This chapter takes up again the issue raised at the end of Chapter 3, the relationship between the expected costs of a building at the design stage, as estimated by the design team an the actual costs as incurred by the builder; for however carefully the initial designs are costed and however buildable the design, there is still scope for major discrepancies between estimates and actual cost if the basis of the cost analyses and the system of cost planning and control do not reflect the realities of construction.

The chapter looks in a little more detail than Chapter 3 at cost prediction, planning and control methods, identifying both their very real virtues but also the theoretical and practical difficulties to which they give rise. There is a very brief discussion of some of the attempts made in the past to overcome the deficiencies and create a better representation of construction costs at the design stage. The chapter proposes recommend-ations for improving the compatibility of information carried by the design documents and the information required for construction. A better understanding of the interaction between those two may help designers, surveyors and contractors to achieve the combination of cost and quality which all clients, building owners and building users are looking for.

13.2 Current methods of cost estimation, planning and control

The central question asked at the beginning of Chapter 1 was: how can all the parties engaged in the building process ensure that maximum value for money, in all senses of value, is achieved – or approximated as closely as possible – in a world of great uncertainty? The thrust of the argument throughout has been that the issue is one at least partly of mutual understanding, whereas what the system often seems to produce at present is maximum conflict.

Yet however hard everybody tries, however sophisticated systems become, there remain two critical difficulties which are inherent in the process of building itself and which explain why accurate cost reduction has always been such an intractable problem. The first difficulty is that a really accurate estimate of a building's cost cannot be made until the details of the designs are known – except in the case of standard repeated building types. However, the client wanting to have a building constructed needs to know how much it is going to cost before committing him or herself to the contract and its detailed design. The second difficulty is that the information about the building as presented by the designers and analysed by the quantity surveyors does not relate directly enough to the process of construction as perceived by the contractor.

The techniques developed over the years to overcome these central difficulties may be criticized as relatively crude but the fact that a hundred years of ingenuity has ultimately failed to come up with a perfect solution perhaps indicates the depth of the problem. With the development of integrated computer models and more co-ordinated information systems, success may be nearer, but it will still require mutual understanding and considerable determination on the part of all the people involved if any real advance is to be made.

13.2.1 The initial estimate

The cost-prediction and cost-planning techniques which have been developed to try to make the best use of information available at each stage in the development of the design. Figure 13.1 derived from the diagram by Ferry and Brandon (Ferry and Brandon, 1970) represents neatly the relationship between the different stages of design and the cost procedures required.

At the very beginning, even before the brief itself has been formulated, clients may be approaching their decision from one of two different directions (or from somewhere in between). First they may have a clear idea of the building required, in terms of its function and size, and need to know how much it is likely to cost; having been given a rough estimate they can then adjust their expectations of the buildings specification – or

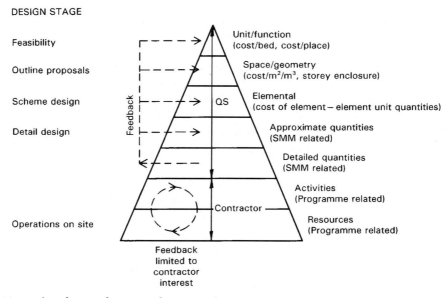

Figure 13.1 Hierarchy of cost information for use at design stage.
Source: Adapted from Ferry and Brandon (1970), p.1030

perhaps look again at the budget to see if it can be raised. Examples of this sort of situation might be a factory owner wishing to expand production by a certain amount; a commercial concern increasing staff by a known number; a veterinary surgeon requiring premises with specific functions and a specific number of staff.

Alternatively, a client may have a very firmly fixed budget and want to know what kind of building can be expected for the money – perhaps also what trade-offs are possible between, say, quality of finish and size. Examples here include a local authority education director needing to build a primary school but allocated a fixed capital sum (or borrowing limit).

Obviously estimates made at this stage cannot take account of any specific characteristics the design of the putative building might have. There are ways though as we saw in Chapter 3 of using information about similar building types to make some sensible estimates. Three techniques are commonly used:

- estimates based on function or performance;
- estimates based on size or space;
- estimates based on the geometry of the proposed building.

Function – or performance related. This is extremely simple and can be used when minimal information is available; it is not however applicable where the function of a proposed building is new, unique or its proposed design very different from the conventional. The principle is to use information available on other buildings of similar function to identify some kind of unit cost – for example cost per student for a college, cost per bedspace for a hospital, the population to be served by a library.

Size or space related. With this technique the cost per square metre of buildings of a similar sort are used as the basic data, as discussed in Chapter 3; the data are adjusted for time and location by the use of the indices published by the BCIS. A slightly more sophisticated version is to identify the areas for various uses within the building (teaching, circulation etc.), develop separate estimates for each area and create an overall estimate.

Geometry related. The problem with the first two techniques is that they take no account of the building shape in plan or section, which as discussed in Chapter 9 is a significant determinant of cost. One method of overcoming this problem was known as the 'storey enclosure method' (see Ferry and Brandon, *op. cit.*) – but now more complex modelling of shape and size is possible with computers. However before any model of this sort can be used, design proposals have to have been developed in some detail.

Although there are no alternatives to some sort of approximate estimating before the design is developed, there is a real and perhaps unnecessary problem which is imported into the whole cost-control process at this early stage. Each of the techniques produces a single-figure estimate; such a figure becomes quickly fixed in the minds of clients, finance providers, designers and surveyors. It would probably be much more sensible, though more difficult and costly, to present the early estimates as a range of probabilities, showing the sort of features or circumstances which would tend to push costs up or down.

13.2.2. The cost plan

Nevertheless, using these methods, together in many cases with the in-house expertise of the design or QS practice (which might have experience in a particular field), a budget will be determined as the brief is consolidated. This should happen at Stage C, the Outline Proposals Stage of the RIBA plan of work (see Figure 2.3 above). Then the next stage of the design and control process can commence: the production of the cost plan.

The cost plan serves two important purposes:

- ■ to confirm the budget already set;
- ■ to allow the distribution of costs within the various functional elements to be made and to ensure that the distribution is appropriate for the needs of the building. For example, it would not be sensible to specify an expensive floor finish with a life of fifty years and a low-cost roofing material designed for ten years in a building with a designed 0life of twenty years. No architect would consciously specify such obviously inconsistent specifications, but at a more subtle level careful cost planning can throw up the same type of incompatibility.

In principle, the production of a cost plan is quite straightforward, although in practice it needs judgement and experience.

The procedure uses, as a basic data source, cost analyses of other similar buildings, but because every building is unique (if only in its location), there is no exact comparison. Ideally, if we are designing a three-storey 1500 m^2 air-conditioned office block in London for a major banking organization, then what is needed is an elemental cost analysis for a three-storey 1500 m^2 air-conditioned office block in London built as recently as possible. Usually all that can be done is to select the nearest match in as many respects as possible and then make suitable adjustments.

Once the relevant analyses have been selected, cost targets can be established for each element; that is the amount of expenditure likely to be required for each element can be determined and used as an indicator of the cost-effectiveness of that part of the proposed design (see again Figure 13.1). For example, if the floor finishes for a building of that sort usually cost £8 per m^2 but the floor costs of the proposed building work out at £15 per m^2, that at least raises questions which the designer and client has to consider: reduce that specification, save money elsewhere, increase the budget (or hope for the best, leave things as they are and trust the additional cost will get lost somewhere?).

The order of establishing targets will depend on the sequence of information being produced by the architect but clearly the more important elements such as substructure and superstructure should be considered first, as considerable additional work will be required should they be changed at a late stage. For example, changes in the external wall geometry and specification in terms of whether, for example, it is to be load-bearing or not, will have a major effect on nearly all the remaining elements. On the other hand, changes in the internal floor finishes will have little influence on any of the other elements.

The process of establishing a cost plan is based on three separate adjustments to the source data, that is the information derived from cost analyses of similar buildings.

Quantitative adjustments. This is solely a measure of how much of the particular element there is. Initially the allocation of costs for each element will be based on its cost per square metre of floor area as this is the only information available from the base cost analyses.

However many elements have little relationship to floor area in terms of the quantity required. While floor and ceiling finishes are directly related to floor area, for example, wall finishes and external walls are not.

As the design develops and the geometry of the building begins to firm up it is possible to use **element unit quantities** from the base cost analyses to establish a cost target for each element of the proposed building. These element unit quantities are the actual amounts of the element used, such as the area of a wall in square metres, or the number of windows; these can then be multiplied by the **element unit rate** (i.e. the actual cost per square metre of wall or cost per window) to give an expected total cost for the element – the total cost of the walls or windows.

Time and location adjustments. As costs change over time and can also vary widely in different parts of the country at the same time, the figures derived from cost analyses for each element have to be adjusted for both time and location. The basic principle of such adjustments – by applying the relevant published indices – has already been explained in Chapter 3:

Qualitative adjustments. This is the most difficult adjustment to make as it is not based on objective data. The uniqueness of each building means that there can be wide differences in specification between the building being designed and the ones being used as the sources of cost analyses. Not all these differences will be identifiable from the published information and some informed guesses might be necessary.

The cost targets established in this way should confirm the budget established at the feasibility stage. If this is not the case then the design team must re-appraise the design and make what adjustments are necessary to match the cost plan to the budget. This can be an iterative – and creative – process, but cannot go on for long as a firm costed solution has to be established by the end of Stage D, the Scheme Design stage of the RIBA plan of work; after that stage there should be no more changes to the brief, otherwise the design team will be involved in much abortive work.

Appendix 3 shows an extract from a typical cost plan.

13.2.3 The cost check

As the design moves into the detailed stage and final decisions are made, a system of cost-checking is used to confirm or not the cost targets set in the cost plan. This is done using approximate quantities, as the design is sufficiently developed for the building economist to measure the quantities of the elements and because the specification is determined, derive an appropriate unit rate or rates for the various constructions making up the elements. Approximate quantities are used as detailed quantities based on the Standard Method of Measurement are time-consuming and therefore costly to prepare – and they achieve little increase in accuracy.

This cost-checking process is essential as it will confirm whether or not the elemental cost targets are realistic. If this is not confirmed the design proposal may have to be modified accordingly.

Finally, when the targets in the cost plan have been validated, the design team can move to the preparation of production information and the Bill of Quantities as a basis for seeking tenders.

Once the tenders have been returned and stage H (tender action) is complete, the winning tender should, if the design cost-control process has been effectively carried out, equate with the budget established during the Feasibility and Outline proposals stages.

The priced bill of quantities can now be analysed to see how well it accords with the cost targets set in the cost plan and of course will itself become an elemental cost analysis to be added to the database for future use by building economists.

As Brandon and Ferry point out, the whole of this process is based on a particular model of the building costs – a model which relates costs to elements (Ferry and Brandon, 1970). There are other ways of modelling costs which have been proposed to overcome the basic deficiencies of the elemental method and to make cost information available more quickly and more accurately. None of them has yet made a significant impact on the actual practice of cost estimation planning and control – though regression models are used by the Department of Education and elsewhere and important though the ideas are, we discuss them no further here.

13.3 The fundamental problem restated

Despite the advances made in modelling techniques and the use of microcomputers for assessing alternatives more quickly, it can still be argued that the issues which reflect the real costs of buildings are not fully taken account of in current approaches to building economics. And the reason is that already identified in Chapter 3. Put (relatively) simply it is **that the sources of cost information, primarily generated through the use of bills of quantities reflect the product rather than the process of construction**.

This detachment of the two is indicated by the closed circle at the bottom of Figure 13.1.

The bills of quantities and the Standard Method of Measurement (now in its seventh edition for the building industry) use units of finished work in the main to convey costs rather than identifying the resources needed to achieve the finished work. For example a description in a bill of quantities might be:

One brick wall in common bricks in English bond in cement mortar . . . 100 m²

However it is not the wall which generates the cost but those resources which make up the wall – the bricks, the labour, the mortar and perhaps some plant.

Furthermore the location of the element in the building is ignored. To take an extreme example, in a multi-storey structure it is obvious that it will cost more to cast the concrete floor slabs at the top of the building than those at the bottom (see Figure 9.15 for confirmation of this). Under the Standard Method of Measurement, the floor slabs would be aggregated and simply classified as 'concrete in floor slabs'. This might cause no problem if there are no changes in the design during the construction stage, as the costs will be averaged out, but if there are, the cost implications of such changes are difficult to judge.

More fundamentally, there is mis-match between the way design is represented in the bill of quantities and the contractor's approach to planning and controlling the cost of construction; the contractor will attempt to identify the various activities and their sequence, the time required for each activity and the various resources needed.

The information in the bills of quantities does not help the contractor directly to establish his construction programme. At best this is a considerable inconvenience and liable to lead to errors given the limited time the contractor has to prepare his tender bid. However at worst, it means that the contractor is essentially building an entirely different cost model for his or her own purposes and as pointed out Chapter 12, the payments made to the contractor on the recommendation of the quantity surveyor, usually in arrears at monthly intervals, will not be compatible with the cash flow profile generated by the contractor through his or her construction programme.

This was recognized in the interim Latham Report which, after referring to doubts by clients that such monthly payments are the best way to ensure satisfactory progress on contracts, went on to say that there was increased interest in negotiating agreed stages of work before the start of the contract, with payments being made when these stages are complete (Latham, 1993).

The two fundamental difficulties in using bills as the basis of cost models are, then: first the real cost generators, the resources, are not identified and secondly the unit of finished work represents an amalgamation of resources which are not all subject to the same variables. Both difficulties have been recognized and changes made in the SMM rules of measurement to allow certain resources to be identified separately.

The initiative for this came from civil engineering where, because of the many changes often required to the design during construction, as a result of the level of uncertainty in such projects, the principle of 'method related charges' was established.

This helped to determine the values of changes occurring on site by recognizing that certain resources are not directly related to quantities of work done, but to their utilization on site, the time period for which they are used and the cost of their installation and removal; resources in other words with high fixed costs, such as tower cranes. Sometimes the initial installation of fixed equipment can be extremely expensive. For a large construction project in Riyadh, Saudi Arabia, a tower crane was brought from Germany – a considerable fixed cost to be accounted for.

As has been shown in earlier chapters, however, the bill retains its prominence in the UK and there are good reasons, some of which have already been discussed. Three of these should be re-emphasized here.

■ It does help communication between designers and contractors; a description such as 'reinforced in-situ concrete floor slabs, 150–300 mm thick 50 m^3 immediately conveys what is required. Had the bill stated '1000 kg of cement, 2000 kg of fine aggregate and 4000 kg of coarse aggregate, with labour and mixing plant etc.' it would not be very helpful.

■ The identification of specific resources by designers is difficult and may be impossible; the number of bricks in a wall may be calculable but designers cannot be expected to work out the amount of labour required.

■ The various editions of the standard methods used are produced by groups of experts representing both designers and contractors; they have general support in the industry and are recognized as an important element in the financial management of building projects.

The dissatisfaction with the limitations in the use of bills of quantities, together with poor co-ordination of project information, has been expressed for many years and a number of improvements and alternative approaches put forward. Some have actually been implemented.

13.4 Improvements and proposals for reform

13.4.1 Research into Site Management and the Building Industry Code

During the late 1960s and early 1970s the County Architects Department at Nottingham County Council developed what was known as the Research into Site Management Project (Swain, 1968, 1972).

The principle was that the design staff not only designed the building, but were also directly responsible for its construction. One conclusion they came to after running this project for a number of years was that bills of quantities were irrelevant to the needs of planning and controlling the project on site.

RSM proved very useful in teaching designers about the problems of buildability and the problems associated with general contracting. Unfortunately the scheme was eventually abandoned owing to government legislative changes, aimed at reducing unfair leverage by local authorities. At the same time, the County Council was experimenting with improving data co-ordination and information flow between those involved in the building process. They were forerunners in the development of the use of computers to aid the production of bills of quantities and their subsequent manipulation to provide cost information for various purposes. They developed the Building Industry Code, which did allow cost information to be assembled both for use in design cost control and for the process of construction on site, by facilitating the derivation of construction activities.

Their approach relied on the identification of 'features'* which provided the essential link between the computer needs of design cost control and the dynamic needs of construction itself.

Unfortunately the approach still relied on the rules of the SMM to describe and quantify the building work and therefore retained all the inherent problems identified earlier in this chapter; it was eventually abandoned after attempts were made to apply it to the RSM projects discussed above.

13.4.2 The operational bill

This was devised by the Building Research Station in 1961 under the guidance of two of its researchers, Forbes and Skoyles and attempted to model the bill of quantities to the way the construction work is carried out, thus providing the basis of construction planning and control (Forbes and Skoyles, 1963).

The approach relied on the design team establishing a series of activities and presenting them in the form of a precedence diagram as an integral feature of the project documentation.

Material and labour resources were then presented within each defined activity or operation in the bill of quantities, material resources being presented separately in their normal purchasing units. The labour resource was presented as an omnibus activity against the particular item to be carried out. The remaining resources of plant and management were allowed for within the management section of the bill of quantities (compatible with the Preliminaries section of any normal SMM based bill of quantities).

A further advantage of the approach was that a degree of data co-ordination was provided in that the drawings were presented in operational terms compatible with the bill of quantities which in turn was intended to provide the basis of planning and control for the contractor. The approach failed for the following reasons.

- It required the complete design solution in order to enable the detailed planning of activities and their sequence to be carried out.
- The skills of planning and programming the construction of a building lie with the contractor and the design team was not in a position to decide the activities and their sequence.
- The use of an 'activity' as a basic unit was not compatible with the well-established design cost control procedures discussed earlier in the chapter. An activity tends to be unique to a particular building project and therefore not a useful basis for comparison – the prerequisite of traditional design cost control.

*Feature was defined as a subdivision of an element representing the lowest stable functional attribute of an element, e.g. element: external wall; features: non-structural, structural (CLASP Building Industry Code Onward Office Trust 1969, Table 5).

■ Contractors were reluctant to adopt alternative tendering techniques; unfamiliarity and the greater effort needed would increase their costs – with no greater guarantee of securing a contract. As a result, the operational bill was not welcomed by those for whom it was intended to have direct benefit – the contractors.
■ Similarly it required more effort and new approaches from the design team, with no concomitant increase in fees.

The operational bill was subsequently revised to produce the 'Activity Bill' or Bill of Quantities (Operational Format) which retained the precedence diagram but reverted to the unit of finished work based on the SMM as the resource and cost carrying mechanism. This was a regressive step as it lost many of the advantages of the operational bill.

Had the operational bill been tried with the benefit of today's low-cost micro-computer technology, it might have had more success.

13.4.3 The Construction Planning Unit approach

This was developed under the auspices of the PSA and was an attempt to structure project information for building projects in a series of operational categories termed Construction Planning Units (CPUs); it was described in a document prepared by the Department of the Environment in 1972 concerned with the arrangement and presentation of information for use in design and construction.

The CPU concept recognized that if the contractor was to be aided in establishing his construction solution, the information provided by the designer should recognize, at least at a strategic level, the method of construction to be used. However the approach was essentially only about structuring project information in a way which more clearly modelled the construction process. The unit of finished work, based on the rules of the SMM, was retained.

13.4.4 The British Property Federation system

This approach arose from the frustration of influential clients with the building industry's procedures and the inefficiency of procurement methods (British Property Federation, 1983).

Among many of the innovations included was that the contractor's programme should be used as the tender bid and subsequently as the basis of resource and financial management. The use of bills of quantities was considered unnecessary and the tendering contractors would be presented only with drawings and specifications.

The principle involved is very similar to those underlying the RSM project and the Operational Bills. The approach gained little favour, possibly because of the vested interests of both the RIBA and the RICS, who saw it as a threat to their professional activities.

13.4.5 Co-ordinated Project Information

A study undertaken by the Building Research Establishment (1987) showed a clear link between poorly presented project information and poor quality of work on site. Co-operation between the main organizational groups in the industry, the RIBA, the RICS, the ACE and the BEC, led to the introduction of CPI – Co-ordinated Project Information, an attempt to improve co-ordination of the different forms of project information, the drawings, the specification and the bills of quantities.

The cornerstone of the CPI was the establishment of the Common Arrangement of Work Sections (CAWS). This is a list of approximately 300 different types of work encountered in the building process. One hundred and fifty of these work sections are concerned with on-site skill related work such as in-situ concrete work, formwork, brickwork etc. The remaining 150 are concerned with performance-related concepts – primarily high-level services such as mechanical, electrical and transportation systems. Figure 13.2 is an extract from CAWS showing examples of each of these two types of work sections.

Each listed work section is allocated a code together with a description of what each contains and what is not included. Figure 13.3 is an extract from a CAWS work section showing its code, definition, inclusions and exclusions.

Accompanying the CAWS are three non-mandatory guides relating to drawings, specifications and bills of quantities respectively, which explain how project information is to be prepared in accordance with the CAWS. This means that the relationship of these three essential parcels of information is clearly visible and that duplications, omissions and inconsistencies are eliminated, at least in theory.

Graphical information in the form of drawings is presented, under CPI in accordance with the CI/SfB classification system★ and identified as location, assembly or component drawings, with the name of the initiator (architect, mechanical engineer etc.) clearly shown.

★Appendix 2 reproduces the basic tables from the SfB system. The system itself was developed in the 1940s by the Swedish Co-ordination Committee for the Building Trade (Samarbetskommitten för Byggnadsfragor – hence SfB). It was later adopted as an international standard by the International Council for Building Research Studies and Documentation. The CI prefix stands for Construction Industry and indicates the British version.

E	**In-situ concrete/Large precast concrete**		U	**Ventilation/Air Conditioning Systems**
E10	In situ concrete		U10	General supply/extract
E11	Gun applied concrete		U11	Toilet extract
E20	Formwork for in situ concrete		U12	Kitchen extract
E30	Reinforcement for in situ concrete		U13	Car parking extract
E31	Post tensioned reinforcement for in situ concrete		U14	Smoke extract/Smoke control
			U15	Safety cabinet/Fume cupboard extract
			U16	Fume extract
E40	Designed joints in in situ concrete		U17	Anaesthetic gas extract
E41	Worked finishes/cutting to in situ concrete			
			U20	Dust collection
E42	Accessories cast into in situ concrete			
			U30	Low velocity air conditioning
E50	Precast concrete large units		U31	VAV air conditioning
			U32	Dual-duct air conditioning
E60	Precast/composite concrete decking		U33	Multi-zone air conditioning
			U40	Induction air conditioning
F	**Masonry**		U41	Fan-coil air conditioning
			U42	Terminal re-heat air conditioning
F10	Brick/block walling*		U43	Terminal heat pump air conditioning
F11	Glass/block walling		U50	Hybrid system air conditioning
F20	Natural stone rubble walling		U60	Free standing air conditioning units
F21	Natural stone/ashlar walling/ dressings		U61	Window/Wall air conditioning units
F22	Cast stone walling/dressings			
			U70	Air curtains
F30	Accessories/Sundry items for brick/block/ stone walling			
F31	Precast concrete sills/lintels/copings/ features		V	**Electrical supply/power/lighting systems**
			V10	Electricity generation plant
			V11	HV supply/distribution/public utility supply
G	**Structural/Carcassing metal/timber**		V12	LV supply/public utility supply
G10	Structural steel framing		V20	LV distribution
G11	Structural aluminium framing		V21	General lighting
G12	Isolated structural metal members		V22	General LV power
G20	Carpentry/timber framing/first fixing		V30	Extra low voltage supply services
			V31	DC supply
			V32	Uninterrupted power supply
G30	Metal profiled sheet decking			
G31	Prefabricated timber unit decking		V40	Emergency lighting
G32	Edge supported/reinforced woodwool slab decking		V41	Street/Area/Flood lighting
			V42	Studio/Auditorium/Arena lighting
	* See Fig. 13.3 for details		V50	Electric underfloor heating
			V51	Local electric heating units
			V90	General lighting and power (small scale)

Figure 13.2   CPI: extract from Common Arrangement of Work Sections, 1987.
Source: Co-ordinated Project Information Committee.

F10   BRICK/BLOCK WALLING

Laying bricks and blocks of clay, concrete and calcium silicate in courses on a mortar bed to form walls, chimneys, partitions, plinths, boiler seatings, etc.

Included

Brickwork of clay, concrete and calcium silicate

Blockwork of clay and concrete

Special shape bricks and blocks

Specially faced bricks and blocks

Brick facing slips

Brick dpcs

Firebrick work

Brick bands, copings, sills, arches, etc.

Holes, chases, grooves, mortices, cutting, bonding, pointing other than for engineering services

Forming key for asphalt and other applied finishes

Centring

Mortar (Z21)

Excluded

Concrete cavity fill and concrete fill for hollow blocks or reinforced brickwork/blockwork. (In situ concrete, E10)

Bar reinforcement for reinforced brickwork/blockwork. (Reinforcement for in situ concrete, E30)

Natural stone rubble walling, F20

Natural stone ashlar/dressings, F21

Cast stone walling/dressings, F22

Damp proof courses, wall ties, forming cavities, etc.
(Accessories/Sundry items for brick/block/stone walling, F30)

Proprietary metal, concrete, etc. lintels, sills, copings, etc.
(Accessories/sundry items for brick/block/stone walling, F30)

Non-proprietary concrete sills, lintels, etc.
(Precast concrete sills/lintels/copings/features, F31)

Holes and chases for services
(Holes/chases/covers/supports for services, P31)

Figure 13.3   CPI example of typical work section.
Source: Co-ordinated Project information Committee.

The drawings are presented in elemental form as it is not feasible to prepare them in a work section format. For example, the element of substructure may contain several work sections such as excavation, piling, in-situ concrete, brickwork, asphalt work etc. However, the relationship of information on the drawings to the preambles and the measured work in the bill of quantities is achieved by labelling the drawings with the CAWS codes. Figure 13.4a, b and c show how drawings, preambles and measured work are co-ordinated using the CPI system.

CPI has been reasonably successful in terms of measured work in bills of quantities because the rules contained in the latest standard method of measurement – SMM7 – are set out in accordance with it; it is therefore more difficult to avoid than to use. Unfortunately as the guides referred to are only advisory, the preparation of drawings and preambles has so far tended to ignore CPI, so co-ordination of the information sources is still not being achieved. The CPI system has already involved considerable investment in the development of standard libraries of descriptions both in hard copy and computer forms. Quantity surveyors are now trained in its use, but not, or at least not to the same extent, architects or builders. The Latham Report recommends that the use of CPI should be a contractual requirement and that its application should be extended to the civil engineering industry; whether the recommendation is acted on remains to be seen.

13.5 A way forward

What is needed is the facility to transpose information rather than translate information as is currently done – for this wastes effort and time and leads to errors; and, as we have continually stressed, the emphasis needs to be shifted from the costs of completed units of work to the management of those basic resources described in detail in Part II.

One approach, which goes some way to meeting this objective and takes the Co-ordinated Project Information system one stage further, has been developed by one of the authors as part of his work with the CIB Working Commission W74 (CIB, 1986). This Working Commission was responsible for the development and application of the SfB classification system as an aid to information management, and the suggestions which follow owe a great deal to the stimulus of ideas from the members of that international group.

The approach works on the basis that the building project can be represented by each of the three tables of the SfB system in terms of elements, construction and resources and that it will take a certain time to complete as shown in Figure 13.5. It is in this way possible to represent the design in terms of the product (the elements) and in terms of the process

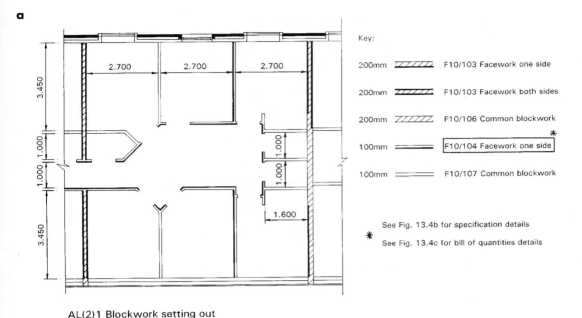

AL(2)1 Blockwork setting out

Figure 13.4a   CPI example of location drawing.
Source: Co-ordinated Project Information Committee.

(the constructions) and the resources. Figure 13.6a illustrates the principle simply: the design is analysed in three levels: the elements, the constructions and the resources required; the process of construction creates the building by converting the resources, through activities, into constructions (e.g. blockwork) and elements and ultimately the whole building. This principle can be taken further by allowing the activities to be identified by the constructor (essential to establish the construction solution as discussed in Chapter 12) while preserving the direct relationship to the design. Figure 13.6b illustrates these linkages.

This is important because up to now that link has not been successfully made. The approach allows contractors to assemble their activities direct from the design information without the need for the time-consuming and error-generating translations used at present.

As can be seen from the SfB tables (Appendix 2) each table has a code assigned to each description. The drawing in Figure 13.7 shows the use of the codes to identify the nature of the information.

Figure 13.8 is the same network diagram referred to in Chapter 12 with one essential difference – the SfB tables 1 and 2 codes have been added. Figure 13.9 is an extract from the Bill of Quantities where the information

b   **F10   BRICK/BLOCK WALLING**

TYPES OF WALLING

101   FACING BRICKWORK ABOVE DPC

102   FACING BRICKWORK BELOW DPC

103   FACING BLOCKWORK, 200MM WALLS

104   FACING BLOCKWORK, 100MM WALLS*

105   COMMON BLOCKWORK BELOW DPC

106   COMMON BLOCKWORK ABOVE DPC, 200 MM WALLS

107   COMMON BLOCKWORK ABOVE DPC, 150 & 100 MM WALLS

108   ENGINEERING BRICKWORK TO MANHOLES

WORKMANSHIP GENERALLY

220   QUALITY OF WORK

230   INCLEMENT WEATHER

260   CONCRETE BRICKS/BLOCKS
         etc.

104   FACING BLOCKWORK, 100 MM WALLS:**

  - Blocks: Dense aggregate concrete to BS6073 : Part 1.
    Type: Solid.
    Work size: 390 x 190 x 140 and 90 mm.
    Finish: Grit blasted on exposed faces as drawing AL(2)1.
    Special shapes (100 mm walls only) : dog leg blocks.
        Closer blocks to door jambs, half blocks
        to curved stair walls, lintel blocks.
        Manufacturer and reference : Edenhall Dense Masonry Blocks.
  - Mortar, bond and joints as tyupe F10/103

    * See also Fig. 13.4a and Fig. 13.4c
    ** Typical Preamble Clause

Figure 13.4b   CPI example of specification details for inclusion in bill of quantities preambles.
Source: Co-ordinated Projects Information Committee.

relating to a particular activity has been assembled enabling the contractor
to allocate the resources needed and identify their cost implications. As can
be seen this idea is very similar to the CPI system except that CPI is only a

c

MASONRY

See also Fig. 13.4a and Fig. 13.4b

F

Item	F10 BRICK/BLOCK WALLING	Qty	Unit	Rate	£	p
	Facing blockwork Spec 104					
	Walls:					
A	100 mm thick; facework one side	438	m²			
B	100 mm thick; curved on plan; 1150 mm radius; facework one side	33	m²			
C	100 mm thick; curved on plan; 1150 mm radius; entirely of half blocks; facework one side	36	m²			
D	Extra for special 90° closer blocks	131	m			
E	Extra for special 90° dog leg blocks	120	m			
F	Extra for special 190 mm deep lintol blocks (concrete and reinforcement measured separately)	99	m			
	Common blockwork Spec 106					
	Walls:					
G	200 mm thick	73	m²			
	Common blockwork Spec 107					
	Walls:					
H	100 mm thick	453	m²			
J	150 mm thick	37	m²			
	Closing Cavities:					
K	50 mm wide; horizontal; blockwork 100 mm thick	26	m			
				To collection £		

Figure 13.4c CPI example of measured work contained in bill of quantities.
Source: Co-ordinated Projects Infotmation Committee.

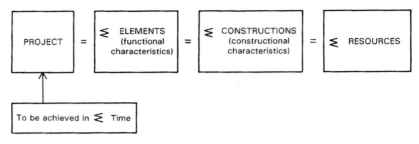

Figure 13.5   The basic principle of the SfB classification system.

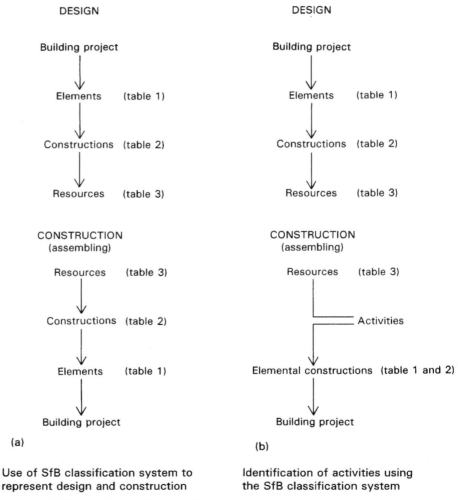

Figure 13.6   Use of SfB classification for co-ordination of design and construction information.

part solution in that it relates only to the organization of the project information as produced by the design team.

In the proposed technique, the SfB classification system has been used to identify all the information of relevance to both the design and the construction but more importantly to facilitate the manipulation and retrieval of information for the specific needs of designers and constructors.

To illustrate this important point, consider the information concerning external walls (21) and blockwork F; this can easily be located on the drawing (Figure 13.7), the contractor's network diagram (Figure 13.8) and the Bill of Quantities (Figure 13.9). Note that the Bill of Quantities shows the specific information relating to the activity H in Figure 13.8, indicating the actual **resources** needed (coded from table 3 of the SfB classification).

The SfB system can therefore be used to manage the flow of information generated and used by those involved in designing and constructing; the management of that information flow is of course greatly facilitated by the use of computers. SfB is particularly helpful here as information can be assembled or disaggregated in various permutations by the use of the codes

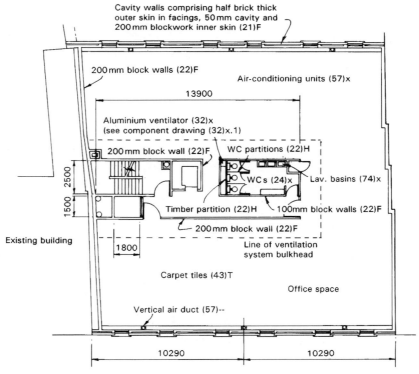

Figure 13.7   SfB classification used to co-ordinate drawings.

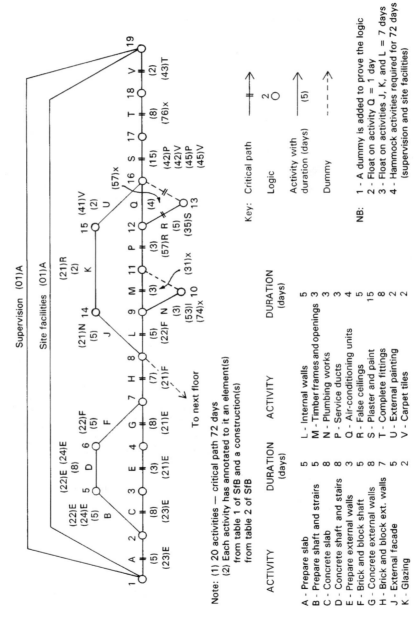

Note: (1) 20 activities — critical path 72 days
(2) Each activity has annotated to it an element(s)
from table 1 of SfB and a construction(s)
from table 2 of SfB

ACTIVITY	DURATION (days)	ACTIVITY	DURATION (days)
A - Prepare slab	5	L - Internal walls	5
B - Prepare shaft and stairs	5	M - Timber frames and openings	3
C - Concrete slab	8	N - Plumbing works	3
D - Concrete shaft and stairs	8	P - Service ducts	3
E - Prepare external walls	3	Q - Air-conditioning units	4
F - Brick and block shaft	5	R - False ceilings	5
G - Concrete external walls	8	S - Plaster and paint	15
H - Brick and block ext. walls	7	T - Complete fittings	8
J - External facade	5	U - External painting	2
K - Glazing	2	V - Carpet tiles	2

Key: Critical path ⟶

Logic ⟹ (with 2 ◯)

Activity with duration (days) ⟶ (5)

Dummy - - - →

NB: 1 - A dummy is added to prove the logic
2 - Float on activity Q = 1 day
3 - Float on activities J, K, and L = 7 days
4 - Hammock activities required for 72 days
(supervision and site facilities)

Figure 13.8 Network diagram for typical floor plan showing use of SfB classification system to co-ordinate construction activities.

ACTIVITY   : Brick and block external walls

ELEMENT   : External walls (21)

CONSTRUCTION : Blockwork F

Item No	Loct	Code	Description	Qty	Unit	Hours	Rate	Total Time (Hours)	Total Cost £	
			RESOURCE : Labour c							
		60	Block walls							
		F30	Blockwork							
		F350	Walls							
		F280	High strength blocks in CLM (1:1:6)							
1	01 *	F1150	200 mm thick	58	M²	1.94	5.00	112.52	562	60
2	01 *	F1152	Rough cutting	3	M	0.81	5.00	2.43	12	15
			RESOURCE : Commodities y							
		60	Block walls							
		f230	High strength blocks							
3	01 *	f2050	450 x 225 x 100 mm	573	NR		0.50		28	65
			C/F					114.95	603	40

* Location 1st floor

Figure 13.9   Resource-based bill of quantities showing use of SfB classification system to co-ordinate measured information.

Extract from bill of quantities showing part of activity : Brick and Block walls (21)F showing labour costs and hours and commodities required

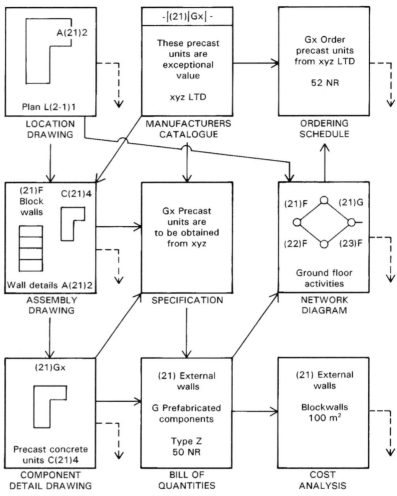

Figure 13.10   Use of SfB classification system to manage information flow in design and construction.

assigned to each description making up the tables. Figure 13.10 shows some examples of the various presentations and permutations of project information which can be activated either manually or with low-cost computer aid.

Recently the Department of the Environment, with matching funds from the Building Project Information Committee representing the four major institutions (RIBA, RICS, BEC, and CIBSE) has recently commissioned research to develop further a classification system for use in the UK construction industry (*Chartered Surveyor Monthly*, 1994). The approach described above is likely to be an important component of this work as documented in a recent report (ISO Technical Committee TC59/SC13 Classification of Information in the Construction Industry, 1993).

Research is currently being undertaken in several places, including the University of Loughborough, Salford University and Liverpool John Moores University to develop information management systems of this sort which will allow effective data exchange between designers and builders based on CAD and CAM (Aoud and Price, 1994).

However it is still very much in its infancy and so far little progress has been made in convincing those concerned with the design and construction of buildings of the need for change. The way forward is the creation of an effective interface between computer-aided design (CAD) and computer-aided management (CAM) to facilitate the building of product/process models allowing the implications of the one for the other to be clearly evident and explored. Ultimately one can see an entirely electronic system of information exchange between all the users of the information which describes a building – its design, its resources, its production and its cost.

13.6 Conclusion

> Better information exchange and better cost prediction will not of themselves necessarily lead to the sort of cost reductions optimistically hoped for by the Latham Report (Latham, 1994). But they should lead, if widely practised, to a better understanding on all sides of the implications for cost and construction of design decisions. Combined with closer co-ordination of activity between architect, surveyor and builder, and improvements in management at all stages, major improvements in the efficiency of the whole process can realistically be expected.

FOR FURTHER STUDY

1 Recommended reading

For a more detailed account of the functions and techniques of design cost control, see Part 3 of Ferry and Brandon's *Cost Planning of Buildings* (1991) 6th edition. The books on construction management referred to at the end of the last chapter are equally relevant here, but none of them looks at the use of the bill of quantities in the management process. The British Property Federation's *BPF System for Building Design and Construction*

(1983) is worth study for its proposals on this issue as is the earlier work of Forbes and Skoyles on operational bills (referred to in the chapter).

The CIB (1986) *Practical Manual of SfB* and the *Co-ordinated Project Information* guides (Co-ordinated Project Information Committee, 1987a, b and c) should be studied for an appreciation of the nature of and need for more effective project information.

2 Discussion or essay questions

a Explain why the problem of integrating the project information relating to the design and to the construction process has proved difficult to resolve. Would a better co-ordination of project information lead to improvements in overall productivity in construction?

b Explain why an interim valuation based on the priced bill of quantities for a multi-storey office block is likely to be inaccurate.

c Why did the British Property Federation's proposals for reform gain little support? Are the proposals in the Latham Report for better co-ordination likely to be successful? Identify in both cases whether barriers to acceptance are simply reluctance to change or the consequence of a firm belief that the proposals will not solve any major problem (see Latham, 1994, pp 25–6).

<table>
<tr><td>

14

</td><td>

The procurement of buildings

</td></tr>
</table>

14.1 Introduction: costs and procurement

Previous chapters have described the many ways in which design decisions influence specific components of a building's cost by determining the type of materials used, the form of construction, the systems of environmental control, the efficiency with which labour and plant can be deployed, and ultimately the building's long-term running costs. However, many people in the industry have argued that the single most significant influence on the total cost of a building to the client is the method of 'procurement' used, that is, in one of many definitions 'the framework of relationships and procedures within which construction is brought about'. The procurement method is seen as so significant because it determines the efficiency with which the whole process of producing a building, from design through construction, can be carried out.

This chapter examines the various procurement systems currently used, their effects on the roles and relationships of the clients, designers, surveyors, managers and builders and their implications for the efficiency of building production.

In any procurement strategy there are two distinct components:

■ the tendering procedure: that is the process through which a contractor is selected to carry out the work and the basis on which a contract can be let, for example a contractor might be selected through limited competition on the basis of a lump sum – or price at which he is prepared to carry out the project;
■ the contractual arrangement: that is the legal definition of the obligations rights and liabilities of the parties and the documentation on which those obligations are based such as drawings, bills of quantities and the JCT80 Standard Form of Contract with Quantities.

These two components determine between them the degree of competition between contractors and the allocation of financial risk; the contractual arrangements also determine the lines of authority and management responsibility between client, design team and contractor.

Although there are, as will be described below, many variations, procurement systems in the 1990s can be divided into two broad categories.

■ those which separate the design and construction phases, precluding any major contribution by the contractor to the design development: the 'traditional' methods;
■ those which attempt to integrate design and construction; these have evolved more recently in attempts to reduce the time from inception to completion, to bring the contractor's expertise in at an early stage and ultimately to reduce construction time and cost. We will refer to them as the 'non-traditional methods of procurement (though in fact there have been design and build types of contract since the last century).

Between each of these categories of procurement system and between the variants in each of the categories, there are significant differences in the role and influence of the architect or design team; in the distribution of risk, between contractor, client, professional consultants and subcontractors; and in the lines of management. Most significantly for the theme of this book, the way in which costs are controlled and the responsibilities for that control also vary from one procurement method to another.

Figure 14.1 shows in outline what the major procurement paths are and how they are related. Table 14.1 shows how their relative importance changed over the period 1984 to 1993. It can be seen there that traditional systems were still the dominant methods of contractor selection in 1993 although there had been a steady decline in the previous decade. The figures show a 35% reduction from 83% to 54% of the value of building contracts being let under traditional arrangements (that is, those shown as 'Firm BQ', 'Lump sum spec. and drawings', and 'remeasurement approx.

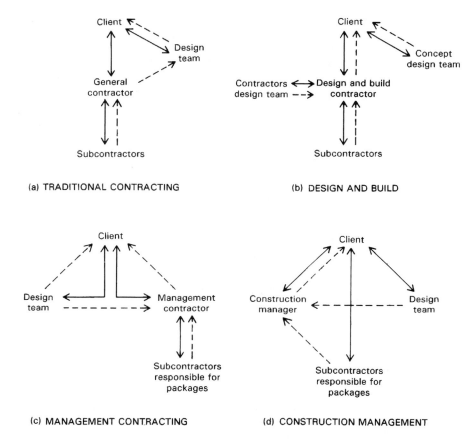

Figure 14.1   Contractual (——) and responsibility (– – –) relationships for major methods of building procurement.

BQ' and 'Prime cost'). Management contracting declined to 6.7%, probably owing to the introduction of construction management which in two years cornered almost 20% of the value of building contracts. The share of design and build grew rapidly – from 5% to 15% and to 36% in 1993 by value.

In a survey reported in *Building* in 1993, 38% of 4000 building professionals still favoured traditional methods, 31% design and build, with only 5% in favour of management contracting and 13% construction management (*Building* 16 Apr. 1993).

Without going into too much detail, this chapter will describe the main features of each of the procurement methods outlined in Figure 3.1 and attempt to indicate the relative effect of each of the main systems on the link between design, costs and quality.

Table 14.1   Trends in methods of procurement.

Procurement method	1984 %	1985 %	1987 %	1989 %	1991 %	1993 %
Lump sum – Firm BQ	58.73	59.26	52.07	52.29	48.26	41.63
Lump sum – spec and drawings	13.13	10.20	17.76	10.26	8.35	9.98
Lump sum – design and build	5.06	8.05	12.16	10.87	14.78	35.70
Remeasurement – approximate BQ	6.62	5.44	3.43	3.58	1.26	2.43
Prime cost plus fixed fee	4.45	2.65	5.17	1.12	0.12	0.15
Management contract	12.01	14.40	9.41	14.99	7.87	7.17
Construction management	—	—	—	6.89	19.36	3.94
Total	100.00	100.00	100.00	100.00	100.00	100.00

14.2 The traditional system

For over a hundred years, from the mid-eighteenth century to the 1970s, what is now seen as the traditional system was (with the important exception of speculative housebuilding) almost the sole way of having a building designed and built. Its essential features were and are those detailed in the RIBA plan of work (described in Chapter 3); in summary, a person or a corporate body needing a new building appoints an architect to develop the design; when the design is complete or virtually complete, contractors are invited to tender to carry out the construction for a particular price; the architect or her agent monitors the process of construction, to ensure that the work is carried out according to the specification. The responsibilities and rights of the various parties are determined by a legal contract between the client and the contractor. Both the design team and the contractors are formally employed by the client, while the architect is paid a fee based, until recently, on the contract value and an agreed scale of rates.

At the beginning of the last century (roughly the period between 1820 and 1850) this system gradually replaced older methods such as payment 'by measure and value' and the employment of craftsmen on an individual basis by the client, architect or a master craftsman (Satoh, 1995). Interestingly the change to new forms of contracting was as bitterly contested in the nineteenth century as it is today. Government and public clients and some architects began to favour the lump sum contract (or 'contract in gross' as it was then called) as it gave a more or less guaranteed price; but many architects, craftsmen and workers' representatives opposed the system. Fierce competition they claimed drove tender prices down; this led to lower quality and lower wages, as contractors were forced to cut corners in an effort to meet their contract price and still make a profit.

Nevertheless the system prevailed and became the standard way of operating in the second half of the nineteenth century and throughout most of the twentieth.

One of the main features of the traditional approach is that design and construction are seen as the responsibility of separate and independent parties – the design team and the contractor. The two groups are brought together when the design generally has been fully developed and documented by the design team. Their documents – the drawings and the bills of quantities – form the basis on which contractors tender; all contractors are therefore tendering on the same information, ensuring that competition is equitable. Once the contractor is selected, the formal contract, usually one of a number of standard forms and currently most often the JCT 80, is signed between client and contractor; but the design team will generally act on the client's behalf in ensuring that the conditions of the contract are fulfilled.

Two critical elements of this modern form of the traditional system have developed during this century in complex and sophisticated ways (some would say much too complex and sophisticated). These are the forms of contract and the use of the bill of quantities.

The establishment of an agreed form of contract came slowly and painfully; the Joint Contracts Tribunal was set up in the 1930s and the JCT contract agreed in 1937, since when it has gone through a considerable and complex evolution. And despite every attempt at devising a standard system, variations on the basic forms continue to proliferate. A table published in the Interim Report of the Latham group refers to 17 different versions in use at the beginning of the 1990s as well as another 19 non-JCT forms of contract (Latham, 1993, pp. 39–40).

The second significant development of the traditional system referred to above – and this was unique to Britain and those countries which followed its systems, mainly the colonies – was the 'bill of quantities' referred to frequently in earlier chapters. The bill defines a project in terms of every item of work needed, expressed qualitatively and quantitively for each element. Although such bills have not been used elsewhere, they have served a critical function in Britain. In 1984, 67% of building contracts were let using bills of quantities although by 1991 this had declined to 50%. This is nevertheless a remarkable record for a document which in many parts of the world, including Japan and the United States of America, is considered entirely superfluous. It is worth therefore emphasizing why bills of quantities are still considered so useful – indeed central to the traditional approach – in Britain.

- They facilitate the process of tendering, eliminating duplication of effort by the contractors thus saving time and money.
- They provide an objective basis for tendering and the subsequent comparison of the tenders. This is because each tenderer is bidding on the same information. Even if there are errors within the bill of quantities, tenders are still based on precisely the same information; the standard forms make provision for the correction of such errors.
- The bill can be used to value the work as it progresses. Contractors are usually paid monthly as described in Chapter 12 and the priced bill's quantity is generally used to ascertain the value of the work completed.
- The bill can be used as a basis to value any changes that might be required. Even in the best designed and managed project, changes will inevitably be required involving variations to the amount of work required. The bill of quantities containing the various unit rates will provide the basis of valuing such changes.
- The bill is used as a basis to settle the final account. Again because of all the various unit rates contained within it, then once the final quantity and quality of work has been determined and agreed, the unit rates where relevant can be used as a basis of settlement.
- Bills of quantities are a source of cost information and the majority of cost prediction techniques rely on the information contained within them.

Usually the cost information is manipulated into different cost categories devised by quantity surveyors as a basis for financial planning and control. The whole of the BCIS system referred to in Chapters 3 and 9 is based on the use of elemental cost analysis derived from the bill of quantities. The widely used price books by Spon's, Laxton's and the like also contain much information derived from priced bills of quantities.

Most of the developments in information technology and its use in the preparation of bills of quantities have been driven by the need to manipulate cost information contained in bills of quantities, as a basis for future cost prediction and management.

However although the developments of construction contracts and the bills of quantities took place in the context of the traditional procurement methods and are an essential part of it, they are also important in the non-traditional approaches discussed below. What is unique to the traditional methods is the relationship between designer and constructor. To some this is one of the strengths of the system, but others see it as its biggest weakness.

From the point of view of the client and designer, the system has the advantage that the design team retains control of the way the design intentions are realized. Although it is the contractor who manages the actual construction process, his or her activities are subject to instructions from the client (the 'employer' in the contract), normally acting through the architect. It is the architect, for example, who frequently provides or appoints the quantity surveyor and the clerk of the works, and it is the members of this design team who hold regular site meetings with the contractor to discuss progress and if necessary issue instructions.

However, this separation has also been seen by very many commentators as the system's critical weakness. As contractors are not appointed until the design is virtually complete, they are not in a position to make a contribution to its development. Contractors' intimate knowledge of their own methods of working, the skills available to them and the current market conditions for materials put them in a better position than architects to judge some aspects of the buildability of a design. Early consultation between architect and contractor must be beneficial and help to prevent the many problems of misunderstanding and many of the errors that do frequently occur leading to costly delays or failures. To say this is not to imply that architects do not take buildability into account – nor that builders should usurp the design function, but just to reiterate an obvious point that only through maximum mutual understanding and co-operation is efficient building possible.

The tendering procedure adopted is certainly one of the strengths of the traditional system for it can achieve the cost benefits of competition but at the same time, through the documentation provided and the rules of tendering adopted, avoid some of its damaging effects; it is clear to all parties exactly what is being tendered for, and the competition is therefore at least at one level, on the basis of like with like.

However, preparing at tender bid is expensive for contractors – and where too many contractors are allowed to bid the total costs involved are very high indeed. The Latham Report identifies poor tendering procedures as one of the most damaging weaknesses of current practice and, as we saw in Chapter 7, quotes instances of absurdly high numbers of tenders for very minor contracts. In such cases the cost of preparation of tenders by all these contractors has to be met somewhere; ultimately the costs of the unsuccessful bidders will be covered in the costs of any successful tenders made for other projects.

There are other problems connected with the high cost of tendering: for example, contractors who do not really want the job may nevertheless bid for fear of not being invited to bid in the future, put little effort into the assembly of the tender. This means that many successful bids are based on tentative, ill-thought-through proposals with little regard for the programming and resource needs of the project. At best this leads to an unsatisfactory construction solution and at worst constant antagonism throughout the post-tender phase as the successful contractor tries to make good financial losses that are the almost inevitable outcome of a superficially considered tender bid (NJCC Code of Procedure for Single Stage Competitive Tendering).

It is because tendering is so expensive and excessive tendering counter-productive that most reports that have been conducted over the years have among other things recommended the use of limited or selective rather than open tendering.

The code of practice on selective tendering sets out precisely the method of conducting the process of carrying out limited competitive tendering and one of its recommendations is that a maximum of six firms should be invited to bid with two names in reserve in case one or more of the initial six decline to tender.

Finally, in terms of strengths and weaknesses under the traditional system – and this of course is an advantage or disadvantage depending on which side of the fence you are standing – although the architect bears long-term liability for any design faults, much of the financial risk of the project is borne by the contractor (see Figure 14.2 based on the Latham Report). As we saw in Chapter 7, any building project is subject to a whole range of risks and one of the major differences between the various forms of procurement is the way that risk is allocated between the parties; whoever carries the risk has the heavy and costly responsibility of managing it. As Figure 14.2 shows risk allocation varies considerably between one procurement method and another from the client's point of view. This is one of the most important factors in deciding on the procurement route to be followed. The implications of this are fully explored in a number of specialized texts, and are not dealt with any further here.

14.3 Variations on the traditional system

14.3.1 Lump sum with approximate quantities

There are a number of variations on the basic lump sum, competitive tender, traditional approach.

Often the design team, for very good reasons, will not have fully determined the detailed solution although the overall design has been established. This is generally the case in civil engineering projects, especially where much of the work is underground and the specific conditions are difficult to determine in advance (ground water, rock etc.)

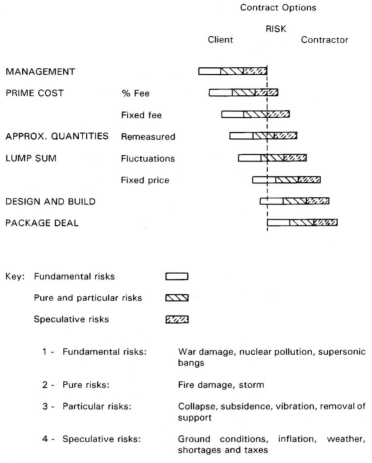

Figure 14.2 The distribution of risk under different methods of building procurement.
Source: Latham Report.

or where the unique nature of the project makes it difficult to determine a final solution (such as a hydro-electric power station).

Such contracts are often described as lump sum contracts with approximate bills of quantities, the use of the word approximate or provisional implying the need for re-measurement where there is a degree of uncertainty.

However 'lump sum with approximate quantities' is a contradiction in terms. The contract is really a measurement contract where the uncertainty of the situation is recognized and within the contractual arrangements specific mechanisms are identified to account for this uncertainty. An extreme version of such an approach is the use of the schedule of rates where specific unit rates for anticipated parts of the work are determined in advance in order that the final settlement can be reached when the true quantities involved are determined by measurement.

It has been recognized for a number of years that the use of unit rates in this way is not an equitable or accurate approach to the financial settlement. As a result the standard method of measurement for building works and civil engineering works have both set up within their rules mechanisms to ensure that the context within which the changes in the amount of work take place are highlighted and the implications accounted for.

The problems relate to the point made at the end of Chapter 3 and discussed in more detail in Chapter 13, that the costs of building works are not merely quantity related; some of the resources involved are influenced by other factors such as the fixed costs and time related costs. For example a large tower crane will have a high installation cost which will remain the same no matter how much work it subsequently does. It will also incur a time-related cost determined by the number of weeks it is on site; costs will not therefore be directly related to the physical quantity of goods and materials lifted.

14.3.2 Lump sum without quantities

A further variant on the traditional system is one without bills of quantities. In such cases a specification is prepared of the work to be carried out and the quality of materials and workmanship to be used. This creates a difficulty for the contractor in that before they can prepare their own bid they must first ascertain the quantities of work involved. Clearly such an approach is time-consuming and error-producing as each tendering contractor may well incorrectly quantify the work involved and thus base the tender on incorrect information.

However when projects are relatively standard and uncomplicated or small in size (perhaps under £250 000) the advantages gained from using a bill of quantities may be outweighed by the cost of preparing them.

Nevertheless, despite the disadvantages attributed to the system in the UK, it is this particular approach – lump-sum tendering without the use of the bill of quantities – which is the predominant way of executing procurement within the United States of America and many other parts of the world where British influence has been negligible. In fact the British Property Federation system referred to in the last chapter advocated a similar approach. It recommended the use of the contractors' programme both of the financial management of the contract during its execution and as the basis of the tender submission.

14.3.3 Weaknesses and an adaptation of the traditional system

However the traditional approach to procurement, based primarily on the use of bills of quantities, still remains the most usual approach within the United Kingdom.

Among the main reasons for its success are undoubtedly its familiarity, the general inertia of the industry, and the vested interests of the professions involved. However, especially in the current climate of fierce debate on the future of the whole procurement process, it should not be forgotten that the traditional approach has shown real strengths and has produced many buildings which have been well designed, well built, constructed in time and within cost limit.

Yet analyses of the sources of many of the industry's problems have shown its procedures to be cumbersome and inefficient and therefore, in comparison with those of other countries and with other industries, expensive. These problems have been attributed to the failings of the traditional design approaches which can be summarized as follows:

- the overall project programme was perceived as being longer than necessary mainly because the design and construction processes are sequential;
- the contractor and his or her team have no involvement in the design process and may never have worked with any of the design team before; it is often difficult to establish a well-motivated project team;
- resource utilization: the construction team has no opportunity to contribute to the development of the design solution, which may not have placed enough emphasis on optimal resource use and construction times;
- profit: the fact that the contractor and his or her team have tendered with a view to maximizing their profit within the constraints of the bidding process means their interests may not necessarily be project focused.

There are other forms of procurement which have a long history and are suitable for specific circumstances. One of these is the Prime Cost or Cost Reimbursement contract under which the contractor is appointed to carry out the work for the payment of a 'prime cost' for the basic resources used in the project, together with a fee for general overheads, profit and project overheads. The fee is either fixed or a percentage figure related to the prime cost.

Such contracts can be the subject of competition but they are generally most appropriate in unique circumstances where immediate work on site is required such as after storm or fire damage when seeking competitive bids will be the last thing on the client's mind. They are often the only way of carrying out investigative work.

The obvious difficulties with such an arrangement can be summarized as follows:

■ The client's ultimate commitment is not known and as can be seen in Figure 14.2 the majority of the risk is carried by the client, especially when a percentage fee is used.
■ There is limited incentive for contractors to use their resources efficiently as they know they will receive recompense for them under prime cost. However when a fixed fee is used contractors will generally manage the construction process more efficiently as the longer the project takes and the higher the client resource costs committed, the smaller the proportion of the total cost will be the fixed fee.
■ A major difficulty with such contracts is the process of checking the prime cost. The client has to install costly on site monitoring personnel to check the quality and utilization of the resources.

A variant of the cost reimbursement arrangement is the target cost contract. This is an attempt to provide more incentive for contractors to ensure that they effectively manage the resources paid for under the prime cost. The difference between the actual and estimated cost, whether this is an excess or a saving, is shared between the client and the contractor in a predetermined way.

In the search to overcome the perceived weaknesses of the traditional system, other approaches proliferated. Some were further variants of the traditional system – such as two-stage tendering. This attempted to retain the advantages of financial competition while enabling the contractor's expertise to contribute to the design process. Contractors are invited to tender on a financial competition basis on the major cost items likely to occur in the project such as labour, major plant, supervision and general overheads, together with the information about their utilization. Unit rates for major works items such as concrete and brickwork are also asked for, together with a copy of a recent priced bill of quantities.

From this information the contractor is selected and then in conjunction with the design team becomes involved in developing the design solution. As the solution evolves the initial cost information provided by the contractor is used to negotiate the ultimate price of the work. This particular approach seems to have fallen out of favour, superseded by other more radical different approach to be described in the next few pages. But it was suggested in the Interim Report of the Latham Committee that it might be a good idea to resuscitate it.

14.4 The 'non-traditional' methods of procurement

The main non-traditional procurement strategies are Management Contracting, Construction Management and Design and Build; each has a number of variants and new variants seem to be constantly devised. The basic relationship implied between client, contractor and architect in each of these methods is shown in Figure 14.1 and can be compared with the traditional approach. As Table 14.1 shows, the most serious contender as the main alternative to the traditional route is some form of Design and Build. Indeed one commentator has gone so far as to argue that the management contract is set to disappear. So this section will discuss briefly the first four of the non-traditional routes and conclude with a longer discussion of Design and Build, especially its implications for cost and quality.

14.4.1 Management contracts and contract management

Management contracting became very popular in the 1970s and '80s but was partly replaced by its derivative Construction Management which in turn seems to have lost some of its attraction (Table 14.1). These techniques appeared to some clients and builders to offer a panacea for many of the industry's problems by establishing a spirit of co-operation and teamwork and by allowing the design and construction process to overlap.

The management contract works in its basic form as follows: the client appoints a management contractor who is paid a fee to manage the actual construction of the building on the client's behalf. He or she is appointed to manage, programme and supervise rather than build and in essence acts as a member of the design team.

The construction work itself is split down into sub-contracts known as packages. These packages relate to the various specialist tasks required such as earthworks, formwork, brick and blockwork, mechanical and electrical services. Each package is let usually in limited competition to a number of interested subcontractors who submit tenders for the particular package. As well as drawings, bills of quantities are usually prepared for each package.

The management contractor provides the site management team together with the general site facilities such as canteens, offices, hoardings, storage and possibly major plant such as cranage. The basic fee he receives covers general overheads and profit usually as a percentage of the prime cost of the works (that is the sum of the costs of the packages). Direct costs for the general site requirements are usually reimbursed at cost.

Alternatively the management contractor may be paid a fixed fee based entirely on the estimated prime cost, providing a strong incentive to work as efficiently as possible.

Prior to the management contractor being appointed, a cost plan is prepared and once appointed the management contractor works closely with the client's quantity surveyor to prepare an estimate of the prime cost showing the value of, first, the various packages and, second, the site management costs. It is also not unusual for the client to specify a guaranteed maximum price (GMP) above which no expenditure will be reimbursed.

The management contractor may be selected by negotiation but more usually through competition. In this case a number of firms will be invited to submit proposals based on tender documentation which will include: general arrangement drawings together with such specification information as is available, the anticipated contract value and key dates and the form of contract documentation to be used.

The tendering management contractor's submission will include the management fee together with an estimate of site management and overhead costs. There will be a method statement showing how the work is to be carried out, with a list of potential work packages.

The main advantages of the management contracting route are that it allows the project to be on site earlier than most other methods as all the detailed design work does not have to be completed before work starts on site; the project therefore can be completed earlier than under conventional methods (hence the label 'fast track', applied to both this and the Construction Management variant).

It gives the client and designers total flexibility to develop the scheme so that a range of possible solutions can be assessed for time cost and quality. It is also claimed that management contractors have no conflict of interest as they have nothing to gain or lose by the effects of their advice.

Some clients however are unhappy about entering into a contract which does not have a predetermined contract sum but only an estimate of prime cost. The system also requires the client to carry a greater degree of risk, as Figure 14.2 indicates.

Richard Rogers and Partners' Channel 4 building in Horseferry Road was built using this route, with Bovis as management contractor; the advantages are clearly shown in the two accounts of the project published in *Building* and the *Architects' Journal* (*Building*, 29 Oct. 1993 and *AJ*, 20 Apr. 1994). The package system 'spread the time for the design. The building reflects ideas and decisions taken up to the last moment' yet 'because the client sought as much cost certainty as possible, 70% of the packages had been pre-tendered with the others estimated providing 90% certainty about the outcome (*AJ*, *ibid.*, p. 35). Bovis were seen 'as part of the professional team rather than purely as a contractor . . . we avoided any possibility of a confrontational relationship between the management and contractor which could have led to design decisions being unravelled later... this would have affected the programme and costs' (*Building, ibid,* p. 24).

The Nottingham Inland Revenue Offices, mentioned earlier, also successfully used the management contract route.

Since the mid 1980s a version of management contracting known as construction management has become popular for some types of project; the main difference is that all subcontractors' contracts are with the client not the manager; managers therefore have virtually no risk and their sole allegiance is to the client and the project. However, clients have little real sanction in the event of poor performance by managers and the method has been used mainly by clients who regularly commission work and have some in-house expertise in project procurement, such as the large retailers like Marks & Spencer, Sainsbury's and Tesco. However major projects like the Glyndebourne Opera House have also used the system where there was continuous close involvement by the client (*New Builder,* 24 Apr. 94).

14.4.2 Design and build

It is the design and build method of procurement however which has generated the most acrimonious debate in recent years and which has become the favoured procurement route for very many types of project. It is controversial quite simply because experience has been so varied and because it affects so critically the interests of the many parties involved. To its advocates it solves what is seen as the fundamental weakness of the traditional system – the separation of design and construction; it offers a guaranteed price to the client; it offers speed and efficient construction. To sceptics and to outright opponents, however, design and build, by devaluing the role of the architect also devalues the importance of design; this is a view expressed by some significant clients and contractors as well as by architects themselves.

The following quotations give a flavour of the strength of opinion and the variety of perceptions of what design and build is and what it may imply.

First, the enthusiast:

> *the idea that design and build produces an inferior product is an old wives' tale put about by designers . . . It costs 15% less to put up a building using D&B compared with JCT80. Contractors can cut 5% off materials prices because they have greater flexibility . . . also skim 5% off tender prices due to lower level of aggravation (Neil Kenworthy, director of MDA management, who has managed nearly 700 D&B projects since 1985, (quoted in Building,* Aug. 1992).

Second the sceptic:

> *I'm not a great enthusiast; if tried and tested clients ask for it, you don't tell them to jump in a lake. But we know the end product is not as good* (Robin Nicholson, Associate at Edward Cullinan Architects).

Third the outright opponent:

> *In a debate on Design and Build at the RIBA, Richard McCormac, past president of the RIBA, described 'new methods of procurement which eroded the architect's role'; they had developed 'because of inexperienced clients with an ignorance of design' whose ethos 'was one of middle management, with short term opportunistic and low aspirations. They sustain a legacy of cheapness that is bringing us back to the 1960s'.*

One of the difficulties in making any objective assessment of the advantages and disadvantages – in terms of cost, time and quality – of the design and build as a procurement system is that there are so many variants of the basic principle. At its simplest, a contract is let to a contractor on a negotiated or competitive bid basis to design and build the whole project; design teams will be appointed by and under the control of the contractor; the contractor might also provide financing (so-called turnkey projects). The advantages of such a system are clear – the client has a firm price, the full responsibility is taken by the contractor who in turn has control over the whole process from design to completion. The disadvantages and dangers are equally clear. It can be a rigid system, which does not allow the client to develop his or her requirements and ideas; the original brief has to be precise and variations after the signing of the contract difficult to effect. But as the above quotations show, the real danger many perceive is reduction in design standards and perhaps even quality of construction. (A services engineer has complained: 'when buildings are procured by the design and build route, no-one seems to think about the services until far too late and you end up with a compromise' (*Building*, 19 Nov. 1993)).

It is in response to these recognized dangers that the system 'has evolved all manner of hybrids. At one end of the spectrum it equates to traditional contracting with more risk. At the other it is management contracting with more muscle. Another 57 varieties fall somewhere in between, often with little to differentiate them' (*Building*, Design and Build Supplement Special Feature, 14 Aug. 1992).

One version involves the 'novation' of an architect to the contract; that is the architect is appointed by the client, not the contractor. Experience seems to be very mixed with neither architects nor contractors particularly satisfied with the results. Then there are architect-led design and build schemes and schemes in which, though the contractor in fact appoints an architectural team, it is one already familiar with the client's requirements. This was the case with Laing's hospital development for an advanced medical centre at Clydebank (*Building, ibid.*). New hybrids are proposed, such as 'partnering' which 'give architects the chance to be team leaders but not all the time' (*Building*, 8 July, 1994, p. 13).

One of the most revealing and interesting case studies of design and build in operation was published by *Building's* July 1993 Design and Build Supplements (Spring 1993) on MacCormac Jamieson Prichard's student halls of residence at Queen Mary and Westfield College in east London. There were in fact three projects: the first hall was built under a traditional contract, the second a contractor's all-in package (design and build) while the third was what has been described (here and in other reports of the same project) as 'hybrid design and build'.

Martin Spring's report makes a very interesting analysis:

> *The appearance of all three conforms to their stereotypes. The package deal looks like a block of flats of 1970s vintage . . . the architect design block, by contrast, is flamboyantly picked out in red and blue metal panels and is a flurry of intricate modelling and clever detailing . . . and the two design and build blocks look like a pared down version of the architect-designed block.*
>
> *Judging purely on appearances, it would seem that the more the contractor has taken over from the architect, the more basic the end product becomes. Such a conclusion only confirms the architectural profession's worst suspicions.*
>
> *But deeper investigation reveals this as false logic. The difference in appearance of the three projects is actually the result of widely varying client brief and budgets that dropped by as much as 40%.*

But it was not just a matter of appearance: the client had other concerns. In the 'pure design build version: the quality of detailing was poor . . . toilet overflow pipes wind round the walls . . . sloppy tolerances are filled in by mastic.' In the third, hybrid version however, results were better; still relatively low cost, with better quality. In a remarkable reversal of received wisdom, the team found the design and build more flexible than the conventional projects; and the architect commented:

> *In the first project, we were very circumspect about instruction changes because disputes by the contractor would put the client at financial risk . . . but in the Design and Build project, we issued some 52 change orders . . . it was useful that the QS had them priced in advance . . . it largely came down to a very relaxed and co-operative attitude by Willmot Dixon (the contractor).*

The client's final quoted comment was that the system worked under certain conditions, including clear, detailed specification for 'appropriate design quality' . . . 'but I wouldn't use it for a new one-off faculty building'.

This of course is only one case; other projects have yielded different conclusions; a RIBA exhibition in January 1994 ('Before and After Design and Build') showed a range of projects from good to bad, built under various forms of design and build and management contracts. Roger Hawkins commented.

> *The most alarming and depressing exhibits are those where the architectural input has been ignored and overruled by a subsequent D&B contractor . . . it is not perhaps the specific form of contract which is to blame for 'the cost of everything and the value of nothing' mentality. The exhibition shows that better quality building can be produced where time and energy are allowed for the design process.*

(See also *Architects' Journal*, 20 Oct. 1994, 'Pickett's lock: a cautionary tale.').

14.5 Conclusion: the critical interface

The last three chapters have discussed apparently different topics – the contractor's programme, cash flow, cost prediction, presentation of information, systems of communication and, in this chapter, methods of building procurement. Yet they are all actually concerned with the same issue: the critical interface between the work of the designer and the work of the contractor. The lessons from the debates of the last few years on these topics seem to point to a very obvious conclusion: good buildings at reasonable cost are produced when there is a close and enthusiastic collaboration between on the one hand a well-managed and high-quality design team of good designers who understand issues of buildability and cost and on the other hand a well-managed construction team of people who understand and appreciate the architectural aims of the project, and are able to make a creative input.

What is also clear from the experience of the last few years, the proliferation of contracts and procedures, the development of new initiatives, the constant debate on issues of procurement and the respective roles of all the parties involved in the production of a building, is that there are no easy ways of ensuring this ideal. Each attempt to improve the inadequacies of the current system seems to have thrown up examples of successful projects, but also to have brought new forms of problem.

The Latham Report is undoubtedly the most authoritative summary of the current issues and its recommendations for a way forward need to be taken seriously. In total there are 30 different proposals; their focus is on simpler standardized contractual and tendering procedures, better communication, simpler dispute resolution, improved design and construction management and improvement in skills and knowledge. In fact many of the recommendations are for the implementation of ideas already tried.

The proposals for a simpler form of contract (a revised version of the New Engineering Contract) and many of the other recommendations could perhaps if implemented bring about a marked reduction in conflict.

Perhaps the biggest indictment of the industry's current practices is the way it has become more reliant on the legal profession to resolve its ever increasing number of project-related disputes. The proliferation of standard forms of contract each presented in complex legal terminology provides an open invitation for lawyers to expand their role in the resolution of consequent problems. New approaches to dispute resolution are being tried, many from the United States where the industry has suffered from similar increases in adversarial problems leading to expensive and time-consuming litigation. As a result 'Alternative Dispute Resolution', based on adjudication, conciliation and mediation, is firmly in favour in the US in order to engender a sense of trust and partnership between the various parties to the contract. This approach is now finding favour in the UK as more and more clients become dissatisfied with the current situation. Under these arrangements, the parties accept the appointment of an adjudicator or more than one in large complex projects who, if a dispute arises, makes recommendations with which they all agree in order that work can proceed without interruption. Of course such an approach does not prevent arbitration or litigation being resorted to if the parties are not all in agreement with the original adjudication. One recommendation of the Latham Report is that adjudication should be the normal method of dispute resolution.

The increase in the international opportunities and the globalization of the construction market should also help the industry to take a more open-minded approach to the development and use of procurement strategies by bringing it into contact with the way different countries and organizations go about their business. Membership of the European Community is already having some effect though it is not dramatically evident yet.

The CIB set up a working commission in 1989 concerned purely with Procurement Systems, which has an international membership and has among its terms of reference the aim of studying how present procurement is developing on a global basis and to report back to the international construction community. Latham recommends a levy to finance further research of this and other kinds relevant to construction.

Given all this activity, research and expanding knowledge, solutions to the 'problems of the interface' should be within reach. Greater efficiency in the whole management process is clearly needed; a recent study produced by Reading University has argued that more effective management of the design process itself could make a major contribution to the reduction in total construction costs (Gray *et al.*, 1994). And the need for further improvements in management skills in the construction process itself has long been recognized and much action taken.

However none of these proposals will by themselves bring about the increase in real understanding and co-operation between the professions that seems to be required. The Latham Report itself merely supports the educational initiatives that are already taking place (pp. 72–3), without making recommendations. Yet it may be at the educational and training level (including continuing professional development training) that real solutions lie.

One comment of the Latham Report needs to be taken to heart: none of the previous reports has been acted upon with any degree of success or enthusiasm. Whether Latham will be any more successful than the previous reports in actually improving the efficiency of the industry or even getting more than half-hearted agreement to its analysis remains, at the time of writing, to be seen.

1 Recommended reading

J. W. E. Masterman's *An Introduction to Building Procurement Systems* (1992) is a key text and the Treasury's handbook *Strategy Selection for Major Projects* (1992) is an excellently clear presentation of the different procurement routes. However, the discussion on procurement systems is moving so quickly that any recommended reading will tend to become quickly out of date. *Building* magazine produces a regular Design and Build supplement and all the professional journals report on new developments and the continuing debate. There is really no alternative to regular reading of the relevant magazines and papers.

The Latham Report itself should be looked at, but it is by no means an introductory document and assumes considerable familiarity with current practice; summaries and discussions appeared in several journals (e.g. *Building*, 22 July 1994).

2 Discussion or essay questions

a In what circumstances and in what ways is the involvement of the contractor in the design process desirable? If desirable, how can it be achieved?

b Would not most of the 'interface' problems be solved if the architect was fully in control of the construction process? (See for example R. Slavid

(1993) and Harding (1994), for opposing views, as well as the RIBA study of the future of the profession.)

3 Project

The advantages and disadvantages of the various forms of procurement are usually discussed in terms of risk, cost and time. Discuss the probable implications of each for the **quality** of design and construction. How can quality be maintained in the face of commercial pressures? In searching for answers, study the reports on major buildings in the construction press (e.g. Glyndebourne, Nottingham Tax Office, Channel Four Headquarters, Western Morning News, The Ark, Manchester Airport Terminal 2 (where there was major conflict between designers and clients).

PART

V

Cost limits and values

15 Commercial values and the property market

15.1 Introduction

As has been stressed throughout the book, the need to design within cost limits, and to forecast and control costs accurately, arises from the inevitable reality that building owners expect value for money. That is, they expect the value of the building when completed to be worth the money paid for it and this may well not be the case if costs are not carefully considered and controlled. But how is 'value' assessed? There are in fact many different answers depending on the type of client, the function of the building and the purposes for which the value is being determined. The value of a new cathedral must obviously be reckoned on different criteria from the value of a factory; the value of a school depends on different factors than the value of an office block. In this chapter we look at the establishment of commercial values and their implications for design and cost, leaving non-commercial criteria to be discussed later.

Architects are sometimes dismayed at the effect commercial valuations have on the possibilities for design; and indeed it is often true that cost limits determined by commercial factors are so low that it is difficult to design buildings of any real quality within them. However by understanding the principles on which commercial values are determined, designers have a better chance of establishing possible trade-offs between different aspects of design quality and cost. For example, the simple knowledge that maximizing rental space in an office development is important allows an architect to concentrate on a design which reduces unnecessary circulation and other non-rentable areas and may therefore allow a higher quality of specification in the main office areas.

The following paragraphs attempt to explain briefly and without going too deeply into the theory of property valuation or the complexities of the modern property market, the basis on which the commercial value of a typical office or similar building is determined. For the expected value of a proposed new building and its relationship to expected costs are the critical factors in determining whether the project is likely to go ahead; if value is not above cost there are basically three alternatives: the project is abandoned, its design specification may have to be reduced to bring cost down or, perhaps the most difficult to achieve, the building may have to be redesigned to increase its value. Whatever the situation, 'value' is critical to the success of the design.

15.2 The property market

Before, however, defining value in this sense and showing how it is derived, we need to understand a little about the nature of the property market. For values are ultimately determined by the relationship of supply and demand for accommodation of a particular type – that is by the working of market forces. The point is obvious but worth stressing, because the property market has historically been particularly sensitive to economic cycles. There have been times when the shortage of office space in some areas, London particularly, has been so acute that property values have soared and property development has been an extremely profitable business. At other times – and the beginning of the 1990s has been one of those periods – demand has dropped and many buildings have become vacant; because of the long time lags in office building, new properties have continued to come onto the market nevertheless. Office vacancy rates in London went up from 2% in 1987 to 20% in 1992 before dropping back again in 1993; prime rents having reached £70 per square foot in 1989, dropped to below £40 by 1992, before levelling off a little by 1994. The result has been precipitate falls in property values leading to heavy losses and business failures among the developers.

Nowhere has this been better illustrated than in the case of the Canary Wharf development in London Docklands. The development was begun at the very time when vacant rate were at their lowest (1987) and was ready for letting when they were at their highest. The developers, the UK division Olympia and York, collapsed owing 11 banks £600 million.

The property market as something distinct from other markets with its own ways of operating and its particular methods of funding is a relatively modern phenomenon; and it is still evolving. It has become more international, developed a great range of financial techniques and given birth to a new industry of property specialists. In the period before the Second World War, buildings tended to be built mainly for companies who were going to use them; and many of the grander builders of the first half of this century still bear the names of their first occupiers and owners.

Many large developments are still produced specifically for the eventual owners and users but many others are large multi-purpose speculative developments which are let or sold to various occupiers. The proportion of speculative developments changes over the property cycle; in 1988 it was over three-quarters of the total available space on offer in London (including second-hand space); by 1992 it was only 2%. However many properties which are built for particular clients and particular functions are now designed with an eye to possible future changes and future marketability, the Channel Four building in Horseferry Road, London, designed by the Richard Rogers Partnership is a case in point; although designed specifically to accommodate the very specialized functions and technology of a television production studio, it is also convertible into office space so that it could be sold for a different ort of occupier in the future.

Most commercial buildings are seen therefore as tradable commodities on an active property market; it is a market in which there are many players; large property trading companies continually looking to buy and sell, developers, large and small, producing buildings of one sort or another and many commercial clients looking for suitable buildings to rent or buy; and there are the professional surveying firms, one of whose main functions is to bring the demand and supply sides together both by helping to establish values and by organizing or advising on the financing of the various transactions needed to obtain, sell or produce office industrial retail and leisure accommodation.

However the three major participants are:

■ the occupiers (who may or may not be the owners),
■ the developers, and
■ the providers of finance.

All three may under different circumstances be the actual owners of the buildings.

15.2.1 The building occupier

Occupiers may be any kind of commercial organization from very large businesses occupying the whole of a major building, to small businesses occupying a single floor or even just a single office. A firm of whatever size looking for new premises has basically the following options: it may have a new building built; it may purchase (and possibly refurbish) and existing building, including a building newly completed; it may rent part or the whole of a new or existing building.

Most commercial organizations, even the very large, do not have available the considerable funds to buy or to finance the construction of a major building, whether an office block or a retail development or an hotel; even if they do have the funds available they may not wish to tie them up for long periods in property; the return they can achieve on capital invested in their own business activities will probably be far higher than they can earn from property investment.

Furthermore they may not have the interest or expertise to become involved in the highly risky business of property development; there are exceptions, such as the major retail chains, which will be discussed further below, but most companies will simply want to obtain their required accommodation by paying an appropriate sum of money as rent – or more rarely as the purchase price.

It is for these reasons – unwillingness or inability to fund property from own resources and lack of expertise or enthusiasm for development – on the part of eventual users of buildings that the two major participants in the market have come to play such an important role – the specialist property developers and the financial institutions.

15.2.2 The developers

The property development company is by no means a new phenomenon, but it has become much more common in the last fifty years. As pointed out above, most buildings in the pre-war period were built for specific owners; it was only after 1952 that property companies existing solely to develop commercial properties became really significant. The story of their growth is told in two very different books; one highly critical and highly readable is Oliver Marriott's *The Property Boom* (Marriott, 1967), which details the astonishing expansion from virtually no capital of companies such as Oldham Estates, Ravenseft, City Centre, and shows how some of the people who set up and ran those companies and who quickly became household names, such as Charles Clore, Jack Cotton and Harry Hyams, made fortunes by identifying undervalued land or property, borrowing large sums and then building properties to yield very high capital profits. The other book, Whitehouse's *Partners in Property* (Whitehouse, 1964), tells the story from the developers' point of view and shows how financial institutions, contractors and a host of other organizations created joint development companies to exploit the opportunities the property shortage offered and to share in the high returns.

Those heady days did not last and property development is a more sober business today – but fortunes are still nevertheless made and lost. The major companies are sometimes divided into those which trade – that is buy and sell – and those which concentrate on actual development; but there is much overlap. Some are the well-known property companies quoted on the Stock Exchange and frequently in the news after some dramatic gain or loss, such as British Land, Land Securities, Slough Estates, MEPC.

But almost any type of company may at some time become a 'developer'. Many of the large contracting companies now have their own property development divisions and have become developers in their own right. Amec for example is involved in major developments with local authorities and other public bodies throughout the north of England particularly and have specialized in regeneration projects. At the other extreme, for a very small scheme, the 'developer' may be an individual who sees an opportunity to make a profit by buying a plot of land, having a building built, then sold or let. It is also now quite possible that architects and surveyors will themselves be developers, looking for opportunities to use their specific skills in an entrepreneurial way rather than acting as consultants for a fee (a significant reason of course for their training to incorporate some understanding of the development process).

The developers' functions may vary considerably but essentially they organize the purchase of the land (or property), carry out feasibility studies to determine the most profitable form of project, arrange finance, have the building designed and built, then ultimately sold or rented out. All these functions may actually be performed by different consultant organizations – but the developer will often be the main co-ordinator and organizer.

The way in which a development comes about may also vary from one scheme to another. Developers may identify an opportunity – a vacant site, a derelict building – or may be approached by an owner of land, a local authority, or a potential user of a new building. They will then explore the possibilities; for example it might seem that a mixed development of offices and shops could be appropriate; or maybe it is an ideal site for a hotel. They will do a series of feasibility studies on the likely costs and profitability of various alternatives and, having decided on them, may then approach a contractor, a firm of architects and surveyors to produce outline schemes.

However large the development company, it will probably not have the free funds available for financing of major schemes; most of the money required will be borrowed from the financial institutions. There are a host of ways to raise the necessary finance; the company may seek partners (which may include the main contractors for the construction) or set up a joint company specifically for a particular project, including funding institutions, public authorities and other interested parties. It may borrow money for the short term from one institution such as a bank and seek long-term funding from pension funds and insurance companies and other financial intermediaries. All the providers of finance will want to know details about the development – its potential value as a capital asset and its earning capacity. The detailed mechanisms of the funding process can these days be quite extraordinarily complex and need not detain us here. Interested readers should consult the specialist texts. We will simply describe the major sources and the basic principles of funding.

15.2.3 The financial institutions

Whatever the scheme it will require two types of finance; first money will need to be borrowed to cover the construction period – to pay for the land, the building itself and all the associated costs of bringing a project to the stage where it can be occupied. Secondly, long-term finance will be required; developers may want to sell the property and reap their profit quickly; but at some point one organization or another has to be prepared to forgo cash for a long period of time – to sink money in the property, which will yield a return only over many years.

The institutions which provide this finance include banks (not just the 'high street' banks but dozens of others including foreign banks), the large pension fund and insurance companies.

Traditionally, banks provided only short-term funds to cover the period from land purchase to first letting or even part of that period; they were unwilling to become deeply involved in long-term property investment. As Marriott has described the position in the 1950s, the banks' rôle was crucial in making development possible at all; although in theory they were only supposed to lend if long-term money had been agreed (from other sources) and the building pre-let, in fact the rules were frequently ignored.

In the 1980s the high-street banks relaxed their views on the risks of long-term property and became major investors; however at the end of the decade as the boom collapsed, they found themselves with huge amounts of outstanding loans which the borrowing developers could not afford to repay. The involvement of the banks in Canary Wharf was referred to above. Many fingers were burnt and the banks may not be so willing to play with fire again.

The main providers of long-term finance have been and are two major types of institution: the pension funds and the insurance companies. Both types of organization act as depositories for long-term savings and have acquired vast funds which they need to invest on behalf of their clients. To give some examples, the British Telecom Pension Fund stands at about £12 billion, British Rail about £7 billion, the Universities Superannuation Schemes nearly £6 billion.

Figure 15.1 shows both the relative levels of investment in property by the two types of institution and the fluctuations over the past 25 years. The

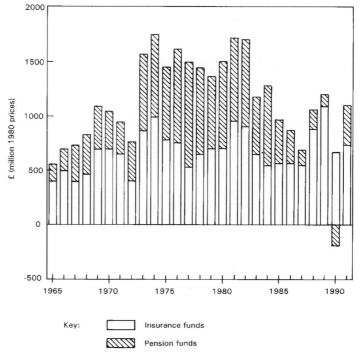

Figure 15.1   Property investment by institutions.
Source: Guy (1994).

exceptional nature of the 1990 recession is shown by the fact that it appears to have been the only year during the whole of that period when the pension funds actually reduced the level of their investment – that is they took more money out of property than they put in (Guy, 1994, p. 57).

All of these organizations have a policy of spreading their portfolio of investments or loans, both in terms of time and in types of investment, simply to spread the risks. They hold a range of different investments from those considered low-risk but long-term such as government bonds, to the higher risk but potentially more profitable such as property, shares in major companies and many shorter-term investments which can be quickly realized if they have large calls for cash (as insurance companies do after major disasters).

Because they are providing the bulk of the money to finance property development, they play a critical part in determining the criteria on which property values are assessed. A developer will only be able to acquire the funding required, and therefore go ahead with a scheme, if he can persuade a financial institution that the project will yield a good return at low risk and in particular that its commercial value when completed will be higher than the costs of its development.

15.3 Establishing the building's value

All three groups involved in the property market therefore have as a prime concern the value of the development in one sense or another. Occupiers will only be prepared to pay a rent at a level they perceived the property to be worth to them; developers will only make a profit if the building's value is greater than it cost to develop it; and the funding institutions will only provide finance if the returns – which depend ultimately on the rents obtainable – are high enough to compensate for the risk involved, compared with the returns they could receive on safer investments such as government stocks. In fact the critical requirement for all the participants can be translated into the simple relationship already referred to many times: the value has to exceed the cost. Obviously no one – least of all financial specialists with experience and expertise in property – is going to lend money on a scheme which cost more to build than it is actually worth. (Though of course, given the volatility of the property market, this does in fact frequently happen.)

How then is this 'value' determined and how is it related to income earning capacity and to costs? The next section attempts to answer these questions, defining some basic concepts used in the property business; this involves a little, not very formidable, mathematics.

15.3.1 Yield and years purchase: a simple example

The value of a commercial building will reflect current conditions in the property market and the particular characteristics of the building itself. Because of the range of possible situations and the complexity of property law the assessment of such values is a big subject on its own to which the attention of a whole profession is directed. It requires some years of study to understand fully and all that is attempted here is to outline the fundamental principles.

In fact that are a number of different ways in which a building is valued, each relevant to different situations; but underlying them all is the same mathematical principle explained in Chapter 8 in the discussion of life-cycle costing, that is relating a stream of income (and/or expenditure) in the future to capital value in the present. An investment in property implies essentially the same kind of decision process as the investment in a new heating system such as described in Chapter 11.

If we consider first the case of a building owned by a property company and leased to a commercial concern, the ownership of the building is only worth the income it generates; its value therefore depends on the level of that income; but if it yields, net after all costs, say £10 000 a year, what is it actually worth as a capital sum; how much could it be sold for?

To answer that question it is essential to understand two basic terms common in the property industry: 'yield' and 'years purchase'.

Yield usually means the income earned from a property investment expressed as a percentage of the investment in the value of the property. So if £500 000 is invested in a property from which, after expenses, £50 000 is received in rent, the yield is 10%. (But there are complications: see, for example, Baum and Mackmin, 1987, pp. 204–19 for a full discussion).

The level of yields in the property market bears some relationship to returns obtainable on other sorts of investment, or from the point of view of the financial institutions, property and other ways of investing their money are alternatives; if they can receive 5% from a secure investment such as government gilts, they will expect a higher yield (2% is often quoted) from the riskier investment in property; and the more risky a particular property appears, the higher the expected yield will be. When there are good prospects for increases in capital values of buildings, investors will be content with lower yields. In general yields have been stable but in the early 1990s they began to rise markedly (see Guy, 1994, p. 60–1).

The second concept which has to be understood is that of 'years purchase'; it is a phrase which goes back several centuries and in one sense can be defined and explained very simply. It is the reciprocal of the yield. If the yield on a property is 8%, the years purchase is 10.08 = 12.5. It offers a simple way of calculating the value of a building from the level of rents and the expected yield. The value is simply the annual income multiplied by the years purchase (YP).

For example assume an 8% yield is required from a building and the net income (rents less costs) is £20 000 a year; the following must be true, if V is the value of the building:

£20 000 is 8% of V, i.e. £20 000 = 0.08 × V
then V = £20 000/0.8
that is £20 000 × 12.5 (i.e. the years purchase)
or £250 000

It should also be clear from the example why the expression is called years purchase; it would take 12½ years of income to 'pay for' the building. However it should be recognized that this way of looking at the relationship between yield and value is a short cut. The real mathematical justification for using the reciprocal of the yield multiplied by the income as a measure of value is the result of a curious mathematical fact, that when incomes are considered to be earned to infinity ('in perpetuity' in the property terminology), the sum of their discounted values can be shown also to equal to the reciprocal of the rate of discount used multiplied by the annual income. This is difficult to grasp at first reading and is explained in greater detail in Figure 15.2. The reader has a choice at this point therefore: to read on, accepting simply that a building's value can estimated by using YP or (the better alternative!) to understand the concept more fully by studying Figure 15.2 carefully.

However a very simple hypothetical, and perhaps unlikely, example should help make the principle clear. Assume you have a spare plot of land big enough to build a small lock-up garage; you also know that some neighbours, tired of having their cars vandalized, are prepared to rent such a garage from you and it seems likely that you can charge £12 per week. To make it simple, assume your maintenance costs are £124 and therefore the net income will be £500 a year. You obviously do not want to pay more to have the garage built than it is actually worth; how much is it worth? The answer depends on what level of return you expect on your money and how long you think the building will last We will look at two possible ways of coming to a value first on the basis of a limited, 15-year life and secondly

Derivation of expression for Years Purchase in Perpetuity

The expression derived in Chapter 8 for the Present Value of an amount £A per annum received over n years and discounted at (ix100)% interest was :

$$\frac{A(1-(1+i)^{-n})}{i}$$

As the number of years(n) increases, the expression $(1+i)^{-n}$ becomes smaller; after very many years it will be close to zero. This effect can be seen quite clearly in Fig.8.5a,where at the high rate of 10% the present value of £1, i.e $(1+i)^{-n}$, is virtually zero by the time n reaches 40.

If $(1+i)^{-n}$ is treated as equivalent to zero the expression above obviously reduces to:

$$A(1-0)/i \text{ or } A/i$$

i.e. the present value of an amount £A per annum received in perpetuity discounted at (i x100)% is A divided by i or A multiplied by 1/i, the Years Purchase. E.g.if the rate is 5% then 1/.05 = 20. 20 is the YP

Figure 15.2   The derivation of expression for years purchase in perpetuity.

on the basis of a permanent income. Assume then that you feel you need at least 8% return (as you can get 6% without risk in a savings account).

If the garage will last 15 years, then be worth nothing, the calculation of its value could then be made as follows:

> Present value of £500 p.a. at 8% for 15 years (using the present value of £1 per annual tables – sometimes called years purchase table) = £4279.
>
> If you paid £4279 for the garage to be built it would be equivalent to putting money in the bank at 8%; you could then draw £500 a year for 15 years, at the end of which time you would have nothing left. In other words, having an income of £500 p.a. for 15 years is the same as having £4279 now; the garage can therefore be said to be worth £500 a year or £4279.

However, if optimistically you reckoned that with regular maintenance the building would last for ever then its value is the present value of £500 at 8% 'in perpetuity'; this as explained in Figure 15.2 is equal to £500 × 1/0.08 or 500 × 12.5 (the 'years purchase in perpetuity') or £6250.

Another way of putting this is that, should you pay £6250 for the garage and receive a net rent of £500, you will receive a yield of 8%; your position would be exactly the same as if you put money in the bank at 8% and left it there for good; you could draw an income of £500 every year leaving the capital intact. In this case the value of the garage can again be expressed as either '£500 p.a. in perpetuity' or £6250; the two are equivalent; the capital value is the income multiplied by the YP.

Now assume that you intend to borrow the money (and this is the unlikely bit!) from an institution which wishes to make a permanent investment in it, and that the lending institution has the same requirement for an 8% yield. If the income is £500 the institution will also value the building at £6250. It might either lend the money on that basis or actually wish to take over the garage by buying it off you at that sum (while you retain the freehold of the land). However there would be no point in the operation from your point of view if the garage cost that amount to build. You would either have to hand over all the income to the funders or sell it to them at no profit to yourself at all.

If however you could have it built for £5000 you could either sell it to the bank at a profit (of £1250) or borrow only the necessary £5000. In the second case the position would be as follows:

cost = £5000
loan = £5000

interest payments to the funders (8% on £5000) = £400 p.a.
income from rent = £500
therefore net income = £100 p.a.

You would then be making a profit of £100 per year. Interestingly if you capitalize that annual profit on the same YP principle at 8% the answer is £100 × 12.5 = £1250, the same figure as the profit made by selling to the funders. Either way you can be said to have made a capital profit of £1250. To take it one stage further and emphasize the equivalence, you could put your £1250 in a savings account at 8% and draw £100 a year without ever touching your capital.

Trivial though this example is, it actually contains in essence all the basic principles of property development; financing institutions do calculate values on the basis of YP; they do often take over ownership of the property and may then lease it back to the developer who makes his or her own return by letting it out at a total higher rent than was paid to the funder.

The example could be extended to illustrate many other aspects of property development and some suggestions are made at the end of the chapter.

We can, however, move a little closer to reality by considering the development and financing of an office block at its very simplest.

15.3.2 The developer's budget

To illustrate the application of these ideas in the context of property development, we can assume a very simple, but not totally untypical, situation. A developer intends to build an office block on a vacant piece of urban land, hoping to rent it to a single tenant. He does not have the funds to pay for the building himself and will therefore need to borrow. He borrows from bank funds to finance the building process itself, but needs to take out long-term funding once the building is completed. If the long-term funding is coming from an insurance company or a pension fund they will expect a return which in the light of alternative ways of investing their money is seen as sufficient to cover the risk involved.

Before committing himself to the project or attempting to raise finance the developer needs to know just how much it is going to cost, how much it will be worth when it is finished and of course whether he will be able to borrow the necessary finance. The calculations and assumptions he has to make are often shown in the form of a 'developer's budget'; there are several ways of presenting this and all oversimplify the reality to some degree but they are a useful vehicle for explaining and understanding. In the example presented in Figure 15.3, it is assumed that the price of obtaining the plot is fixed, that the height and total accommodation feasible are approximately known (very much influenced by planning requirements). The developer wants to assess whether he is likely to make an adequate profit.

The assessment of the scheme's feasibility is based on calculating the difference between 'development value' and the 'total development costs'. In calculating these totals there are obviously many uncertainties; for example the value of the building is going to depend in the way described above, on both the income that will be generated and the YP figure used. The YP will be determined by current yields on similar properties; if

Outline of a Simplified Development Appraisal

Development Value:

Estimated rental value: 10,000 sq.ft net
lettable area @ £20 per sq ft...................£200,000
assuming expected yield is 7.7%
Years Purchase at 7.7% (i.e.100/7.7)   x   13

Development value   **£2.600.000**

Development costs

Acquisition of site..........................   £950,000
 acquisition costs(e.g.legal and surveyors
 fees)   £40,000

Construction costs
12000 gross sq ft at £85 per sq.ft   £1.020,000

Professional fees...............................£200,000

Financing costs:
 land and acquisition
 18 months @ 6%   £89,000

 construction
 9 months @ 6%(averaged)   £23,000

Total development costs...................   £2,322,000

therfore developer's profit(£2,600,000-£2,322,000)= £278,000

Figure 15.3   The developer's budget: a simplified example.

financial institutions are expecting 8%, for example, then the YP is $1/0.08$ which is 12.5. This would reduce the value of the building in the example to £200 000 × 12.5 = £2 500 000. If, at the same time, the rents turned out to be only £18 per square foot, the building's value would be reduced to £180 000 × 12.5 = £2 225 000 – thus wiping out the developer's potential profit.

The rent will depend on many different factors; first the current demand for office space of that type in that location and the price of other alternatives. If demand is low and there is already some vacant office space in the area, then the proposed development might be difficult to let and will certainly not produce high rents; if however demand is high and alternatives few then obviously rents will rise. But it is at this point that the issue of design can be reintroduced as of critical importance; for the total rent obtainable from any commercial property depends not just on current supply and demand conditions but on the quality and amount of space a particular development can offer; these are both issues of design.

Before that point is pursued any further, the rest of the developer's budget calculation needs to be explained. The major costs in Figure 15.3 are the costs of acquiring the land (to which may be added in many cases the cost of buying and demolishing an older building), the costs of construction and various ancillary costs including the costs of short-term finance and various fees. If the developer's calculations (or the calculations of the institution which is going to provide long-term finance) indicate that the development's value is likely to be little more or even less than its cost, the scheme is most unlikely to go ahead. There have been periods, as we indicated earlier, when the shortage of property of a particular sort has been so severe that it seemed easy to make high profits; Marriott gives some spectacular examples. His figures for Centre Point indicate a notional capital profit for the developer, Oldham Estates of £11.7 million on a cost of £5 million! But there have also been long periods when profitable development has been extremely difficult to achieve; and it is in these periods that skilful economic designs become critical.

Obvious what the developer and the financial institutions will be looking for is the highest rents achievable for the lowest cost. There are therefore three primary requirements of the design. First it has to produce the highest lettable area possible; this issue has already been discussed in Chapter 9. Secondly it has to produce what will be perceived as good-quality space by potential tenants – providing the facilities they need as well as good working conditions. There are here as elsewhere many dimensions to the 'quality' of office space but, as suggested in Chapter 11, quality now includes low running costs and high-energy efficiency in particular. A particularly interesting current issue is the effect of changing perceptions and priorities. To take two quite different examples, full air conditioning and accessibility for disabled people. As awareness of the environmental and running costs of air conditioning grows and designers learn to offer good environmental conditions without it, its desirability will decrease. Again as the importance of accessibility is realized (and reinforced by Building Regulations), occupiers' perceptions of what is required are changing and with changing perceptions, rental values and hence capital values will also change. 'Interior landscape' has come to be expected, as part of good office environment and its design has developed as an area of special expertise (Duffy *et al.* 1976, 1993).

Thirdly a commercial development has to be buildable quickly, efficiently and inexpensively. As can be seen from the example in Figure 15.3, the costs of financing during the building period are high; in that for example if the project took six months longer to build than predicted, short-term finance costs would rise by about £40 000 – eroding the profitability considerably.

In the terms of the developer's budget as set out in Figure 15.3 then, the designer has major responsibility in the determination both of the value of the building and its costs – for ensuring in fact that the first is higher than the second. It does not follow by any means of course that the balancing of that equation necessarily results in high-quality building. Values higher than costs can be achieved at very different levels.

Where very high rents can be achieved – for prestigious offices in the centre of the major cities, for example, the quality expected will be commensurably high; land costs and building costs will also be high. At the other end of the scale very low rents might be all that are possible to achieve in a suburban area; it will not be possible to provide high specifications at those rents (although lower land and building costs will help). But the basic principle will still apply – the building has to offer accommodation good enough to yield a value above the cost of construction.

15.3.3 A real example

The sort of model discussed so far is a very simple one; in the real world of property development life is much more complicated. Instead of a single developer building one building for rent and simply borrowing money to do so, there are a multitude of alternative arrangements between financiers, developers, contractors and owners involving different types of letting in one development.

During the early post-war property boom, funding bodies – the pension funds and insurance companies – very quickly became aware that they were often lending money to developers on terms which allowed any capital gains to accrue to the developers themselves, while the return to the lenders was limited to repayment of the initial loans with interest. The institutions understandably came to expect a greater share in the high returns from successful and very profitable development, and many new methods of funding were developed both to give the institutions a share in the equity of the property and to protect them against risk. There are now many ways of doing this but one example, based on an actual recent development, will illustrate the principles involved.

The scheme was a 49 000 sq. ft. speculative office development in a major Midlands city, built by a property company with finance from a major pension fund. The total costs were estimated as follows (the figures have been rounded for simplicity):

Acquisition of land and buildings:	£2 500 000
Developer's preliminary cost	500 000
Professional, agents, legal fees etc.	750 000
Construction costs	4 250 000
Contingency	150 000
Total development costs	£8 150 000

In addition, interest charges for finance during the period of construction were reckoned at 7.25% and estimated to amount to £550 000 over the 20 month development. Rents for office space in that area at that period were approximately £19 per square foot; as the fund required a return of 8%, the value of the building (i.e. at 12.5 YP) could be estimated as £49 000 × 12.5 = £11 637 500.

The pension fund agreed to provide the finance through what is known as a profit erosion scheme, through which they become owners of the building and the developer's profit depends on the final levels of rent achieved, the time of letting and a number of other factors. The return is in effect shared between the developer and the funder, but if things go wrong, if the building is not let for example, the developer's share can be completely 'eroded'.

In this case the funders acquired the existing land (and buildings) then provided the developer with finance for the development process itself, that is they provided the short-term as well as the long-term financing. The short-term loan was on a lower interest rate of 7.25% to be 'rolled up' an then incorporated in the total cost of the building. The agreement with the developer was complex as it included the procedures for and financial implications of a whole range of possible outcomes, for example: that the project was not let for a long period; that it was only partly let; that rents were higher or lower than predicted; that the net lettable area turned out to be less than predicted and so on.

In the event the development was let only nine months after completion at a rent higher than that used in the initial calculation. Under the agreement this meant that the developer received a bonus equivalent to the difference between the valuation at the original rent and the actual total commitment the fund had originally been prepared to make (with a number of minor adjustments). Furthermore he received some of the difference between predicted and actual rents, capitalized and shared on an agreed basis.

Even this scheme was a relatively simply project in financing terms compared with many – but again it illustrates the basic principles and the vulnerability of 'value' to changes (or incorrect estimates) in rent levels and to the particular requirements of funding institutions.

15.3.4 Developments by the owner occupiers

The other form of commercial development which we will refer to very briefly is the construction of a building or buildings specifically for (and by) a company or other organization for its own use. Examples are many: the retail developments of companies such as Sainsbury's, Tesco, Marks & Spencer, B & Q, factories in industrial parks, office headquarters such as for Barclays Bank.

The supermarket chains are now major owners of very large property portfolios. Sainsbury's and Tesco each have nearly £2.5 billion of freehold property as well as over £500 million pounds worth of long and short leases. Marks & Spencer's properties were worth something in the order of £1.5 billion in 1992 (Guy, 1994, p. 116).

Very large organizations like these may be able to generate the finance from their own resources but, perhaps because they wish to invest their own cash elsewhere, may still borrow from the financial institutions. According to Guy retailers have in recent years funded their developments through a mixture of loans and share issues. Many different financing techniques have been used, including sale and leaseback arrangements, where the occupier sells its property to a finance or property company then takes out a long lease. Guy quotes a number of recent examples in the retail business, such as Gateway's sale of 31 stores to British Land in 1991 for nearly £400 million. Such a deal means that the retailer does not have its capital tied up in the property but can use it to develop its main business (or indeed use it as the initial finance of new stores).

In these non–speculative developments – i.e. bespoke developments for a

Signs of recession, 1994.

particular client – commercial property criteria still apply but other factors relevant to the particular business will also come into play. A business might have its own budget constraints and its own clear ideas as to value for money. Their appraisal of their own property investments, for example, will not be based on its lettable value to others, but in the increases in income or profits which the new premises is going to make possible. The basis of its valuation should still in principle be the same. A company investing in a new factory, for example, should require the net increase in its income, flowing as a direct result of the new facilities, to have an estimated present value higher than the cost of the investment. Whether companies make or can make such calculations with any degree of accuracy is a different matter.

A hotel chain building a new hotel will make calculations based on the number of bedrooms, the average charge per night, the expected level of occupancy, the opportunities for earning from conferences and meetings and 'special occasions' (a very important source of income today). The expected expenses of running the hotel will be deducted from the total of all these sources of revenue to give a net income.

That net income has then to be compared with the cost of building the hotel in the first place, which might be done in one of several ways. One way would be to compare the present value of the future income with the capital cost using an appropriate discount rate. But the hotel might in fact take a quite short-term view; the investment could be financed on a relatively short loan like a mortgage, with capital and interest paid over say ten years. The decision to invest in a new hotel will then depend on whether the net income each year is sufficient to service the loan – and leave a profit for the owners. Another alternative would be a sale and leaseback arrangement as with the retail stores mentioned above.

The design criteria that are likely to arise from these conditions should be fairly clear: the owner will want the maximum number of bedrooms of sufficient standard to justify a reasonable charge, plus facilities for dining conference and meeting. Cynics might feel that one result of the commercial pressures on hotels is, judging by some recently built examples, that the appearance of relative luxury has become more significant than architectural quality – but that is not a necessary consequence of the financing system itself.

However, although firms might determine their own budgets and investment criteria in ways appropriate to their particular business, the commercial market value will still be an important consideration, particularly if the scheme is funded by a financial institution; for it may one day be necessary to sell it to another owner.

15.4 Conclusion

Commercial pressures are bound to operate in the private sector; there is no escape from the iron law that value has to be more than cost. This does not inevitably mean poor-quality building, unless the budget is absurdly low. But it does mean that architects have to be able to design in ways which allow the money available to generate maximum value – and not be lost for example in inefficient construction. It also means that architects have to be able to persuade clients of the commercial value of good-quality design; if quality is correctly perceived and understood as incorporating the best facilities, energy efficiency, low maintenance and the provision of enjoyable as well as efficient working environment, that should not be impossible.

FOR FURTHER STUDY

1 Recommended reading

O. Marriott's *The Property Boom* (1967) is still worth reading. It was a remarkable piece of first class journalism which put in the shade much academic writing on the subject. For a fairly detailed modern examination of the property market, see D. Cadman and L. Austin Crowe's *Property Development* (1991).

There are many books on property valuation; Richmond's *Introduction to Valuation* (3rd edn, 1994) has recently been revised; Baum and Mackmin's *The Income Approach to Property Valuation* (1989) sets out the basic mathematics clearly then explores its application different methods of valuation. Although specialized, Clifford Guy's *The Retail Development Process* (1994) contains a readable and up-to-date introduction to the whole system. *Responsive Environments* (Bentley *et al.*, 1985) has an excellently clear exposition with examples of the financing and design principles of mixed commercial developments.

On the relationship between design and costs for offices see Duffy, Cave and Worthington (1976) and Duffy, Laing and Crisp (1994).

Over the years the *Architects' Journal* has published many special reports and studies on the economics of various sorts of development, both commercial and public sector, which often discuss financing as well as costs.

2 Exercises

a Take the simple example of the garage development in the chapter and work out the consequences of the following changes in circumstances:

■ a drop in the general level of interest rates;
■ an increase in the rent which could be earned;
■ an increase in building costs.

b A commercial development of 40 000 sq. ft. lettable area is expected to produce a rent of £21.75 per square foot; construction costs, fees, and development finance are estimated at £7.2 million. If the building's value is calculated on the basis of an 8% yield, what is the maximum amount that could be paid for the site and demolition of any existing building on it?

3 Discussion or essay questions

a Using references from the financial press, explore the story of the Canary Wharf development; in what ways and on what criteria has it become a success or failure?
b What arguments could you use to persuade a client wanting new office premises that design 'quality' is worth paying for, taking account of all the likely pressures to keep costs down?

Values, cost limits and prices: the case of housing

16.1 Introduction

In the last chapter it was shown how the amount of money that can be spent on a commercial building will be limited by its value as determined in the market. In the public sector, at least until recently, the cost limits were determined by different criteria; the notion of 'value for money' has been differently defined. Very often – perhaps most often – it has been defined in terms of standards and cost norms or limits. For example the allowable costs of schools were determined on the standards required by the Ministry (later Department) of Education and how much it should cost to achieve those standards. So the amount of space per pupil was one of the criteria of 'standards'; and costs were calculated on the basis of what was thought to be reasonable at a particular time in a particular place. Efforts were (and are) constantly made to improve the value achievable for given costs by research into design production methods and the dissemination of results. The CLASP system was an outcome of one such programme.

Over the last few years attitudes and procedures have been changing both with privatization of many formerly public-sector activities and with the application of private-sector investment criteria to public construction investment. It is difficult at present to make a realistic assessment of practice across all public-sector construction activities and some references or further study are given at the end of the chapter. Instead we will concentrate on one special case which spans both sectors and illustrates quite vividly the difference between a 'market' approach and a 'norm-based' approach – the building of houses.

Housebuilding in Britain has been conventionally categorized, at least since the series of Housing Acts after the First World War, into public-sector and private-sector; the public sector consisted almost entirely of local authority housing departments which from 1919 onward particularly built low-cost subsidized housing on a substantial scale. The private sector included the speculative housebuilders and the developers of housing for private renting but became completely dominated by building for owner occupation as the private rented market declined.

Since 1969 a third group of providers, the housing associations, has become increasingly significant. At one time included in official statistics as 'private', they became recognized as unequivocally 'public' when they became dependent on government subsidy and government loan finance. Since the Housing Act 1988, their status – public or private – has become increasingly ambiguous as government has reduced grant levels, insisted on associations raising funds from the private market and officially defined them as 'businesses'. Meanwhile the local authorities' powers to develop have been strictly curtailed, leaving the associations virtually the only organizations currently producing what has come to be called, in a phrase adopted from abroad and much disliked by many (for both political and grammatical reasons) 'social housing'; it is an unfortunate phrase but difficult at present to avoid. Other public/private sector hybrids are emerging – such as housing trusts and 'housing companies'.

For ease of exposition, this chapter therefore adopts a simple division into two sectors. The first part, section 16.2, examines the cost and financing of housing which is supported by government capital subsidies, that is most housing produced formerly by local authorities but mainly by housing associations – 'social housing'. Both local authorities and housing associations have at various times built for sale – but mostly for renting to people on relatively low incomes. The second half of the chapter, section 16.3 looks at the economic factors which affect houses built by developers for profit and sold to owner occupiers or less often private landlords. The private sector is by far the largest sector, as Figure 16.1(a) and (b) shows, but makes relatively little use of consultant architects, quantity surveyors or small general contractors, for reasons which will be explained.

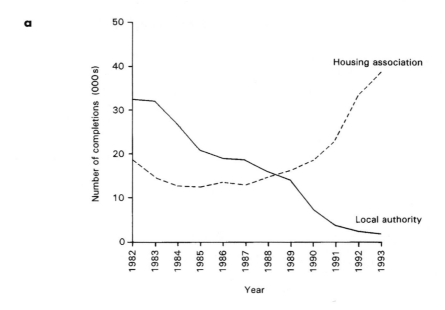

Note: Private sector starts range from 221 000 in 1980 to 120 000 in 1992

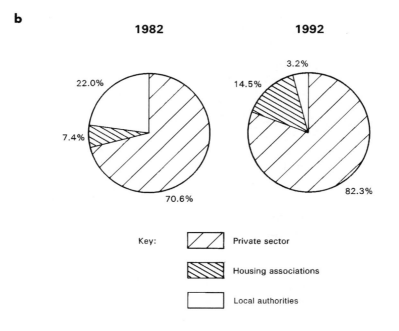

Figure 16.1   Housing completions by type of developer.
(a) and (b)   *Source*: Housing and Construction Statistics.

16.2 The 'social-housing' sector

Even more often perhaps than in the case of the building types discussed in the previous chapter, architects designing for this sector have usually had to work within often very restrictive budgets for very exacting clients. Cost limits or guidelines have been set and monitored by the subsidizing authorities (once the Ministry of Housing, then Department of the Environment and now the Housing Corporation) and, at times of rising materials and labour prices, have often made high standards difficult to achieve.

Some form of cost control is an inevitable consequence of subsidy, as governments realized very quickly when such controls have not been in operation. The reason is very simple: if subsidies are available without control on costs, they might simply have the effect of encouraging inefficiency or, if given to the private sector, of being diverted into excess profits; indeed it has often been alleged that this always happens. It was also quickly realized, but sometimes seems to have been forgotten, that once cost controls are imposed, it is necessary to have some way of maintaining standards, otherwise cost limits might be met by reducing the size of houses built and quality of specification. Often in the history of British council housing quality and cost standards have been part of a single system; sometimes as when the recommendations of the Parker Morris report were implemented after 1968, standards have been defined and mandatory; at other times they have been advisory and less well defined, but designs for houses by local authorities made subject to ministerial approval.

The actual techniques of control have varied throughout the 70-year history of subsidized housing in Britain and there is a wide range of different systems in all countries where subsidized housing is produced. The possibilities are many. Sometimes allowable cost levels have been explicitly linked to market values of similar houses in the owner-occupied sector. But more often, limits have been established on the basis of what are deemed to be reasonable costs for a particular size and standard of dwelling.

The history of these cost controls and subsidy systems, in the UK alone, is complex and readers interested should refer to the texts recommended at the end of the chapter. We will concentrate here on the current position. Furthermore as most housing built with government capital subsidy is now provided by housing associations (though most of the public sector **stock** is still owned by local authorities), the focus will be on them. The discussion will also be limited to new building for although originally most associations concentrated on rehabilitation, this is now a very small part of their operations.

Before delving into the way the cost limits and financing system operate, it is necessary to explain what the associations are and to describe the role of the Housing Corporation, which monitors and controls their activities.

16.2.1 The housing associations and the Housing Corporation

Although many of the organizations which are now housing associations can trace histories back into the last century and beyond (in the case of the oldest, a continuous line back to the thirteenth century almshouses) the modern form of association has developed essentially since 1969 when the Housing Act of that year increased there eligibility for subsidy. From 1974, they became a recognized arm of the public sector and many new associations were formed, some expanding very rapidly indeed. Most of the older associations were originally charitable bodies as were many of the new, but there were also non-charity associations which consequently had a different tax status and fewer restrictions on their activities; the distinction became particularly significant when tenants of non-charitable associations were given the 'right-to-buy'. All housing associations are managed by voluntary management committees (at the time of writing but there are signs that this could change).

There are approximately 1600 associations, most of which are very small; the largest however now have more houses under management than some local authorities. Table 16.1 shows the range and size of associations in 1993.

However the largest category in the table includes associations like North British which has 27 000 homes throughout the country and the largest regional association, Merseyside Improved Houses with over 17 000.

The Housing Corporation, originally established with a very minor role in 1964, was given responsibility in 1974 for the oversight of all associations receiving government subsidy; to continue to receive support, associations were required to register with the Corporation and had to meet a range of criteria. At the time, the associations were making a relatively modest

Table 16.1   Size of housing associations by number of units in management. *Source: NFHA Directory and Year Book 1994.*

No of units managed	No of associations	Total stock
0–249	1275	54 000
250–2499	271	256 000
over 2500	88	588 000
Total	1634	898 000

contribution to new housing developments in the public sector, but as government policy shifted towards a reduction in the local authorities' housing role and increased that of the associations, the Housing Corporation's responsibilities and powers expanded; and the complexity of its procedures and requirements grew.

By the beginning of the 1990s housing associations accounted for over 80% of all development assisted by government capital grants and they also account for quite a large proportion (though it is difficult to establish exactly) of the work of small to medium-sized architectural practices. An understanding of the grant and cost control regime has become essential for successful work in this field and this in turn requires some knowledge of the finance and control system as a whole. Unfortunately it is a system which is continually under review with the details changing virtually every year but the broad principles have remained more or less the same since the Housing Act 1988.

16.2.2 Finance, costs and standards

The current system in England (it operates with some differences in Scotland and Wales) is described in outline in the following paragraphs.

Housing association's developments now receive capital finance from two major sources, the Housing Corporation which provides capital grants, and the financial institutions which provide long-term finance on commercial terms. The second source is relatively recent; before 1988, the state (through the local authorities or the Housing Corporation) was the source of long-term loans as well as grants.

The Corporation controls the scale of the total development programme and the costs of those developments through two major mechanisms.

1. It approves associations' development programmes and allocates money in the form of grants – mainly Housing Association grant; an association which does not receive such an allocation will normally not be able to build.
2. It sets cost indicators to which associations have to work if they are to receive funding: these are currently known as total cost indicators.

Figure 16.2 shows schematically and in a very simplified way the parallel sets of decisions made by the Corporation and a small association, though the decisions only coincide **in time** in the second part of the diagram. For larger associations, so-called 'programme associations' the sequence of decisions will be different as they will be considering rolling programmes rather than individual schemes. The diagram should help to make the following discussion of the system and procedures clearer.

BUILDHOLME HOUSING ASSOCIATION LTD	HOUSING CORPORATION (regional office)
wishes to build block of 14 flats for elderly people on identified cleared inner city site	Receives allocation from London (based on Housing Needs Index for region)
Requests architects for costed feasibility study	
establishes that (a)scheme can be built within Total Cost Indicator (b) assuming levels of grant and cost of loan finance, rents will be reasonable	
Includes scheme in bid for funds to Housing Corporation	Receives bids from housing associations in region
	Decides which schemes it can support and what levels of funding (grant) for each association or scheme
Scheme approved Grant level agreed with HC Private finance negotiated	approves specific programmes
Detailed design, planning permission etc.	
Scheme out to tender	
Tenders returned all above TCI Detailed plan adjusted to reduce costs	(approves final cost estimate)
Lowest tender accepted	
Scheme on site	pays grant in stages as scheme develops

Figure 16.2   The Housing Corporation and housing association decision processes.

Each year the Housing Corporation receives an allocation of funds from the Government which in turn it allocates to its nine English regions; this regional allocation is made on the basis of the 'Housing Needs Indicator', a formula which is intended to reflect the relative housing needs of each region on a number of different criteria such as the balance between number of households and dwellings, the condition of the current housing stock, and, after a reversal of a decision to remove it, the level of homelessness.

Individual housing associations make bids to the regional offices of the Corporation for their proposed development programme. For smaller associations the bids will be for money for specific schemes but in the case of the larger ones which have what is known as a 'cash programme agreement' with the Housing Corporation, it will be for a rolling three-year programme of development, individual schemes not being specified in detail. The region will then allocate money in the form of grants to associations according to their (and the Government's) perception of the current priorities.

This will itself be affected by local authorities' view of what is required, for local authorities are still seen as having a 'strategic responsibility' for housing in their areas. For example, a particular authority may have identified a need for some five-bedroomed family houses and for some special housing under the community care scheme, but reckon there is sufficient accommodation for fit elderly people. The Housing Corporation regional office responsible for that local authority area will take these priorities into account when allocating funds to particular associations. They will also consider many other factors, including the associations' financial strength, capacity to manage the proposed development, track record of efficient performance and perhaps most importantly, whether they believe the proposed scheme represents good value for money.

Given that the total requests for money from associations are always far in excess of the funds available, most associations will be disappointed; they are unlikely to receive enough to fund all their proposals and they may not receive any allocation at all.

The general level of housing association grant – that is the percentage on average of each scheme's cost that will be financed by the Corporation is determined each year (essentially by the government in consultation with the Corporation).

From 1989 to 1991, 73% of costs were met from HAG; by 1994/95 this was down to 62%. The government proposed to reduce this to 60% and to 55% in 1995/96; there was strong opposition not only from the associations but from the private funders, afraid that rents might reach unaffordable levels; in the event rates were actually cut to an average of 58%.

The Government's stated policy was to continue to reduce these levels on the grounds that each pound of public money can be made to produce more housing (through leveraging larger proportions of private finance).

The actual amount of grant available for an individual scheme, however, can vary widely, from 100% on some forms of development to virtually none in some exceptional circumstances. The rates are set out in a complex table related to the cost indicators discussed below and each association has to calculate the level for which each scheme will be eligible.

For the small or medium-sized association which has authority for a particular development, the grant will be a fixed percentage of the **actual cost** of the scheme. In the case of the large associations, which have agreements for funding over several years, the grant will be a fixed percentage of the total cost indicator (explained below) for the programme as a whole, and associations may apply this differently to different specific projects. There are signs that associations prepared to produce schemes using less than the official grant proportions will receive favourable treatment.

16.2.3 Private finance

As housing association grant covers only a proportion of the total costs of development; the difference, which used to be funded by a loan from the Housing Corporation itself, now has to be found privately, that is, borrowed from institutions such as building societies and similar financial agencies; some small proportion of capital costs may be met from the capital reserves of the association itself or from charitable sources.

Most of the money comes from banks and building societies but there are now organizations specifically set up to act as intermediaries between City institutions and the association. The most important of these is the Housing Finance Corporation, which operates on a large scale and for bigger associations. Some large associations are now financially strong enough to issue their own bonds while at the other end smaller associations have to raise the money by borrowing directly from banks or building societies on terms little different from a conventional mortgage.

Figure 16.3(a) and (b) show the growth of private finance in the 1990s and the main sources of the money.

The cost of this finance is critical for the viability of schemes and the introduction of private funds has added new pressures and requirements on associations. Repayments on the loans have to be met from rents; the higher the proportion of costs which have to be met from borrowing and the higher the costs of borrowing, the higher the rents will be. Associations in the early 1990s have claimed that as grant rates have reduced, the costs of financing loans is pushing up rents to unacceptable levels. The Housing Corporation's response has been to press associations to bring total costs down by whatever means they can, including building on a large scale, using design build contracts and private developers' standard house types.

On the other hand the financial institutions themselves are not anxious to see grant rates drop too far; for if they do the proportion of rents paid by housing benefit will increase; the future income stream from which loans will be repaid therefore becomes more vulnerable to political decisions, on

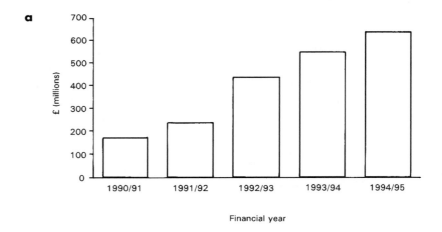

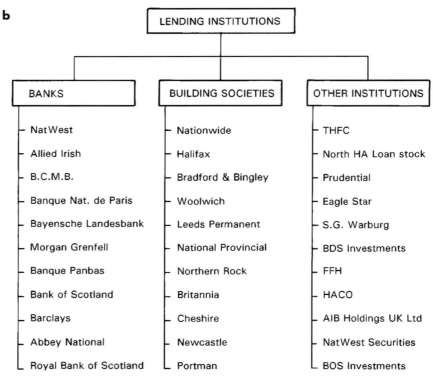

Figure 16.3   Growth and sources of private finance for housing associations.
(a) and (b)   *Source:* National Federation of Housing Associations – Financial Monitor

the levels and eligibility of tenants for benefit. Partly as a consequence of this, institutions expect high levels of collateral in the form of (conservatively valued) properties, for every loan.

16.2.4 The total cost indicator

The limit on the costs of houses built for associations is set generally by what is now known as the total cost indicator (TCI); the word generally is used because there are circumstances where costs may be higher or lower; nevertheless TCI sets the generally allowable level.

Associations will not normally submit bids unless they believe their schemes can be built at or below TCI which is based on the Housing Corporation assessment of what buildings of a particular size and type ought to cost if designed and built efficiently.

Tables showing the relevant TCI for schemes of different types, sizes and regions are published annually by the Housing Corporation; extracts are shown in Table 16.2. A base table sets out indicative costs for houses categorized by floor area and by what is termed their 'cost group'; these

Table 16.2   Extract from the Housing Cooporation's Total Cost Indicator tables, 1995–96

(a) Total unit costs 1995/6: all self-contained accommodation

Unit floor area m²	Probable occupancy (persons)	Cost group		
		A	C	F
up to 25	1	£45 200	34 600	31 300
exceeding/ not exceeding				
25/30	1	49 900	37 600	33 800
30/45	1 & 2	54 500	40 600	36 300
35/40	1 & 2	59 100	43 600	38 800
etc.				
65/70	3 & 4	86 800	61 700	53 700
70/75	3, 4 & 5	91 400	64 700	56 200
115/120	6. 7 & 8	127 500	87 800	75 100

(b) Supplementary multipliers (examples)

Frail elderly	1.37	1.43	1.46
Special needs	1.23	1.28	1.29

cost groups are regions of the country where building costs are considered to be approximately the same. Cost group A, for example, includes the more expensive London Boroughs, whereas the lowest cost group, group F, covers boroughs in mainly northern counties. There is a second base table, for shared housing, in which costs are related to number of people sharing, not floor area.

However the system is not quite that simple. The costs in the basic table relate to the acquisition of site and works. Many adjustments have to be made before the appropriate cost can be determined for a particular scheme. Most of these are defined as 'multipliers' to be applied to the basic cost indicators. For example, in group A the multiplier for works only is 0.65, whereas in group F it is 0.84. This reflects the fact that, in London, a higher proportion of the cost of new buildings will be for land.

For rehabilitation schemes the multipliers vary depending on the state of the house when acquired, the type of tenancy and, again, the region of the country. Other multipliers are used to allow for the special costs (or savings) rising from particular characteristics of the accommodation or form of contract. For example, special needs accommodation for frail elderly people carries a multiplier of 1.37 in area A and 1.46 in area F. Design and build contracts are expected to produce lower costs and have a common multiplier of 0.98.

Furthermore there is a second set of adjustments to cover on-costs such as legal fees, valuations, insurance premiums etc. These range from 8% (i.e. a multiplier of 1.08) for buildings bought off the shelf from a private developer, to 30% for re-improvements; and there are additional on-cost allowances for special schemes.

Put briefly and in summary form like this, the system sounds complicated though it is reasonably logical. However, it does show how cost control systems of this type inevitably generate complex rules and criteria if they are to be fairly applicable to many different circumstances; and the more complex they become the more they lend themselves to conflicting interpretation and manipulation.

Some flexibility is essential. These cost indicators are not applied mechanically; they are not absolute cost limits and are intended, as their name suggests, to indicate to the associations level of cost to be expected in particular circumstances. Furthermore they do not necessarily apply in all circumstances to individual buildings; there can be a degree of pooling of costs across different dwellings in a scheme and, for housing associations running larger, agreed development programmes, cost can in effect be pooled across a number of different schemes.

For most purposes, the TCI is an upper limit on the amount an association can spend on a particular scheme. But there is now considerable pressures on associations to bid below these costs. They might be able to do this for a number of reasons. First they may be willing and able to subsidize a scheme themselves, from their own reserves. Secondly they may be prepared to see rents rise high enough to finance a higher level of private funding.

Thirdly they might reduce standards. This is, naturally, a highly controversial issue and when a research report (Joseph Rowntree Trust, 1994) claimed that housing associations were producing unacceptably small homes, there was a considerable outcry. The Housing Corporation issues guidance (*Scheme Development Standards*: Housing Corporation, 1994) which lays down its expectations in regard to such aspects of quality: external environment, internal environment, accessibility, safety and security, energy efficiency and building practice. Associations' schemes are tested for compliance with these expectations during what is known as the scheme audit. However there is a highly significant omission from these requirements: there are no space standards. And while it is true that many of the other standards could not be met unless space was adequate, it still allows scope for homes to be built, for example below the Parker Morris standards (originally proposed as absolute minima) (Parker Morris Committee, 1961).

There are also circumstances in which an association may spend above TCI levels on a particular scheme if they can provide the extra funding from another source, or persuade the Housing Corporation that there are exceptional reasons for such extra spending. Any extra unsubsidized costs will normally imply higher rent levels and as housing associations exist to provide low-rent accommodation, they will want to avoid extra costs of this sort.

As mentioned briefly above, the actual grant levels for particular schemes are also tied to the category and costs of dwelling provided. The relationship is set out in a separately published table of grant rates each year. As this changes, there is no point in describing it in detail.

16.2.5 The consultant's role

In a system like this the role of the architect and quantity surveyor in the early stages of a scheme is critical. This is even more true now that the risks of any overspend on a scheme have to be borne by the association itself. The extra costs will have to be met from reserves if they are available or passed on to tenants in the form of higher rent, undermining the whole object of the subsidized scheme.

An architect working with an association will therefore have a brief which will state the number and type of dwellings required, the site, and the cost limit calculated by the association on the basis of the TCI table, grant rates and other factors specific to them (such as the expected cost of private finance).

The brief will also require certain quality standards to be met, determined by the association which may also have very specific preferences on aspects of the design itself. Associations which have been operating for many years have become very knowledgeable clients and know exactly what they require. However, the architect who understands the operation of the TCI tables, for example, may well be able to suggest alternative mixes or arrangements of accommodation which will allow more cost effective – or grant effective – schemes. For example, by designing so that an extra unit can be incorporated on a given site (within the constraints imposed by the local planning policies), land costs as a proportion of total scheme costs might be reduced. Or by having more one-bedroom and fewer two-bedroom units, more grant might be available for a particular building cost.

An interesting example of the possibilities of reducing costs and increasing standards is the use of the Lifetime Homes concept by Edwin Trotter Associates for Habinteg Housing Association (Joseph Rowntree Trust, 1994). A range of standard house types has been designed 'which enables any developer of housing to put together a full mix of dwelling types on a site of any shape or size. Using the standard design route means that the features required by the Lifetime Homes concept (including full accessibility for disabled people) cost no more' (Edwin Trotter Associates, 1993) (see Figure 16.4). As the TCI allows extra for homes designed with full wheelchair access for example, this design should allow more money to be put into other aspects of the houses without exceeding cost limits. Unfortunately the reality is that it will merely mean such houses can actually still be built as grant rates reduce.

It is obviously important in any housing association scheme to get the design and cost relationship right from the beginning; the cost limits are known and there is relatively little flexibility. Some compromises may be necessary but right from the early stages the architect and client association have to be very clear what these might be, and where it is possible to save money without reducing quality.

The architects and QS have to have a good knowledge not only of how particular forms of building levels of accommodation and standards can be achieved, but also of current tendering climate and the direction in which tender prices are likely to move. The initial design proposals may well be produced several years before the building work begins. If decisions to cut costs have to be made at a late stage, for example after tenders have been received, or even worse after a scheme has started, it may be necessary to reduce standards in ways which neither the architect or client wants.

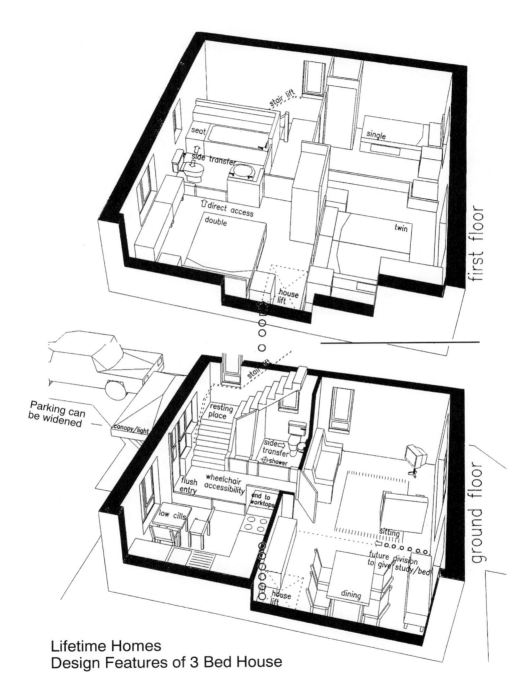

first floor

ground floor

stair lift

seat

single

side transfer

⇧direct access

double

twin

house lift

Parking can be widened

stair lift

resting place

canopy/light

side transfer
shower

flush entry

wheelchair accessibility

end to worktops

low cills

sitting

future division to give study/bed

house lift

dining

Lifetime Homes
Design Features of 3 Bed House

Figure 16.4   Lifetime Homes.
Source: Edwin Trotter Associates, 1993.

Throughout the 1980s, the collaboration between architects and housing associations has produced much housing which has been widely recognized as of excellent quality at many different levels. The level of tenant satisfaction has been high, as shown by many general and individual association surveys. Subsidized housing producers generally, both those local authorities which are still building and housing associations, have been consistently winners of housing and civic design awards; in 1993 for example 13 of the 16 regional Housing Design Awards were won by public sector schemes. Housing associations have also gained a reputation for the development of innovative energy conserving designs.

Until recently, most schemes have been built under a traditional procurement method, using JCT 80 or similar, but it is now increasingly the case that the associations will use design and build or some form of management contracting. The reason is pressure from the Housing Corporation to do so in the belief that overall costs will be reduced. Perhaps because of this, but almost certainly because of the pressure to exploit economies of scale and the reduction in grant etc., there are sure indicators in 1994 that the reputation for quality is beginning to crumble. It can only be restored and maintained with a combination of careful design and careful costing – but there are, as has been pointed out in the other chapters, always lower limits below which the maintenance of quality is impossible and without adequate finance the best will not reappear.

16.3 The speculative housebuilding market

There are naturally many similarities and connections between the building of houses for the private home ownership market and for the housing associations. Many housebuilding firms are involved in both sectors, some with major divisions specializing in each: Laing, and Lovell Homes and Westbury are three which have depended heavily on the housing association sector during the housing market recession of the early 1990s. As housing associations are pushed further into volume development, there are likely to be more linkages of this sort.

However there are major differences between the two markets. To begin with private housebuilders are normally both developers and builders – they are concerned with everything from design through construction to marketing.

Though drawing on the same resources as contractors and though subject to the same basic input costs – for land, materials and labour – they face quite different financial and cost constraints. The upper limits on the cost of the houses themselves for example are essentially determined by the difference between land costs and the prices at which the houses can be sold. These prices are in turn governed by, mainly, the price and availability of mortgages and the income security of potential purchasers – all extremely difficult to predict.

The recent history of the industry abounds with dramatic successes and equally dramatic failures, gambles that paid off and more that did not, of flamboyant personalities, bitter take-over battles and the steady devouring of small firms by large. That history is not relevant here except to make the point that it provides a picture of an industry very sensitive to economic fluctuations where success or failure depends very much on how cleverly – or luckily – the firms ride the upswings and downswings.

The sector is dominated by a small number of large firms; some of these are almost solely housebuilders, others divisions of even larger organizations and others parent companies with subsidiaries of their own. There are approximately 25 firms building over 2000 houses a year (see Chapter 7) and although the largest are currently building about 7000, at peak times a few firms, such as Barratts, have reached over 12 000 a year.

But there are also very many small firms building only a few houses a year; these are usually contractors extending their operations but at times of booming markets and really high prices, when profits have appeared to be easily available, all sorts of organizations have entered the field, usually to leave rapidly when the downturn came.

As there are so many different types of firm and such variations in market conditions, it is difficult to generalize about the relationships between finance, costs and quality on the speculative building market. All housebuilders are operating under similar economic forces, but the larger ones can respond in different ways from the smaller.

First, for the volume builders the costs and production of the houses themselves become almost a minor issue, in the sense that the control of costs and the production system is not their major problem – or rather it is a problem very much under control. This is because they use a range of standard designs, produced in large numbers; they can programme, cost and build with considerable accuracy.

For many years, as we saw in Chapter 6, housebuilders have aimed to match the techniques of mass production manufacturing and hence achieve the same high levels of productivity and low unit costs. In the United States in the 1940s, William Levitt was quite explicit about his imitation of the Ford production line in the building of his two Levittowns (Long Island and Pennsylvania); as was also shown in Chapter 6, computers are bringing the objective of production line systems for housing much closer.

The large-scale developers have other advantages of size, not all strictly economies of scale in the sense defined in Chapter 4, advantages, for example, of bulk purchase of materials, even having components made

End of one experiment: demolition of flats. Hyde Park, Sheffield, 1992.

The new social housing: can quality be maintained?

specifically for them in mass-produced quantities. They will of course suffer, like all builders, if the price of their materials or labour increases rapidly but again because they are big, they are in a strong position to control the impact of such increases. Collectively they represent the major market for any materials and even individually they are important customers for the materials suppliers; they are therefore in a strong bargaining position.

The houses are virtually mass-produced objects, which like cars can be varied to provide different models and even customized but which essentially have to cover average costs over a large output to return a profit. The volume builders look for high turnover rather than high unit profits. But the real fundamental issues for them are the price and availability of land, the price and availability of funding, and the buoyancy of the housing market.

Nearly all housebuilding firms suffer severely in recessions; but it is the smallest which suffer the most. This is mainly because of their relative financial weakness. In order to buy land and materials they will almost certainly have to borrow money from the banks, money which banks willingly lend while markets are buoyant. Once it becomes difficult to sell houses and prices drop, small housebuilders find their profits disappear but more importantly they cannot finance the loans and finally their creditors are likely to take action.

Even relatively large builders can find themselves in severe financial difficulties when recession is prolonged. Trencherwood and Lovell were among major housebuilders rescued by banks in 1993; and as the recession ends, difficulties can increase as materials and land prices rise, forcing firms to borrow more if they are to continue production. Bovis Homes and Ideal Homes lost £62 million and £72 million respectively in 1992 and could have been in very serious trouble had they not been subsidiaries of larger organizations (P & O and Trafalgar House); and Tarmac's huge losses of £350 million in 1992/93 were in part attributable to the collapse of house sales.

However most companies – large and medium – have shown considerable resilience; they have acquired more secure long-term funding and they may have a range of other assets which can be disposed of to maintain their balance sheet positions in the short term. Some indeed have benefited from depression. Barratt became established and expanded rapidly by mopping up smaller builders and their land banks during the house market slump of the early 1970s. And in the early 1980s, in Sir Lawrie Barratt's own words, 'we went from strength to strength . . . we are happier working in a recession' (*Building*, 5 Feb. 1993). Firms like Barratt which can hold on to or acquire land banks in times of recession are of course then in a very strong position to compete when the upturn comes – if it does.

The particular circumstances of the housebuilding market have meant that housebuilders have a different perception of quality and of standards than say the housing associations or than architects designing houses for private individuals. Minimum construction standards are to a degree determined by the building regulations and by the requirements of the National Housebuilding Council. Builders themselves, in competitive times are increasingly aware of the need to match the more demanding standards of purchasers, and after many highly publicized cases of poor quality in the boom periods of the 1970s and '80s, anxious to avoid any accusations of shoddy construction.

But beyond that, housebuilders have given 'added value' a special meaning. Essentially they will try to incorporate features which are unattractive or can be made to seem attractive to potential purchasers and which will tend to raise house prices more than costs: fitted kitchens, for example, carpets to client's choice, central heating, choice of high-quality bathroom suites. Many now consider nostalgic or vernacular features to be particularly strong selling points (Bryant Homes, for example, have a style they call Vicwardian). Such features incorporating special brickwork, carved wood fascias, leaded lights, and a host of others can be expensive, so builders are constantly looking for ways, often with manufacturers, of reducing these or other costs to compensate.

Customer appeal and marketing rather than any architectural concepts of design quality have come to predominate in many market sectors. It is nothing new; historical nostalgia and eclecticism and symbols of status have been features of housing design for centuries.

Despite the scale and importance of the volume of housebuilders' output, they make, as was pointed out at the beginning of the chapter, relatively limited use of consultant architects and surveyors; their own in-house staff will be used to develop and adapt the standard styles and to control costs. One of the most important design roles is often to plan site layouts so as to maximize the number of units on a site, while allowing each house appropriate space for gardens, access and privacy and of course meeting the local planners and road engineers' requirements. The problem can require considerable ingenuity and the viability of a scheme may be dependent even on whether one more unit can be fitted in; if the site looks overcrowded, prices will be difficult to achieve; spaciousness will raise the possible price but may increase the land cost element more than proportionately.

It is the smaller builders who are more likely to produce individually 'architect designed housing'; and because of the economics of mass production which make it very difficult for them to compete in the low-cost market, their houses tend to be in the higher cost brackets. The one private-sector winner of a regional housing design award in 1993 was Beechcroft homes, for a development of 'spacious houses for young retired people' designed by the Wallace & Hoblyn Partnership; clearly a relatively high-cost scheme.

Architects working in this field have, once again, to be acutely aware of the economic pressures. They have to be thoroughly familiar with expected price and quality levels for a specific location (and price levels can vary considerably over very small distances, particularly in suburban areas); they need to know what the cost of land is per plot (or the value at which that land is held in the builder's balance sheet); and they need to know the costs and availability of materials and labour. A salutary but true story might underline the point. When one of the authors was interviewing the director of a medium-sized housebuilding firm in the 1970s, he mentioned the name of a local architect with a good reputation who was known to have designed houses for this particular builder. 'Never again', said the builder. 'Wonderful designs – but we just couldn't build them at the going prices.' The architect, when also interviewed, naturally agreed with the builder's assessment of the quality of the design, but argued that the economies had been carefully considered. There is no simple solution to such a difference of perception – but the problem is clear.

16.4 Conclusion

The contrast between the establishment of cost limits in the two housing sectors, determined in the one case by centrally imposed cost criteria and in the other by market conditions, is interesting partly because it points to no obvious conclusion. The combination of defined standards and employment of good architects should have produced and did produce excellent housing in the public sector; but during the later 1960s and 1970s in particular, quality was undermined by financial pressures and, perhaps, over-ambition in the face of pressing housing need. On the other hand commercial pressures in the private market might have been expected to keep standards at a minimum; again at the bottom end of the market some would argue that this is exactly what has happened. But there has been a countervailing pressure towards higher standards as a result of consumer pressures, advertising and tighter control of constructional standards through for example the National Housebuilders Federation and pressure from building societies. To take one small example, the standard of bathroom and kitchen fitments in moderately priced houses today is far higher than a decade ago; anything less would not be saleable.

The economic and social issues raised here are considerable – the issues of public- versus private-sector provision and of fair distribution of housing opportunity. The reader is left to explore them in the very large literature on the subject now available.

FOR FURTHER STUDY

1 Recommended reading

There is a great deal written on housing policy and housing economics but relatively little on the subject of this chapter which is the design implications of the different methods of finance and production; Scoffham's *The Shape of British Housing* (1984) is an excellent historical account. And a new history specifically of the high-rise building period in the UK has been recently published (Glendinning and Muthesius, 1994). The Parker Morris report (1961) is still worth looking at (see questions below).

On the general operation of Housing Associations the National Federation of Housing Associations (NFHA)'s *Committee Members' Handbook* (1990) is probably as clear as anything. There are many other NFHA publications listed in their quarterly regular lists.

2 Exercises

Use the TCI base table and supplementary factors (Table 16.1) to work out the approximate cost limit on special needs scheme of 118 m² designed to be occupied by 6 people.

3 Discussion and essay questions

a Given the increase in prosperity over the past 30 years, why is subsidized housing still deemed necessary in all European countries? In discussing this question try to establish the relationship between the costs of housebuilding, the income levels of the lowest income groups (say the bottom 20%) and the amount people can afford to spend on housing.

b Why is it necessary to have an elaborate system of cost control for grant-aided housing and what measures can be taken to ensure the maintenance of standards in such a system?

c It has been argued (by the sociologist Conrad Jamieson, for example) that housing doesn't need architects. Discuss.

d Is a high quality of architectural design achievable in the lower price ranges of the private market? Is it actually achieved?

4 Projects

a Read the Parker Morris report (1961). How many of its recommendations are still relevant? What would you now add or alter? How do space standards in (i) the private sector and (ii) the housing association sector compare to Parker Morris (find examples). As the gross national product has grown in real terms by over 40% since 1961, why, do you think, have housing space standards not improved?

b Visit a local housing association and its current developments to discover the impact of recent changes in the financial regime on the standard of design and accommodation offered.

17 The value of architecture

This book has been about achieving value for money in building. In the last two chapters 'value' has been defined in monetary terms only and shown to be defined in different ways by, for example, the operation of the property market in the case of speculative office and housing development or in terms of prescribed norms as frequently has been the case for public-sector buildings.

Achieving value even in those evidently narrow senses requires, as has been seen, some essential pre-conditions. First there must be real understanding on the part of architects and contractors of each other's functions, objectives, problems and modes of working. There must be realistic cost estimation and rigorous cost control based on actual resource costs and building programmes. Designers need to be aware of the cost implications of their decisions, first, in terms of the resource use they imply, secondly in terms of the way they facilitate the contractors' programming and cash flow and thirdly in terms of the long-run effects on the costs incurred by building owners and occupiers. If all these conditions exist, value for money might be achieved.

But, architects will protest, doesn't this ignore the **real** values of architecture? Isn't architecture worth much more than the mere monetary value of buildings determined by market forces? And, of course, it is; buildings are particularly rich in the range of values they hold for different people at different times: aesthetic value, historical value, political value, symbolic value.

Clearly, these values are not measurable simply in monetary terms. It is true that many people would argue that there are ways of attributing monetary values to them; and there are established techniques which attempt to do precisely that. When a decision has to be made whether to preserve an old building or to demolish it to make way for something new, arguments about relative values have to be tackled; very often decisions are made on the basis of investment appraisals which give some kind of implied value for the qualities of the older architecture.

The techniques of cost benefit analysis were at one time a popular approach to handling such decisions. But as the very highly charged discussions on some recent proposals in London, such as Paternoster Square and the extension to the National Gallery, have shown, the decisions cannot actually be made on cost benefit grounds alone or through straightforward investment appraisal.

Underlying the cost benefit approach is the view that there must be some limit to what individuals or societies are prepared to pay to safeguard or create architectural values; and that there are ways of establishing those limits. The complex problems – theoretical and practical – of actually identifying such monetary figures have been widely discussed over the last thirty years – without any real consensus emerging; there are certainly strong arguments to suggest that such an enterprise is philosophically flawed anyway. There are no 'correct' methods of making decisions, on behalf of society, about the worth of a great building, or the value, for example, of an uninterrupted view of St. Pauls, still less of making decisions on behalf of future generations. Such decisions **are** made – they have to be; but they are made through debate, political process, individual whim, the exercise of influence and in all sorts of other ways. They are not made by establishing absolute monetary values.

The Sydney Opera House was referred to in the first chapter; it is often used as an example of financial and administrative fiasco – even appearing as one of the 'Great Planning Disasters' in Peter Hall's book of that name. Yet it is now established as one of the great opera houses of the world – giving pleasure to its thousands of users and visitors every year. But, further, it has come to represent Sydney itself; it is the only building that most people outside Australia could identify as being in Sydney. It was used as a powerful symbol in the city's campaign to be the site of the 2000 Olympics; it is used widely in travel advertisements for Australia as a whole. So it

Sydney Opera House.

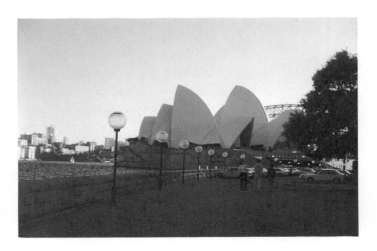

would now be very difficult indeed to answer the apparently simple question: was it far too expensive?

Of course it could have been built more efficiently; there could have been better relationships between client, engineers, architect and builders; but then it could have been a square box.

But Sydney's opera house is not unusual. The symbolic values of architecture have always been powerful. Cathedrals and temples, palaces and villas, town halls and head offices have been built for more than functional purposes. Sometimes the objective has been to show the extent of a community's devotion to their god, sometimes to display power and authority of rulers; sometimes to display wealth; sometimes, as in the great series of Victorian town halls, to express civic pride; sometimes as a form of commercial display.

And it is not just the grand or even well-designed buildings that have acquired powerful meanings. A famous photograph originally published in the *Daily Mirror* in 1969 and reproduced in Martin Pawley's *Architecture Versus Housing* (Pawley, 1971, p. 98) shows a man threatening to leap in despair from the upper window of his tiny terraced house, which was about to be bulldozed as part of a slum clearance programme. He was of course eligible for rehousing in a 'better' home; there were rules for calculating the value of the house for compensation purposes (to the owner – not the tenant); but nothing, it seemed, could match the man's own valuation of his home.

Anglican Cathedral, Liverpool.

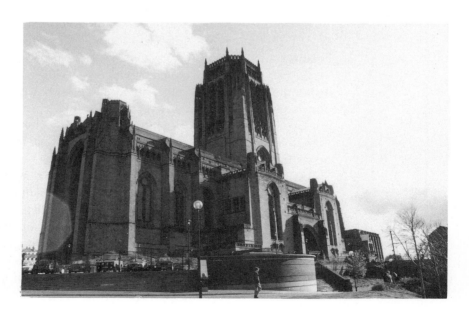

The meaning we attach to buildings may indeed have no connection whatever to their architectural quality; but architectural quality itself is certainly one of those unquantifiable values which people and societies can come to deem important. The notion of architectural quality as life-enhancing can seem fairly irrelevant to families struggling to survive in run-down (and sometimes architect-designed) housing estates. Yet if 'good architecture' is defined to include all those qualities summed up in Virtruvius' 'commoditie, firmnesse and delight' – that is to refer to buildings that work well, are built well and give pleasure to users, passers-by and visitors – then it is surely worth paying for: it must have a real value over and above mere minimal building.

The argument about the value of architecture itself can become quickly tangled with issues of taste and of style; arguments about 'style' have always been vigorous. In the last century, the battles of the styles, gothic versus classical, industrial versus craft (described well in Mordaunt Crook, 1989) were prolonged and bitter. There is and rarely has been agreement even among the cognoscenti about what is the 'right' way of building, even about the criteria on which architecture should be based; whether for example architecture should express in some way the 'spirit of its age' (whatever that might mean), some fundamental principles of harmony and proportion or be the personal expression of individual aesthetic values. (For a vigorous and controversial view of these issues see David Watkin's *The Morality of Architecture* (Watkin, 1977).)

Our perceptions of quality, superficially at least, seem to change radically over time. What we now see as the magnificent railway stations of the Victorian era in Britain were at the time often perceived as mere massive sheds. The Liverpool historian Picton referred to the Albert Dock buildings in that city as 'that hideous pile of brickwork'. It was a view shared by many city councillors in the 1970s when it came close to demolition. A campaign not only locally but on a national scale, pointing out its qualities as a fine feat of engineering, a masterly use of iron and brickwork and simply a beautiful building, led ultimately and despite the very doubtful economics of the whole operation to its rehabilitation. It now attracts millions of visitors a year.

What these examples show is that there are aspects of quality that transcend style; and it is these that make good buildings. It is perhaps easier to put the argument by looking at the issue negatively: poor buildings can be defined more easily than good ones. No building can be thought of as having real quality if its internal planning is ill thought through and does not work well for its users, if it uses poor materials and elements which do not last or do not function well; if it rapidly develops structural faults. However one has to add – 'or if it is outstandingly ugly'; there is in the end no escape from aesthetics – and no escape from the need for imagination and talent in the creation of architecture. Indeed there are those architects who would argue that some sacrifice of 'commoditie' is worth while if it is compensated for by beautiful design: what matters, they say, a little inconvenience and discomfort against the pleasures of working in a fine building? That is a debate which has no end.

Arguments which contrast 'value for money' as defined in the terms discussed in the two previous chapters as somehow inevitably in conflict with the value of architecture as discussed here are perhaps based on a fundamental misunderstanding both of the nature of architecture and on the nature of values. It is certainly the case that if clients are not prepared to pay for enough time and talent to be devoted to the design of buildings, if the budget simply does not allow good quality materials to be used, if the construction industry is under continuous pressure to produce as fast as possible, then we are hardly likely to get good buildings or good value in any sense. On the other hand economic constraints are inevitable; and clients are not and should not be interested in paying for inefficiencies in the design management, the construction management or the interface between them.

We have to remember that even the building of great Gothic cathedrals was dominated by the availability of money; as Kraus's book, *Gold Was the Mortar* (1979) showed in great detail sometimes little work was done for decades, even centuries, because the money was not available; at other

Albert Dock, Liverpool, 1994.

*Cathedral of Christ
the King, Liverpool.*

times the work progressed rapidly as funds (often from quite unchristian activities) were made available. Modern cathedrals are no different; the building of Liverpool's Anglican cathedral has taken over 70 years, been dogged by many problems (including two world wars) but is finally achieved; to many it is the last great Gothic cathedral, a triumphant assertion of the determination to build a great church; its costs (including its considerable running costs) have to be accepted as the price that must be paid for that achievement. To other people, however, it seems a huge and expensive anachronism in the modern age.

Its companion, the Roman Catholic Cathedral of Christ the King, was originally to have been built on the same sort of scale to a design by Edwin Lutyens; only the crypt of that original design was built; by the end of the Second World War, the costs of achieving the original design were prohibitive. Eventually a competition was held for a new design; it was won by a leading architect, Sir Frederick Gibbard, with a scheme which was seen as different, exciting and more appropriate in scale, cost and design to the late twentieth century. The original budget was £1 million; it eventually cost £4 million and was built in little over four years (late 1962 to early 1967). It was admired, but not universally. The architectural critic Charles Jencks chose it as an example of a building which failed architecturally because of its 'univalence' – its lack of multiple meanings (though this view is difficult to reconcile with the variety of local nicknames it rapidly acquired!) (Jencks, 1973, pp. 20–5).

But there were other more practical problems. In 1986 the cathedral authorities sued the architects and the engineers, Lowe and Rodin, alleging negligence in the design and construction, in particular the use of poor materials leading to severe leaks in the roof. The comments of the QC for the architects are highly relevant to the general theme of this book: 'Sir Frederick Gibbard was one of the great architects of the post war period and this cathedral one of the great buildings of that period [but he] and the engineers were faced with the almost impossible task of building a great building on a shoestring.' Another report of the proceedings said: 'Liability had been denied by the architects and engineers who blamed each other for the defects.' Settlement was eventually agreed at £1.3 million. In an agreed statement after the final hearing the trustees said, 'we have always acknowledged the brilliance of the original conception' (*Building*, 14 Feb. 1986).

Cathedrals are rather exceptional sorts of buildings; but from this story there are many lessons to be drawn; interestingly different people draw different lessons. Readers are left to draw their own and then perhaps to ask the question: does my assessment of where the blame lay depend on my own professional perspective?

To finish, we quote an even more special case, perhaps the world's most famous 'great building', the Parthenon on the Acropolis at Athens, a fascinating example of both the conflict and the possible coincidence of economic, political, symbolic and aesthetic values. The original plans were for a building smaller than the one which was eventually dedicated in 438BC. If Rhys Carpenter is to be believed, there were in fact two early plans, one before and one after the Persian invasion (Carpenter, 1970). When the leader of the 'People's Party', Pericles, came to power, he wanted to build a temple grander and greater than anything yet seen in Greece. It was ostensibly to show the gratitude and devotion of the Athenian people to Athena for deliverance from the Persians; it was to house a gold-covered giant statue of the goddess. Yet there is little doubt that it was also intended to secure Pericles' political position, and to symbolize the moral, economic and cultural superiority of Athens over the other Greek city states.

The building was of course going to be extremely expensive; but this was seen as a not wholly negative aspect of the operation. First it enabled Pericles to put to good use the funds collected to maintain the armed forces against any further invasion, and which were not needed immediately. (The other city states which had contributed the money were not happy with this idea or with the Athenian argument that the building was to the glory of all Greece.) Secondly it provided work for thousands of Athenians including the redundant sailors and soldiers and according to the historian Pausanias every type of craftsman:

carpenters, moulders, bronze casters, embossers, furnishers and transporters of materials, among which were dealers and sailors and steersmen by sea, wheel wrights and waggoners and breeders of yoke animals, by land. And also there were rope-makers, weavers, leatherworkers, road builders and miners. And as each craft had its own company of slave and free under its orders, one might say that every age and every capacity were marshalled into service.

It might indeed be the case that this was one of the earliest government construction training schemes and the effective use of construction to drag the economy out of recession on true Keynesian principles!

Two and a half thousand years later, millions of people swarm over the Acropolis to admire what remains of the great temple which despite (and also, admittedly, because of) its ruined state still has a hypnotic power. Perhaps Pericles did not realize what he had created; he certainly made no attempt at life-cycle cost analysis but at least he knew that the values of great architecture and the realities of economics were not irreconcilably opposed.

Introduction to the tender price and building cost indices

Index numbers are used in economics mainly to describe changes over time in prices, costs or output, but they can also be used to indicate geographical variation; for example, variations in income level between one part of a country and others – or between different countries. The principle is very simple: one particular point in time or space is taken as the standard (the base) from which others are measured; the relevant measure at the base date or place is given the value 100. So, for example, if an index were being developed for materials prices using January 1990 as the base date, the price of timber in 1990 would be assigned the index number 100; if prices rose 5% by January 1981 the index would then be 105; if it fell by 5% the index would be 95.

An index could be used as in that example just to show a change in price of one particular commodity, but the most usual function of index numbers is to amalgamate a range of different prices into one single **indicator**; and it is important to remember index numbers are just that – indicators of difference; they are never mathematically accurate measures.

There are two problems which arise in trying to create a good index series for a range of different prices.

Problem 1: prices changing at different rates

Individual prices might be changing at different rates; but some prices might be more important, for one reason or another, than others. This problem is tackled by 'weighting' the different constituent prices in an index by some measure of their relative importance.

For example: assume we want a simple index of building costs, that we already have information on the costs of labour, materials and plant, and that investigation has shown that on most projects costs are split 40% labour, 50% materials and 10% plant. Assume the cost of plant rose very much more rapidly (this is unlikely – an exaggerated example is used to show the effect of weighting); the situation might be as follows:

	Year 1 (the base year)	Year 2
Index of plant cost	100	130
Index of labour cost	100	110
Index of materials cost	100	112

To derive a simple index of all costs for year 2 we could simply average the three numbers in the last column, giving $(130 + 110 + 112)/3 = 117.3$

But this gives too much importance to the rise in plant costs which only account for 10% of the total. So if we weigh the figures by their relative importance we get the following:

Plant	130×10	$=$	1300
Labour	110×40	$=$	4400
Materials	112×50	$=$	5600
Total (indices × weights)			11 300

To derive the index we now divide by the total weights (100) – for we now have 100 units of measurement, not three; this gives us an index of 113, considerably lower than the first one (117.3) and, because it reduces the effect of the increase in plant costs is a better reflection of the general increase in total costs.

Problem 2: change in significance of items indexed

The second basic problem with index numbers is that the weights used in a base year may not be appropriate in later years; over long periods of time they may become quite inappropriate. The best-known index of all – the retail price index – is particularly sensitive to this sort of change. At one time household coal was an important item in the average household budget; expenditure on cars was not. This has now of course completely changed.

There are no real solutions to this problem – just ways of making it less serious. Usually new base years are selected, with updated weightings; or current year weightings are used – that is the weights are changed as circumstances change. The difficulty with both these solutions is that they strictly invalidate comparisons over long periods; one is no longer comparing like with like.

(These issues are fully dealt with in all basic text statistics and will not be pursued further here.)

The tender and building cost indices

There are a number of published indices developed for both building and civil engineering but the most well-known and most widely used are those published by the BCIS (the Building Cost Information Service).

The BCIS all-in tender price index is based on a random sample of priced bills of quantities for accepted tenders; a project index is calculated for each one in relation to a set of base date prices; then all the projects in the sample are averaged to produce the published tender price index, which, it is claimed, 'provides an accurate and effective measure of the variations in contractors' prices over time'. There is a range of other tender price indices focusing on one type of tender, such as the 'private commercial' and the public-sector TPIs.

There are several building cost indices published, some for particular types of construction such as the Steel Framed Buildings Cost index but also one general building cost index, which is a weighted average of three of the special ones. The difference between the tender and the cost indices is that the latter are derived from changes in national labour rates, materials prices and plant costs, and are produced by applying the changes in these costs to cost models of average buildings. Some 30 work categories such as excavation, masonry, hardwood joinery, are given percentage weights to reflect their significance in the total cost of an 'average' building, then the effect of changing resource prices (also weighted) calculated for each category.

To take one example, for electrical work labour is weighted 40% and material 60%; the weighted index of electrical work costs is then given a weight of almost 10% in the total index.

The final cost index produced is therefore a weighted index of weighted indexes. So much averaging is bound to lead to a very broad 'indicator' indeed; a rise of say 5% in the building cost index can give only an approximate indication of the general effect of increases in building prices on the costs of a particular building.

As well as these nationally available series, many large client bodies and quantity surveying practices produce indices for their own purposes; this is because indices produced in-house, based on data which is primary rather than secondary to the user, are felt to be more reliable.

Manipulating the indices

The indices are used by building economists in a number of ways and for a number of purposes. The technique of manipulating them is in principle very simple but the results have to be interpreted very carefully.

Using indices to update building prices for budgeting purposes

We have data for a building of a particular type in a particular place and wish to get some idea of what a similar building might cost at a different time in the same place. The calculation may be set out as follows:

Cost per m^2* of comparison building 1989 = £500:
All in Tender Price Index (1985 mean = 100)
   1989 4th quarter: 134
   1994 4th quarter: 110

Therefore the probable cost to the client of a similar building in 1994 = £500 × 110/135 = £407.4 per m^2.

Note how important it is to use the right index. If we had used the BCIS general building cost index the answer would have been very different.

General building cost index   1989: 4th quarter: 127
                                 1994: 4th quarter: 154

The calculation therefore would be: £500 × 154/127 = £606.3 per m^2.

The difference between the two results shows that while tender prices fell as a consequence of severe competition for work, basic resource costs continued to rise. It is not surprising that many contractors went out of business in these circumstances.

Calculation of price fluctuations

The contractual arrangements for building projects specially over 12 months' duration and of significant value usually allow fluctuations to be accounted for. The traditional way of allowing for fluctuations was to record the basic costs of the various resources needed in the project at the time the contractor priced for them (the tender date) and at the time of incorporation into the project and then paying or retaining any differences. Although this is an arithmetically straightforward process, it is extremely time-consuming. As a result, the National Economic Development Organization initiated an index-based approach reflecting changes in resource costs for a number of works categories. This approach, known as Formula Price Adjustment, has proved extremely effective in dealing with fluctuations during the construction. In this case of course it is the building cost indices which are relevant.

---

*i.e. in this case, cost means the price charged by the builder in his tender, that is the cost paid by the client (part of the procurement cost in Figure 3.2).

Assessment of changes in cost and price relationships

Indices can be used to estimate the consequences of changes in costs and prices resulting from using different construction methods or building in different locations.

For example the building cost indices show that costs for concrete-framed construction since 1989 have increased less than the costs of either steel-frame or brick construction. It does not of course follow that concrete frame is cheaper; this is a very easy trap to fall into, especially when reading from graphs of index numbers on which the lines inevitably meet at the level representing the base year. Whether one is cheaper than the other depends of course both on what the relationship was at the base year as well as on how prices have moved since.

Extrapolation

Indices can also be used, through extrapolating past trends, to predict future prices. It is a technique which needs to be used very cautiously and can, at points of change in the building cycle particularly, lead to serious errors. For example, predictions made in August 1989 on the basis of the trend over the previous years in the all-in tender price index would have been seriously misleading as an indication of what prices were likely to be in 1994.

SfB Classification System: basic tables

SfB Basic Table 1 - Elements

SITE

(00) *Reserved*

(10) PREPARED SITE

(20) SITE STRUCTURE

(30) SITE ENCLOSURES

(40) ROADS, PATHS, PAVINGS

(50) SITE SERVICES (piped and ducted)

(60) SITE SERVICES (electrical)

(70) SITE FITTINGS

(80) LANDSCAPE, PLAY AREAS

(90) SUMMARY SITE
Information applicable to two or more of the groups (10) to (80).
All general information applicable to the site as a whole.

(-0) *Reserved*

(1) GROUND SUBSTRUCTURE

Parts below underside of lowest screed or where no screed exists to underside of lowest floor finish.

(10) *See Site*

(11) GROUND, EARTH SHAPES

(12) *Free*

(13) FLOOR BEDS

(14) *Free*

(15) *Free*

(16) FOUNDATIONS (other than pile foundations)

(17) PILE FOUNDATIONS

(18) *Reserved*

(19) SUMMARY GROUND SUBSTRUCTURE (building)
Information applicable to two or more of the groups (11) to (18)

(1-) *Reserved*

(2) STRUCTURE (incl. carcass)

(20) *See Site*

(21) WALLS, EXTERNAL WALLS

(22) INTERNAL WALLS, PARTITIONS

(23) FLOORS, GALLERIES

(24) STAIRS, RAMPS

(25) *Free*

(26) *Free*

(27) ROOFS

(28) *Reserved*

(29) SUMMARY STRUCTURE (building)
Information applicable to two or more of the groups (21) to (28)

(2-) *Reserved*

(3) COMPLETIONS
(to structure incl. openings in structure)

(30) *See Site*

(31) EXTERNAL WALLS' COMPLETIONS

(32) INTERNAL WALLS' COMPLETIONS

(33) FLOORS', GALLERIES' COMPLETIONS

(34) STAIRS', RAMPS' COMPLETIONS

(35) SUSPENDED CEILINGS

(36) *Free*

(37) ROOFS' COMPLETIONS

(38) *Reserved*

(39) SUMMARY COMPLETIONS (building)
Information applicable to two or more of the groups (31) to (38)

(3-) *Reserved*

(4) FINISHES (to structure)

(40) *See Site*

(41) WALL FINISHES EXTERNALLY

(42) WALL FINISHES INTERNALLY

(43) FLOOR FINISHES

(44) STAIR, RAMP FINISHES

(45) CEILING FINISHES

(46) *Free*

(47) ROOF FINISHES

(48) *Reserved*

(49) SUMMARY FINISHES (building)
Information applicable to two or more of the groups (41) to (48)

(4-) *Reserved*

(5) SERVICES (mainly piped, ducted)

(50) *See Site*

(51) SERVICES CENTRE (mainly piped, ducted)

(52) DRAINAGE, REFUSE DISPOSAL

(53) LIQUIDS SUPPLY SERVICES

(54) GASES SUPPLY SERVICES

(55) SPACE COOLING SERVICES

(56) SPACE HEATING SERVICES

(57) VENTILATION AND AIR CONDITIONING SERVICES

(58) *Reserved*

(59) SUMMARY SERVICES (mainly piped and ducted, Building)
Information applicable to two or more of the groups (51) to (58)

(5-) *Reserved*

(6) SERVICES (mainly electrical)

(60) *See Site*

(61) ELECTRICAL CENTRE

(62) POWER DISTRIBUTION SERVICES

(63) LIGHTING SERVICES

(64) COMMUNICATION SERVICES

(65) *Free*

(66) TRANSPORT

(67) *Free*

(68) *Reserved*

(69) SUMMARY SERVICES (mainly electrical, Building)
Information applicable to two or more of the groups (61) to (68)

(6-) *Reserved*

(7) FITTINGS

(70) *See Site*

(71) DISPLAY, CIRCULATION FITTINGS

(72) REST, WORK, PLAY FITTINGS

(73) CULINARY, EATING, DRINKING FITTINGS

(74) SANITARY, HYGIENE FITTINGS

(75) CLEANING, MAINTENANCE FITTINGS

(76) STORAGE, SCREENING FITTINGS

(77) *Free*

(78) *Reserved*

(79) SUMMARY FITTINGS (building)
Information applicable to two or more of the groups (71) to (78)

(7-) *Reserved*

RESERVED GROUPS OTHER THAN THOSE PREVIOUSLY MENTIONED

(01)/(09) and (0-)
(81)/(89) and (8-)
(91)/(99) and (9-)
(-1)/(-9) and (--)

SfB Basic Table 2 - Constructions

A PRELIMINARIES, GENERAL CONDITIONS, GENERAL COSTS AND GENERAL WORK INCL. GENERAL TEMPORARY WORK.

B DEMOLITION AND SHORING WORK

C EXCAVATIONS AND LOOSE FILL WORK

D *Reserved*

E CAST IN-SITU WORK

F BLOCK WORK

G WORKS OF PREFABRICATED COMPONENTS FOR CARCASS AND SUBSTRUCTURE

H SECTION WORK

I PIPE WORK

J WIRE WORK, MESH WORK

K QUILT WORK, INSULATION WORK

L FLEXIBLE SHEET WORK (PROOFING)

M MALLEABLE SHEET WORK

N RIGID SHEET OVERLAP WORK

O *Reserved*

P THICK COATING WORK

Q *Free*

R RIGID SHEET WORK

S RIGID TILE WORK

T FLEXIBLE SHEET WORK (except L)

U *Free*

V FILM COATING AND IMPREGNATION WORK

W PLANTING WORK
(work with living forms)

X WORKS OF PREFABRICATED COMPONENTS FOR COMPLETIONS, FINISHES AND SERVICES

Y *Reserved*

Z *Reserved*

- *Reserved*

Part of SfB Basic Table 3 - Materials and other Resources

a **ADMINISTRATION** (or General)
b **PLANT, TOOLS**
c **LABOUR**
d *Reserved*

e/o FORMED MATERIALS:

e NATURAL STONE
0 GENERAL
1 GRANITE, BASALT, OTHER IGNEOUS
2 MARBLE
3 LIMESTONE (other than marble)
4 SANDSTONE
5 SLATE
6 *Reserved*
7 *Reserved*
8 *Reserved*
9 OTHER FORMED NATURAL STONE MATERIALS

f PRE-CAST WITH BINDER
0 GENERAL
1 SANDLIME CONCRETE (precast)
2 ALL-IN AGGREGATE CONCRETE (precast) HEAVY CONCRETE (precast)
3 TERRAZZO (precast)
4 LIGHTWEIGHT, CELLULAR CONCRETE (precast)
5 LIGHTWEIGHT AGGREGATE CONCRETE (precast)
6 ASBESTOS-BASED MATERIALS (preformed)
7 GYPSUM (preformed)
8 MAGNESIAN MATERIALS (preformed)
9 OTHER MATERIALS PRE-CAST WITH BINDER

g CLAY (DRIED, FIRED)
0 GENERAL
1 DRIED CLAY e.g. sun dried, un-burnt
2 FIRED CLAY, UNGLAZED FIRED CLAY
3 GLAZED FIRED CLAY, VITRIFIED CLAY
4 *Reserved*
5 *Reserved*
6 REFRACTORY MATERIALS, HEAT RESISTANT MATERIALS
7 *Reserved*
8 *Reserved*
9 OTHER DRIED OR FIRED CLAYS

i WOOD*
0 GENERAL
1 TIMBER (strength graded, unwrot)
2 SOFTWOOD (in general, and wrot)
3 HARDWOOD
4 WOOD LAMINATES, e.g. plywood, laminboard, blockboard, faced wood laminates
5 WOOD VENEERS
6 *Reserved*
7 *Reserved*
8 *Reserved*
9 OTHER WOOD MATERIALS (other than those at j1, j7, j8)

* including impregnated wood

p/s FORMLESS MATERIALS:

c AGGREGATES, LOOSE FILLS
0 GENERAL
1 NATURAL FILLS AGGREGATES
2 ARTIFICIAL AGGREGATES IN GENERAL ARTIFICIAL GRANULAR (heavy)
3 ARTIFICIAL GRANULAR (light)
4 ARTIFICIAL ASH
5 SHAVINGS
6 POWDER
7 FIBRES
8 *Reserved*
9 OTHER AGGREGATES, LOOSE FILLS

q LIME AND CEMENT BINDERS, MORTARS, CONCRETES
0 GENERAL
1 LIME
2 CEMENT
3 LIME-CEMENT (mixed hydraulic binders)
4 MORTARS, CONCRETES IN GENERAL LIME CEMENT-AGGREGATE MIXES
5 TERRAZZO, GRANOLITHIC MIXES
6 LIGHTWEIGHT, CELLULAR CONCRETE MIXES
7 LIGHTWEIGHT AGGREGATE CONCRETE MIXES
8 *Reserved*
9 OTHER LIME-CEMENT-AGGREGATE MIXES ASBESTOS CEMENT

t/v FUNCTIONAL MATERIALS:

t FIXING AND JOINTING AGENTS
0 GENERAL
1 WELDING MATERIALS
2 SOLDERING MATERIALS
3 ADHESIVES, BONDING MATERIALS
4 JOINT FILLERS, PUTTY, MASTICS
5 *Reserved*
6 FASTENERS
7 IRONMONGERY
8 *Reserved*
9 OTHER FIXING AND JOINTING AGENTS

u PROTECTIVE, PROCESS/PROPERTY MODIFYING AGENTS
0 GENERAL
1 ANTI-CORROSIVE MATERIALS
2 MODIFYING AGENTS, ADMIXTURES
3 ROT PROOFERS, FUNGICIDES, GERMICIDES, INSECTICIDES
4 FLAME RETARDANTS
5 POLISHES, SEALS, HARDENERS, SIZE
6 WATER REPELLANTS
7 *Reserved*
8 *Reserved*
9 OTHER PROTECTIVE PROCESS/ PROPERTY MODIFYING AGENTS (other than v) e.g. anti-static agents

w ANCILLARY MATERIALS
0 GENERAL
1 RUST REMOVING AGENTS
2 *Reserved*
3 FUELS (gases, liquids and solids)
4 WATER
5 ACIDS, ALKALIS
6 FERTILISERS
7 CLEANING MATERIALS, ABRASIVES
8 *Reserved*
9 OTHER ANCILLARY MATERIALS

X COMPONENTS (by function)
y *Reserved*
z *Reserved*
- *Reserved*

Example of a cost plan

BCIS on-line – AEP – cost plan Ref. 100 Number 90150 C – 1 – 634

HEADING

Job Title:	TYPICAL PRIMARY SCHOOL
CI/SfB code:	712
	Primary schools
Type of work:	BB
Last updated:	29 August 1994
Date of pricing:	01 January 1995
Date of tender/ base month:	01 December 1994
Date of possession:	01 February 1995

PROJECT DESCRIPTION

Single-storey primary school on raft founds with loadbearing brick/block walls, timber pitched roof with clay tiles, associated site works and drainage.

LOCATION
NORTH OF ENGLAND
Location code: BB

SITE
Good access, water table 1.8 m below ground level, storage space adequate, poor gbc, gently sloping site.

MARKET CONDITIONS
Very competititive

CONTRACT PARTICULARS
Client: LOCAL AUTHORITY
Contract period (months) – stipulated: 9

ACCOMMODATION AND DESIGN FEATURES
Single-storey to accommodate 130 Nr. pupils, accommodation includes 1 Nr. hall, 2 Nr. infant classrooms, 2 Nr. junior classrooms, servery kitchen, storage, wc, admin. and boilerhouse. Brick/block construction on raft foundations with timber pitched roofs with clay tile coverings.

AREAS

Basement	0 m²	Area of external walls	4110 m²
Ground floor	590 m²		
Upper floors	0 m²	Average storey heights	
Gross floor area	590 m²	basement	0.00 m²
		ground	2.41 m²
		upper	0.00 m

Usable area	340 m²		
Circulation area	37 m²	Internal cube	0 m³
Ancillary area	198 m²		
Internal divisions	15 m²	Number of units	130
Gross floor area	590 m²		
		Spaces not enclosed	0 m²

FUNCTIONAL UNITS AND DESIGN/SHAPE
Design/shape:
1 storey   100.00%

SPECIFICATION

COSTS EXCLUDING PRELIMINARIES

Element		Total cost	Cost/m^2	Element unit quantity	Element unit cost	%
1.	SUBSTRUCTURE	22 954	36.21	634 m^2	36.21	7
2A	Frame	12 676	19.99	634 m^2	19.99	4
2B	Upper floors					
2C	Roof	31 950	50.39	634 m^2	50.39	9
2D	Stairs					
2E	External walls	19 616	30.94	462 m^2	42.46	6
2F	Windows and external doors	16 952	26.74	38 Nr	446.11	5
2G	Internal walls and partititons	7982	12.59	423 m^2	18.87	2
2H	Internal doors	6083	9.59	30 Nr	202.77	2
2.	SUPERSTRUCTURE	95 259	150.25			27
3A	Wall finishes	15 353	24.22	1308 m^2	11.78	4
3B	Floor finishes	11 821	18.65	634 m^2	18.65	3
3C	Ceiling finishes	12 969	20.46	634 m^2	20.46	4
3.	INTERNAL FINISHES	40 143	63.32	–		12
4.	FITTINGS	12 542	19.78	1 Itm	12 542.00	4
5A	Sanitary appliances	4410	6.96	29 Nr	152.07	1
5B	Services equipment	329	0.52	1 Nr	329.00	0
5C	Disposal installations	456	0.72	75 m	6.08	0
5D	Water installations					
5E	Heat source	41 571	65.57	1 Itm	41 572.00	12
5F	Space heating and air treatment					
5G	Ventilating systems					
5H	Electrical installations	22 306	35.18	1 Itm	22 306.00	6
	Gas installlations					
5J	Lift and conveyer installations					
5K	Protective installations	2839	4.48	8 Nr	354.88	1
5L	Communications installations					
5M	Special installations					
5N	Builder's work in connection	1858	2.93	–		1
5O	Builder's profit and attendance	1797	2.83	–		1
5.	SERVICES	75 566	119.19	–		22
	BUILDING SUB-TOTAL	246 464	388.74	–		71
6A	Site works	34 982	55.18	2966 m^2	11.79	10
6B	Drainage	12 547	19.79	550 m	22.81	4
6C	External services	2288	3.61	1 Itm	2288.00	1
6D	Minor building works	3042	4.80	2 Nr	1521.00	1
6.	EXTERNAL WORKS	52 859	83.37	–		15
7.	PRELIMINARIES	37 445	59.06	–		11
	TOTAL (less contingencies)	336 768	531.18	–		97
8.	CONTINGENCIES	10 102	15.93	–		3
	CONTRACT SUM	346 870	547.11	–		100

Element 1   SUBSTRUCTURE
Raft foundation on poor ground strata, 400 mm top soil excavation, 150 mm reinforced concrete slab with edge thickening.

Element 2A   FRAME
Steel frame incorporating cranked beams, fabricated by welding with bolted site connections.

Element 2C   ROOF
Timber-pitched roof on steel joists, 10 m span. Red clay pantile coverings on underfelt. Velux double skin clear glass rooflights. UPVC drainpipes and fittings.

Element 2E   EXTERNAL WALLS
Cavity walls with Thircroft Berkeley mixture facings externally, 60 mm cavity with Dritherm bonded glass fibre wall insulation and 140 mm Celcon block inner leaf.

Element 2F   WINDOWS AND EXTERNAL DOORS
Pine framed windows with Hinchcliffe aluminium inserts with 4 mm toughened float glass (95 m^2). Pine panelled doors and screens with aluminium inserts (44 m^2). Precast concrete and steel lintels.

Element 2G   INTERNAL WALLS AND PARTITIONS
100, 140 and 215 mm block partitions. Melaboard wc cubicles.

Element 2H   INTERNAL DOORS
Hills solid flush doors in pine frames (38 Nr.)

Element 3A   WALL FINISHES
Plaster and emulsion paint (740 m^2) or eggshell paint (213 m^2). Wrought softwood boarding and framing with fire retardant paint.

Element 3B   FLOOR FINISHES
Wrought maple T & G board flooring (135 m^2). Hawkins smooth paviours on screed (80 m^2), vinyl tiles on screed (225 m^2). Softwood or vinyl skirtings.

Element 3C   CEILING FINISHES
Plasterboard and skim with emulsion (429 m^2). Softwood T & G boarding with retardant paint (154 m^2). Insulation (578 m^2).

Element 4   FITTINGS
Softwood, hardwood and blockboard shelving and cupboards. Sink cupboard units. Cloak rails and seat units.

Element 5A   SANITARY APPLIANCES
Stainless steel sink top (2 Nr), cleaners sink (1 Nr), Belfast sink (1 Nr), shower tray (1 Nr), wash hand basins (11 Nr), wc suites (11 Nr), slab urinals (2 Nr).

Element 5B   SERVICES EQUIPMENT
Stainless steel sterilizing sink

Element 5C   DISPOSAL INSTALLATIONS
Plastic soil and vent pipes, serving 30 Nr sanitary appliances.

Element 5D   WATER INSTALLATIONS
See 5E

Element 5E HEAT SOURCE
PC sum for supply and fix of LPHW central heating and air conditioning plant.

Element 5F SPACE HEATING AND AIR TREATMENT
See 5E

Element 5G VENTILATING SYSTEMS
See 5E

Element 5H ELECTRICAL INSTALLATIONS
PC sum for supply and fix of electrical installations including 139 Nr. lighting points, 5 Nr power points, 43 Nr equipment points.

Element 5K PROTECTIVE INSTALLATIONS
Fire hose reels, fire extinguishers, asbestos fire blankets.

Element 6A SITE WORKS
Site preparation, removing topsoil etc. surface treatments including excavations and tarmacadam paving, concrete flags, gates and fences etc.

Element 6B   DRAINAGE
Excavation and filling for drainage runs, clay pipes and fittings, manholes etc.

Element 6C   EXTERNAL SERVICES
Normal, water, gas and electric mains

Element 6D   MINOR BUILDING WORKS
Oil storage bins

Bibliography

Achard, P. and Gicquel, R. (1986) *European Passive Solar Handbook Preliminary Edition*, Commission of the European Communities.

Adams, S. (1989) *Practical Buildability*, Butterworth.

Ambrose, P. and Colelnutt, B. (1975) *The Property Machine*, Penguin Books.

Aoud, G. and Price, A. D. (1994) *Application of Computer Systems to Improve Construction Planning*, The ICON Project, *Acorn Tenth Annual Conference Papers*.

Aqua Group (1990a) *Contract Administration for the Building Team*, BSP.

Aqua Group (1990b) *Tender and Contracts for Building*, Blackwell.

Architects' Journal (1974) The costs of office, p. 685, Table vii.

Architects' Journal (1993a) Architects slam Government proposals on insulation standards, 3 Feb., pp. 31–40.

Architects' Journal (1993b) Product approvals and standards, 12 May, pp. 19–26.

Architects' Journal (1993c) Why are insulation standards here the lowest in Europe? 26 May, p. 4.

Architects' Journal (1993d) Glazing and curtain walling. *AJ* Focus, Sept.

Architects' Journal (1993e) Automation in Japan, 10 Oct., p. 31.

Architects' Journal (1994a) Campus focus and city landmark, 13 Apr., pp. 31–40.

Architects' Journal (1994b) A purpose built television station, 20 Apr., pp. 29–39.

Architects' Journal (1994c) Youth prevails in 1994, *AJ*/Bovis Awards, pp. 18–20.

Arts Council (1993) *Architecture and Executive Agencies*, The Arts Council.

Ashworth, A. (1988) *Cost Studies of Buildings*, Longman.

Ashworth, A. and Skitmore, M. (1982) *Accuracy in Estimating*, Occasional Paper No. 27, CIOB.

Ball, Michael (1988) *Rebuilding Construction: Economic Change in the Construction Industry*, Routledge.

Barker, T. C. (1977) In Supple, B. (ed.), *Essays in British History*, Clarendon Press.

Barnes, N. M. L. and Thompson, P. A. (1971) CIRIA Report 34, *Civil Engineering Bills of Quantities*, CIRIA.

Baum, A. and Mackimm, D. (1989) *The Income Approach to Property Valuation*, 3rd edn, Routledge & Kegan Paul.

Baume, M. (1967) *The Sydney Opera House Affair*, Thomas Nelson (Australia) Ltd.

BCIS (1994) *Tender Price and Building Cost Indices*.

Bentley, I., Alcock, A., Murrain, P., Mcglynn, S. and Smith, G. (1985) *Responsive Environments – A Manual for Designers*, Architectural Press.

Bishop, D. (1975) Productivity in the Construction Industry, in D. A. Turin (ed). *Aspects of the Economics of the Construction Industry*, George Godwin.

Bon, R. (1989) *Building as an Economic Process*, Prentice Hall, New Jersey.

Bonke, S. and Pedersen, E. F. (1991) Computer control and working conditions on site in the Danish construction industry, in Rainbird and Syben (eds), *Restructuring a Traditional Industry*, Berg.

Bonnell, D. G. (1959) The mechanisation of the construction process, *Journal of the Royal Society of Arts*, April.

Bowley, M. (1960) *Innovations in Building Materials – an Economic Study*, Gerald Duckworth & Co.

Bowley, M. (1966) *The British Building Industry – Four Studies in Response and Resistance to Change*, Cambridge University Press.

Brandon P. S. (ed.) (1990) *Quantity Surveying Techniques, New Directions*, BSP.

BRECSU (1992) *Annual Review 1991/2*.

BRECSU *Digest 339* (1988).

Briscoe, G. (1988) *Economics of the Construction Industry*, Mitchell.

British Property Federation (1983) *The BPF System for Building Design and Construction*, British Property Federation.

British Standards Institution (1992) BS 7543: *Guide to Durability of Buildings and Building Elements, Products and Components*.

Broadbent, G. (1973) *Design in Architecture*, John Wiley & Sons.

Broadbent G. (1984) In P. S. Brandon and J. A. Powell (eds), *Quality and Profit in Building Design*, E. & F. N. Spon.

Brookes A. J. (1983) *Cladding of Buildings*, Construction Press.

Brookes A. J. and Grech, C. (1990) *The Building Envelope: Application of New Technology Cladding*, Butterworth, London.

Building Research Establishment (1976) *The Building Game*.

Building Research Establishment (1994) IP13/94, *Passive Stack Ventilation Systems: Design and Installation*.

Building (1991) *Canary Wharf – A Landmark in Construction*, The Builder Group.

Building (1992a) Roofing Supplement, 28 Feb.

Building (1992b) Redesigning the architect, 22 May, pp. 16–20.

Building (1992c) Dispatches from the Front, 24 July, pp. 30–1.

Building (1992d) City calls for cutbacks in brick production, 18 Sept.

Building (1993a) Contractors face price hikes, 22 Jan., p. 7.

Building (1993b) Report says US building cost less, 16 Apr., p. 9.

Building (1993c) US cost comparison – architects reply, 30 Apr., pp. 42–5.

Building (1993d) Contractors eroding architects' role, 21 May, p. 56.

Building (1993e) IT breakthrough will slash building costs, 11 June, p. 30.

Building (1993f) Materials hike chokes builders, 18 June, p. 12.

Building (1993g) Bovis US/UK cost comparison: findings criticized by architects and engineer participants, 14 July, p. 10.

Building (1993h) Skills gap threatens recovery, 1 Oct., p. 13.

Building (1993i) Contractors face price hikes, 1 Oct.

Building (1993j) 4 site saga, 20 Oct., pp. 22–30.

Building (1993k) 13 Dec., p. 63.

Building (1994a) King cash, 4 Mar., p. 26.

Building (1994b) A mouse in the house, 15 Apr., p. 47.

Building (1994c) Treasury bans pay when paid, 30 July.

Building Research Establishment (1987) *Co-ordinated Project Information for Building Works – a Guide with Examples*, p. 3, Fig. 4.

Burberry, P. (1994) Ruling on energy and ventilation *Architects' Journal*, 18 Aug.

Burberry, P. (ed.) (1994) *Designing for Production*, 3 Vols, Building Research Establishment.

Cadman, D. and Austin-Crowe, L. (1991) *Property Development*, 3rd edn, E. & F. N. Spon.

Campagnac (1991) Computerisation strategies in large French firm and their effect on working conditions, in H. Rainbird and G. Syben (eds), *Restructuring a Traditional Industry: Construction Employment and Skills in Europe*, Berg.

Carpenter, R. (1970) *The Architects of the Parthenon*, Penguin Books.

Central Purchasing Unit (1992) *Contract Strategy Selection for Major Projects*, HMSO.

Chamberlain, D. A. (ed.) (1994) *Automation and Properties in Construction XI*, Elsevier.

Chartered Surveyor Monthly (1974) Classification Tables – research begins, Oct., **4**(1), p 4.

Chau, K. W. and Walker, A. (1988) The measurement of total factor productivity in the Hong Kong construction industry, *Construction Management and Economics*.

Chevin, D. (1992) Last judgement, *Building*, 15 May, p. 62.

Chevin, D. (1993) IT Breakthrough will slash building costs, *Building*, 11 June.

CIB W92 (1991) *Papers Presented at the Meeting held in Las Palmas, December 1991*, CIB.

CIB Working Commission (1973) *The SfB System*, CIB.

CIB Working Commission 74 (1986) *A Practical Manual on the use of SfB*, CIB.

CIOB (1987) *Code of Estimating Practice*, CIOB.

CIOB (1995) *Effects of Accelerated Working, Delays and Disruption on Labour Productivity*.

CITB Joint Action Group on New Entrant Training (1994) *Training Proposal for the Construction Industry Training Scheme for Craft and Operative New Entrants*, Construction Industry Training Board.

Clamp, H. (1993) *The Shorter Forms of Building Contract*, 3rd edn, Blackwell Scientific Publications.

Clapp, M. A. and Cullen, B. (May 1968) Maintenance and running costs of school buildings, *Chartered Surveyor*.

Clarke, L. (1984) On the concepts of skill and training in the construction industry, *Production of the Built Environment*, 5, Bartlett International Summer School.

Clarke, L. (1986) Determinants of training in the construction industry, *Production of the Built Environment,* 7, Bartlett International Summer School

Clarke, L. (1987) *Production of the Building Environment*, Bartlett International Summer School.

Clarke, L. (1988) Value/output/time relationships in British construction, *Production of the Built Environment*, 9, Bartlett International Summer School.

Clarke, L. (1992a) *Building Capitalism*, Routledge.

Clarke, L. (1992b) The problems of piecework in the British construction industry, *Production of the Built Environnment*, 11, Bartlett International Summer School.

CLASP (1969) *Building Industry Code*, ONWARD office.

Construction Industry Manpower Board (1980) *Final Report to the Secretary of State for the Environment*, Department of the Environment.

Cooke, B. (1985) *Construction Planning Case Studies*, Macmillan.

Coordinated Project Information Committee (1987a) *Common Arrangement of Work Sections for Building Works*, Co-ordinated Project Information Committee.

Coordinated Project Information Committee (1987b) *Production Drawings – A Code of Practice for Building Works*, Coordinated Project Information Committee.

Coordinated Project Information Committee (1987c) *Project Specification: A Code of Practice for Building Works*, Coordinated Project Information Committee

Cullen, B. and Jeffrey, I. (1967) *Running Costs of Hospital Buildings*, Building Research Station Current Paper Design Series, No. 65.

Department of the Environment (1971) *Costs in Use: A Study of 24 Crow Office Buildings*, HMSO.

Department of the Environment (1994) *Housing and Construction Statistics, 1983–1993*, HMSO.

Dolan, E. G. (1971) *TANSTAAFL – The Economic Strategy for Environmental Crisis*, Holt, Rinehart and Wilson.

Draper, K. (1984) Systematic quality appraisal. In P. S. Brandon and J. A. Powell (eds), *Quality and Profit in Building Design*, E. & F. N. Spon.

Duffy F., Cave, C. and Worthington (eds) (1976) *Planning Office Space*, Architectural Press.

Duffy, F., Laing, A. and Crisp, V. (1993) *The Responsible Workplace: The Re-design of Work and Offices*, Butterworth Architecture/Estates Gazette.

Eccles, R. G. (1981) The quasi firm in the construction industry, *Journal of Economic Behaviour and Organization*.

ECD Partnership (1991) *Solar Architecture in Europe*, Prism Press.

Eden, J. F. (1975) Mechanisation, in D. Turin (ed.), *Aspect of the Economics of Construction*, George Godwin.

Edwards, B. (1993) New environmental duties for architects, Architects' Journal, 8 Dec.

Edwin Trotter Associates (1993) *Lifetime Homes – A Range of Adaptable and Accessible Standard House Types for All Generations*, Habinteg Housing Association.

Essex, T. (1993) Counting the cost, *Building*, Doors and Window Supplement, 30 Apr., pp. 26–8.

Evans, B. (1993a) An alternative to air conditioning, *Architects' Journal*, 10 Feb.

Evans, B. (1993b) Prefabricating the superstructure, 16 June, *Architects' Journal*.

Evans, B. (1994a) Low cost energy offices, *Architects' Journal*, 6 Apr.

Evans, B. (1994b) Perfecting component engineering, *Architects' Journal*, 20 Apr.

Evans, B. (1994c) Automating construction, 20 July, *Architects' Journal*.

Ferguson, I. (1989) *Buildability in Practice*, Mitchell.

Ferry, D. J. (1964) *Cost Planning of Buildings*, Crosby Lockwood & Sons.

Ferry, D. J. and Brandon, P. (1970) *Cost Planning of Buildings*, Crosby Lockwood & Sons, 6th edn, 1991.

Fitch, J. Marston (1973) *American Building – The Historical Forces that Shaped It*, Shocken Books.

Flanagan, R., Meadows, J. and Robinson, J. (1989) *Life Cycle Costing*, BSP Professional Books.

Forbes, W. S. and Skoyles, E. R. (1963) The operational bill, *RICS Journal*, Feb.

Fryendal-Pedersen, E. (1990) Still waiting for better cranes, *The Production of the Built Environment, 12,* Bartlett International Summer School.

Fryer, B. (1990) *The Practice of Construction Management*, BSP Professional.

Gann, D. (1991) *Future Skill Needs of the Construction Industry*, IPRA Ltd for the Department of Employment.

Gardiner, L. (ed.) (1979) *Mechanical Plant in Construction,* George Godwin, London.

Gill, S. (1994) *Imprint*, Lincoln College, Oxford.

Glendinning, M. and Muthesius, S. (1994) *Tower Block: Modern Public Housing in England, Scotland, Wales and Northern Ireland*, Yale University Press.

Goodchild, C. H. (1993) *A Report on the Comparative Costs of Concrete and Steel Framed Office Buildings*, British Cement Association.

Gray, C. and Flanaghan, R. (1989) *The Changing Role of Specialist and Trade Subcontractors*, Chartered Institute of Building.

Gray, C., Hughes, W. and Bennett, J. (1994) *The Successful Management of Design*, Centre for Strategic Studies, Reading University.

Green, R. (1986) *The Architects Guide to Running a Job*, Butterworth Heinemann.

Groak, S. (1992) *The Idea of Building*, E. & F. N. Spon.

Guy, C. (1994) *The Retail Development Process*, Routledge.

Hall, A. D. and Cheetham, D. W. (1987) Labour productivity and investment in power tools, *International Journal of Construction Management and Technology*, **1,**(3).

Hall, P. (1980) *Great Planning Disasters*, Weidenfeld & Nicholson.

Harding C. (1994) Time for architects to reliquish their leadership, *Building*, 11 Feb.

Harper, D. R. (1990) *Building: The Process and the Product*, Chartered Institute of Building.

Harris, F. and McCaffer, R. (1981) *Modern Construction Management*, 3rd edn, BSP Professional.

Harvey, R. C. and Ashworth, A. (1993) *The Construction Industry of Great Britain*, Butterworth-Heinemann.

Hawkes, D. (1994) User control in a passive building, *Architects' Journal*, 9 Mar.

Hillebrandt, P. (1971) *Small Firms in the Construction Industry*, Committee of Inquiry on Small Firms Research Report No. 10, HMSO.

Hillebrandt, P. M. and Cannon J. (eds) (1989) *The Modern Construction Firms*, Macmillan, London.

Hilton, W. S. (1968) *Industrial Relations in Construction*, Pergamon.

HMSO (1994a) *Approved Document F: Ventilation* (1995 edn), HMSO.

HMSO (1994b) *Approved Document L: Conversation of Fuel and Power* (1995 edn), HMSO.

HMSO (1994c) *S11850 Building Regulations (Amendment) 1994*, HMSO.

HMSO (1994d) *Sustainable Development: The UK Strategy*, HMSO.

HM Treasury (1992) *Strategy Selection for Major Projects*, Cental Unit for Purchasing Guide No. 36: Construction.

Horner, R. M. and Ab-Hamid, M. (1993) The influence of wall panel characteristics on the productivity of bricklayers, CIB W-65, proceedings.

Housing Corporation (1994) *Scheme Development Standards*, The Housing Corporation.

Hudson, L. (1972) *Building Materials*, Longman Group.

Hutchinson, M. (1993) The need to stick to the specification, *Architects' Journal*, 20 Oct.

Hutton, G. H. and Devonald, A. D. G. (1973) *Value in Building*, Applied Science Publishers.

Illingworth, J. R. (1993) *Construction Methods and Planning*, E. & F. N. Spon.

Inland Revenue (1994) *Construction Industry Tax Deduction Scheme*, Leaflet IRI/15, Inland Revenue.

Institute of Civil Engineers and Federation of Civil Engineering Contractors (1992) *The Civil Engineering Standard Method of Measurement*, 3rd edn, Institution of Civil Engineers.

ISO Technical Committee (1993) *Classification of Information in the Construction Industry*.

Jackson, D. (1982) *Introduction to Economics, Theory and Data*, Macmillan.

Jencks, C. (1973) *Modern Movements in Architecture*, Penguin Books.

Joseph Rowntree Trust (1994) *Lifetime Homes*, Joseph Rowntree Trust.

Kingsford, P. W. (1973) *Builders and Building Workers*, Edward Arnold.

Kostoff, S. (1977) *The Architect: Chapters in the History of a Profession*, Oxford University Press.

Kraus, H. (1979) *Gold was the Mortar: The Economics of Cathedral Building,* Routledge & Kegan Paul.

Lamb, D. (1974) *The Lump – An Heretical Analysis*, Solidarity.

Langford, D. A. (1982) *Direct Labour Organizations in the Construction Industry*, Gower.

Langridge, R. J. (1975) *Material Changes in the Traditional House during Period 1964–1974*, unpublished dissertation, Liverpool Polytechnic.

Latham, M. (1993) *Trust and Money*, Interim report of the Joint Government/Industry Review of the Procurement and Contractual Arrangement in the United Kingdom Construction Industry, HMSO.

Latham, M. (1994) *Constructing the Team*, Final Report of the Joint Government/Industry Review of Procurement and Contractual Agreement in the United Kingdom Construction Industry, HMSO.

Lawson, B. (1980) *How Designers Think*, Architectural Press, London.

Lawson, B. (1994) *Design in Mind*, Butterworth Architecture.

Lawson, R. M. (1993) *Comparative Structure Cost of Modern Commercial Buildings*, Steel Construction Institute.

Levy, S. (1990) *Japanese Construction – an American Perspective*, Van Nostrand Reinhold.

McHale, J. R. (1962) *Buckminster Fuller*, Prentice Hall.

Mackinder, M. (1980) *The Selection and Specification of Building Materials and Components*, Research Paper 17, York Institute of Advanced Architectural Education.

Mackiners, M. and Marvin, H. (1982) *Design Decision Making in Architectural Practice*, Building Research Establishment, BRE Information Paper, IP 11/82.

McKinlay, A. (1987) Management of diversity: oganizational change in the British construction industry, *Production of the Build Environment 8*, Bartlett International Summer School.

Mann, T. (1992) *Building Economics for Architects*, Van Nostrand Reinhold.

Manser, J. E. (1994) *Economics: A Foundation Course for the Built Environment*, E. & F. N. Spon.

Markus, T. A. (1967) *The Real Costs of a Window – an Exercise in Cost Benefit Analysis*, Report no. 62, University of Strathclyde Dept. of Architecture and Building Science.

Marriott, O. (1967) *The Property Boom*, Hamish Hamilton.

Marsh, A., Heady, P. and Matheson, J. (1980) *Labour Mobility in the Construction Industry: Final Report to the Construction Industry Manpower Board*, Department of the Environment.

Marvin, H. (1985) *Information and Experience in Architectural Design*, Institute of Advanced Architectural Studies.

Massey, D. and Meegan, R. (1982) *The Anatomy of Job Loss*, Methuen.

Masterman, J. W. E. (1992) *An Introduction to Building Procurement Systems* E. & F. N. Spon.

Midlands Builder and Engineer (1994) Five storeys high, Apr., p. 17.

Mordaunt Crook, J. (1989) *The Dilemma of Style*, John Murray.

Morton, R. R. (1990) Professional ideologies and the quality of the built environment, *Production of the Built Environment 12*, Bartlett International Summer School.

Morton, R. R. (1991) *The Teaching of Economics in Schools of Architecture*, unpublished report to RIBA.

Mower, G. (1977) *Gaudi*, Oresko Books.

Moxley, R. (1993) *Building Management for Professionals*, Butterworth.

National Federation of Housing Associations (1990) *Committee Members' Handbook*, National Federation of Housing Associations.

National Joint Council for the Building Industry (1994) *National Working Rule Agreement (1994 edn)*.

Newsday (1994) William Levitt, 30 Jan.

Nicholson, M. P. (1992) *Architecture Management*, E. & F. N. Spon.

Ormerod, P. (1994) *The Death of Economics*, Faber and Faber.

Osborne, J. (1991) Plastic Money, 25 Oct., *Building, Doors and Windows Supplement*.

Parker Morris Committee (1961) *Homes for To-day and To-morrow*, HMSO.

Pawley, M. (1971) *Architecture Versus Housing*, Studio Vista.

Pawley, M. (1991) Commenting on Stansted Airport, *Building*, 10 May, pp. 49–50.

Pawley, M. (1993) Solar Architecture Conference Review, *Building*, 11 June, p. 22.

Pearce, D. Markandya and A. Barbier, E. B. (1989) *Blueprint for a Green Economy*, Earthscan

Publications Ltd.

Pedersen, E. (1990) Still waiting for better cranes, *The Production of the Built Environment*, 12.

Pezzey, J. (1984) *An Economic Assessment of Energy Conservation Measures in Housing and Other Buildings*, Building Research Establishment.

Phelps Brown (1968) *Report of the Committee of Enquiry into Certain Matters Concerning Labour in Building and Civil Engineering*, HMSO.

Postgate, R. (1923) *The Builders' History*, National Federation of Building.

Powell, C. G. (1980) *An Economic History of the British Building Industry 1815–1979*, Architectural Press.

Powell, J. A., Cooper, I. and Lera, S. (eds) (1984) *Designing for Building Utilisation*, E. & F. N. Spon.

Powell, K. (1994) A day in the life of Glyndebourne, 13 Oct., *Architects' Journal*.

Prais, S. J. and Steedman, H. (1986) Vocational training in France and Britain: the building trades, *National Insitute Economic Review*, 116.

Pratt, M. W. J. (1975) *An Account of Working Class Housing Built under Subsidy by the Liverpool Corporation between 1918 and 1932*, unpublished MA thesis, Liverpool University.

Raftery, J. (1993a) *Principles of Building Economics: An Introduction*, E. & F. N. Spon.

Raftery, J. (1993b) *Risk Analysis in Project Management,* E. & F. N. Spon.

Rainbird, H. (1991c) Labour force fragmentation and skills supply in the British construction industry, in H. Rainbird and G. Syben (eds), *Restructuring a Traditional Industry: Construction Employment and Skills in Europe*, Berg.

Rainbird, H. and Gerd, S. (eds) (1991) *Restructuring a Traditional Industry: Construction Employment and Skills in Europe*, Berg.

Randolph, B. (ed.) (1992) *Housing Associations after the Act*, Research Report 19, National Federation of Housing Associations.

Rapoport, A. (1969) *House Form and Culture*, Prentice Hall.

RIBA (1980) *Handbook of Architectural Practice and Management*, 4th edn, RIBA Publications.

RIBA (1992) *Strategic Study of the Profession*, RIBA.

Richmond, D. (1975) *Introduction to Valuation*, Macmillan Press.

Richmond, D. (1994) *Introduction to Property Valuation*, 3rd edn, Macmillan.

RICS (1989) *Standard Method of Measurement*, 7th edn, RICS.

Rogers, R. (1990) *Architecture: A Modern View*, Thames & Hudson.

Ruegg, R. T. and Marshall, H. E. (1990) *Building Economics – Theory and Practice*, Van Nostrand Reinhold.

Rutter, D. K. (1993) *Construction Economics: Is There Such a Thing?* Construction Papers No. 18, CIOB.

Satoh, A. (English edn by Morton, R. R.) (1995) *Building in Britain, The Origins of a Modern Industry*, Scolar Press.

Schutt, R. C. (1982, 2nd edn 1988) *Economics for the Construction Industry*, Longman Group.

Scoffham, E. R. (1984) *The Shape of British Housing*, George Godwin, Longman Group.

Seeley, I. H. (1972) *Building Economics*, Macmillan.

Shanley, L. F. (1969) *Cost Control for Medium and Large Builders*, An Foras Forbartha.

Skoyles, E. R. (1968) *Introducing Bills of Quantities (Operational Format)*, Current Paper 62/68, Building Research Station.

Slavid, R. (1993) Should architects become construction managers? *Architects' Journal*, 17 Nov., p. 18.

Spencer-Chapman, F. F. and Grandjean, C. (1991) *The Construction Industry and the European Community*.

Spring, M. (1994) Landmark, *Building*, 10 May.

Steel, M. J. and Cheetham, D. W. (1993) Frank Bunker Gilbreth: building contractor, inventor and pioneer industrial engineer, *Construction History*, Vol. 9.

Stewart, A. (1992) Profile: dispatches from the Front, *Building*, 24 July.

Stone, P. A. (1966) *Building Economy*, Pergamon Press.

Stone, P. A. (1967) *Building Design Evaluation: Costs in Use*, E. & F. Spon.

Stone, P. A. (1970) *Urban Development in Britain: Standards, Costs and Resources 1967–2004*, Vol. 1, Cambridge University Press.

Swain, H. (1968) Project R.S.M., *Architects' Journal*, 11 Sept.

Swain, H. (1972) Project R.S.M., *Architects' Journal*, 12 Jan.

Syben, G. (1993) Strategies of growth of productivity in the absence of technological change, in H. Rainbird and G. Syben (eds) *Restructuring a Traditional Industry: Construction Employment and Skills in Europe*, Berg.

Tailby, S. and Whitston, C. (1989) In S. Evans and R. Lewis (eds), *Manufacturing Change: Industrial Relations and Restructuring*, Blackwell, Oxford.

Turner, D. (1987) The construction industry of Great Britain, *Midland Bank Review*, Autumn.

Turner, R. G. (1986) *Construction Economics and Building Design: an Historical Approach*, Van Nostrand.

Vale, B. and Vale, R. (1991a) *Green Architecture: Design for a Sustainable Future*, Thames & Hudson.

Vale, B. and Vale, R. (1991b) *Toward a Green Architecture: Six Practical Case Studies*, RIBA Publications.

Venturi, R. (1955) *Complexity and Contradiction in Architecture*, Museum of Modern Art.

Walentowicz, P. (1992) *Housing Standards After the Act*, Research report 15, National Federation of Housing Associations.

Walker, A. (1989) *Project Management in Construction*, BSP Professional.

Watkin, D. (1977) *Morality and Architecture*, Oxford University Press.

Watkin, D. (1986) *A History of Western Architecture*, Laurence King.

Whitehouse, B. (1994) *Partners in Property*, Bern Shaw.

Winch, G. (1985) Labour only and the labour process, *Production of the Built Environment*, **6.**

Winch, G. (1991), Computer-aided design and project management in the British construction industry. In H. Rainbird and G. Syben, *Restructuring a Traditional Industry: Construction Employment and Skills in Europe*, Berg.

Zevi, B. (1985) *Erich Mendelsohn*, Architectural Press.

Index